Lord of the Dance

A MONCREIFFE MISCELLANY

Lord of the Dance

A MONCREIFFE
MISCELLANY

Diverse Writings of
Sir Iain Moncreiffe of that Ilk, Bt
CVO DL QC FSA PHD
Albany Herald of Arms

Edited by
HUGH MONTGOMERY-
MASSINGBERD

Debrett's Peerage Limited
MCMLXXXVI

Copyright © Lady Moncreiffe of that Ilk 1986
ISBN 0 905649 81 8

Published by Debrett's Peerage Limited
73–77 Britannia Road, London SW6 2JR

Represented by
Michael Joseph Limited
27 Wright's Lane, Kensington
London W8

Distributed by
TBL Book Distribution Services
17–23 Nelson Way
Tuscan Trading Estate, Camberley
Surrey

Designed by Humphrey Stone
Typesetting by P&M Typesetting Ltd, Exeter, Devon
Printed and bound by R. J. Acford, Chichester, Sussex

Contents

Foreword

There are many people far better qualified than I to write a Foreword to this particular book, but although I only had the pleasure of knowing Iain Moncreiffe for the last eight years of his life I shared the same admiration of, and fondness for him as those who may have known him all his lifetime.

Iain first came into my life when he was invited to become Chairman of Debrett in 1977, and nobody could have brought more to an institution such as Debrett. His quite extraordinary store of genealogical knowledge combined with his famous, indeed infamous, sense of humour, made working with him an absolute delight and an unusual education.

Any meeting attended by Iain was never allowed to become too serious or too pompous, and his contributions, although frequently obscure at first hearing, often went straight to the heart of the matter. Iain's scholarship was always tinged with a slight irreverence, and his conversation was seldom without humour.

It is impossible to think of him now without a smile crossing one's face, and like so many of his friends I have greatly missed his mischeivous sense of humour and his superb companionship.

When thinking of a suitable title for this collection of his writings, I was determined to avoid any dull, academic phrase. I was reminded of Iain's Memorial Service at the Guards Chapel when one of the songs sung by the choir was 'I am the Lord of the Dance', and this seemed to capture his great enthusiasm for life and his sense of fun. Hence the title of this book.

Iain was immensely proud of his own family's history and the Hill of Moncreiffe from which his family took its name. Visiting Iain at Easter Moncreiffe was like walking into another world in which the present was inextricably mixed up with the past.

This typical old Scottish house was full of paintings, books and heirlooms covering almost every aspect of Iain's ancestry, and he delighted in giving guests a guided tour of this historical treasure trove. To be with Iain in this environment was a unique experience and one from which visitors emerged exhausted, but amazed at Iain's encyclopaedic knowledge of Scottish history.

One of Iain's greatest gifts was the ability to impart this knowledge to others without condescension or any trace of intellectual snobbery. He loved sharing his knowledge and always managed to make history come alive by his vivid interpretation of characters and events.

It is therefore a particular sadness that he died before being able to translate so much of his knowledge into the written word, and it is no exaggeration to say that many books literally died with him, inasmuch as he was the *only* person who could have written them.

We are fortunate however that there was nevertheless a huge reservoir of Iain's writings from which to draw when preparing this book, and few people were as well equipped to undertake this task as Hugh Montgomery-Massingberd.

Faced with such an *embarras de richesses*, Hugh has cleverly managed to combine the serious and learned with the fun and flippant sides of Iain's character. Indeed if the maxim that 'you can tell a lot about a man by the books in his library' is correct, then in Iain Moncreiffe's case this is even more true of his writings which show every side of his multi-faceted character.

However, the task of selecting and editing Iain's writings was obviously a daunting experience as Hugh Montgomery-Massingberd admits in his Introduction; for Iain did not take kindly to having his writing 'tampered' with. In a stern letter of rebuke Iain once wrote me for allowing an editor to attempt to correct his grammar he ended with the Churchillian words: This is something up with which I will not put.

I can only hope therefore that Iain will look kindly upon our labours and excuse any indiscretions which we may be guilty of on the grounds that we are trying to share so much of what we loved and considered valuable about 'the Ilk'.

Anyone who knew Iain will no doubt find much in the pages which follow to remind them of him, and to any readers of this book who did not have the pleasure of knowing him I can only say that I hope we have captured something of his originality, knowledge and humour.

Eccentricity might be another quality fairly attributed to Iain Moncreiffe, who frequently ended conversations with the parting words: 'Woof Woof'; which was, I believe, his equivalent to *'Au Revoir'* as an alternative to the rather more mundane and final, 'Goodbye'.

ROBERT JARMAN
Managing Director of Debrett's Peerage Limited
July 1986

Editor's Introduction

Herald, genealogist, advocate, scholar, courtier and clubman, Sir Iain Moncreiffe of that Ilk, 11th Baronet, was surely one of the most colourful, funny and engagingly eccentric characters that the monochrome 20th century has produced. Since his death in February 1985, at the early age of 65, it has constantly struck many of his wide acquaintance how utterly irreplaceable Sir Iain is as a source of far-flung intelligence and recondite erudition. The purpose of this book is to collect together some of his diverse writing from various sources which might otherwise be overlooked so as to help ensure the survival of 'the Ilk's' unquenchable spirit.

I first came into contact with Sir Iain when I joined the editorial staff of Burke's Peerage publications in the 1960s. He was undoubtedly the star contributor to *Burke's Peerage* which he wanted to make 'a treasure-house of family tales'. I found his attitude to genealogy both a revelation and an inspiration. Family history, too often the preserve of the batty, the boastful and the bore, was sheer fun to Sir Iain. In his rollicking accounts of the Moncreiffes of that Ilk, the Stuarts, Earls of Moray, the O'Neills and other families, he gave a new meaning to the term 'narrative pedigree'. He relished the chance to put some flesh and blood into the traditionally skeletal studbook. Nobody did more to remove what he called 'the eyewash and the whitewash' from a subject hitherto generally considered dry, dusty and debilitating.

While other more nervous genealogists would make out priggish *apologias* for the study of pedigrees ('important part of social history' etc) Sir Iain would, with typical bravado, face the clichetic charge of snobbery head-on. He positively delighted in the Mitfordian-style tease (as an old friend and correspondent of Nancy) that he was 'the world's Master Snob'. Gossip columnists would, as usual, always get this slightly wrong, referring to him as the 'world's greatest snob'. Sir Iain used to enjoy chiding them that when they told a juicy story about, say, Lady Molly Snodgrass, he felt less inclined to believe in its verisimilitude if they referred to her as 'Lady Snodgrass'.

Delightfully – and indeed often outrageously – unpompous, Sir Iain never minded being made into a figure of fun in the gossip columns or in *Private Eye*. For their part, the journalists, sated by the self-important and the self-publicist, certainly recognised 'the Ilk' for a thoroughly good egg and held him in great affection. Sir Iain was wise enough to know that the trivial often tells much more than high-minded attempts to be profound. He always insisted on the vital place of contemporary gossip in the study of family history.

In reality, of course, Sir Iain was anything but a snob. Like all truly great scholars he had the refreshing knack of expressing his learned studies in simple and supremely entertaining terms. No family, he would stress, is older than any other family, though some lines can be traced back further than others – and no one could trace them further than Sir Iain.

The Moncreiffes of that Ilk may have held the lands of Moncreiffe ('that Ilk' means the place of the same name) near the City of Perth for some 1,500 years. Sir Iain's father, Lieutenant-Commander Gerald Moncreiffe, a big game hunter and coffee planter in Kenya, was the grandson of Sir Thomas Moncreiffe of that Ilk, 7th Bt (whose wife, significantly, was the daughter of the Lord Lyon King of Arms, the 11th Earl of Kinnoull). Sir Iain's mother was Hinda Meredyth whose father styled himself Count de Miremont. His maternal ancestry, which included a descent from Erszebet Báthory, the 'Blood Countess', is discussed in the opening chapter of this book.

Sadly Sir Iain never wrote his intended memoirs. It would, however, be possible for a more skilful editorial hand than my own to piece together much useful source material from this miscellany. Apart from his splendid Game Book (extracts from which form CHAPTER VII), many of the pieces reprinted here contain hilarious autobiographical diversions from their ostensible themes. Sir Iain, to say the least, was not always the most disciplined of writers and we therefore owe a considerable debt to the late Philip Dossé, the eccentric publisher of *Books & Bookmen*, who encouraged him to say what he liked and at as great a length as he wished. One review (of a book edited by myself as it happens, though this is, and was, of little relevance) ran to over 20,000 words. Thanks largely to Sir Iain and to Auberon Waugh (his sometime fellow Gun – see CHAPTER VII) this engagingly idiosyncratic literary magazine enjoyed a golden period in the 1970s.

Thus, in the pages that follow, we come across such random snippets as how little Rupert (his first name) was 'kidnapped from Kenya at the age of four', had two pythons and a boa constrictor put round his neck 'to teach me not to be alarmed by snakes' and was taken by his grandmother to visit Princess Beatrice. We learn how he was taught to eat porridge by his MacGregor cousins and was sent to Switzerland at the age of eleven on account of his health 'to a literally revolting school' where the staff tortured their charges. At his last private school, Stowe House at Broadstairs (founded, incidentally, by a forbear of this book's designer), the headmaster 'placed me under a misapprehension' as to the Facts of Life.

From Stowe, he went on to Heidelberg University where he watched '(with Goebbels in the royal box) a floodlit performance in the ruined Castle there of a play by my coz Will Shakespeare'. Up at 'the House' he joined 'Loder's *alias* the Christ Church Society, in my time the most happily inebriated dining club at Oxford'. We learn how at 'Pinkie' Brett's deb dance he met 'a dark eyed Scottish descendant of Nell Gwyn' and, two years later, proposed to her – the surprising reply he took as a refusal. By this time it was the Second World War in which he served with the Scots Guards.

Of his Army days, he records such happenings as being blown up at Monte Camino, arranging for Vera Lynn to serenade a kilted Bing Crosby to the sound of the Scots Guards pipes and entertaining Emerald Lady Cunard (whose features he likens to Elizabeth Tudor) at 'bizarre luncheons when I was Captain of the late King's Guard'. After the war I.M. was private secretary to Our Man in Moscow. Like Marx he studied in the British Museum Library although 'wearing a morning coat on my way to Ascot'.

When he married 'Puffin' Countess of Erroll in 1946 he wanted a live falcon (the Erroll crest) at the ceremony, but 'my then bride's Sackville relations were too English to permit anything so Celtic and bizarre'. At his second wedding, however, 20 years later to Hermione Faulkner in the ruined mediaeval chapel of Moncreiffe, the bride's page carried a live falcon (also her family crest) 'albeit hooded'.

Sir Iain inherited the Moncreiffe baronetcy in 1957 when the House of Moncreiffe was, to quote Peter Reid's memorably crisp caption to its illustration in the catalogue of *The Destruction of the Country House* exhibition, 'burnt with the Baronet'. He had been called to the Scottish Bar in 1950 and took silk 30 years later. He was also Honorary Sheriff of Perth and Angus ('can give you up to two years imprisonment if you deserve it'), a Deputy Lieutenant for Perthshire and a member of the Queen's Body Guard for Scotland (Royal Company of Archers). In one aside, he describes himself as the Archers' 'second worst shot with a bow until Admiral Sir Angus Cunninghame Graham retired from the butts'. Apparently the admiral once managed to land an arrow on the roof of Holyroodhouse.

In 1961 Sir Iain, who had previously been Unicorn Pursuivant of Arms, was appointed Albany Herald at the Court of the Lord Lyon. In this capacity he memorably proclaimed the full styles and titles of the late Dukes of Argyll and Buccleuch at their funerals.

Sir Iain's publications included the joyfully comprehensible (all cheerfully illustrated by the late Don Pottinger) *Simple Heraldry*, *Simple Custom* and *Blood Royal*; a masterly survey of *The Highland Clans*; and *Royal Highness*, a study of the ancestry of Prince William of Wales. While these books are naturally full of good stuff, the major corpus of his scholarship – the projected great works on Scottish genealogy, the Picts, Dawn religion and sacral royalty – remained unpublished at the time of his death. He once wrote:

I will in due course – when time affords – demonstrate that much of the art of heraldry developed out of the symbolism of royal ancestor cults derived in turn from the dawn religion of *sacral royalty*...

Time, alas, did not afford.

The particular tragedy of Sir Iain's death was that so much wonderful knowledge died with him. Recalling some of his old postcards, written in his tiny, neat, almost cubic manuscript and covering such varied subjects as the High Kings of Ireland, Vlad the Impaler (otherwise 'Dracula'), Scottish castles, African royalty, Indian princes, our shared cousinship with Charles Darwin (*inter multos alios*), it gives me a pang to realize how many things I will always regret not being able to ask him.

The contents of this volume are arranged in eight Chapters. The first, 'The Fun of Genealogy', includes a general *hors d'oeuvres* on the subject of family history, a taste of I.M's narrative pedigrees, and one of his papers (on the descendants of Chaucer) to the International Congress of Genealogical and Heraldic Sciences. Sir Iain enjoyed travelling to such gatherings whether they were in Salt Lake City or Salzburg and kept in touch with a worldwide network of scholarly pen pals.

CHAPTER II brings together some of this distinguished Commander of the Royal Victorian Order's writings on royalty – including 'The King's Evil'; Mary Queen of Scots, Nell Gwyn, Queen Victoria and their descendants; the present Queen and the modern style of monarchy. 'The Master Snob' (CHAPTER III) includes I.M's polemics on the hereditary principle and the House of Lords; an anecdotal analysis of the peerage and baronetage; and assorted pieces on etiquette, 'U' and 'Non-U', aristocracy, clubs and one of I.M's great heroes, P.G. Wodehouse.

CHAPTER IV is devoted to heraldic matters. It contains a couple of general essays on armory; an erudite discussion of 'double coats' at the dawn of Northumbrian and Scottish heraldry and a paper on the

Ravaillac dagger. Scottish subjects form the basis for CHAPTER V, 'Spirit of Caledonia'. This includes an essay on the continuity of the Royal House of Scotland; a hitherto unpublished evaluation of the Massacre of Glencoe; good-natured put-downs of Messrs Prebble, Johnson (the contemporary flame-haired polymath not the 'Great Cham'), Gale and MacLean (Alistair, not Fitzroy as should, of course, be clear from this spelling); as well as pieces expressing I.M's love of the islands, lochs, portraits, kirks and steam trains of his native land.

'Abroad', as Sir Iain used to say, 'begins at Berwick'. CHAPTER VI follows him on his travels by way of Hungary and the old Holy Roman Empire, Transylvania, the Orient and Texas. Other exotic locations such as Chile, Isla Alejandra Selkirk in the Pacific, Sarawak and India are to be found in CHAPTER VII, 'Mixed Bag', which consists of extracts from I.M's Game Book. The 'Remarks' column is full of good things and sometimes the other columns spring a surprise or two. (Don't miss, for example, the entry for 7 December 1943.)

The last Chapter begins with a round-up of family *banshees* and ends with another couple of hitherto unpublished items. The first is an all-too-brief scrap of I.M's cod obituary and the second is 'The Last Will & Testament of Angus MacSnort of that Ilk and Auchinbuidle, CSI'. This gloriously funny document was executed on I.M's 15th birthday in 1934, when he was a schoolboy at Stowe. It affords early evidence of his remarkable talents and personality. The ten pages of foolscap, complete with seal and ribbon, are bursting with exuberant colour, romance, chivalry, tradition, extraordinarily precocious 'spoof' scholarship and, as ever, a cornucopia of broad jokes. There is also – as in the MacSnort's reference to his toy rabbit Bunny 'which I have cherished since my fifth birthday' – a touchingly child-like quality which happily Sir Iain never lost.

One of the most illuminating insights into the Moncreiffe *persona* is to be found in his *tour-de-force* 'Reflections of a Praetorian Guard' (in CHAPTER II). After describing some royal horseplay, I.M says:

For when royal people get the rare chance to let their hair down, they do it straightforwardly like us: like romping children and not self-consciously like pompous 'grown-ups'. Goodness, I feel sorry for grown-ups: chairmen of companies, social democrats, civil servants – 'no longer servants and no longer civil' in Churchill's phrase – retired majors, *etc.*

Characteristically he then adds a rider about his own days as a Major (in the Perthshire Home Guard). However, all those – like myself – who never feel they belong in the hostile world of 'grown-ups' will rejoicingly identify with such a life-enhancing soul.

Sir Iain's own soulmate, Hermione Moncreiffe, has been of the utmost help in the assembling of this memorial miscellany. She generously made available a mass of material from the book room at Easter Moncreiffe ('Monckers'), as well as many of the illustrations. I am especially grateful to Lady Moncreiffe for her constant advice and guidance throughout the preparation, editing and production of the book.

Although Sir Iain wisely retained the copyright in all his work, which has passed to his widow, it is fitting to acknowledge the publishers of *Books & Bookmen, The Spectator, The Times Literary Supplement, The Armorial, The Genealogists Magazine*, and other organs in which much of the text in this book first appeared. The source is generally given at the end of each item.

In arranging the material for publication I have consciously mixed the learned and the lighthearted. The book reviews are, in any event, a splendid mixture of both – as Sir Iain was himself – but I have not hesitated to include a few representative monographs in which the erudite Dr. R.I.K. Moncreiffe, QC, FSA, FZS, PhD, MA, LLB, does his serious best to keep a straight face. However, as this is essentially intended to be a book for the general reader I have regretfully eliminated I.M's copious footnotes. Sometimes, though, I have taken the editorial liberty of promoting the spicier ones up into his main text.

Sir Iain went off in pursuit of so many delicious red herrings that there was no question of a conventional editorial exercise. I have cut as little as possible, merely trimming excessive repetition (inevitably, given the style of I.M., a fair amount remains) or rehashes of the book ostensibly under review. As a result the reprinted reviews may read even less like criticisms of a particular book than they did in the first place – although that is not saying much. Anyway, I have taken the view that readers will want to read Moncreiffe. For those who want to track down the books he discusses, I have given the relevant publication details wherever possible.

My italicised editorial notes are inserted in square brackets within the text itself – again to avoid footnotes. I have tried to keep these to the minimum – a date, a subsequent event, a cross reference, etc. – and have seldom indulged myself in a comment. Naturally I have not interferred with I.M's idiosyncrasies – such as 'don't', 'ain't', '&', 'Ld', 'coz' and so forth. I need hardly add that I have endeavoured to correct misprints or the very rare author's slip.

In editing this book I have been haunted by a letter I came across among I.M's papers written from Easter Moncreiffe in 1983, it reads as follows:

Gentlemen

This is an oblique letter of thanks for *A History of the Clan Shaw* which awaited my return home yesterday.

Now on my mother's side I descend from Anton *Fugger*, Count of Kirchberg (1493–1560) who was then the richest man in Europe.

So I hope you will take it in good part when I describe as a fugger whoever 'corrected' & edited my Foreword into such a mess *without giving me any chance to correct proofs of any sort?* There is nobody else living who had the knowledge to write that foreword – it's [*sic* – ED] content was certainly worth as much as any QC might charge some silly fugger to get him off the sort of offences committed against scholarship by 'editing' me – all to be spoilt by 'Maclaggan' (a mispelt surname) for 'Murlaggan' (a place) & *all* the other howlers imposed on me (even to the Scottish dipthong in my own surname).

Has no fugger in your office ever heard of The Mackintosh?

Nevertheless, many thanks for the book, from that descendant of the grandest Fugger of them all,

IAIN MONCREIFFE OF THAT ILK

While brooding on the number of offences I have doubtless 'committed against scholarship by "editing"' I.M. in this book, it is at least some consolation that he himself got 'It's' and 'mispelt' wrong.

Notwithstanding its justified magisterial authority, this remonstrance to the publishers of a clan history also nicely illustrates the essential good humour and benevolence of the man. The simple truth is that for all his pose as a snob and the schoolboyish pranks that earned him a certain notoriety, Sir Iain was the kindest and gentlest of men, a boon companion to all who knew him.

Anyone who did not experience the hilarity of accompanying 'the Ilk' on what can only be described as a 'bender' around his numerous clubs could be said not to have lived. On the occasions I was privileged to do so I felt rather like P.G. Wodehouse's Pongo Twistleton to Sir Iain's irrepressible Earl of Ickenham. Like the immortal Uncle Fred, Sir Iain certainly spread sweetness and light. (I.M. would doubtless have pointed out, incidentally, the genealogical connection between P.G.W. and Matt Arnold, the originator of that happy and appropriate phrase.)

HUGH MONTGOMERY-MASSINGBERD

July 1986

I

The Fun of Genealogy

The Jigsaw of Family History

Genealogy is fun. Just as a piece of furniture or a picture takes on much more interest if you know its provenance, so does an individual the more the diverse ancestral elements that went to form him or her are known. The provenance of genealogy lies within the greatest gift of all: life. True family history in depth is a tapestry of *all* those who ever lived and to whom we owe our existence, and the threads woven across it are the connected lives of their interwoven generations. Tracing it, to change the metaphor, is like a detective trying to fit together a jigsaw puzzle whose pieces have been scattered throughout the world over the centuries. It is not only natural but instructive to want to know not just the broad generalized history of the country in which you live, but the actual life-histories of the people from whom you derive your individual existence. When you have discovered who as many as possible of your ancestors were – not merely the line of your father's surname – you will find a new thrill in learning the strange vicissitudes of their lives in diverse walks of life. Visiting the houses or places where they lived, seeking out their likenesses or their graves, handling the coins they used centuries ago – everything takes on a special interest when you know that, as it were, something of you has been there before. For families are seldom static; the rich are not always rich, nor the poor nothing but the offspring of untold centuries of poverty.

Sir Anthony Wagner, former Garter Principal King of Arms, has pointed out in *Pedigree and Progress* that it is a myth to think of social classes as distinct, self-perpetuating, hereditary corporations. On the contrary, it is easy to demonstrate that this is no more than a figment of the imagination, fostered by politicians of both Left and Right to serve their own party dogmas. Even the middle classes, whose social movement up or down was often rapid enough to be visible to the naked eye, did their best to hide this movement in the anonymity of city life.

And never forget that you each owe your very existence not just to

1

your parents, but to *every single one* of your personal ancestors since mankind began. It is impossible to knock out one brief link at any time in history and keep the whole chain together. Abraham Lincoln and the Aga Khan, and many more readers of these words than perhaps realize it, could never have been born had Alfred the Great's mother died in childhood.

Ponder this. None of you could ever have been born if your mother's mother's mother's mother had died in infancy. But do you know offhand who she was? It would have been no good your direct maternal great-great-grandfather marrying somebody else instead, for the child of such a marriage would have been quite different genetically from your real great-grandmother, and no descendants could ever have been *you*.

The extraordinary variety of genealogy may perhaps be illustrated by a case well known to me. The child of a Kenya settler wanted to find out about his mother's side of the family. She vaguely believed herself to be of a titled family ultimately French in origin, and her mother, a British general's daughter, believed herself to descend maternally from Admiral Bradley who had taken part in the first coastal survey of Australia and after whom Bradley Head, a landmark at Sydney in New South Wales, was named. It seemed a fairly solid Victorian background.

Admiral Bradley turned out to be a *Sergeant* Jonas Bradley who had settled in Australia and whose son had been so successful as a sheep farmer that he has an entry in the Australian *Dictionary of Biography*. Young Bradley married the daughter of an Australian explorer called Hovell; her natural brother Albert Hovell, Master Mariner of the good ship *Young Australia*, was convicted in 1869, together with two of his crew of aborigines, of murdering three persons, names unknown, on the high seas: a story reminiscent of an adventure by Joseph Conrad. The farmer Bradley's daughter married General Pearse, of the 'Fighting Fifth'; and their daughter married the natural son of a dashing Austrian count of French origin called Rességuier de Miremont, whose father sprang in the female line from industrious Pierre-Paul Riquet (1604–1680), the Baron de Bon Repos who had built the Canal du Midi from the Mediterranean to the Atlantic. The Austrian count's mother, a Hungarian countess, Amelie Festetics, belonged to what had become a very grand family (descended in the female line from Erszebet Báthory, the 'Blood Countess' who tops the list under 'murderer' in the *Guinness Book of Records*) whose founder had been Peter Ferstetych, born before 1504, a manumitted *serf* of the Bishop of Zagreb at Sassinovec in Croatia (now Yugoslavia). This then, was my mother's background, for I was that Kenya settler's son. The Midi of Languedoc, the Carpathians, the Balkans and the Australian outback alike took on a new interest for me.

2

It is a pity that some people seem interested only in grand descents, others only in respectable ones. Yet others seek only what is rare. I once told somebody that he descended from Charlemagne, which he hadn't known before. His only reaction was a shrug since an enormous number of other people must share in that descent. It seemed dull to me not to be excited, or at least interested, in identifying an actual flesh-and-blood forefather who lived in the eighth century, and to be able to know so much about him and even visit the chapel where he worshipped, whether he was a serf or an emperor. Indeed, quite literally, Charlemagne can be regarded as the Father of Europe; his was a most vigorous stock. If he and his third Queen, Hildegard, had bever been born, no single one of his descendants would ever have been born; not George Washington nor George III, not Herman Goëring nor Winston Churchill, not Bonnie Prince Charlie nor President Nixon. Moreover, neither could any of these people have been born if the future William the Conqueror had never been born as William the Bastard, illegitimate son of the original Harlot (Harlotte of Falaise) the tanner's attractive daughter to whose prowess in bed one single night in 1027 so many of us thus owe our very being. All our ancestors are interesting, for they were *all* necessary in handing down life to us even if they lived long, long ago.

In the quest, there are so many things that are fun too. As I have already observed, there is the discovery, if possible, of their photographs or their portraits: their iconography, as it is called. Then there are pictures of their houses or belongings. One of the oldest residences whose former occupants can still be traced is the drystone fortress of Ailech in Northern Ireland, where the ancestors of the present O'Neills of Clanaboy had their stronghold from the 5th until the 11th century. To come to more recent times, I was shown on Lake Toba in the interior of Sumatra the ancestral stone table, stone benches and decapitation stone where cannibal feasts had been held until 1912 by the family of our hosts, the elder members of which recollected them well and described them shyly: 'But this was before we became Lutherans.'

There are so many side-lines of genealogy. I have noticed, for example, that a characteristic handwriting can sometimes be inherited as in the case of some of the Argyll family. Any study of genealogy among the early Celts requires an understanding of what social anthropologists call the 'classificatory' system, which extended among Indo-European peoples from India to Ireland, and was patrilinear. It seems probable that the Picts had a similar 'classificatory' system for purposes of succession law, but that it was matrilinear – such a system still exists among the Bemba of Zambia – which is of genealogical importance in working out the ramifications of the Pictish royal house because innumerable people now living in many countries can trace themselves back to Kenneth MacAlpin's Pictish grandmother, who was alive *circa* AD800.

Einstein said 'Science without religion is lame, religion without science is blind.' And early human genealogy and religion are inextricably entwined, as I will explain. This is not perhaps the place to discuss in detail my agreement with the scholastic axiom of my 25 times great-grand-uncle Saint Thomas Aquinas that (to quote Dr T. M. Lindsay) 'while reason and revelation are two distinct sources of truths, the truths are not contradictory: for in the last resort they rest on *one* absolute truth – they come from the one source of knowledge, God, the Absolute One'. But it has a profound bearing on the evolutionary theories of my fifth cousin four times removed – Charles Darwin – with whom I am equally in general agreement.

For nobody can fail to observe how extraordinarily the allegory of creation in the book of Genesis fits the sequence of evolution as revealed for us by the scientists. Epochs are poetically expressed as days, in much the same way as we say 'in Neanderthal Man's day'. We are told in Genesis that in the beginning 'there was light'. The scientists say that the Earth was a ball of fire. In the second epoch, as the Earth cooled, there was vapour: when the waters beneath were divided from 'the waters which were above'. Next, the waters gathered together to form seas, and the dry land appeared. Then vegetation sprang up, depending on the sunlight of the firmament for life. Next *out of the seas* came forth amphibious reptiles – 'let the waters bring forth abundantly the moving creature that hath life' – and from these reptiles evolved, notice how the order in Genesis is still correct, 'fowl' before 'beast of the earth', i.e. birds before mammals. And the last in time to be evolved was Man.

How the correct sequence of evolution was revealed to the talented Hebrews centuries before Darwin's explorations, and how much of it was known to even earlier civilizations, is beyond our present knowledge; but their poetic use of the words 'day' for 'epoch' and 'created' for 'evolved' should not obscure the wonder of it.

A moment's reflection will show that, at some single stage and in some single place, within a little family group of primates, the single anthropoid common forefather of every man living today walked this Earth. Nobody really thinks different human beings, all with ten fingers and an appendix, were separately evolved from different amoebae in separate parts of the world. The myriad coincidences would be beyond ordinary mathematical comprehension. However much other warm-

4

blooded mammals may have branched off as our yet more remote kin at some far earlier pre-anthropoid primordial stage, 'a man's a man for a' that'. To paraphrase Kipling: we are all brothers under the skin. And to quote him: 'We be of one blood, thou and I.'

So it cannot be stressed often enough that no family is older than any other family. Some lines can be traced back further than others, but none for much more than just over a couple of millennia. Some people adopted surnames earlier than others, so that one can trace the history of an old name, especially if it is mentioned in surviving records over a long period. But I repeat for emphasis, nobody suggests that two separate human families were evolved from two different amoebae, or even from two different quadrupeds, or even from two different monkeys. If every man alive today was able to trace back the source of his 'Y'-chromosome – the chromosome which can only be given him by his father and which alone can make him a man, and which his forefathers in turn could only have received from their forefathers – we would all find that we had each inherited our individual 'Y'-chromosome from the very same source in the testicle of a single, joint, man-like ancestor, one individual at the anthropoid stage of evolution. That individual anthropoid's issue may have had to intermarry for generations before his distributed 'Y'-chromosome produced men who were fully entitled to be called *Homo sapiens*, but we may nevertheless accord him the archaic name of Adam. For we all descend from him. All families spring from his. And to the age-old question, 'When Adam delved and Eve span, who was then the gentleman?' the answer is clear: Adam. How could it have been Eve? From that illustrious 'Y'-chromosome sprang all the immemorial nobility in the world.

Throughout the world the early legends of every civilization attribute the discovery of agriculture and the arts to God-like royal ancestors. These early food producers perceived divine power in the life force which impregnated matter with energy. By concentrated prayer and ritual, part of this life-force, as it were the lucky spirit of the community, was embodied in the talisman king, successor to the wise horned-priest figure of Stone Age cave paintings. Respect for sacral royalty is the earliest religion of which there is any certain knowledge. It spread with civilization throughout the world. Sacral royalty 'was the early inspiration of drama, astronomy, architecture, sculpture, painting, music, dancing, games and costume'. It also inspired the earliest ancestral records, whether oral, passed by repetition from generation to generation by bardic herald-priests, or kept by them in newly invented writing.

It is not surprising, therefore, that the earliest genealogies that have come down to us are royal ones, or those of sacred families. And since kings have tended to marry princesses and often foreign ones, throughout the centuries, it is usually through royal intermarriages over the millennia that we can trace the most ancient descent of people actully living today. Most people have royal blood; the difficulty is to trace it.

Thus nearly all the longest traceable direct male-line descents, invaluable for the tracing of the human 'Y'-chromosomes over long periods, are those of royal or sacred houses. In Japan, for instance, the oldest great historic families go back to the imperial house itself and to priestly court nobility, all traceable since the very first written records, and already then immemorial.

When I was a Guards Officer during the Second World War, one of my comrades was Lieutenant Louis Kung, Scots Guards, *alias* K'ung Lingchieh. His parentage linked modern Chinese history with the remote past. His mother was one of the three sisters of T.V. Soong, the former Foreign Minister of China; the other two Soong sisters had married respectively Sun Yat Sen, first President of China after the overthrow of the Manchu dynasty in 1912, and Generalissimo Chiang Kai-shek. His father was Dr H. H. Kung, then Finance Minister, and I understand that they belonged to the K'ung clan who have evolved over more than 75 generations around the tomb of their illustrious forefather K'ung tsze, better known as the sage K'ung Fu-tze or Confucius (551–479 BC) and their genealogy had been treasured by Chinese scholars thoughout two and a half millennia in their great Chia Pu or family name book. But I don't know whether any copy of this has survived the Communist 'burning of the books' throughout China. Moreover we are told that Confucius himself was a scion in the direct male line, through the Dukes of Sung, of the proto-historic Shang dynasty (traditionally 1766–1121 BC). It was estimated in 1911 that some 40 to 50,000 male-line descendants of the K'ung family were living in the neighbouring city of K'iuh-fow; I would add, with possibly the oldest traceable human 'Y'-chromosomes in the world.

In this connection, incidentally, I cannot sufficiently stress the grievous mental injustice, and the heartless blocking of all scholarly research, including medical and scientific research, caused by the operation of the Adoption Acts, even as amended by the Children Act (1975). Briefly, an adopted child, after reaching the age of 18 can with great difficulty obtain access to some legal information about his true parentage. The reasons for and against this are well understood. But the *descendant* of an adopted child, long after the need for concealment is dead, has no means of gaining access to the important original birth certificate of the adoptee. The unnecessary cruelty of this thoughtless ban is obvious.

To return to descents traceable over a long period, ancient dynastic families of the Caucasus have survived into the 20th century. Some of them, such as Bagration, are traceable in the direct male line since before the Conversion of Armenia in AD 314.

Yearning backwards to the earliest sources of identifiable ancestors, I have so far discussed mainly royal or sacred lineages, only because it is usually through them that there is the best chance of getting furthest back, following all possible lines, male or female. To recapitulate: kings marry into even older dynasties across nations, their daughters marry local nobles whose daughters in turn marry lesser landowners in their districts, and so on downwards to the farmer's younger sons' daughters who marry labourers in the villages. Thus a given Mackay clansman living in Strathnaver in the remotest north-west of Scotland in 1370 was not likely to be the ancestor of a given Robertson clansman living in Atholl in the central highlands by 1870. But King Robert II, living in 1370, had a daughter who married the Macdonald Lord of the Isles, and their daughter married the Mackay chief. As a result of local intermarriage generation after generation among the Mackay cadets in Strathnaver, there is a strong likelihood of a given clansman there in 1870 descending from King Robert II. Similarly, another of Robert II's daughters married the thane of Glamis, and in the following century Lord Glamis's daughter married the Robertson chief: again, owing to local intermarriage generation after generation among the Robertson cadets in Atholl, there is a similarly strong likelihood of a given clansman there in 1870 descending from Robert II. And from Robert II, the genealogy can of course then be carried back without difficulty into the Dark Ages. It is the royal house that is the most probable unifying factor between the two widely separated clansmen's genealogies.

Finally, there is the question as to which are the oldest traceable native American descendants. Many noteworthy people including modern Europe's great benefactor General Marshall of the 'Marshall Plan' have sprung from the marriage of the colonist John Rolfe and the famous Virginian princess, Pocahontas (1595–1619), daughter of Powhatan, king of all the redskin tribes from the Alleghenies to the Atlantic seaboard. There are also the Spanish dukes of Moctezuma, descended from the maternal grandson of Halco Hucpantzin (Don Pedro of Moctezuma), son of the celebrated Montezuma, actually Moteuczoma II, Emperor of Mexico, who perished in 1520; and whose ancestry, we are given to understand in Stokvis' *Manuel d'Histoire, de Généalogie et de Chronologie* (Leyden, 1888), was traceable through twelve further generations by way of the Aztec king Acamapechtli of Tenochtitlan

(1350–1404) back to the Toltec king Totepeuh II (985–1026). By a happy combination of the proud native and the conquistador, the then Conde de Moctezuma was Spanish Viceroy of Mexico 1696–1701. It is to be hoped that as many other people as possible who have any redskin ancestry will record as much of it as is known while there is yet time.

We should all set to and emulate the effort behind Alex Haley's remarkable *Roots*, where he may have been misled about the exact village in Africa but nevertheless tracked down his American slave ancestry across the wide Atlantic to the aristocratic Mandinka kindred who bore the surname of Kinte in the former kingdom of Baddibu on the Gambia. And Mandinka history in general is known for the last thousand years, though it is rather an irony that although they abolished cannibalism throughout their conquests in West Africa they were themselves famous as slave-traders. Apart from the records kept in the Moslem and Christian north, such as those of the sultans of Morocco and the former imperial dynasty of Ethiopia, most black African genealogies are oral (as in Polynesia), but none the less valuable for all that, as their keeping was a sacred task. Thus the forefathers of the present Sabataka of the Baganda, son of my late friend 'King Freddie', the last Kabaka of Buganda, at whose ancestral court some of the ritual ceremonies went back to Ancient Egypt, are known through some thirty-five generations back to prince Kintu, the first Kabaka about 1300, an incoming royalty from a neighbouring kingdom whose dynasty is believed to have come by way of Abyssinia. In Africa, we may have come full circle, back to the cradle of Mankind.

From I. M.'s Introduction to *Debrett's Family Historian* (1981)

A Treasure-House of Family Tales

I. M. used to say that he wanted Burke's Peerage & Baronetage to become 'a treasure-house of family tales'. His rollicking accounts of genealogy certainly gave a new meaning to the term 'narrative pedigree'. Here are some extracts from the prize specimens he contributed:

MONCREIFFE OF THAT ILK

Lineage – The Moncreiffe family derive their name from the feudal Barony of Moncreiffe in Perthshire, which is itself derived from the old Gaelic place-name *Monadh Craoibhe*, 'the Hill of the Sacred Bough' (presumably oak, immemorially the family plant-badge), and has been in their possession since before surnames were first adopted in Scotland. They are the oldest family in Perthshire to have retained their original lands in the male line.

On the summit of Moncreiffe Hill the ancient Kings of the Picts had their principal stronghold, evidently called Dun Monaidh; and the early tenures of the Moncreiffe family connect them with Atholl and Dundas, both held by yr. branches of the old Picto-Scottish Royal House. The Moncreiffe Arms with the royal lyon red on silver, the colours of the house of Maldred, Regent of the Cumbrians and brother of King Duncan slain by Macbeth 1040, indicate them to have been early cadets of the same branch of Maldred's line as Dundas, their neighbours at Fingask and Dunbarny which sandwich Moncreiffe (c.f. the same 13th century 'chief ermine' heraldic differencing of Fitzmaurice on FitzGerald). So it seems probable that the Moncreiffes were also scions (although in the female line from Maldred's mother backwards through the Dark Ages) of the ancient Celtic dynasty whose *dun* was on the Hill, and that they have inherited Moncreiffe from the mists before the dawn of our national history, perhaps 1,500 years ago. In the male line, Maldred himself belonged to the Kindred of St Columba, sprung from Niall of the Nine Hostages, pagan sacral King of Ireland, living in 400 AD at Tara.

There are three main lines left in Scotland today, all descended from the 8th Laird of Moncreiffe, who d. 1496: that of Lord Moncreiff of Tulliebole, that of MONCRIEFF *of Bandirran*, including in the female line SCOTT-MONCRIEFF *formerly of Fossaway* and MONCRIEFF *of Kinmonth* and that of the present chiefs. Each line is differentiated by its spelling of the name. Another line settled abroad in the 16th century as Archers of the Scots Guard of the Kings of France, and formed three branches of French seigneurs. But one branch ended in an Academician, one of the 'Immortals'; another finished when the Marquis de Moncrif was guillotined in the Terror; the third was ended by a cannon-ball at Eylau.

The Moncreiffes' mediaeval obligations are still maintained: thus they are even now (1970) obliged to pay Perth Hospital £2 4s. 5d. annually (soon to be converted to new pence), because in ROBERT BRUCE's reign Sir John Moncreiffe of that Ilk granted a charter to the Black Friars of Perth allowing them corn from Moncreiffe that they should pray for the souls of the Moncreiffe family, this right being transferred at the Reformation to JAMES VI's Hosp., and commuted to money in 1591. The names of the early Lairds are only

traditional (RAMER, GASPAR, GERARD and ROGER: Frankish names that may derive from the important local marriage alliance of an heiress of the house of Maldred to a powerful baron of the great Norman house of Mowbray) and so Sir MATHEW, the first to be recorded in a Royal Charter, is now counted as 1st Laird of Moncreiffe.

SIR MATHEW OF MONCREIFFE had a charter dated 1 Feb. 1248 (which is still preserved at Moncreiffe) confirming him in the lands of Moncreiffe. He also held Balgony near Abernethy in the Clan Macduff country, and the Atholl lands of Culdares and Duneaves in the mouth of Glenlyon. He m. Marjorie, sister of John of Dundemor, lord of Dundemor in Fife, co-Regent of Scotland during the minority of King ALEXANDER III, and was given with her the lands of Dunbarrow near Strathmiglo, also in Fife. Sir Mathew was s. by

SIR JOHN MONCREIFFE OF THAT ILK, 2nd Laird, was forced to do homage to EDWARD I of England 1296, but according to tradition sheltered Sir William Wallace in a cave on Moncreiffe Hill. In 1312 he resigned Easter Moncreiffe at the Feast of St. Benedict to a yr. son Mathew, ancestor of the first line of Moncreiffes of Easter Moncreiffe, the ruins of whose Tower still survive. Sir John's eldest son,

WILLIAM MONCREIFFE OF THAT ILK, 3rd Laird, rode with the Earl of Atholl and a number of other Scottish barons on the great raid into Northumberland in 1296, when they burnt Corbridge and Hexham, but on their return the Scots were defeated at Dunbar, where his near relation Thomas of Moncreiffe was captured; and as 'William de Mouncrefe' he was obliged to add his name to the Ragman Roll. His son,

DUNCAN MONCREIFFE OF THAT ILK, 4th Laird, d. 1357 and is *bur.* in the ruined chapel of Moncreiffe, where his red tombstone is the oldest to survive. His successor,

JOHN MONCREIFFE OF THAT ILK, 5th Laird, mentioned in Sir Walter Scott's *Fair Maid of Perth, d.* 1410, and was s. by his son,

MALCOLM MONCREIFFE OF THAT ILK, 6th Laird ('Malcolmus de Moncreiffe de codem'), a member of King JAMES II's Council which acted as Lords Auditors (the effective Government), received a new charter incorporating both his Highland and his Lowland estates into the free Barony of

Moncreiffe, with the usual jurisdiction of life and death 1 Dec. 1455, *m.* Elena (*d.* 1458), dau. of Sir David Murray of Tullibardine, and *d.* 1464/5. His son,

JOHN MONCREIFFE OF THAT ILK, 7th Laird Chamberlain and personal Squire to the boy King JAMES III 1464, *m.* Beatrix, dau. of James Dundas of that Ilk by his wife Cristina Stewart, sister of the 'Black Knight of Lorn' (who *m.* Joan Beaufort, Queen Dowager of Scotland, and was murdered by Flemish pirates). The 7th Laird *d.* between 1466 and 1475, having had with other issue,

JOHN MONCREIFFE OF THAT ILK, 8th Laird, was convicted of wrongfully occupying the lands of Kinmonth (the *Ceann-monaidh* or 'Head of the Hill' of Moncreiffe) 1484, and was at feud with John Ramsay of Kilgour, who slew his brother and was ordered to pay 'Johnne Moncreif of that Ilk . . . 300 merks for infefting a perpetuale priest for the soul of umquhile Andrew Moncreif', 1494–5, the dispute being about the teind-sheaves of Abernethy and Dunbarny. By his 1st wife Margaret, dau. of Sir Robert Levingston of Drumry, Laird of Easter Wemyss, he had, with other issue,

JOHN (Sir), 9th Laird.
The 8th Laird of Moncreiffe *m.* 2ndly, Janet Strathauchin (Strachan), sister of Mr Gilbert Strathauchin, Canon of Aberdeen and Prothonotary Apostolic, and after the laird's death *ca.* 1496 her family carried off the matrix of his heraldic seal and a number of Moncreiffe family deeds (an impression of this seal in 1476 is in the possession of the Duke of Atholl). His eldest son,

SIR JOHN MONCREIFFE OF THAT ILK, 9th Laird, was one of the 14 peers and lairds who entered into a personal bond with King JAMES IV for the suppression of crimes 27 May, 1501, his autograph as 'Jhon of Muncreff of that Ilk' survives on another document of that year, *m.* Beatrix, niece of Andrew Forman, Archbishop of St. Andrews, and was *k.* with his kinsman John Moncreiffe of Easter Moncreiffe and the other 'Flowers of the Forest' at the battle of Flodden, fighting the English, 9 Sept. 1513, leaving with other issue,

WILLIAM MONCREIFFE OF THAT ILK, 10th Laird, supported the Red Douglas (the Earl of Angus) at the battle of Manuel 1526, was fined for refusing to sit on the assize that condemned Lady Glamis to be burnt as a witch 1532, was captured at Solway Moss and imprisoned in the Tower of London, being apparelled at HENRY VIII's expense in a gown of black damask, a coat of black velvet and a doublet of black satin, as mourning for his own King, JAMES V 1542, was one of the 16 captured peers and lairds who signed the Articles of Agreement with the English king at Hampton Court, relating to a marriage between the king's son and the infant MARY, Queen of Scots 1542, took part with 10 other Moncreiffe gentlemen on the side of the 4 earls who were arrayed in battle at Leith against the Regent Arran 1543/4, and again with Lennox against Arran on the Muir of Glasgow 1544, fought for the Master of Ruthven against Lord Gray in the private battle on the Brig of Perth 1544, became a Protestant at the Reformation, acting unsuccessfully as their emissary to his cousin Adam Forman, Prior of the Charterhouse at Perth, before the mob despoiled the place 1559, had a blood feud with Lord Oliphant from 1560, was among the Barons who subscribed the Articles in the General Assembly of the Church of Scotland 1567, was forfeited by the Queen's Parl. in Edinburgh, but sat in the rival King's Parl. at Stirling that forfeited the Queen's supporters 1571, *m. ca.* 1526, Margaret, dau. of Sir Andrew Murray of Balvaird, and *d.* 15 Dec. 1579, having had, with other issue,

WILLIAM MONCREIFFE, APPARENT OF THAT ILK, a hostage in England for his father's ransom 1543, was released (the ransom never paid) to take part in Lennox's rebellion 1544, entered the French Service 1552, rode with Moray, Châtelherault and John Knox on the 'Roundabout Raid', and fled to England 1565, signed the Band of Association after MARY's abdication 1567, was forfeited by the Queen's party 1571, raised and cmd'd. Moncreiffe's Regt. of Scottish mercenaries in the Swedish Service, entered into a plot to reinstate mad King Eric XIV by killing King John during an exhibition sword dance at the royal palace (to secure arrears of pay), but the plot was betrayed, 1573, was arrested, April 1574, and never heard of again. He was *b. ca.* 1526, *m.* 1550, Jean, dau. of Laurence, 3rd Lord Oliphant, and had with other issue,

WILLIAM MONCREIFFE OF THAT ILK, 11th Laird, was the last to have the hereditary right to sit in Parl. as a feudal Baron before the statute providing for the election of

Commissioners to represent the barons, took part with other Moncreiffes in slaying Arthur Jardine 1578, was chosen a Gentleman of the King's Chamber to guard JAMES VI from Morton 1580, joined in the Band of Association of the whole Name of Murray 'for the assurance and taking order of our own estates, the defence of our rooms, tacks, steadings, goods and gear, which by the incursions of Broken Men, and unthankful and unnatural neighbours, may appear to be in danger', this treaty setting up a Council of Murray lairds and the Laird of Moncreiffe under the presidency of Tullibardine, with powers to settle quarrels within the Murray league and to initiate action against outside aggressors 1586, sold his Highland lands of Culdares and Duneaves to pay for the acquisition of the Fife barony of Carnbee 1599, *m.* 1586, Anne, dau. of Robert Moray of Abercairny, and *d.* 27 Sept. 1624, being *s.* by his eldest son,

SIR JOHN MONCREIFFE OF THAT ILK, 12th Laird and 1st Bt., Sheriff of Perthshire, was *cr.* a *Baronet of Nova Scotia*, being granted a nominal 16,000 acres (never taken up) in that dominion, incorporated by King CHARLES I into the free Barony and Regality of New Moncreiffe 1626, signed 'for Perthescheir' the National Covenant 1638, also signed for Perthshire the commission appointing Leslie to comd. the Covenanting Forces, and *d.* Jan. 1651. By his 2nd wife Lady Mary Murray, dau. of 2nd Earl of Tullibardine, and sister of 1st Earl of Atholl, Sir John left an eldest son.

SIR JOHN MONCREIFFE OF THAT ILK, 13th Laird and 2nd Bt., Capt. and Lt.-Col. Scots Guards, personally raised No. IX Company Scots Guards (now Right Flank 2nd Bn.) for the Regt. by Warrant from CHARLES II 1674, being childless and in debt the Crown confirmed a family arrangement whereby in 1667 he sold the Barony of Moncreiffe, with its Tower and Fortalice, to his kinsman Thomas Moncreiffe (*see above* under the 8th Laird), who was accordingly ranked immediately next to him at the family conclave held at Tippermaloch, 6 Apr. 1668, and at Sir John's death after 2 May, 1683, he was *s.* in his Baronetcy by his *unm.* brother, David, but as chief of the Name by his kinsman [descended from the 2nd son of the 8th Laird – *see above*],

Sir Thomas Moncreiffe of that Ilk, 1st Bt, who thus became 14th Laird. In 1674

CHARLES II united in his favour the formerly separate Baronies of Moncreiffe and Easter Moncreiffe, and on 30 Nov. 1685, he was *cr.* a Baronet as MONCREIFFE OF THAT ILK by JAMES VII, to whom he had been a close adviser while that king, as Duke of York, had governed Scotland. An original mem. of the Royal Co. of Archers, during the Commonwealth he acted as Clerk of the Secret but Royal Cttee., who sent him several times to visit CHARLES II in exile, he was Clerk of the Exchequer and Treas. in Scotland (completely modernising the Treas. as its permanent head) during 5 reigns from the Restoration, pulled down the old castle of Moncreiffe and erected a new seat, the first complete country house ever to be designed by Sir William Bruce 1679, took the Test as heritable Bailie, Steward, Justiciar, Crowner and Adm. of the Regality of St. Andrews 'and as having right to the coquet thereof' (the Customs seal of office) 1682, signed the order for the payment of compensation to the victims of the Massacre of Glencoe 1692, augmented the existing (1567) family patronage of two bursaries at St. Andrews (still held by Eilsabeth Moncreiffe of Moncreiffe) 1703, and endowed by the Moncreiffe Mortification the right of presenting a maiden for education by the Edinburgh Merchant Maiden school (still held by the present Baronet) 1708. Sir Thomas was *b.* 1626, *m.* 1stly, Bethia (*d.* 1703), dau. of Alexander Hamilton of Hill, Lord Justice Clerk during the Protectorate. He *m.* 2ndly, Mary (*d.* Nov. 1723), dau. of Sir Thomas Hope of Kerse, Lord Justice Gen., and widow of Sir John Young of Leny, and *d.s.p.* 15 Jan. 1715, aged 89, when he was *s.* by his nephew,

Sir Thomas Moncreiffe of that Ilk, 2nd Bt, and 15th Laird, mem. Royal Company of Archers, *educ.* St. Andrews and on the Grand Tour, had a dispute with the City of Perth over a new sandbank that appeared near Moncreiffe Island in the Tay, the Perth fisherfolk cutting the nets and threatening to 'cutt the noses' of the Moncreiffe fishermen 1714, during the subsequent litigation was threatened with attack 'as a suspected persone', presumably for Jacobite leanings, 1715, *bapt.* 3 Oct. 1678, *m.* (contract 22 Dec. 1701) Margaret, dau. of Patrick Smythe of Methven, and *d* Oct 1738, leaving issue,

Sir Thomas Moncreiffe of that Ilk, 3rd Bt,

and 16th Laird, mem. Royal Company of Archers, *educ.* Edin. Univ., and on the Grand Tour, sued his father for an increased allowance (Moncreiffe being an entailed estate to which he was next heir) and won in the Court of Session, but lost the appeal to the House of Lords, his father having retained his neighbour Lord Stormont's son, William Murray (afterwards Lord Chief Justice Mansfield), in one of his first three cases as counsel at the bar of the Lords, 1734, knocked out his brother David with a cane at the Perth Ball 1738, *b.* 31 Dec. 1704, *m.* (an elopement) 2 June, 1730, Katharine (*d.* 24 June, 1735), dau. of the Jacobite Sir William Murray of Ochtertyre, 3rd Bt; descended through her paternal grandmother Margaret Haldane of Gleneagles from such great Highland chiefs as Grant of Grant, the Mackintosh and Macdonald of Clanranald, and through her maternal grandmother Lady Amelia Murray (*m.* the 9th and was abducted by the 11th Lord Lovat), dau. of 1st Marquis of Atholl and Lady Amelia Stanley (eventual heiress of the Isle of Man), from among others HENRY VII of England, William Cecil the great Lord Burghley, William the Silent prince of Orange and his 3rd wife Charlotte de Bourbon, Anne de Montmorency the Constable of France 'sans peur et sans reproche', the Lascaris and Commenus' emperors of Byzantium, and many of the most historic houses of mediaeval Christendom and beyond. By her he had, with other issue,

WILLIAM (Sir), **4th** Bt.

Sir Thomas *d.* 3 May, 1739, and was *s.* by his elder surv. son,

Sir William Moncreiffe of that Ilk, 4th Bt, and 17th Laird, said to have been crippled by a nurse dropping him from a window, *educ.* Glasgow Univ., and Holland, during his childhood the Dowager Duchess of Atholl (who was staying at Moncreiffe) reported that a party of Jacobite 'ruffians' had robbed her and Lady Moncreiffe of their horses, but they were returned through the personal exertions of her son Lord George Murray who was also Sir William's cousin 1745, *b.* 11 Feb. 1732, *m.* Clara (*d.* 31 March, 1785), dau. of Robert Guthrie, brother of James Guthrie, 1st of Craigie, and *d.* 28 Sept. 1784, leaving issue (with a dau. Jean, *m.* Andrew Cunningham of Bonnington) a son,

Sir Thomas Moncreiffe of that Ilk, 5th Bt,

and 18th Laird, an early mem. of the Royal Caledonian Hunt, *educ.* St. Andrews, and on the Grand Tour, Ensign 36th Foot (aged 16) 1774, Cornet 10th Dragoons 1776, replanted Moncreiffe Hill 1786, mental eccentricity obscured his reason to the extent that the estate was put in charge of tutors 1791, thereafter drew many talented but irrelevant sketches in books in the library at Moncreiffe, and *d.* 26 March, 1818. He was *b.* 7 Jan. 1758, *m.* 13 Aug. 1786, Lady Elisabeth Ramsay (then aged 16), dau. of 8th Earl of Dalhousie and sister of the future Gov. of Canada. By her, a nature lover and botanist (who *d.* 3 June, 1848, when her night-cap took fire from a candle), he had issue,

DAVID (Sir), **6th** Bt.

Georgina Elisabeth, *b.* 20 Aug. 1790, *m.* 5 March, 1818, 2nd Earl of Bradford, and *d.* 12 Oct. 1842, leaving issue. Her husband remarried her brother's widow, Lady Moncreiffe.

Sir Thomas was *s.* by his only son,

Sir David Moncreiffe of that Ilk, 6th Bt, and 19th Laird, D.L. Perthshire, Capt. of the Royal & Ancient Golf Club, St. Andrews (gold medallist twice), mem. Royal Co. of Archers, Preses of the Royal Caledonian Hunt, Major 3rd King's Own Light Dragoons (aged 24) 1814, *educ.* Eton, a keen Regency sportsman, built kennels at Moncreiffe for the Fife foxhounds to visit, one of his Manton shotguns is preserved in H.M. Armouries at the Tower, kept a racing stable at Easter Moncreiffe, drew up the present Perth Hunt rules as Preses 1818, and won many trophies coursing and cockfighting, *b.* 31 Dec. 1788, *m.* 12 Jan. 1819 (as the result of a successful wager) Helen (who *m.* 2ndly, 30 Oct. 1849, George Augustus, 2nd Earl of Bradford, and *d.* 25 April, 1869), dau. of Capt. Æneas Mackay of Scotstoun (descended from Donald, 1st Lord Reay, Chief of the Clan Mackay), who had been chained to Sir David Baird for over three years after being captured by Hyder Ali at the battle of Conjeveram, and by her had, with two daus.,

1. THOMAS (Sir), **7th** Bt.

2. William Æneas, respected for 'his kindness and simplicity' but 'proud and honourable to an absurdity', an Offr. 92nd Highrs., exchanged as Major into the 72nd (then in India) after a row with his colonel, got sunstroke, settled in Australia where he 'fell into bad hands, trusted everybody and

12

was robbed on all sides', spent 18 months alone in the bush tracking a favourite mare, and at 62 could still ride a bucking colt, *b.* 19 Jan. 1825; *d. unm.* in Queensland, 5 Jan. 1906.

Sir David *d.* 20 Nov. 1830 (winning as a result a bet with Whyte Melville, who was obliged to give the famous Silver Putter, bearing both their Arms, to the R. & A. at St. Andrews for not dying first), and was *s.* by his elder son,

Sir Thomas Moncreiffe of that Ilk, 7th Bt., and 20th Laird, Vice-Lieut. of Perthshire, hon. Col. Royal Perthshire Rifles, mem. (aged 15) of the Queen's Body Guard for Scotland (Royal Co. of Archers), Capt. of the Royal & Ancient Golf Club, St. Andrews (gold medallist), and of the Golfers of Blackheath, Chm. Perthshire Conservative Assoc., *educ.* Harrow, Lieut. Gren. Guards 1839–43, keen on hunting, stalking and entomology (the Perth Natural History Museum was dedicated to his memory), mem. of White's but a founder mem. of the Turf Club and an original mem. of Pratt's, *b.* 9 Jan. 1822, *m.* 2 May, 1843, Lady Louisa Hay (*d.* 4 Sept. 1898), eldest dau. of 11th Earl of Kinnoull, Lord Lyon King of Arms, whose mother was the last surviving Lady Patroness of Almack's, and had issue,

1. David Maule, *b.* 12 Dec. 1854, *d.* 25 April, 1857.
2. ROBERT DRUMMOND (Sir), **8th Bt.**
3. (Thomas George) Harry, planter in India, *b.* 9 Oct. 1861, *educ.* Harrow, *m.* 31 Aug. 1883, Elisabeth (*d.* 20 Feb. 1947), dau. of Sir John Muir of Deanston, 1st Bt., Lord Provost of Glasgow, and *d.* of fever at Calcutta 26 March, 1887, leaving issue,
   1. (JOHN ROBERT) GUY (Sir), **9th Bt.**
   2. (Thomas) Gerald Auckland, Lt.-Cmdr. R.N., served in World War I 1914–18 (wounded as Gunnery Lieut. of H.M.S. *Mersey* at the sinking in the Rufigi Delta, E. Africa, of the raiding cruiser S.M.S. *Koenigsberg*, 1915), keen big game hunter, cleared the jungle scrub and set up a coffee plantation at Fort Ternan in Kenya 1913, *b.* 13 Sept. 1886, *educ. Britannia, m.* 17 June, 1918, Hinda (who *m.* 2ndly, 7 April, 1923, Capt. Geoffrey Lionel Smith, of Chile Estate, Koru, Kenya, yst. son of late Sir William Smith; and 3rdly, 1931, late Charles Arthur Gordon McMinn, of

Nanyuki, Kenya, and *d.* 14 Jan. 1960), dau. of Comte François de Miremont, and *d.* 3 June, 1922, leaving issue,
   (RUPERT) IAIN KAY (Sir), **11th Bt.**
4. William, family historian, rancher in Wyoming 1888-1923, his Moncreiffe Ranch on Little Goose Creek being now the Brinton Memorial Ranch museum, friend of Col. 'Buffalo Bill' Cody and President 'Teddy' Roosevelt, served in Roosevelt's Rough-Riders in the Spanish-American War, bagged a wapiti considered by Selous the most beautiful deer head ever shot, 1896, provided (with his bro.) 22,500 horses for the Boer War, *b.* 19 Jan. 1863, *educ.* Harrow, and Trin. Coll. Camb., *m.* 9 March, 1909, Edith Mary (*d.* 21 Dec. 1957), dau. of Hugh Conyngham Boyd, of Ash Grove, Newry, Ireland, late of Woodside, Torquay, and *d.s.p.* 31 May, 1944.
5. Ronald, Capt. Worcestershire Imp. Yeo., served in Matabele War 1896, and in S. African War (on Baden Powell's staff, throughout Siege of Mafeking, when not in close arrest) 1900–02, a celebrated clubman and drinker in White's and on the Turf, keen shot and polo player, friend of QUEEN ALEXANDRA and Cecil Rhodes, took part in the Jameson Raid, *b.* 3 May, 1864, *educ.* Harrow, *m.* 8 Oct. 1906, Edith Evelyn Kathleen (who *m.* 2ndly, Guy Hylton Gardiner), only dau. of Arthur Arthington Worsley, and *d.s.p.* 6 Aug. 1909.
6. Malcolm, rancher in Wyoming, located on the old T.J. Ranch with Hon. Fred Bennet on the Powder River 1895, and acquired Polo Ranch in Sheridan co. 1904, *b* Oct. 1866, *educ.* Harrow, *m.* 23 April, 1901, Amy Morehead (*d.* 22 Sept. 1954), sister of the late Countess of Portsmouth, dau. of Samuel Morehead, Governor of Kentucky during the American Civil War, and *d.s.p.* 15 June, 1948.
7. Claude, *b.* 21 June, 1869, *d.* an infant.
8. John Alexander, M.C., D.C.M., Major Oxfordshire Hus., served in the Boer War, severely wounded as Sergeant Warwickshire Imp. Yeo. at Kleis Drift on the Orange River (D.C.M. and immediate commn.), 1900, Lieut. Younghusband's Horse operations Cape Colony 1902, served in World War I 1914–19, cmd'd Cavalry Machine Gun Squadrons in France

13

and Flanders (wounded, despatches, M.C., French Croix de Guerre with palm), *b.* 2 Aug. 1871, *educ.* Harrow, *m.* 4 Oct. 1910, Lady Beatrice Constance Grosvenor (*d.* 12 Jan. 1911), widow of 3rd Baron Chesham, and 2nd dau. of 1st Duke of Westminster, K.G., and *d.s.p.* 21 June, 1933.

1. Louisa, *b.* 11 June, 1844, *m.* 29 Oct. 1863, 7th Duke of Atholl, K.T., and *d.* 8 July, 1902, leaving issue. He *d.* 20 Jan. 1917.

2. Helen, *b.* 18 July, 1845, *m.* 5 April, 1864, Sir Charles John Forbes of Newe, 4th Bt., and *d.* 12 Nov. 1913, leaving issue. He *d.* 24 July, 1884. In his well-known memoirs, Lord Frederic Hamilton thought her 'the most perfect example of classical beauty I have ever seen, had features as clean-cut as those of a cameo'.

3. Georgina Elisabeth, R.R.C., D.J.St.J., *b.* 9 Aug. 1846, *m.* 21 Nov. 1865, 1st Earl of Dudley and *d.* 2 Feb. 1929, leaving issue. He *d.* 7 May, 1885, Lord Frederic Hamilton's memoirs call her 'a radiant apparition', while the Official Report commented on her toil for sick and wounded in the Boer and First World Wars: 'The history of women's work for the Red Cross in this country provides, so far as we are aware, no similar example of equally sustained labour producing results of the same value'.

4. Harriet Sarah, *b.* 7 Feb. 1848, *m.* 7 Dec. 1866 (*m.* diss. by div. 1875), Sir Charles Mordaunt, 10th Bt., M.P., and *d.* 9 May, 1906, leaving issue. He *d.* 15 Oct. 1897.

5. Blanche, *b.* 2 June, 1849, *m.* 11 June, 1878, Charles Archibald Murray of Taymount, and *d.* 4 July, 1926, leaving issue.

6. Frances Rose, *b.* 22 Sept. 1850, *m.* 21 Feb. 1871, Sir Alexander Muir-Mackenzie of Delvine, 3rd Bt., and *d.s.p.* 7 July, 1923. He *d.* 25 June, 1909.

7. Selina, *b.* 4 Oct. 1851, *m.* 20 July, 1869, as his 2nd wife, Major-Gen. William Arbuthnot, C.B., 14th Hus., and *d.* 26 Nov. 1877, leaving issue.

8. Mary Katherine, a pioneer in setting up shop as interior decorator, *b.* 3 Dec. 1859, *m.* 26 Oct. 1880 (*m.* diss. by div. 1905), Sir Basil Templer Graham Montgomery, 5th Bt., Laird of Lochleven, and *d.* 30 July, 1910, having had issue. He *d.* 4 Oct. 1928.

Sir Thomas, whose daus. were celebrated Victorian beauties, *d.* 15 Aug. 1879, when a unique Atholl Highrs. firing party attended his funeral in the Chapel of Moncreiffe, and was *s.* by his eldest surv. son,

Sir Robert Drummond Moncreiffe of that Ilk, 8th Bt, and 21st Laird, C.B., C.M.G., V.D., T.D., D.L. Perthshire, A.D.C. to KING GEORGE V, hon. Col. 6th (Perthshire) Bn. The Black Watch (Royal Highlrs.), Capt. Atholl Highrs., *educ.* Harrow, Lieut. Scots Guards 1876–81, served in World War I, cmd'd Perthshire Bn. The Black Watch (aged 58, and after an apparently hopeless stomach operation) at the battles of Festubert, La Boiselle and Thiepval (despatches twice, mil. C.M.G.) 1915, cmd'd. at Edinburgh Castle 1918, *b.* 3 Nov. 1856, *m.* 6 April, 1880, his cousin Evelyn Elisabeth Vane (*d.* 16 Jan. 1938), eldest dau. of Col. Hon. Charles Rowley Hay Drummond of Cromlix, and *d.s.p.* 8 June, 1931, when he was *s.* by his nephew,

Sir (John Robert) Guy Moncreiffe of that Ilk, 9th Bt., and 22nd Laird, Cmdr. R.N., served in blockade of Venezuela (bombardment of Puerto Cabello) 1902–03, on Royal Yacht *Victoria and Albert*, and in World War I as a Submarine Cmdr. (wrecked off Texel), Lieut. Atholl Highrs., a keen big game shot, *b.* 30 June, 1884, *educ. Britannia, m.* 29 April, 1919, Mary, Offr. Order of Orange-Nassau of the Netherlands, dau. of late John Balli, of London and Paris, and had issue,

DAVID GERALD (Sir), **10th Bt.**

(Katharine) Elisabeth, 24th of Moncreiffe, served in World War II in W.R.N.S. (*Moncreiffe, Perthshire*), *b.* 23 May, 1920.

Sir Guy *d.* 7 Sept. 1934, and was *s.* by his only son,

Sir David Gerald Moncreiffe of that Ilk, 10th Bt., and 23rd Laird, M.C., mem. of the Queen's Body Guard for Scotland (Royal Co. of Archers), Capt. Scots Guards, served in World War II, fought in Right Flank (the Company raised by the 13th Laird – *see above*) together with his cousin Iain (afterwards 11th Bt.) in both battles of Monte Camino, now a battle honour on the Colours 1943, sniped German snipers on the Arno (M.C.) 1944, wounded twice as Patrol Offr., Capt. Atholl Highrs., *b.* 29 July, 1922, *educ.* Eton, and Edin. Univ., *d. unm.* in a fire which destroyed his family seat, 17 Nov. 1957, when he was *s.* by his cousin . . .

O'NEILL

Lineage – The great dynastic House of O'Neill is the most famous branch of the ancient royal family of Tara, whose recorded filiation is accepted by scholars from about 360 AD, and which is the oldest traceable family left in Europe. It was of their palace that the poet Thomas Moore wrote the celebrated verses that begin 'The harp that once through Tara's halls'. When they first appear in written history (after the conversion of Ireland) they had already been pagan sacral kings from time immemorial, and were the greatest royalty among the ancient Gaels. They gave High Kings to all Ireland from the 5th century until the 13th century, and reigned from 425 until 1603 in Northern Ireland, where the Lords O'Neill owe their position to descent from an heiress of this dynasty. Their surname, the first ever to be adopted in Ireland, means 'Grandson of Niall' and was originally assumed by their forefather King Domnall, grandson of King Niall 'Black-Knee', during the period 944-956 when he was rightful heir to the temporarily usurped Kingdom of Ireland.

The Gaels invaded Ireland before the dawn of the Christian era, and eventually established their sacral kings at Tara. These pagan Iron Age kings belonged to the royal family that claimed descent through the semi-legendary god-king Cormac (traditionally King of Tara 254–277) from incarnations of their ancestral spirit, Conn 'of the Hundred Battles'. They were associated with human sacrifice of royal victims from within their own dynastic family, for 'as in the sacred grove of the Golden Bough, the king of Tara reigned, as a rule, by virtue of having slain his predecessor'. If by mischance the king died a natural death, the druids performed a white-bull sacrifice to determine into which prince of the dynasty the lucky spirit of the Conn-folk had passed. Each king underwent the mystery of four tests, including a horse ritual, and was inaugurated to the weird sound of a bull-roarer, on the celebrated *Lid Fal* or Stone of Destiny still to be seen at Tara.

EOCHU *Mugmedon* 'Slaves-Lord', KING OF TARA, living 360 AD, earned his nickname by slave raids on Roman Britain, in one of which he carried off and married a princess of the Ancient Britons called Carina, by whom he had a son,

NIALL *Noigiallach* 'of the Nine Hostages', KING OF IRELAND, living 400 AD, in whose time the royal house of Tara asserted a nominal suzerainty over the whole island. He was possibly the Irish king who campaigned against Stilicho, father-in-law of the Roman emperor Honorius; and was anyway slain (whether by a thunder-bolt or by a hostage King of Leinster) while engaged in the wars abroad . . .

NIALL *Frasach* 'of the Showers', KING OF IRELAND 763–770, whose reign opened with three months of snow and continued in famine, earthquakes and pestilence, so that in 770 he abdicated and became a monk at Iona, where he *d.* 778. He *m.* Eithne (who *d.* 768), dau. of Breasal of Brega . . .

NIALL *Glundubh* 'Black-Knee', KING OF IRELAND 916–919 captured and drowned a murderer who had violated the sanctuary of Armagh 907, revived the ancient Fair of Taltiu 916, campaigned repeatedly against the Danes and Norse in Ireland, but was mortally wounded in battle near Dublin against their king, Sigtryg (King of Dublin, afterwards King of York), and was shriven on the battlefield, 15 Sept. 919. From him, the O'Neills derive their name. He *m.* Gormfhlaith (who *d.* 947 after accidentally falling on the sharp-pointed post of her bed), widow of Cormac, King of Munster, and of Cearbhall, King of Leinster, and dau. of his predecessor Fiann *Sionna* 'the Fox', King of Ireland (876-916), Head of the Southern Ui Neill, and by her had issue . . .

MUIRCHEARTACH *na Cochall Craicenn* 'of the Leather Cloaks', KING OF AILECH 938–943, Royal Heir of Ireland, 'the Hector of the West of the World', one of the greatest of Irish commanders, generous to his enemies, often defeated the Danes or Norsemen and overran their territory around Dublin, slew his rebellious tributary Goach, local King of Keenaght 927, was surprised in his own stone fortress of Allech by the Norse, and carried prisoner to their ships on Lough Swilly, but escaped 939, fitted out his own fleet, and pursued them to their Hebridean islands, which he plundered 941, made his famous Circuit of Ireland in midwinter with a picked force of the Cenel Eoghain equipped with leather cloaks, carrying off the local kings in chains, feasting them splendidly at Ailech and sending them as hostages to his father-in-law the High King 941, his bard commemorated this expedition with a celebrated poem 942, had long yellow hair, and was *k.* in battle at Ardee against Blacar, King of Dublin, March, 943 . . .

AEDH *Macaemh Tóinleasg* 'the Lazy-Arsed Youth', KING OF CENEL EOGHAIN 1176–1177, Royal Heir of Ireland, slew his father's slayer, 1160, restored O'Neill power by his energy after his inauguration at Tulach Og, established his rule over all Tir Eoghain (Tyrone), and became supreme in the North of Ireland 1176, a 13th-century Norman-French poem records his help to the high-king Ruaridh O'Conor against the English invaders in Meath, 'De Kineloyin, O'Nel Il Reis od sei menad tri mil Yrreis' (O'Neill, the King of Cenel Eoghain, brought with him 3,000 Irishmen), but he was slain in battle against his successor Maelsechlainn Mac Lochlainn, whose son Ardgal he cut down in the fray, 1177 . . .

WAKE

Lineage – The famous House of Wake is among the very few surviving families of the old pre-parliamentary Anglo-Norman baronage, who were already Peers of the Realm when the Mother of Parliaments was first evolved. Indeed, a Wake baron was imprisoned by King John, and their banner was displayed in battle for Simon de Montfort's cause. Their battle-shield was also carried on Crusade in the Holy Land. The last Lord Wake died in 1349, married to a Royal Duke's sister. His own sister had married first the son of the Red Cummin, claimant to the throne of Scotland, and then a son of Kind Edward I – and her daughter 'the Fair Maid of Kent,' who married the Black Prince and was mother of King Richard II, became Baroness Wake in her own right. She was almost certainly the bewitching lady in honour of whose Garter the noble Order was founded.

The Fair Maid's descendants carried the senior female-line representation of the Wakes into the royal House of York, who were proud to label the Wake *torteaux* on their own ducal coat of arms: and thus the representation passed down through King Edward IV to the present Duke of Bavaria. But the male line of the Wakes has continued in Northamptonshire to this day, through Sir Thomas Wake whose pennon waved at Crécy. Many of their manorial lands were lost when the then Wake put on his armour to fight for the White Rose in 1485, as the Middle Ages went down on Bosworth Field. More yet had to be sold to pay Roundhead fines in 1647, because a troop of horse had been raised for King Charles by the second Wake baronet, who was a gallant Cavalier. Since then, the Wakes have given to England three Admirals, a General, an Ambassador in Paris, and an Archbishop of Canterbury.

But perhaps the chief distinction of the Wakes is that their surname has been popularly and independently accorded – although retrospectively – certainly from the 14th century onwards, to the Anglo-Saxon epic hero Hereward the Outlaw: from whom in fact they only claim descent in the female line. For it is evident that the valiant Mercian thegn Hereward was posthumously nick-named 'the Wake' precisely because he was locally remembered in the fenland as an ancester of the Wakes. They certainly inherited lands which had been Hereward's, and their descent from his daughter is indicated in later mediaval MSS., at least one of which is otherwise inimical to the family. When of course no direct contemporary evidence is known to have survived, there is no evidence to disprove the tradition of this descent, the existing form of which can be demonstrated to go back at least to the 13th century; and all the circumstantial evidence as far back as Domesday Book in 1086 tends to corroborate it . . .

The Descendants of Chaucer

Until recently, scholarly genealogists were convinced that the progeny of the world-famous poet Geoffrey Chaucer were extinct. Now, it would seem, we've found them a-plenty, alive and kicking in that part of

France which long thought of itself as English (to the fury of us Francophile Scots), and with any luck further research will perhaps trace some of them – besides the Durfort-Duras Earl of Feversham – back to England itself.

There have already been two-fold false hopes. Everybody remembers that the great Captal de Buch was a Founder Knight of the Garter. Most experienced genealogists will also remember the exciting prospect we once mistakenly viewed of a continuing Chaucerian descent through the marriage of a later Captal de Buch (also given the Garter, when he was created Earl of Kendal in 1446), demolished when the *Complete Peerage* (volume VII), demonstrated that his wife Margaret de la Pole was a *niece* and not a *daughter* of the Duke of Suffolk who married the Chaucerian heiress.

(It is of course essential that scholars following my text don't muddle the *de la Poles* with the *Poles* as is so easily done by the unwary with only a superficial knowledge of that period. The 'atte Poole' or de la Pole mercantile family, that rose to be dukes of Suffolk and to which this article refers, ended its role on the European stage when 'White Rose', the general whom François I had recognised as 'King Richard IV of England', was slain commanding a division at Pavia in 1525. This family had no connection whatsoever with that of Pole lord Montague, a completely different but equally Yorkist semi-royal family epitomised by Cardinal Reynold Pole, and whose name was pronounced 'Polle' not 'Poole'. For a genealogist to confuse the two families would be like attributing to W. H. Smith the descendants of F. E. Smith because both Hambleden and Birkenhead have 'grass roots' coronets).

The second false clue was the ancestress of the Stonors of Stonor, now Lords Camoys. For it turned out that, although indeed the daughter of William de la Pole, then earl and future 1st Duke of Suffolk who was in 1430 to marry Alice Chaucer, the Stonor lady was begotten thus: 'The nighte before that he was yolden' (*i.e.* Suffolk yielded himself up in surrender to the Franco-Scottish forces of Joan of Arc on 12 June 1429) 'he laye in bede with a Nonne whom he toke oute of holy profession and defouled, whose name was Malyne de Cay, by whom he gate a daughter, nowe married to Stonard of Oxonfordshire' (*Hist. MSS Com.* 3rd Rep., pp. 279–280).

Curiously enough, if there's no flaw in the third line of enquiry now to be set out here, it would appear that the historically Anglophile family of Durfort who later inherited for a while that *chanson de geste* title of 'Captal de Buch' have also produced Chaucer's still thriving offspring. The way of it is this.

In his *La Maison de Durfort à L'Epoque Moderne*, Professor Yves

Durand gives us at pp. 28–30 an account of the career of Gailhard de Durfort, Seigneur de Duras, Blanquefort & Villandraut, one of the two members of this great Gascon family to have been Knights of the Garter [the second was no. 493 in the list of the Order: Louis de Durfort (called de Duras) Marquis de Blanquefort and Earl of Feversham, British Ambassador to France – nominated 30 July and installed 25 August 1685]. At p. 297 the professor gives also a shorter summary of this career, as part of the Durfort genealogy appended.

Gailhard de Durfort, Seigneur de Duras, came of an old seigneural family who had risen to prominence in Aquitane through their maternal relationship to Pope Clement V (Avignon, 1305–1314). Gailhard lived in London during his youth. Torn between his particlar allegiance to the Duc d'Aquitaine (King Henry VI of England who claimed also to be King of France) and his more general allegiance to King Charles VII of France, he negotiated in 1451 the surrender of Bordeaux to the French, who failed however to keep their part of the bargain; whereupon in 1452 he renounced the homage he had done to Charles VII and joined in the pro-English revolt of the province of Guyenne. After the crushing defeat of the English Cause at Castillon in 1453, his lands were forfeited and he fled to England. There at first 'le proscrit vit fort mal'.

'*Puis commence la guerre des Deux-Roses*:; *Gaillard de Durfort choisit le parti d'York, celui qui finit par triompher. Edouard IV le fait chevalier de la Jarretière et gouverneur de Calais. Ses revenus s'augmentent de rentes dans le duché de Lancastre. Il épouse une Anglaise, Anne, fille du duc de Suffolk*'. There follows an account of his conduct of important military and diplomatic missions to Brittany and Burgundy. '*Survient alors la paix de Picquigny en 1457, et Louis XI octroie son pardon en juin 1476 aux exilés de 1453. Gaillard de Durfort recouvre alórs Duras, Blanquefort et Villandraut. . . . Il mourut en 1481, après avoir demande dans un testament rédigé à Duras un an auparavant, d'êntre enterré dans le tombeau de sa famille, chez les Frères Mineurs de Bordeaux*'.

There is a list of the successive Knights of the Garter at Appendix B to the *Complete Peerage*, vol. ii. Of these no. 193 is 'Galhard de Durfort, Seigneur de Duras. Nom. before 22 Apr. 1463, degraded 4 Nov. 1476, d. 1487 (*sic*)'. It may be noted that he was nominated by the victorious King Edward IV *vice* no. 110, namely Erik, King of Denmark, Norway and Sweden, who had died in 1459, the year before the Yorkists' temporary eclipse. Moreover, it is interesting to note that Edward IV's six nominations in 1463 were, in the following order: no. 192 Ferdinando, King of Naples; no. 193 Galhard de Durfort, Seigneur de Duras; no. 194 John, Lord Scrope of Bolton; no. 195 Francesco Sforza,

Duke of Milan; no. 196 James, Earl of Douglas (exiled from Scotland where his family had been next to the King in power); no. 197 Sir Robert Harcourt – and that no further Garter was given until 1465, when the Sovereign's own brother Richard Plantagenet, Duke of Gloucester, afterwards Sovereign of the Garter himself as King Richard III, was first nominated.

The extraordinary honour thus paid to this exiled Gascon lord is most easily accounted for if his wife was indeed '*Anne fille du duc de Suffolk*', as Professor Durand tells us not only at p. 29, but also at p.297 whereafter he traces her Durfort descendants down to the present-day Armand de Durfort, Duc de Lorge. For in April 1463 (when Durfort received the Garter from Edward IV) she could have been none other than sister of John de la Pole, 2nd Duke of Suffolk (not then 21, as he was born 27 September 1442) who before October 1460 had married King Edward IV's own sister Elizabeth (daughter of Richard, 3rd Duke of York, KG, Protector of England, Regent of France and Lord Lieutenant of Ireland, slain in battle December 1460). Young Suffolk himself had to wait for the Garter until he was thirty.

There is no mention of Anne, Dame de Duras as such in any of the ordinary English works on the Suffolk family – such as the *Complete Peerage*, Burke's *Extinct Peerage* or Napier's *Historical Notices of Swyncombe and Ewelme*. But the *Dictionary of National Biography*, in its article by C. L. Kingsford under 'POLE, William de la', on the 1st Duke of Suffolk, tells us of his children by his only wife Alice that 'Her son John succeeded his father as second Duke of Suffolk. She is credited with another son, William, and a daughter Anna'. If Professor Durand's French sources are correct, as the very grand circumstances in which the Seigneur de Duras received the Garter suggest, we have in this lady Anna de la Pole the prolific Anne, Dame de Duras.

Sir Anthony Wagner, Garter Principal King of Arms, in a letter to the present writer about this Durfort-Suffolk marriage, writes: 'whereas I have found no reference to it in any English record so far, I have found it in Père Anselme, *Histoire Généraloqique* . . . Tome V, Paris 1730, page 734, where it is stated that the wife of Galhard de Durfort IV, who died in 1487 [*sic*] 'was Anne de Sufolc, fille du duc de Sulfolc en Angleterre'. The authority for the statement is unfortunately not given, but Anselme is generally most reliable and as everything seems to fit I should be surprised if he were not basing himself on some good authority. One would have thought that when the English genealogists of the 17th century came to look at the pedigree of the Earl of Feversham, KG, they would have spotted who this lady was, but in fact I find a pedigree of Feversham in Simon Segar's Manuscript Baronage here [The College of

Arms] giving her simply as "Anne of the House of Suffolk in England".'

In this context, it may be worth observing that, at some time after the marriage of John 2nd Duke of Suffolk to the sister of Kings Edward IV and Richard III, the family seems to have preferred the surname 'of Suffolk' or simply 'Suffolk' to that of 'atte Poole' or 'de la Pole'. Whether this was only after the Suffolks' eldest son John, Earl of Lincoln, had been declared next heir to the Crown by his uncle Richard III in about May 1485 (*Complete Peerage xii, pt. i, p. 450*) is not clear. But, for instance, two of their younger sons, Lord William of Suffolk and Lord Richard of Suffolk appear in an official list in 1500 (*Complete Peerage, same vol., App. I, p. 22, note c*). Nicholas Talbot's testament proved in 1501 makes bequests to 'my Lord William of Suffolk' (*Bury St Edmund's Wills & Inventories*, ed. Samuel Tymms, 1850, pp. 87–88, 91). And indeed, in 1505–6, Lord Richard of Suffolk wrote to his elder brother, Lincoln's survivor Edmund Earl of Suffolk (formerly 3rd Duke, and Lord Richard styles him 'Your Grace' in the letter), signing himself 'your loving brother, RICHARD SUFFOLK' (Napier, *op. cit.*, p. 183). After Earl Edmund had been beheaded, Lord William of Suffolk was committed to the Tower for life, dying there in 1539; see the *Complete Peerage, vol. xii, pt. i, App. I, pp. 22–23*; and Lord Richard of Suffolk, now styling himself duke and called *White Rose* as nearest Yorkist claimant to the throne still at large, was slain on the side of France at Pavia in 1524/5. These facts are perhaps relevant in demonstrating the contemporary significance of the Suffolk family *as such* (not as Pole) from the point of view of subsequent Durfort chroniclers, and as illustrating the use of the *surname* 'Suffolk' by the de la Pole ducal family itself. The only other English family known to have used the surname 'Suffolk' at all near this period were a non-armigerous Warwickshire family of yeomen and butchers in 1589 – hardly likely to have supplied a wife to a Gascon lord who was a Knight of the Garter during the Wars of the Roses.

A minor yet perhaps relevant pointer, is that the Duc de Lorge tells me the name 'Georges', borne by the third son of Gailhard de Durfort and Anne of Suffolk, was very rare in 15th-century France (an exception that leaps to mind was Georges de la Trémouille, who lived much earlier and was politically on the opposite side). Now, a glance at the *Complete Peerage, vol. iii, App. C*, 'Some observations on Mediaeval Names', and especially p. 630, will show that at that period the name 'George' was equally rare in England despite her patron saint. However, any historian will at once recollect a marked exception: that of the immediate family of Cicely Nevill, Duchess of York, the mother of Kings Edward IV and Richard III and of the Duchess of Suffolk. This included her (the

Duchess of York's) brother George Nevill, Lord Latymer, of age in 1431; her nephew George Nevill, Archbishop of York, born about 1433, and George Nevill, 4th Lord Bergavenny, born about 1440; also her grand-nephews George Nevill, Duke of Bedford, born about 1457, and George Nevill, 5th Lord Bergavenny, born about 1469. Above all, they included her own son George Plantagenet, Duke of Clarence, born in 1449 (and fated for that death in a butt of Malmsey wine in 1477), brother of the Duchess of Suffolk. In view of the great rarity of the name in both France and England, it may therefore not seem too unreasonable to suggest that the Duchess of Suffolk's brother George, Duke of Clarence, KG., was the godfather of Anne of Suffolk's son *Georges* de Durfort – the more especially as there was then only one family bearing the surname of 'Suffolk' among the whole nobility and gentry of England.

That Lady Anne of Suffolk's French marriage should have passed unnoticed by modern English genealogists may be partly explained by her husband having been degraded from the Garter by the Yorkists on returning to his French allegiance in 1476, followed soon after in 1485 by the overthrow of the Yorkists themselves.

However, the matter is of more than usual genealogical importance. For there are otherwise no known descendants of Alice, wife of William de la Pole, 4th Earl and 1st Duke of Suffolk, KG, PC, also Earl of Pembroke and Comte de Dreux, Lord Chamberlain and Lord High Admiral of England. He was born 16 October 1396; succeeded his brother the 3rd Earl who was slain at Agincourt in 1415 (and whose body was then 'parboiled through the night till the flesh came away and the bones were then dried for removal with the Army to England'); was leader of the party for peace with France then seized in the Channel by political enemies on his way to temporary exile in May 1450, and his head hacked off clumsily on the gunwale of an open boat with half a dozen strokes by a rusty sword.

And the 1st Duke of Suffolk's duchess Alice, the widowed Countess of Salisbury whom he had married by a licence of 11 November 1430, was only child of Thomas Chaucer, MP, Speaker of the House of Commons, son and heir of Geoffrey Chaucer, the poet.

As Chaucer himself wrote: 'Wedlock is so easy and so clene'.

From I. M.'s paper to the XIII International Congress of Genealogical and Heraldic Sciences, 1976.

II

Blood Royal

The King's Evil

I say you chaps, there's something rather beastly about scrofula. The face becomes 'putrid' and the sores give forth a 'foetid odour'. Most of us wouldn't touch it with a barge pole. It's not very British to agree with that Orientalist genius James Elroy Flecker's song of the beggars of Baghdad:

> Show your most revolting scar;
> People never weary of it.
> The more nauseous you are . . .

Yet for many centuries the mighty Sovereigns of France and England, supermen like Richard *Coeur-de-Lion* and Saint Louis and *le Roi Soleil*, were not so squeamish when invited to fondle scrofulous folk with their own hands. They were only too eager to prove their sanctified legitimate claims by 'touching for the King's Evil'.

So did pretenders to these uneasy crowns. Always remember that 'pretender' formerly only meant 'claimant'. 'King Monmouth 'touched' during his unhappy rebellion; which he undertook secure in the prophecy that he would meet his fate on the Rhine so that he knew he was safe to invade England, only to be foiled by his particular Delphic python-priestess when his ragtag-and-bobtail pitchfork-men were baffled on that ditch called the Bussex Rhine at Sedgemoor – else my mother-in-law would have been a Royal Highness now. Similarly, Prince Charles Edward 'touched' at the Palace of Holyroodhouse in his capacity as Prince Regent during the heady swirl of the 'Forty-Five Rising. Did Henri IV 'touch' before he decided Paris was worth a Mass? He certainly did later.

The last King of France, Charles X, who like his brother may have learnt nothing (would you have wanted to learn to be like Fouché?) but had certainly forgotten nothing, 'touched' ten dozen tuberculous lumpy oozing necks on May 31 1825. Our last *de facto* ruler to do so had been Queen Anne. Although the book under review [*The Royal Touch:*

Sacred Monarchy and Scrofula in England and France, Marc Bloch (Routledge & Kegan Paul, 1973)] oddly don't mention it, the future Dr Samuel Johnson was among her patients. He remembered her from his involuntarily nauseous but meritoriously precocious childhood as a 'lady in diamonds and a long black hood' when his revolting ailment was lovingly brought to Her Majesty to prod. Yet the English beat the Frogs in the end, for a handkerchief stained with the hallowed blood of Henry Stuart, Cardinal York (Jacobite titular King Henry IX) was considered capable of curing 'the King's Evil' in Ireland as late as 1901.

Some years ago, a loyal Bavarian told me that on appointment to be German Ambassador to the Court of St James's he had called on the Duke of Bavaria (senior descendant of the Stuarts) at Nymphenburg, and been asked in ironic jest: 'Are you visiting me as King of Bavaria or as King of England?' But as a lawyer, I've worked out sound reasons, published so far only in brief in my book *The Highland Clans*, for ruling that the Cardinal York's lawful successor in 1807 was King George III. The Cardinal himself didn't know this, for he was no lawyer, but I believe he'd have been glad if he had. The soundest arguments against me are those of my forefather Sir Thomas Craig, the 16th-century lawyer, in his celebrated *Jus Fendale*: though I'm sure he could be persuaded he was mistaken if we could talk it over today. So it is my considered opinion as counsel that our Queen could nowadays rightfully 'touch' for scrofula. However, it seems just possible that Her Majesty wouldn't be immensely pleased at receiving a petition to revive such an emetically emotive ceremony.

Afterwards to be tortured and shot by the Gestapo for his gallant role in the Resistance that redoubtable French historian Professor Marc Bloch had compiled by 1923 *Les Rois thaumaturges*. This gold-mine of off-beat information now appears in English for the first time as *The Royal Touch: Sacred Monarchy and Scrofula in England and France*. The translator is J. E. Anderson, who has done his self-effacing but intricate task so well that it's hard to believe the original wasn't written in our own tongue. Perhaps it would have been better to call King Harold's controversial Anglo-Saxon father 'Earl' rather than 'Count' Godwin, and the 17th-century Irish scrofula-treater Valentine Greatrakes a 'gentleman' rather than a 'nobleman' (although you'll find his entertaining career was found worth an entry in the *DNB*): but these are minor quibbles. It usually seems unfair how little credit translators get, though it was sometimes said of C. K. Scott-Moncrieff (my 13th cousin twice removed but a loyal member of our kindred who used to come to our funerals at Moncreiffe) that his translations of Proust were almost better than the original.

We all know how Saint Martin is supposed to have divided his cloak with a beggar; but I never understood how the relic Hugh Capet wore as hereditary lay abbot of St Martin of Tours, a side-line to being King of France, could have been half a cape. So I for one am incidentally indebted to Anthony Goodman, who translated Appendix IV of this book, and who renders what I've usually called the *cape* of St Martin as the *cap* of St Martin. Thus it turns out that the family relic which probably gave their generic name to the dumbfounding *Capetian* dynasty – Valois, Bourbon and Braganza alike – was a woollen cap. Furthermore, Professor Bloch tells us of 'a huge tribe of magicians', faith-healers who claimed to belong to 'the race of St Martin'. Now, in Celtic countries anyway, abbots were usually elected from the kindred who had dedicated the abbey-lands to that saint. Nobody has made any deep study of hereditary abbacies outside Scotland and Ireland. So it would be interesting to work out exactly why Lord Mountbatten's Brabantine forefathers held such abbacies in early medieval Belgium. And in the present context, it would be fascinating to discover exactly why the Capetian dynasty held certain hereditary abbacies in France, and whether there was originally any connection between the French sovereigns' healing powers and their abbacy of St Martin.

However, these healing powers got popularly limited to scrofula, in particular those revolting tumours caused by tuberculous inflammation of the lymph nodes and leading to smelly suppurations, usually on the neck. The popular mind associated 'bad neck' with *mar con*, a corruption of the name of St Marculf. Therefore the anointed Kings of France from the 14th century onwards touched the shrivelled head of St Marcoul in order to reinforce their healing powers, which were already derived from the sacred unction at their Coronation. Thereafter they were ready for the doubtful but dutiful pleasure of passing on the touch to those whom their bureaucrats considered to be genuinely scruffy.

Nevertheless, it was the *anointing*, both in France and in England, that really conferred the faith-healing hands. Now, anointing with oil at royal inaugurations goes back to the embalming of the beloved sacral Pharaohs whose bodies were felt to emanate communal welfare even after death. Therefore, just as a royal mummy was anointed with oil when embalmed, so was the Spirit of Good Luck for the people sealed into each new Sovereign by ritual anointing. The living king was specially endued with this part of the divine spirit that moves us all, to be the national mascot through the communal will and prayer whereby quantity can change into quality. The spirit sealed with sacred oil in the living king was symbolised in Egypt by the falcon and the lotus: succeeded millennia later in India, and in Europe by the eagle and the

24

fleur-de-lys (Xians symbolise everybody's tiny personal feather from that royal sky-bird by a dove). Jean Golein, writing as recently as 1372, was thus wrong in attributing the ultimate origin of the Roman imperial eagle to those of Brutus' brutal Republic. This bird had merely been derived (I hate to tell my American friends so, who resurrected their world-respected eagle out of classical Roman Republican sources) from the sacred bird incarnate in the Tarquinian kings – a *rex sacrorum* survived throughout the SPQR period just as an *archon bacileus* survived throughout Periclean Athens – and must be equated with the eagle of Zeus that lived in the kings of archaic Greece and far back beyond. Flowering sceptres and the eagle-shaped ampulla for the holy oil at the Coronation are moving reminders of our flowing continuity as we advance steadfastly with our feet still securely planted on what has been our sympathetic base since the very dawn of all civilisation.

That the *fleur-de-lys* is not a lily but a stylised lotus is perhaps obvious enough from looking at ancient representations. But it's tempting to suggest that the very name *fleur-de-lys alias fleur-de-luce* is Flower of Louis, thus of Clovis (Chlodwig, Ludwig, Ludovic. Lewis, rough-hew it any way). What a pity George III gave up quartering the *fleurs-de-lys* in the Royal Arms at the very moment when there was no rival King of France and that they're not placed first in the Queen of Canada's coat: for the blood of St Louis runs strong in her veins. Professor Bloch tells us that the royal heirs of France had to have the birth-mark of a *fleur-de-lys* on their right shoulder. Since it's said for instance that Shakespeare's Dauphin did, it may be wondered whether the wise precaution was taken of so branding the heir at birth – rather as the naughty countess got so branded for essentially different reasons in Dumas's *Three Musketeers*. Apparently the custom was very ancient, for the professor tells us that Seleucids were said to have been born with an anchor mark on their thigh; and what we would call the Bagration kings of Georgia were born with an eagle on the right shoulder, according to Marco Polo (the only Bagration I know is our former ambassadress Natasha Lady Johnston, whose shoulders I've never had the honour to scrutinise for such a familiar or rather a family mark). But among the Franks, before they became separated into French and Germans only to be united once again by the Common Greed of today, this sacred royal birth-mark appears to have been a Cross, until among the West Franks or French it became the *fleur-de-lys*.

Among the East Franks or Germans, of Charlemagne's former united empire, the Cross appeared as a birth-mark much longer. We learn from this book that 'the heads of the House of Hapsburg, the imperial line, all had this mark on their backs at birth, "in the form of white hairs in the shape of a cross", that at least was the contention of the Swabian monk Felix Febri at the end of the 15th century'. Perhaps this really was an hereditary curiosity, like their jaw, or the Talbot fingers and that family on Fair Isle who are covered in scales. On the other hand, the late Jam Sahib of Nawanagar assured me that the *on dit* among his fellow Indian princes was that the dynasty of the Maharajas of Bandarpur are all born with tails, but anybody who read Kipling's *Jungle Book* as a child must suspect a social leg-pull from memories that the bandar-log were the monkey folk.

Professor Bloch was fundamentally a medievalist looking forwards into the rational economies that laid the ground-stones onto which we cement our modern world. He looked backwards only with that suspicion which scholars reserve for those who operate outside of, yet clumsily intrude into, their well-thought-out field. To him it was the early Capetians who were the first royal faith-healers among the Franks, and it seemed the ambition of William the Bastard's son Henry I of England that foisted faith-touching's origin in England onto his politically invaluable wife's great-uncle Saint Edward the Confessor. If only the deeply-informed professor had not been murdered by those licensed thugs, it would have been useful to strike each other's flints and gaze with enlightenment upon the flame we lit. For I don't share his doubts whether my Capetian ancestors had Merovingian blood, nor his belief that my forefather Henry I – perhaps a murderer who's got away with it until caught by a 20th century detective, but that's another story – could have foisted a faith-healing fable on people still alive who had known St Edward. Groping nervously among the Baltic forests and marshes whence these horrific yet sometimes kindly great dynasties had ridden sword in hand, as vigorous conquerors in the Dark Ages, we must remember that our Queen's forefathers of the Royal House of Wessex, like the Merovingian kings, sprang from the pagaen sacral kings who had incarnated through a self-sacrificing doom-ritual their people's safe-guard: the storm-spirit Woden. Unlike the professor, who's interested in the Gregorian attack on ancient feelings (though he don't take sides), I would therefore still search for the Dark Ages source of healing by 'touch'. That Dark Age evidence is scantily illuminated is perhaps because the Ages were Dark.

The title of the book is so modest that it would be impossible here to relate the fascinating goodies by way of side-lines that it contains: an enticing curiosity shop of cramp-rings, seventh sons of seventh sons, angel coins and many another surprise. We learn that kings are safe from lions, and that Edward III sent an emissary to the Doge of Venice pointing out that he was willing to acknowledge Philip of Valois as king

26

of France 'if he would expose his person to hungry lions and could escape unscathed from their claws' (there was no hint that this offer was reciprocal). My wife tells me that her ancestor Monmouth received a similar offer. But at least Professor Bloch informs us that her ancestral uncle Robert Boyle, renowned among scientists for 'Boyle's Law', believed in the efficacy of the royal 'touch'. The professor also discloses that the House of the Prophet can help over rabies. The first descendant of Muhammad personally encountered by me was Judge Waris Ameer Ali, who put two pythons and a boa constrictor round my neck as a boy to teach me not to be alarmed by snakes (he afterwards made me a very young Fellow of the Zoo), and since then I've avoided assassination by association after being the guest in Amman of King Hussein (the Prophet's most vital living descendant, and that ain't tautology), also shot a cobra with a shotgun given by Nasser to my host in Malaysia, the Raja of Perlis, who was yet another scion of the holy man who made the immortal offer to go to that obstinately immovable mountain. Curiously enough, the Aga Khan, whose rabid-fingering descent from the Prophet is disputed by the enemies of his cult founded on the Rock of Alamut by the Old Man of the Mountains, is undoubtedly descended through his mother from scrofulous-touching Saint Louis.

My doctors tell me scrofula comes and goes, and so temporary cures may appear to be effected, and the royal 'touch' may cheer the patient up. Dr Ian Olsen draws my attention to the accounts of the Lord High Treasurer of Scotland in 1508, when James IV paid money 'to a poor child took the king by the hand'. But it was probably a typically Stuart friendly gesture to one of the have-nots. James VI was the first king to 'touch' officially, and he did it as James I of England: refusing as a well-trained Calvinist to make the usual sign of the Cross over the sores. So as a proud Scot I must go to the Queen of England for what we used to call 'remede'. I have two rather nasty lumps on my neck.

Books & Bookmen, May 1973

A Fecund Womb

There may be old Anglican priests writ large who feel that the Royal Marriages Act should be stiffened up a bit, rather on the lines recently enforced by our economic sheikhs and masters in Saudi Arabia [*an allusion to the execution of Princess Mashaa'il of Saudia Arabia for adultery at Jeddah, November 1977* – ED] Most of us, on the other hand, feel that it's high time the C of E got more genuinely oecumenic, and the antiquated law was abolished that prohibits the Heir to the Throne – alone among British subjects – from marrying a Catholic: even though the children be brought up as good little Anglicans. That HRH may not want to do so in practice is neither here nor there; that such a law remains unrepealed in what is known as This Day & Age is insulting in principle to all Her Majesty's innumerable Catholic subjects and indeed to the common sense of the rest of us. HRH may not want to marry a Moslem or a Hindu either, but the Race Relations industry would create a wondrous how-d'you-do if a Bill were gratuitously introduced into Parliament to prevent him.

Time was when the dynastic houses of Christendom were like the inhabitants of one enormous parish: happily marrying each other across Europe. Royalty married royalty, moving easily from realm to realm, and soon acquiring the characteristcs of the particular country in which they came to reign. People think of them as in-bred because they tended to marry within their rank, but they were usually no more in-bred than the peasantry of an ordinary parish before the coming of the railways. And despite suffering like us all from the occasional weakling, no family ever remained in the royal group for long without possessing in general tremendous inherited stamina. Henry VIII's royal ancestors extended from Sweden to Sicily, and from Iceland to Kiev. In breeding, the royal families of Europe were really as one.

Then suddenly, there came the Reformation. When the incense had settled down, the enormous royal parish was split into two family groups: almost as bitterly as had been Verona in the time of my ancestral uncle Bartolomeo della Scala (1301-1304) whose subjects, we are told by Girolano della Corte, the families of Montecchio and Capulet (I forget what the latter were called in Italian) had made such a fuss about Romeo wanting to marry Juliet. From the 17th century onwards, each nubile Catholic princess was separated from every Protestant potential Prince Charming.

And so it has remained ever since. On the Catholic side of this anachronistic divide are ranged the pre-eminent names of Hapsburg and Bourbon, Wittelsbach and Savoy: with direct male-line descendants of *le Roi Soleil* still reigning in Spain and Luxembourg. A distinguished British diplomatist once remarked to me what a sad waste it was that the present generation of Hapsburgs were so much the most brilliant for a long time. The great Saxon royal house from which our own Queen springs is divided now, either side of the outmoded religious chasm, between Protestant Britain and Catholic Belgium, but no longer reigning in Orthodox Bulgaria because of the Iron Curtain. The equally great agnatic stock to which Prince Philip and Prince Charles belong springs from Christian I, King of Denmark (1448-1481): it still reigns in Protestant Denmark and Norway, though no longer in Orthodox Greece and Russia. But all the royal families of Europe, reigning or deposed, have this in common: they all (except for Albania) descend from the Royal House of Stuart.

Now, I'm often asked about the spellings Stewart and Stuart. There were two separable dynasties in Scotland, of common origin but whom it is convenient to call the Stewarts and the Stuarts, descended from two sons of Alexander, 4th Great Steward of Scotland (died 1285), and taking their name from that office.

The eldest son was James, 5th Great Steward, whose son married Robert Bruce's daughter and was ancestor of the *Stewart* kings from Robert II (succeeded 1370) to James V (died 1542). This was the most usual Scottish spelling of the name.

The younger son of the 4th Great Steward was Sir John Stewart of Bonkyl, 'whose bravery Wallace praised above all men', killed fighting the English at Falkirk in 1298. His descendants, lords of Darnley and earls of Lennox, frequently commanded the Scots troops during the Auld Alliance in the service of France, where they became Seigneurs d'Aubigny. Since the French were little used to the letter '*w*', they tended to spell their name *Stuart*.

When the then Lennox's son Henry Stuart, Lord Darnley, became King Consort of Scots by marriage to James V's daughter, Mary Queen of Scots, he founded the new *Stuart* dynasty of which James VI and I was the first, and which expired with the death of Bonnie Prince Charlie's brother. According to this method, Mary should be regarded as the last Stewart sovereign of Scots, but as queen dowager of France she was already accustomed to the spelling Stuart before her Stuart of Darnley marriage.

However, these spellings are merely convenient to distinguish the two dynasties. Before the 18th century there was no standardised spelling of Scottish surnames. As for the office itself, it has been inherited from his Stewart/Stuart forefathers by Prince Charles, who is the present Great Steward of Scotland.

Similarly, I'm often asked who may wear Royal Stuart tartan: what I was taught to call more precisely the Royal or Stuart tartan. This is a difficult question: and in any case a matter of convention rather than regulation, for we have few sumptory laws outside the Armed Forces. It is of course favoured by the bastard lines sprung from the mediaeval Stewart kings, such as Stewart of Ardvorlich, or Lords Bute and Moray who, indeed, spell their name Stuart. Curiously enough, the later Stuart royal bastards who received or adopted other names such as FitzRoy or

Montagu-Douglas-Scott – James VII and II's grand illegitimate ducal FitzJames descendants in Spain have resumed the name of Stuart – seem to prefer the Hunting Stewart tartan: to be seen, for instance, at Drumlanrig and Bowhill in strange preference to the perfectly well-known Douglas and Scott tartans.

The Royal Stuart tartan is still used, on occasion, by the Royal House of Bavaria, who are of course the senior heirs female of the Royal House of Stuart. Prince Henry of Bavaria was up at 'the House' at Oxford with me before the War, and in the summer vacation, on a so-called 'walking tour' of the Highlands, three of us took him to luncheon with the late Cameron of Lochiel. Henry was wearing his Royal Stuart kilt, and at first crusty old Lochiel seemed about to take umbrage at a Bavarian prince in the Garb of Old Gaul. But when Lochiel realised that, but for Culloden, it was the Duke of York he was entertaining, it was as though the table was suddenly festooned with cockades of the White Rose. For many years now, however, I've been working on a legal argument to demonstrate that (by pre-1688 and therefore Jacobite common law) our own Queen, and not Henry's brother the Duke of Bavaria, is the rightful heir of the Jacobite sovereigns: Prince Charles today the heir apparent of Bonnie Prince Charlie then. But this would make no difference to the wearing of the Royal or Stuart Tartan by both lines of descendants of the Royal House of Stuart.

I myself incline to place the emphasis on *Royal* rather than on Stuart in considering who, outside the actual name, should wear Royal Stuart tartan: that is to say, I regard it as Royal as opposed to Government tartan. By Government tartan I mean the dark green type of tartan, adopted by the Royal Company of Archers during the period 1789–1829 and crystallised in the ordinary uniform Black Watch tartan. By Royal tartan I mean the bright red type of tartan, worn by the Royal Company of Archers before the '45 Rising, and crystallised in the tartan worn by the *pipers* of those Scottish regiments who are Household Troops or have been honoured with the prefix 'Royal': *e.g.* the Scots Guards and the Black Watch (Royal Highland Regiment). Once, when I was Parade Adjutant of a battalion of Scots Guards at Chelsea Barracks, Bing Crosby called on me in the Orderly Room. He was helping with a film called *We'll Meet Again* in which Vera Lynn fell in love with a guardsman wearing a kilt. I explained that the only guardsmen to do so were our pipers, and we dressed her hero in a Royal Stuart uniform kilt while Vera Lynn, her face painted bright yellow, sang 'Coming through the Rye' to our bagpipes. Now, it's obvious that with the Scots Guards that tartan is Royal rather than Stuart.

This brings us to consider who are the far-flung members of the royal clan, the spreading kindred to whom such a wide Royal tartan is appropriate. Since the Crown is heritable by females as well as by males, and Master Peter Phillips is as much (if not more) a member of the royal family as Prince Michael of Kent, the extended royal kindred may be taken to be both the male and female-line descendants of King James I, founder of the British Royal House. He had only two children who left decendants: King Charles I and Elizabeth Stuart, the 'Winter Queen'. And although for reasons of political religion the Act of Succession has cut out the whole line of the former in favour of that of the latter, blood is thicker than communion wine in matters of clanship. I therefore regard the royal clan, who may appropriately use this royal tartan, as the very people so comprehensively set out, with their places and dates of birth, marriage and death, in the three sumptuous volumes of A. C. Addington's *The Royal House of Stuart* (Charles Skilton, 1969/76), the descendants of King James the First of Great Britain.

It struck me forcibly, when the first volume of this mighty boon of reference to historians and genealogists alike came out, how innocent the author was of any intent to subsidise scholarship with skilful publicity. For, since James I was her only child (apart from Bothwell's still-born twins in her lake-girt castle prison on Lochleven), this book is actually the register of all the lawful descendants of Mary Queen of Scots. And it's hard to believe that, had her name been included in the title, many of the distinguished foreign families who appear in it wouldn't have gladly forked out for a book placing them among the progeny of tragic 'Marie Stuart'.

I once wrote that Prince Charles descends from her 17 times over. Now, with Mr Addington's years of research at our disposal, I stand corrected. Prince Charles descends through no less than 22 different lines from Mary Queen of Scots. This is worth stressing, since anonymous letters from what I trust is beyond the fringe of the Scots Nats refer to HRH's 'extremely tenuous link' with the old Scottish royal line. These are the sort of cranks who take immense trouble to use a special stamp with the crowned cypher EIR on it, but give no address to which a herald can reply pointing out that they are using by mistake the English instead of the Scottish form of Crown: ours has *fleurs-de-lys* at the foot of the arches and *crosses patée* in between: the English reverse the position of the crosses and *fleurs-de-lys*.

The Appendices of Mr Addington's work include the 128 Quarters of James VI & I and his wife Anne of Denmark; of these, *all* the ancestors of King Charles I and the Winter Queen back for seven generations, *only one* is missing. This is the name of the wife of Alexander Sutherland of Dunbeath, whose daughter married before 15 Nov, 1456 William

Sinclair, last Jarl of Orkney and 1st Earl of Caithness. I was consulted some years ago about the missing lady's identity, but couldn't help at the time. Since then, however, when our motor car was overwhelmed in a blizzard and we were snow-bound overnight at Cawdor Castle, Lord Cawdor, the present Thane, gave me a copy of *The Book of the Thanes of Cawdor 1236–1742* (Spalding Club, Edinburgh 1859). From documents printed at pp 16 and 54 of this careful compilation of charters it became clear that the then Lady Cawdor was another daughter of the same Alexander Sutherland of Dunbeath, and that their mother (the missing lady) was Marion of the Isles, sister of Alexander, Earl of Ross and thus daughter of Donald, Lord of the Isles, the mighty Macdonald of the battle of Harlaw. I was then able to track down at p 110 of Lord Hailes's *Additional Case for Elizabeth Countess of Sutherland*, the original grant of Dunbeath itself to Alexander Sutherland on 24 Oct 1429 on the occasion of his marriage to this Macdonald lady. This hitherto unpublished discovery is of considerable genealogical importance, as it reveals a direct descent of Prince Charles, the present Lord of the Isles, from his predecessors the Macdonalds of the Isles at the height of their power. 1978 is the bicentenary year of the famous Highland Society of London, our most distinguished body of its kind; and in accepting the Presidency this year, the Prince of Wales has informed us that he wishes to be known in that capacity as 'HRH Prince Charles, Lord of the Isles'. Incidentally, King James VI & I was born Lord of the Isles too.

From Appendix IV of Mr Addington's work we learn that in all, at the time of going to press, Mary Queen of Scots had had only 14,891 legal descendants, altogether, in 16 generations of whom 10,534 are now living. Among her heraldic badges, or perhaps more exactly as an *impresa*, Mary Stuart, as claimant to the English throne now occupied by her descendants, assumed a device which was clearly a dig at her barren coz Queen Elizabeth I of England. It is a vine with two branches, one of which is leafless; a hand issuing from the clouds, and holding a pruning-bill, cuts off the withered branch, in order that the green branch may flourish and bear forth more grapes. However, unlike the Prophet Mohammad's descendants who are 'as numberless as the leaves in the forest', Mary Stuart's progeny are still only to be counted in thousands. This goes to show what rot one so often reads about everybody being descended from everybody, based on the phoney mathematics of doubling up every generation and then comparing the total with that of the population at any given time in past history: thus completely ignoring the implexity of ancestors through constantly repeated inter-marriage.

In the case of this book, nevertheless, we must remember that the author is only setting out the Royal Stuarts' *lawful* descendants. Some, like the McCorkle grandchildren of Princess Croy, are to be found in the United States. But *the great majority of them belong to the famous names of Europe* – the great royal houses already mentioned, of course, with the Protestant and Orthodox sheep (from the C of E point of view) such as Romanoff and Hohenzollern, Baden and Hesse, Württemberg and Mecklenburg, separated from the Catholic goats like Hapsburg and Bourbon, Bavaria and Savoy, but Saxony divided into both camps as its Frenchified form Saxe gets hyphenated – and the other grand names too, Alvarez de Toledo, Colonna and Orsini, La Rochefoucauld and Noailles, Croy and Ligne, Lobkowicz and Esterhazy, Benckendorff and Czatoryski, Radziwill and Bagration, to give but a few examples. There are very few industrial names such as Agnelli and the great banking firm of Fugger: but there is naturally my foreign friend The O'Neill of Clanaboy, who is of course a Portuguese nobleman. Many a romantic tale is evoked by a glance at the names. To give but two examples, taken at random, my old acquaintance the Stuart-descended Prince George Galitzine was married to Anna-Marie Slatin, daughter of the extraordinary character General Baron Sir Rudolf Slatin Pasha, Governor of Darfur in the Sudan when Gordon perished at Khartoum; some years ago I was saddened when she told me she had given away to Durham University the chains which her father had worn as a slave of the Mahdi: what an heirloom to part with except on long loan! Slatin Pasha's brother was the civil servant in charge of hushing up the tragedy at Mayerling; the Crown Prince Rudolf was very much a descendant of Mary Queen of Scots, as was Prince Philip of Coburg who was there that fatal night – Count Hoyos was not a descendant, though the present generation of the Hoyos family are.

But the great English names are almost entirely missing. Apart from close relations of the immediate Royal Family – such as the royal dukes and the Duke of Fife, Lords Mountbatten and Harewood – I could find, after several hours' search, no single British peer among Mary Stuart's lawful descendants. This is the result of a combination of the Royal Marriages Act and the special ban on Protestant royal inter-marriages with her prolific Catholic progeny. Among the few English names, there is that of an old Catholic family descended through the Windisch-Graetzes from that same Crown Prince Rudolf, the central figure in the Mayerling tragedy. This is the present generation of Blundell-Hollinshead-Blundell. When their uncle, Major Victor B-H-B of my regiment, gave his name on being challenged by one of our Scots Guards sentries, he got the classic reply: 'Advance *one*, and be recognised'. The pre-eminent Scottish House of Douglas is represented here only by some of the Swedish Counts Douglas. But the House of Hamilton, ever its rival, is I think the first Protestant peerage family to have produced as its future head in the young courtesy Lord Strabane [*now styled Marquess of Hamilton*] a lawful descendant of Mary Queen of Scots: the [4th] Duke of Abercorn's son James, Lord Hamilton [*now the 5th Duke*], having married a daughter of the late Lady Zia Wernher who so strangely mingled the Royal Stuart blood with that of the half-Ethiopian, half-Russian poet Pushkin.

For my part, I married two illegitimate descendants of Mary Stuart, the one through King William IV and the FitzClarences, the other through King Charles II and the Buccleuchs. And this brings me to this point: *whereas none of the British peerage are to be found among the lawful scions of Mary Stuart, a great concentration of the higher peerage families are to be found among her descendants' natural posterity.* For instance, the Dukes of Richmond, Grafton, St Albans, Bedford, Devonshire, Marlborough, Hamilton, Buccleuch, Northumberland, Leinster, Sutherland and Abercorn all descend from her through natural sons of Charles II or James VII & II. It is very much to be hoped, therefore, that Mr Addington will continue his immense pioneer work by giving us a further volume with the officially recognised *illegitimate* descendants of the Royal House of Stuart. For there seem to have been very few inter-marriages between her lawful (mostly Catholic) and her natural (mostly Protestant) descendants, despite the latter's distinguished role in Britain over three centuries. Looking carefully through Mr Addington's index, I could find only two: my wife's coz, Lady Alice Montagu-Douglas-Scott, now Princess Alice, Duchess of Gloucester (descended from a brace of Charles II's natural sons); and my son's godmother 'Tana' FitzJames Stuart, Duchess of Alba in her own right (sprung from James II's natural son the Marshal Duke of Berwick), whose late husband, of the Spanish grandee ducal house of Sotomayor, appears himself among the lawful scions of the Royal House of Stuart: among the illustrations is a charming likeness of their son Don Carlos Martinez de Irujo y FitzJames Stuart, Duque de Huescar.

The volumes have beautiful coloured frontispieces of King James VI & I by Isaac Oliver, his wife Queen Anne of Denmark by Nicholas Hilliard, and his mother Mary Queen of Scots herself by François Clouet. Among the black-&-white illustrations of their descendants, I am delighted to see opposite vol 1 p 302 the distinguished face of that truly *grand seigneur* Alphy Clary, kindest of men, the greatest gentleman still [*1978*] surviving from the *ancien régime* before the lights went out all over Europe in 1914; when that fatal shot at Serajevo slew another of

Mary Queen of Scots' scions in the Archduke Francis Ferdinand and has been ricocheting round the world killing myriad people ever since. Prince Clary himself won the Gold Medal, the Austrian equivalent of the VC, in the Carpathians during that opening holocaust.

Meanwhile, I hope readers will realise the value of Mr Addington's tremendous work to historians and genealogists alike; and if they had thought to find this a mere review of some glorified 'List of the Huntingdonshire Cabmen', that they will think again.

Books & Bookman, March 1978

Queen of Hearts

We needn't doubt that Mary Queen of Scots was *indescribably* attractive in the most literal sense. As with the photographs of her leading descendant our present Sovereign, her *aura* doesn't come across in any of her surviving portraits. Annigoni's is the nearest to catch our reigning queen's radiant *aura* of regal goodness. While staying with Mary Stuart's Cranborne descendants last week [1975], I saw for the first time at Hatfield a portrait always believed to be of Mary Queen of Scots that seemed to catch something of that equally regal yet enticing essence of what her gaoler Sir Francis Knollys (my wife's ancestor) could not restrain himself from calling 'such a lady and princess', and which I know so well in the hereditary charm that radiates from her reincarnated phoenixes to this day. Typically, it wasn't the dull official portrait also there, but the one the 'experts' think to be a 17th century copy very possibly of a Clouet. Something may have been lost by the copyist, but there is still enough to recognise the lady of my heart. But falling in love takes people in different ways. To me, it means that when the lady enters the room, everything is suddenly brighter. I never fall out of love, and most gals I've found enticing have on later investigation turned out to be Mary Stuart's descendants. Indeed, I've married two of 'em. All the same, I don't think sex much stirred her otherwise generous mind. She pardoned the amorous poet Châtelard the first time he was found under her bed (who ought to have known it was searched nightly by two Grooms of the Bedchamber) but got too fed up with the poor romantick similarly losing his head about her a second time: so he jolly well did lose it, on the block. Anyway, I dote on the lady, even though the then Moncreiffe of the Ilk was against her for reasons of policy.

Note, that for a character who was no walking shadow on Life's brief stage, but on the contrary made such a mark on popular history abroad

('abroad' for us starts at Berwick, just as the English think it starts at Calais), her whole career was but as a passing hour-glass in her own realm. Her active rule in Scotland covered less than 7 years, and she was only 25 when she left her native land for ever and went into life imprisonment followed by 'capital punishment' in England. However, 'One crowded hour of glorious life Is worth an age without a name' (provided this isn't taken too literally, as it was by that nut-case Herostratos who in 356 BC burnt down the beautiful temple of Artemis at Ephesus just in order to get his name into the history books).

There have been so many books about our tragic queen. She is certainly far better known and written about throughout the civilised world than any other Scottish monarch. As a boy, I made the mistake of trying to read Emil Ludwig's *Maria Stuart* in German – as big a blunder as when I attempted Corporal Schickelgrueber's *Mein Strife* – a language I never really mastered, like too much porridge, despite going to Heidelberg University and watching (with Goebbels in the 'royal box') a floodlit performance in the ruined Castle there of a play by my coz Will Shakespeare, whom the Nazis assured me was a *ganz arische* Poet. It included his famous soliliquy: *'sein oder nicht sein, das ist hier die Frage'*, a question my other coz Queen Elizabeth Tudor resolved for my ancestral half-aunt Queen Mary Stuart in the manner used by Lizzie Borden, who took an ax and gave her mother forty whacks. Margaret Swain's *Mary Queen of Scots: Needlewoman* (Van Nostrand Reinhold, 1973) contains a specially worthwhile domestic biography of the queen's everyday life, and should be in every Marian's book-room. Among Queen Mary Stuart's most talented progeny, Lady Antonia Fraser (one of Charles II's ultimate love-children out of Barbara Villiers) recently projected with charming skill and hard work on to a world canvas what Professor Donaldson calls 'the best full-length study in print' of her historically captivating yet captive foremother in *Mary Queen of Scots* (Weidenfeld & Nicolson, 1969). In particular she places Mary's troubadour-style romantic-yet-platonic Queen-of-Hearts-in-distress image in the European rather than the Scottish context, as indeed the queen's training and true purpose as well as Don Juan of Austria's epic saga all befitted.

However, for years people have been banging on to me to recommend a short unbiased and accurate biography of Mary Stuart from the Scottish historians' viewpoint. Well here it is. The authorised version, so to speak, has at last been given us in Dr Gordon Donaldson's lucid *Mary Queen of Scots* (English Universities Press, 1975). Nobody living has better qualifications to have taken on the task than its author, the Professor of Scottish history and palaeography at the University of

Edinburgh, who combines private modesty with straightforward authority based on intricate knowledge. To anybody who has the strength of mind to struggle with original texts, I also firmly recommend his colleague Dr Grant G. Simpson's new book. *Scottish Handwriting 1150–1650* (Bratton Publishing Co, Edinburgh). To over-simplify by generalisation: the more leisurely aristocracy wrote in a legible 'Italianate hand'; while the busy equivalent of typists used the 'secretarial hand' that reminds me of my wife's 'speed-write' that she can't read herself. Going through our own family documents, I find those of the 1200s far easier to read than much of the stuff written in Mary Queen of Scots's lifetime and that of her son, though the Royal Families still wrote legibly enough then as one knows from other papers: which (with reference to the *Casket Letters*) would have made Mary's handwriting easy to forge. Like Queen Victoria, the Kirk about whose foundation Professor Donaldson knows so much prays sitting down. I personally sit in awe of the professor, as do our other colleagues on the Advisory Committee of the Scottish National Portrait Gallery.

He gives a succinct summary of her cruel father James V's reign, followed by a *précis* of politics during her minority. My own forefather King James was like Haroun al-Rashid (our probable eighth cousin), enjoying to go about in disguise as the tenant-farmer of Ballengeich. At first he took a liking to the gypsies, and recognised their leader Faa' as 'Earl of Little Egypt', until they mugged him by mistake while in his disguise, after which Faa' was harassed (as *Z Cars* would put it) as 'Captain of the Egyptians' like any brigand highland chief such as the Captain of Clan Chattan (at that time my ancestor The Mackintosh, who ended up under the meat-chopper after being enticed into my ancestress Lady Huntly's kitchen; though not for food). None of this is in Dr Donaldson's book. The reason he's a professor and I'm only a PhD is simply discipline. He avoids the most attractive red herrings, and even manages to dismiss Donald Dubh Macdonald's great Rising in 1545, the last hope of Hebridean autonomy, without mentioning by name their white-hope *Macdonald* 'himself', murdered by an IRA harper (curses be upon that man), except as the 'figurehead of the administration was soon killed'. The professor poses a minor puzzle associated with his warning, set forth below, not to concentrate on one's senior male line; 'in 1552 . . . it was impossible . . . even to raise a Scottish force for service in the French army'. Yet the Privy Council Register has it that on 12 Dec 1552 William Moncreiffe, 'young lard of that Ilk', and many others, being about to go to France under the Earl of Cassillis 'Lt-General of the army devisit to pas in France, and Patrick, Lord Ruthven, Coronet of the futmen', and 'being their kin and friends', were protected by Act from legal process while in the French service; and he doesn't reappear at Moncreiffe until he rode out in armour with his men to oppose Mary Queen of Scots's marriage to 'Darnley' a dozen years later.

However, the professor more pertinently relates the fate of a proposed 'wealth tax' by the infant queen's Regency in 1556; but note that it was to be levied on everyone, unlike the present system where the Govt who are supposed to be the cops have taken over the role of the principal robbers so long as their victims are a literally talented (think what coin a 'talent' is) élite minority. 'While everyone in the social scale was involved, the nobles naturally led the opposition and withstood the proposal, "affirming that they meant not to put their goods in inventory, as if they were to make their last wills and testaments".' Twingle Feet would have found Robin Hood no excuse in the realistic Scotland of those days.

Meanwhile, of course, the child-queen was away in France as the fiancée of the Dauphin of the Viennois, his correct title; often given wrongly in other books, but not by the professor, as 'Dauphin of France'. The truth of the matter is that the last Dolphin sold the Viennois in 1349 to my ancestor Charles of Valois (afterwards King Charles V) on condition the family always continued to use the title. The Comte de Paris ought to carry out this contract by calling his eldest son Dauphin du Viennois, then let him keep on the title after his succession. Socially, to be the *Dauphin* in France would be just as top grand as to be the *Roi*, with 'Paris Match' writing up his children's Crawfie-type nanny and their other semi-human escapades (for the bourgeois-Trotskyites never really regard royal children as human 'kids'), and would avoid all those silly political tergiversations that made their ancestral grandpop Philippe *Egalité* (another scion of Mary Stuart) lose his head and his much nicer bourgeois son Louis Philippe his throne.

Our most famous queen's happiest childhood is summed up by the professor in his illustration of the Château de Chambord, which I've only visited twice but has that delight of an unexpected sham village on its renaissance roof. But before that, when she was a wee child in Scotland – old enough to remember, as I too remember my childhood Nandi friends before I was kidnapped from Kenya at the age of four – she knew not only Stirling Castle, traditional refuge of heirs to the Scottish throne, but holy Dunkeld and the peaceful island priory of Inchmahome in the Lake of Menteith. How different from that stark foggy ice-bound island Lochleven Castle, where the disloyal Mafia among her subjects imprisoned her in the flower of her adulthood or, as they would have it, adultery. Her gaoler was Mary's own father's adulterous mistress, whose son, my romantic young forefather George

Douglas, arranged her escape with our 'cousin' Willie while ever-loyal Lord Seton (naturally also my ancestor, whose red-&-gold clad portrait is the most splendiferous in the Scot. Nat. Portrait Gallery) lay with two hundred horsemen on the Fife Lomonds overlooking the loch ready to move off at full gallop to her rescue as soon as they saw her tiny boat put off. It was one of the most exciting yet useless escapades in the history of the world. In those days the damp castle walls were completely loch-girt, and our captive queen could only exercise in the tiny windowless high-walled compound; row across sometime, and see what I mean. But the professor's modern illustration can't avoid showing the extra now tree-planted pleasant island around the ruinous keep that was part of the soil-recovery of ground on the banks when my great-uncle Sir Basil Montgomery's agricultural reformist pa lowered the loch's water-level in the last century. Curiously enough, these Montgomerys belonged to the same branch of Eglinton that supplied the Scots Archer Guards in France with its commander, Comte Gabriel de Montgomery, accidental slayer in tournament of my ancestral first cousin King Henry II of France (though some say that, unknown to Montgomery, the royal visor had been misfastened deliberately). This misfortune made Mary Stuart prematurely queen consort of France. Her husband's death soon afterwards made her its queen dowager, and she left for her own sovereign realm of Scotland. But in her time of need it made her look vainly for the grace of aid to the graceless face of her tycoon-bred mother-in-law Catherine de' Medicis, heroine of St Bartholomew's Night, while her brother-in-law 'the shadow of the Valois was yawning at the Mass'.

I am instructed by my anti-fan, the Horble Richard Beaumont, chairman of the most distinguished club which failed to blackball me and got me on its Committee by way of punishment, that he wouldn't mind reading my reviews if I didn't *always* refer to the characters under scrutiny as being my family's relations. I will, therefore, not remind you that the said Horble Richard's delightful wife is herself a descendant of Mary Queen of Scots through Richmond and Albemarle. In 1974, in a lecture to the Scottish Genealogy Society of which I'm a Vice-President, the author Professor Donaldson himself warned us not 'to concentrate on one line of descent, or rather ascent, to the exclusion of others'. By this he meant that he doubted the value of pursuing back only someone's direct male line of ancestry (biologists might call it the 'Y' chromosome) in determining formative influences. As Albany Herald, I accept his challenge, and have therefore *taken at random from his index some* — let's spare you *all* — of my own family's relations who played their part in the strange tales that told their devious tattle to make up the sources necessarily interwoven to make his book as honest as may perhaps ever be possible. All of their lives have long been known to me, and a few selected cracks about them may perhaps serve as glosses on his text or illuminate his characters by way of vignette or mere cartoon.

Let's start with the holy man Knox, who did so much to follow in the other holy man Paul's suppressed squirms in equating – as Our Lord never did – the Xian idea of Sin not with Envy but with Sex: and was for ever bragging on to good advantage like Rabbie Burns (with a side-eye natheless on the guinea-stamp of aristocratic support) about his humble birth. For isn't it rather boastful to attribute one's success to one's own merits, and to downgrade those who bred one so well? So what did Knox do? At the then advanced age of nearly sixty he married a sexy semi-royal child-bride, my wife's ancestral aunt Maggie Stewart, daughter of Lord Ochiltree and sister of the sinister yet majestic 'Captain James Stewart' who was to become semi-regent as Earl of Arran and in the resignation of his retirement to fall victim to an ambush blood-feud bullet photoprinted in text for us three centuries later by S. R. Crockett as vividly as in a Gary Cooper 'western movie'. Sex and grandeur suited Knox when he was cut in on it. His side-kick, the Rev John Craig, was a cousin of my own forefather Sir Thomas Craig, who has been Scotland's leading feudal lawyer until the present day.

While keeping to the religious side, I descend from wise Cardinal Beaton, the murdered pluralist (they hung his blood-dripping corpse in the shape of a St Andrew's Cross outside a window of his castle of St Andrews) with as many titles 'as would have loaded a ship, much less an ass', who took charge of affairs at Mary Stuart's birth and from whom I get life through his daughter's marriage to another character in this book, David, 10th Earl of Crawford, one of Mary's kindest and most civilised supporters. Archbishop Beaton, the cardinal's nephew, and Bishop Chisholm of Dunblane, were naturally my ancestral first cousin and uncle; but we are told that although Marians they were both abroad at the most critical moment. Archbishop Hamilton, another Marian supporter who was later hanged by the godly covenanting winning side, was both my wives' 'ancestral' uncle, as they both spring from the loins of his father the ex-regent Duc de Châtelherault. In future, let's omit 'ancestral' since nobody has an uncle or cousin not so many 'generations removed' after four centuries. Of course, since both my wives also descend from Mary Queen of Scots herself and thus from her mother the Queen Regent Mary, daughter of the Duc de Guise and Antoinette de Bourbon, the Grand-Prior of St John of Jerusalem and both the politically cunning Cardinals of Lorraine were their uncles too. And, to wash the professor's platter of our family foreign religious index-personalities faily clean, my wife's Medici relations in the book include her uncle Pope Leo X, and her first cousin the 25 year old Pope Clement VII whose renaissance bath in the Castel San Angelo *alias* Hadrian's Tomb outrivals even my erstwhile colleague [co-author of *The Highland Clans* – ED] David Hicks's bathroom at Britwell Salome.

Let's now take some of the Scots laymen indexed. My forefather George, 4th Earl of Huntly, Cock o' the North, died of apoplexy when captured by Mary at the battle of Corrichie, so his grisly and badly pickled corpse had to be brought to parliament for trail for treason (by Scots Law in such a case you had to be tried in person); and his son, my uncle Sir John Gordon, was beheaded in her unwilling swooning presence for having plotted to marry her. However, she restored the eldest son (my wife's forefathers) to the earldom of Huntly and he became a grateful Marian, dying democratically years later playing football with his local village team.

Another of my progenitors was Mary Queen of Scots's natural brother (which makes her my aunt), Lord Robert Stewart, who had 'a warm corner in the Queen's heart' and protected the Catholic priest at her first Mass in Scotland. He and their mutual half-sister the Countess of Argyll were supping with the Queen in her tiny dining-room (have you ever gauged how wee a room 'twas for such immortality?), joined unexpectedly by her smelly husband, with Riccio eating at their sideboard. Then the door of her private stair from her husband's bedroom below opened suddenly and another of my forebears, Lord Ruthven, risen from his sickbed deathly pale, clad in black armour and a dressing-gown, burst in followed by the rest of Riccio's murderers. My first cousin Andrew Ker of Faudonside shoved a pistol at the pregnant queen's belly in the obvious hope that she'ld miscarry. But my aunt Argyll showed great presence of mind in overturning the table and seizing a candle to protect my aunt Mary; while my grandpa Lord Robert tried to grapple with my grandpop Ruthven. After the Queen's exile, Lord Robert got into trouble for trying to flog the Orkneys to the King of Denmark (arguably their rightful owner) for a lump sum: but ended up as Earl of Orkney himself instead. As for Lord Ruthven, his son (also my ancestor, and later beheaded as Earl of Gowrie) went to Lochleven Castle to bully his prisoner-queen and ended up on his knees ambitiously offering her his love. Those Ruthvens were popularist forward-looking 'trendy lefties', ever willing to 'demonstrate', and keen on science and medicine.

Others of my forefathers were rather ineffective Marians: William, 2nd Earl of Montrose because he was too old; George, 7th Earl of

Erroll, who had been appointed by 'Francis and Mary, King and Queen of Scots, Dolphin and Dolphiness of the Viennois' to be their Ld Lt of all central Scotland 'from the Earn to the North Water' in 1559 and loyally refused to attend as Lord High Constable the anti-coronation of Mary's infant son James VI during her imprisonment, but was browned off with his own marital family troubles and soon resigned that Great Office to his own son; John and Alexander, 11th and 12th Earls of Sutherland, who were pro-Mary but too remote for their Fiery Cross to bring out their clansmen to double South to reach her in hurried times of need, though highlandmen moved in war as fast as a Zulu impi; a reason which may also have delayed mobilisation by perhaps the roughest of my then grandpas, the grim George, 4th Earl of Caithness, foreman of the jury that acquitted Bothwell (for as a Catholic he was a good Marian), who chained up his eldest son the Master of Caithness during seven years for having been too kind to a defeated enemy and then drove him to a raving death of hell-thirsty madness by giving him salt beef to eat but withholding all drink save brandy. As I descend from the thirsty Master too, I'll tell you the full story another time: like the bit when the Master's younger brother (my uncle George, ancestor of Sir Archie Sinclair, late famous Leader of the Liberal Party) went to mock him for losing the inheritance, but the maddened Master managed to strangle the said Geo. with his chains through the cell-bars. Another of my Marian forefathers was William Keith, 4th Earl Marischal of Scotland, wrongly indexed as 3rd Earl (we pronounced it in the same way as 'Earl Marshal of England', the ceremonial martial job immediately junior to the Lord High Constable), who was so rich that he could 'travel from Berwick to the northern extremity of Scotland, eating every meal and sleeping each night on his own estates'; and whose progressive grandson when criticised for using the revenues of the secularised Abbey of Deer to found the present Marischal College at Aberdeen University replied with the 'Mac-the-Knife' type motto: 'THEY SAY. WHAT SAY THEY? LET THEM SAY.'

Still another forebear, John, 4th Earl of Atholl, gave Mary limited support but lavish entertainment: a great drive of 2,000 red deer in 1564, the bag being 360 deer and five wolves (I myself witnessed, lying in the heather in 1934, the last great deer drive in Atholl, when over 900 beasts covered one side of Glentilt with their movement of massed reddish-brown for an incredible moment). Then of course there were my two uncles, both Marians, who had their foibles. Gilbert, 4th Earl of Cassillis, the 'King of Carrick', though a Catholic who fought well for her at Langside, naturally wanted the titular abbot of Crossraguel to sign over the title-deeds to him. So they tied the abbot naked to the chimney, and 'toasted his buttocks to the fire' slapping on oil 'that the roast might not burn . . . basting as a cook bastes roasted meat'. The abbot signed. My other uncle Archibald, 5th Earl of Argyll, *Mac Cailein Mor*, was rather less successful when commanding on Mary's behalf at the decisive battle of Langside, as his undoubted Campbell brilliance led him to have an epileptic fit at the crucial moment. A third uncle of mine, who appeared rather later on the scene and so is indexed only as Francis Stewart Hepburn, was the 'Wizard Earl' of Bothwell, 'Devil' of the North Berwick Witches' coven, whose diabolical career so curdled the blood of Mary Queen of Scots's son that it led to sickening tortures and persecutions for over a century.

But some of my Marian forefathers were not entirely ineffective, and one was her faithful Lord Fleming. He held Dumbarton Castle for her, the key to the safer north-western passage to France that avoided English waters, even after her cause was lost and she was held fast in England; but lost the castle itself when an aggrieved yeoman warder, whose pretty wife my grandpa Lord Fleming had characteristically caused stript naked and whipt for an alleged theft, betrayed a secret climb-in to the enemy: who were commanded of course by my first cousin Thomas Crawford of Jordanhill, of whom T. F. Henderson wrote that 'although playing necessarily a subordinate part, perhaps no other person was so directly instrumental in finally over-throwing the power of the queen's party. I descend too from Lord Fleming's sister Mary, 'the Flower of the Queen's Maries', and thus especially from her husband William Maitland of Lethington, 'popularly known as Secretary Lethington'. I stick to the great and shrewd Sheriff J. R. N. Macphail's opinion of my grandpa Lethington that 'in both charm and ability he excelled in other Scotsmen of the time . . . in spite of various defections, apparent and strategic rather than real, he remained faithful to the unfortunate Queen until the end'. At his end, he died in the old Roman or Grecian manner by his own cup of poison for her sake. His 'holy' enemies used the 'suicide' excuse to leave his corpse unburied, so that the vermin from it came 'creeping out of the door of the house'.

As for the Regents of Scotland that flit through the book, ever watchful of the dirk behind the arras, the French-bred Regent Duke of Albany was my first cousin and couldn't escape our fogs for his frogs soon enough. The rest were nearer akin to my wife. She descends from the typically vacillating Hamilton Regent Earl of Arran; from the conciliatory Queen-Regent Mary, from the scheming Regent Earl of Lennox slain in an affray; from the dutiful Regent Earl of Mar who had tried to rescue him; and above all from the formidable but assassinated Regent Earl of Moray who dominated Mary's fate. As for the Regent

Earl of Morton, effective head of the Douglases, whom Professor Donaldson gives at last his fair due but nevertheless perished by his own primitive guillotine known as 'Morton's Maiden', he was my wife's uncle. Through 'Darnley', she also descends from the Red Douglas, Archibald, 6th Earl of Angus, the second husband of Queen Margaret Tudor. Angus was so hated by his stepson James V that the King unjustly burned alive as a witch the Earl's sister Lady Glamis (another ancestress of my wife): the poor lady was kept in a dark dungeon so long beforehand that when she was brought forth for the mock 'trial' she had become temporarily blind, but at least the 10th Moncreiffe of that Ilk was one of the barons fined for refusing to sit on the jury.

We may render more exotic by way of contrast the professor's genealogical challenge by selecting some of the foreigners in his index, who affected Mary's childhood or long imprisonment. François Ier and Bluff King Hal with their golden cloth were my uncles: Anne Boleyn and sickly Edward VI and our equally sickly queen-consort Madeleine de Valois my first cousins. Both my wives and I descend from murdered William the Silent, Prince of Orange and founder of the Dutch Republic, also from Anne Duc de Montmorency and Constable of France, whose beautiful captured armour you've probably seen. Coligny, the principal victim of the Massacre of St Bartholomew, was our first cousin; but then his principal murderess, Queen-Dowager Catherine de' Medicis, doubtless in the next world shackled first-to-bar all for black iniquity, was my wife's second cousin; while Louis, Prince de Condé, involved in the catastrophe of Amboise that so upset Mary's childhood, was my wife's uncle. My wives' other joint relations in the professor's index include divorced Catherine of Aragon (aunt); the powerful Duke d'Aumâle and the Marquis d'Elboeuf (uncles): the so batty Don Carlos (but a second cousin), suitor for Mary and son of holy conscientious King Philip II of Spain (first cousin) working away in his tiny admiral's cabin GHQ at the ascetic Escorial, that monastic temple-palace-tomb where little dwarves crept out of it and little dwarves crept in, while all the while Mary languished unrescued in prison lest a Spanish Armada should put a Catholic but Francophile sovereign on Britain's throne. Other joint relations of my American-style harem (I don't approve of divorce, but as it seems the Americans are often polygamous why insist on one at a time? Read Luther on why it was OK for Philip of Hesse to have two wives simultaneously) in the index are the Emperor Charles V (their uncle), who I understand died because his Hapsburg jaw prevented him from masticating his food properly despite all the peppery spices of the Indies (loved chewing raw pepper in Borneo, very digestive); and his natural son Don John of Austria (their first cousin), potential knight-errant yearning to rescue the faery queen Mary from the monstrous Welsh dragon who held her captive. Son John lies buried in the Escorial, his real sword in his effigy's hand, his embalmed body re-sewn piecemeal in the interests of Hapsburg frugality as they had to smuggle his chopped-up corpse in lumps in saddle-bags through enemy France to avoid the expense of sending a warship from Spain to the Netherlands; he, the Admiral of Spain immortalised in Chesterton's paean on his victory at Lepanto, one of the decisive sea-battles of world history, the last and lingering troubadour who once sought in valiant day-dreams our Mary's hand.

The time has come to finish off picking up the professor's genealogical gauntlet by considering our *English* family forebears in his index. The Tudors we've mentioned; and it must be admitted that I descend from Lord Surrey, afterwards 2nd Duke of Norfolk, the victor of Flodden, Scotland's greatest tactical defeat. My wife goes further, and descends from the headless poet Surrey's son Thomas, 4th Duke of Norfolk, equally beheaded in 1572 for having designs on Mary's hand. George Cary (2nd Lord Hunsdon), who was a brief candidate for the same hand, was our third cousin. My wife descends from the Protector Somerset, who as Lord Hertford invaded Scotland brutally in the 'Rough Wooing' of 1547 that led to the infant Mary being sent to queenhood in France instead of England; the last occasion when royal heralds were sent with the Fiery Cross throughout the entire realm to rally the whole nation to arms (my uncle David Moncreiffe was slain, but so – on the opposite side – was P. G. Wodehouse's direct forefather Thomas Wodehouse, MP, whose widow was given the rank of a Knight's wife). Despite having damaged an eye in battle, that shrewd observer John Russell, 1st Earl of Bedford, founded the eccentrically-wise world-influencing house that produced Lord John Russell and Bertrand, Lord Russell, ultimately sired both my wives. My children have as first cousin Charles Nevill, 6th Earl of Westmorland, who lost all in his Rising for Mary Queen of Scots, and died forfeited in exile. Then there struts forth into this genealogical family tapestry Lord Robert Dudley. Earl of Leicester, Elizabeth I's on-the-make favourite (uncle of both my wives and possibly, on further investigation, ancestor of my children), to whose riddance of his wife Amy Robsart the latest Lords Peter Wimsey ought to be just as well applying their minds as to Kirk o' Field. It shows how much more box-office appeal Mary Stuart has than her would-be secret but eventually overt murderess Elizabeth Tudor: consider the attempt to corrupt puritanical Sir Amias Paulet to make away with his prisoner-queen by secret means.

By the way, I think Sir Amias may have been a relation of ours too, but have mislaid the notes. My children certainly descend from the Queen's first official gaoler, the doughty but chivalrous Lord Scrope. My wife, too, descends both from Mary Stuart's kindly gaoler George Talbot, 6th Earl of Shrewsbury and also (through the Cavendishes of Chatsworth) from his wife, the energetic character-builder Bess of Hardwick, who used to help the captive queen with her beautiful tapestry work. However, there is one unexpected index entry: the poet Edmund Spenser, author of the *Faerie Queene* when he wasn't writing porn about my fairy-tale queen Mary. He claimed cousinship and wrote a poem to my children's ancestress Alice Spencer, wife of Ferdinando, Earl of Derby, who didn't deny the cousinship which must therefore have been well-known at the time. This porn must have come in useful to one of Mary's greatest foes, my children's forbear Sir Francis Walsingham, founder of the Elizabethan Secret Service that let few of HM traitorous vassalls escape its racks. But I and both my wives also descend from Mary's sincerest and greatest English foe of all: Sir William Cecil, afterwards 1st Lord Burghley, the chief minister and tireless guardian of Anglican reformed Tudor England.

Mary Queen of Scots was fundamentally a politician, and what is more Professor Donaldson reminds us that she was an astute one. Her mother was a Guise, and her grandmother a Tudor: both families skilled in the accumulation of power. But Mary had neither the financial strength nor the standing army necessary for centralisation. Moreover, Scotland had never been conquered by its king, as the English had been since 1066. It was more a federation of semi-autonomous states, some of which like Crawford and Slains were even 'regalities' (where the Crown writ did not run except in cases of treason), presided over by the Sovereign as Chief of Chiefs. Note that the royal style was 'of Scots' and not 'of Scotland'. And, as the late and great Lord President Cooper reminded us, the parliament of Scotland was never completely sovereign either, since its statutes could fall into desuetude if the people came to think them silly.

Professor Donaldson also analyses the political position of the clergy, the lawyers and burgesses, and comes to the conclusion that 'it has often been said that the aristocratic strength of Mary's party was counter-balanced by middle class support for the regents, but it would seem that this has been too sweeping a generalisation'. An even more topsy-turvy misconception has it that Mary was done dirt by the Scottish nobles *as a whole* and that all of them were self-seeking thugs. G. K. Chesterton put this view in a Father Brown story, crystallised in an old Scottish aristocratic family 'whose valour, insanity and violent cunning had made them terrible even among the sinister nobility of their nation in the sixteenth century. None were deeper in that labyrinthine ambition, in chamber within chamber of the palace of lies that was built up around Mary Queen of Scots.'

This misconception is also untenable. The professor puts in a coco-nutshell the reason why a minority of the more selfish nobles opposed her. He recalls Mary's own claim that the nobles who had revolted against her and driven her out, had done so 'after Mary had entered her twenty-fifth year, the year in which a Scottish sovereign was accustomed to make a revocation of crown grants'. That is to say, at the age of 25 sovereigns could revoke grants of lands or rich livings made by a Regency before they became technically of full age. This is not to say that the nobles in general were against Mary. Indeed, the professor in a brilliant analysis shows that out of our 19 earls about a dozen were committed Marians, whereas only five stood against her; and that she could also command the support of 17 other peers with only eight on the opposite side; together with what appears to have been a majority of the baronial lairds as well.

The trouble was that Mary had not had time to mobilise fully before being intercepted and defeated at Langside by an inferior force under her half-brother the Regent Moray. Even so, I agree with the professor that she would probably still have come out on top in the end if she hadn't placed herself in the implacable power of her even more astute cousin Elizabeth I of England. Mr R. H. Harcourt Williams, librarian and archivist to Lord Salisbury, has most kindly forwarded 'as promised, a copy of the epitaph on Mary Queen of Scots, from the unique pamphlet which you saw at Hatfield'. It was printed at Rouen in 1604, the year after it was no longer dangerous to offend Mary's murderess Elizabeth Tudor. The following three verses extracted from it give a wistful glimpse down these many ages of what Mary's heartbroken devotees thought still of her long headless corpse.

> A Queene I liv'd, now dead I am a Saint,
> Once MARIE calde; my name now Matir is;
> From earthly raigne, debarred by restraint;
> In lieue whereof, I raigne in heavenly blisse.
>
> My Scaffold was the bed where ease I found:
> The blocke a pillow of eternall rest;
> My heads-man cast me in a blisfull sound:
> His axe cut off my cares from cumbred brest.
>
> A Prince by birth, a Prisoner by mishap;
> From crowne to crosse, from Throwne to thrall I fell;
> My right, my ruth, my title wrought my trap;
> My weale my woe, my earthly heaven my hell.

The great Dr Johnson summarised the opposite attitude among the gang who had taken over Scotland: 'Sir, never talk of your independency, who could let your queen remain twenty years in captivity and then be put to death without even a pretence of justice, without your even attempting to rescue her, and such a Queen, too! – as every man of any gallantry of spirit would have sacrificed his life for'. The worthy Mr James Ker (Keeper of the Records), struggling for excuse, replied: 'Half of our nation was bribed by English money'. And got shot down with: 'Sir, that is no defence\ that makes you worse'. Indeed, every Scottish regent relied on English gold, from Moray onwards.

James Stewart, Earl of Moray was first Mary's right-hand adviser and later her most effective enemy. His portrait at Darnaway, home of the present Earl, has always reminded me of a Chicago gangster. He was certainly a tough administrator and (in the words of the ballad lament for his future son-in-law 'the Bonny Earl') 'he mycht hae been a king'. For his father King James V had at one time contemplated marrying his mother, Lord Erskine's daughter, but had been discouraged by Pope Paul III as she did happen to be married officially to the Laird of Lochleven at the time Moray was still the most important living nobleman in the direct male line of the Royal House of Stewart, whose forefathers had been Kings father-to-son without a gap from 1372 until his younger half-sister Mary's accession in 1542 and he must have felt it very hardly that his undoubted royal abilities had been stifled at birth.

It was therefore a great pity that he became alienated from Mary as the result of her marriage to Henry Stuart, a young native of England, but descended from a pre-royal branch of the Stewarts. Henry's father had forfeited the earldom of Lennox and Lordship of Darnley and fled to England before his birth; while in the meantime a natural brother of Queen Mary had been created Lord Darnley instead. The Lennox family clung to their lost titles in England, but used in the English mode 'Lord Darnley' as a courtesy title for young Henry rather than the correct Scottish form 'Master of Lennox'. As Henry's grandmother had been a Tudor, it was thought that marriage to him might strengthen Mary's own Tudor claim to succeed Elizabeth I: her ultimate ambition. So her half-brother resigned his title of Lord Darnley, which was given back to the restored Earl of Lennox. When Henry arrived in Mary's realm the Scots were courteous enough to refer to him by his Anglicised pseudo-title as 'Darnley' (*e.g.* in a unique Great Seal Charter of 15 May 1565), but about three weeks after meeting Mary he was created Earl of Ross and not long afterwards Duke of Albany. *Henry was proclaimed King the day before his wedding*, and it was as 'Henry and Mary, King

ABOVE: 'Little Rupert': I.M. aged five.

RIGHT: I.M. in the Scots Guards

Derek Hill's portrait of I.M.
in Atholl Highlander
uniform, 1970.

and Queen of Scots' that they were married the following day. A coin was struck bearing both their heads and the inscription *Henricus et Maria d Gra R & R Scotorum*, and for the rest of his life Parliaments were summoned in their joint names. But the Privy Council insisted on reversing their names on the coinage, since he was only King Consort.

The Crown Matrimonial, which meant that he would have continued to reign in the event of her death, was denied him. And this had muddled most ordinary readers of history into thinking he was never King Henry. Although they know better, even Antonia Fraser and Professor Donaldson have felt themselves obliged to refer to him throughout as 'Darnley', a name which was never rightfully his, and which he ceased to use when he became an earl and a duke, let alone a king. It's as though historians still insisted on referring to Prince Philip throughout as 'Lieut Mountbatten' when chronicling the present reign. If you can't chronicle a man by the real name used in his own time how can you try to see him through the eyes of his contemporaries? To me, *the* definitive history of that period will only give us a correct impression when the pseudo-Darnley is referred to correctly as King Henry (or at least as the King Consort) throughout his married life.

This marriage temporarily alienated Mary's heirs presumptive, the powerful Hamiltons, the hereditary enemies of the Lennoxes. But worse still, she lost forever the strong council of her half-brother Moray, who was so hurt at being supplanted as her most intimate advisor by what the professor calls 'an empty headed fop of nineteen' that he rose in unsuccessful rebellion. Her consort 'Darnley' alias the King proved a worthless adviser although he did manage to combine syphilis with sodomy, as his sexual tastes were apparently catholic. But Mary was at first very fond of him, and it was not until she found that she shared her bed with a potential Leader of the Opposition that it became clear he would have to be got rid of in the only way known to 16th century politics.

The thing is, she was now increasingly turning for advice to what a Hapsburg would have called 'a patriot for me': that is, somebody who owed his position entirely to her patronage, to herself and not to inherited territorial strength. Her humbly-born Savoyard secretary, the former musician 'Signor Davey' Riccio, was in my opinion ultimately intended to be her minister in helping to control the Scottish nobles, rather in the way her great-uncle Henry VIII had used that 'butcher's dog' Wolsey to pull down 'the finest buck in England' (to quote my wife's ancestral uncle the Holy Roman Emperor about the framing of her magnificent forefather Buckingham).

The main conspirators in the unsurprising bumping off of the haughty and ostentatious Riccio were related to King Henry 'Darnley's' Douglas mother (the most powerful and able man behind them being the Earl of Morton, temporary head of all the Douglases, later to be Regent), and they made it clear that her nasty bedmate was in the plot by using her husband's own dagger to complete Riccio's 56 wounds. Frederick Chamberlain, in *The Sayings of Queen Elizabeth* (John Lane, 1943), cites Spanish Calendar, vol. i, pages 520–521, for a remark of Queen Elizabeth I to de Silva, the Spanish Ambassador, shortly after the cocky Savoyard's liquidation: 'had I been in Mary's place on the night of Riccio's murder, I would have snatched her husband's dagger and stabbed him with it'. She meant stab the 'King', not the minstrel-minister. (At Hatfield, by the way, there is also a profile portrait of Elizabeth Tudor that is the best likeness I've ever seen of Emerald Lady Cunard, who used to ask me to her brilliant dinner parties and come to my bizarre luncheons when I was Captain of the late King's Guard a generation ago.)

Indeed, after his part in this gruesome rebellion, it was clear that King Henry had to go. The only question was, how and when? Meanwhile the Queen was as politic in dissimulation with the traitorous husband she now despised as he was vacillating in his lack of policy after having sanctioned the deed. In retrospect, since he was only King Consort, it might have been better to have tried and executed him for high treason at the earliest opportunity: his position as King of Scotland was rather like that in which Anne Boleyn had been as a Queen of England. But the Scottish Crown was not so powerful as that of Tudor England. So Mary had to use diplomacy. She started by separating her husband from the rest of the conspirators, for which his Douglas kinsmen never forgave him. Then she was told that if she would pardon the other murderers some means would be found to bring her marriage to an end. She was reluctant to seek a decree of nullity on the canonical grounds that they both shared the same Tudor grandmother, lest it bastardised their son, born three months after the murder. But when it was hinted that other means might be found whereby she could be quit of him, 'she stipulated that nothing should be done contrary to her honour and conscience'. Nevertheless, she must have realised sensibly enough that the good of her realm required the riddance of such a nuisance; and that this could hardly be accomplished without violence, so long as she was not personally privy to it. This brings us to the celebrated mystery of Kirk o' Field.

The barely 21-year-old King Henry was lodged temporarily at Kirk o' Field, site of the present Old Quad of Edinburgh University, while recovering from a bout of syphilis. The night before it was thought he would be well enough to sleep with the queen, Kirk o' Field was blown up. Professor Donaldson remains neutral while giving us the pros and cons and a *précis* of the principal works on the subject. The most complicated and amusing of these is perhaps the theory of Robert Gore-Browne in *Lord Bothwell* (1937) that there were three simultaneous plots that night – the king's supporters had put the gunpowder there with a view to blowing up Mary, who had originally intended to spend the night there, and that was why the king didn't even wait to seize some clothes as soon as he smelt fire near the powder; Bothwell had discovered about the powder and set light to it; and Morton's Douglas men, perhaps tipped off, happened to be on the spot to strangle the king should he try to escape. No one will ever really know.

Certainly, as soon as the king smelt burning, he leapt into his night-shirt from a window with his servant, which seems to imply his foreknowledge of the gunpowder: else why run downstairs? As for his stranglers, they must have seen his mother's Douglases for Lennox Stuarts would not have murdered their own chieftain's son and he was heard to cry out 'Pity me, *kinsmen*, for the sake of Jesus Christ who pitied all the world.' This would seem to implicate Mary but the general belief was that it was Bothwell's men who had actually fired the fuse. Further, there is reason to suppose that the powder may have been placed there by that black dyed traitor, my first coz the shifty judge James, Lord Pittendreich, to whose brother Kirk o' Field and the adjoining house with its cellars belonged. Dear coz James was later a suspected tamperer with the Casket Letters, which he conveniently 'produced' to Lord Moray after having been Lord Bothwell's trusted Governor of Edinburgh Castle and was described by the learned Principal Robertson 'the most corrupt man of his age'.

But I don't think Mary herself could have been involved though I wouldn't blame her if she had been. For reasons be discussed later the Queen had been most anxious to sleep with him as soon as possible. While he was there, she twice spent the night in the room beneath his and was expected to sleep again there on what turned out to be the fatal night when she suddenly remembered that she had promised to be at a wedding masque at Holyroodhouse and left him in order to return thither instead. As it was known that she had not slept with her husband for some time, the most reasonable explanation for her specially wanting to sleep with him despite his ghastly syphilitic breath as soon as he was well enough would suggest that she either was, or believed herself to be pregnant by somebody else. If so, it seems fairly obvious that the father was in any case James Hepburn, Earl of Bothwell.

Bothwell, whom she created Duke of Orkney before she married him, had got her in a fix and made it worse by preventing her foisting the unborn twins on her previous husband by slaying him before she could sleep with him in time. She had been trapped, and their brief month of married life (15 may to 15 June 1567) seems to have been bitterly unhappy: 'during the honeymoon Mary was heard to ask for "a knife to stick herself", or else, said she, "I shall drown myself"'.

As for the Casket Letters, the tardy method of their production, the failure to allow any Marian representative to challenge their authenticity at the time, and the disappearance of such important historic originals as soon as convenient, would enable any skilled advocate, myself let alone that legal searchlight (to paraphrase 'luminary' more exactly in his case) our leading criminal lawyer Nicholas Fairbairn of Fordell, QC, MP, to illuminate every flaw and have the case in favour of those letters thrown out in any Scottish court of law. Some may have been genuine, but *all* could *not*, and the slightest taint of forgery invalidates the whole evidence. One clause, for instance, might imply an interpolation into a genuine Marian letter of a love-plaint from abroad from Anna Throndsen, the Norwegian lady whom Bothwell had seduced on a false promise of marriage years before.

There is irony if this was so, for Anna and her powerful family were vengefully waiting there when Bothwell's pirate fleet arrived seeking haven in Norway. It had been chased from Orkney by a Government fleet commanded by my insulted grandpa Sir William Murray of Tullibardine (whom Bothwell had refused to meet in single combat on the pretence that an earl was too grand to fight a mere feudal baron, which was tommy-rot, as all tenants-in-chief in Scotland were then each other's peers and could sit in trial in court on each other) and by Sir William Kirkcaldy of the Grange (apparently my first cousin) a Marian convert who afterwards held Edinburgh Castle last-man-last-round for her exiled Majesty and was the ultimate Scotsman to be hanged in Her service. If only Bothwell, as Duke of Orkney, had stuck to his piratical base in the Shetlands, he might have held on until he could have come to political terms with his fellow Scottish magnates after Mary's death.

But as it turned out, he predeceased her in a manner far *far* more horrible than the headsman's axe that was her doom. Bothwell was no mere swash-buckling Border ruffian to be type-cast like Trevor Howard into a sort of pseudo-Lord Cardigan, though a Border chief of high birth (my reasons for suggesting he was a scion of Niall of the Nine Hostages, pagan King of sacral Tara in the 400s, by way of a brother of Duncan slain by Macbeth, have been printed elsewhere: see *The Armorial* vol vi, no 1, Dec 1970). A polished courtier much abroad, a lover who preceded the late 'Obby' Duke of St Albans by doing a blacksmith's daughter in the steeple of the abbey at Haddington (shades of that 20th century French noblewoman in the tower at Notre Dame!), who had even done a stretch in the Tower of London and collected books on maths, Bothwell a *macédoine* of d'Artagnan, Casanova and Sir Walter Raleigh as if played by Errol Flynn.

While his wife Mary was enduring the agonies of porphyria, worse than the pangs of childbirth, in English 'stately homes', Bothwell was chained in the Danish castle of 'Dragon's Island' to a post half his height so that he could lie but never stand upright, and lying meant trying to snozzle on a mixture of his own excrement and urine, his own filth clogging into his uncut shaggy hairyness (as Zulu warriors used cattle-dung for their ceremonial head-rings) for nearly five years until he died wild and gibbering off his rocker 'living' in a loathsome prison in solitary confinement and no fire in winter and little light even by day, 'where nobody had access to him, but only those that carried such scurvy meat and drink as was allowed, which was given in at a little window'. This was done to the Duke of Orkney, Earl of Bothwell, Lord High Admiral of Scotland, only Lord Warden ever of all the three Marches against England, husband of the Sovereign of the Scots, by the kindly forefather of my two wives and three children, King Frederick II of Denmark, who had oft been Bothwell's genial host in the days of splenderous yore. Needless to say, I owe my life to my descent from Bothwell's sister Lady Jean Hepburn (whose husband the Master of Caithness was driven to death of thirst in fetters on salt-beef and brandy, as related above, in the very same year 1578 of Bothwell's rather similar fate). Bothwell was therefore my uncle: doomed beyond the icy foggiest darkness-depths of all horror, as if our semi-legendary kinsman Beowulf had lost his epic underwater tussle with the monster Grendel in the same viking seas.

Books & Bookmen, May–August 1975

Usherette to Coronets

The first gal to whom I ever proposed marriage was a dark-eyed Scottish descendant of Nell Gwyn. Her father was a statesman who later declined the Viceroyalty of India. We first met while I was an Oxford undergraduate before the War, at the deb dance in London given by Lady Esher for 'Pinkie' Brett: and I made the decision at supper. Being completely inexperienced, however, it took me a couple of years to come to the point. By then I was an officer in the Scots Guards, stationed at the blitzed Tower of London for we were at war, and she was studying medicine at Oxford. So I travelled thither and proposed. She accepted on one condition, that I should buy her Uppark so that we could live in separate wings and never meet. In those days I hadn't met the Meade-Fetherstonhaughs nor yet had been invited to Uppark, so didn't realise the house isn't suitable for making into distant 'wings'. But I rightly took her reply as a refusal. And it was some years before I proposed to anybody again, still inexperienced and equally unsuccessfully, this time to an Anglo-Dutch descendant of Louise de Kéroualle, though I didn't realise this at the time. My wife comes from both Louise de Kéroualle and Lucy Walters.

Donald Adamson and Peter Beauclerk Dewar's *House of Nell Gwyn* (William Kimber, 1975) therefore reminds me at first as much of Charles II as of his particular lady-loves. After all, the Beauclerk Dukes of St Albans, out of her by that king, owe their dukedom to the fact that they are Royal Stuarts in the direct male line. Some time ago, a socialist MP attacked the number of royal bastards among our dukes. This was double-think with grandeur. For the socialists are (in my opinion rightly, since my maternal grandfather was the natural son of a count) the first to say that illegitimate children shouldn't be penalised because their parents didn't go through the formality of marriage, which isn't the child's fault. And the rank of duke, which hurts nobody who hasn't a chip on the shoulder from which a trick-cyclist's services would be the best relief, was originally introduced into this country to mark members of the Royal Family; then extended to ultimately related kinsmen of great historic position. So why should royal natural sons be excluded? There isn't space here to analyse our dukes in detail, but we have thirty-one. Of these, four are royal (Edinburgh, Cornwall, Gloucester & Kent) and five spring from royal bastards (Richmond, Grafton, Beaufort, St Albans and Buccleuch: four Stuarts to one Plantagenet). As for the rest, Marlborough & Wellington are living war memorials to our greatest of soldiers. We are left with such names as Howard & Russell, Douglas & Percy. Do such names mean so little to our national history that they too should not be commemorated in this literally lively way?

But, at second reading, *The House of Nell Gwyn* isn't just an ordinary chronicle of a typically ducal house, such as might be expected of Atholl (I've written one myself) or say the Cavendish Dukes of Devonshire at Chatsworth. Despite the unusual twist in the St Albans dukedom that it isn't linked to one special stately home, but has its housing ups & downs to & fro, this book more than any other reminds me irresistibly of Dennis Price's greatest film, where the hero-villain schemes to be Duke of Chalfont as ultimate heir of the D'Ascoynes in *Kind Hearts and*

Coronets. When she sold her London flat on marriage, my wife bought a cinema projector which now lives alongside the TV in our smoking room. But it's turned out to cost so much to hire a film that it's wiser to go to a cinema, and the Korda films for which we really bought it – Leslie Howard in *The Scarlet Pimpernel*, Aubrey Smith and Ronald Colman and my old acquaintance Douglas Fairbanks jnr in *The Prisoner of Zenda* – have all been withdrawn from film-library circulation. However, my children got *Kind Hearts and Coronets* accompanied by Disney's *Toad of Toad Hall* (preconceived episodes from the life of our gallant present [1975] motor-fiend Lord Hesketh) several years running until they mutinied, and this Xmas got the enticing Ingrid Pitt as our ancestress dubbed incorrectly *Countess Dracula* instead.

Possibly the reason for likening the Dukes of St Albans in real life to those of Chalfont on celluloid, was the wide but completely separate interests of the individuals making up the real family; coupled with such vignette figures with names like Bishop Lord James Beauclerk and Admiral Lord Amelius Beauclerk, of whose HMS *Dryad* capturing the Frog frigate *Proserpine* in 1796 there is an excellent picture which, thank goodness – I, but not all you readers, mean thank God – still belongs to His present Grace. I can't off-hand recollect the Xian name of the Admiral Lord Blankus D'Ascoyne portrayed in the film [*it was Lord Henry* – ED], but it's perhaps only fair to say that he was obviously really modelled on the present Lord Tryon's enigmatic genius of a grandfather, Admiral Sir George Tryon, who like the film's lordly admiral obstinately made his flagship *Victoria* commit suicide with himself and all his crew aboard. Like the imaginary Dukes of Chalfont, too, those of St Albans even had for a while a private banking connection through the 3rd Duke's marriage in 1827 to the widow of Thomas Coutts: how could one ask for more – now that my own Fugger and my wife's Medici blood have receded so much further into the pre-Wedgie Benn past?

It's perhaps worth noting that three of the five delightful mistresses who bore Charles II children were Welsh. Lucy Walters was well-born, having four Garters among her *seize quartiers*. I remember in 1938 hearing the Maharana of Udaipur's pipers playing the plaintive strains of 'My lodging is on the cauld ground, and very hard is my fare' and thinking of how Charles II had been captivated by Moll Davies's singing of it long, long ago, and how the upshot of the king's interview with her offstage afterwards was named Lady Mary Tudor and became mother of Lord Derwentwater beheaded as a Jacobite after the '15 Rising and of his brother similarly executed after '45: and has left us only a few peers like Lords Petre, Granard and Bute, to keep Moll's royal progeny going. Nell Gwyn was born of a rank intermediate between the other two

Welsh beauties. They say her grandfather was a respectable canon, her father a Royalist captain who died in a debtor's goal, and that her sister married a highwayman. Nell herself became an actress after a spell as an orange-girl – what we would now call a soft-drinks cinema usherette – in the theatre pit, and after what turned into an immemorable career died aged 37. She was obviously great fun. Everybody remembers that when her carriage was attacked by an anti-Papist mob thinking it contained Louise de Kéroualle, the Breton-French agent created Duchess of Portsmouth, Nell calmed them: 'Desist, good people, I am the *Protestant* whore.' Also, I seem to remember – probably in Count Anthony Hamilton's memoirs of Gramont – that Nell once invited Louise to enjoy preserved fruits which she'd secretly stuffed with a powerful laxative, knowing her rival was to spend that night with much movement in the king's bed.

Nell's son Charles, 1st Duke of St Albans, who shewed both his parents' spirit when as a youth he fought the Turks with distinction in Hungary as an ordinary volunteer to prove the English colonelcy already conferred on him in childhood no sinecure, married the beautiful blue-blooded heiress of the last surviving male-line branch of the then oldest mediaeval peerage family in England: Lady Diana de Vere, daughter of the 20th & last Earl of Oxford. That earldom had been created in 1142, rather before the days of gunpowder. Owing to the 4th Duke of St Albans being succeeded by a cousin, the representation of these last de Veres passed through an intervening heiress, Lady Charlotte Beauclerk, who married a Drummond – of the family who gave mediaeval Scotland two queens consort and some of my clubs its favourite ex-drunk – down to the present George Drummond (a Godson of King George VI) whose eccentric father used to wear a Household Brigade bow-tie which I copied, and emigrated to our ancestral Isle of Man that I know as well as the native Christians & Stevensons, Quayles & Cubbons. By a coincidence, the heir of the senior extinct stem of the de Veres, the descendants of the poet 17th Earl's eventual heiress (who include myself), is another Drummond, the aptly named Lord Strange [*died 1982*], whom I persuaded to become a peer and live in the Isle of Man as he is also the heir of its mediaeval Kings and 18th century Sovereign Lords. But it's the Beauclerks who continue to quarter the famous Arms of de Vere – whose silver star, worn as a badge by Lord Oxford's men at Barnet battle in the Wars of the Roses being mistaken by his Lancastrian allies in the mist for the sun-rays of York, led to their defeat and the doom of Warwick the King-Maker. Moreover, the present Duke and all his children bear the additional forename 'de Vere', and the courtesy title of his grandson is Lord Vere of Hanworth. So it's to be wished the family would adopt 'de Vere Beauclerk' for surname, just as other natural offspring of Charles II are now called 'Gordon Lennox' or 'Montagu Douglas Scott'. There has indeed been a rumour since my youth that one of them was called 'Ramsay Macdonald'.

On the other hand, it's a pity they weren't all just called 'Stuart' in the first place, which is what they really are and would certainly have been called in Scotland before the Union of the Crowns, cf. my article in *Burke* on the Earls of Moray. To make such matters worse, some of these bastards conceal their own bastards. There is a nice American with whom I correspond called Mr F. R. Howkins, who descends by way of a carpenter and other craftsmen father-to-son from Kings Charles I and II by way of a natural son of the 'Lennox' Dukes of Richmond, themselves royally spawned on Louise Villiers [*a slip later corrected – see below. –* ED] And so Mr Howkins is really a Royal Stuart too, though his coat-of-arms as recorded by the late Lord Lyon doesn't make this as clear as one could wish. The Beauclerks at least named their own natural children by their own bastard surname, proud of the baton sinister (what novelists call a 'bar sinister' which is an heraldic impossibility) across their Royal Arms. And it is one of the many merits of this interesting book that its authors have taken much trouble to track down and include the descendants of such obviously illegitimate Beauclerks. They ploughed the fields and scattered the royal seed on the land, and it was fed and watered by God's Almighty Hand: for one of the double *b*s became Chaplain of Holy Trinity Church in Boulogne in 1875. Many of the St Albans family seem to have inherited Charles II's charm, though not always in their richly-chosen wives' opinion; and although we learn that such-and-such a duke sowed his wild oats in a serving-maid, there is here no such instance as that which caused the extinction of an Irish peerage because the sole heir died from being kicked in the balls by a stuffy but evidently unstuffable milkmaid he was trying to seduce.

This perhaps brings us to some of the exploits of the late 'Obby', 12th Duke of St Albans, whom I used to meet occasionally in our clubs. At that time I belonged like him to Brooks's, and the authors quote his celebrated crack to Newman, our now legendary hall porter: 'wind up my watch for me, there's a good fellow'. He was a strange mixture of de Vere Beauclerk *cum* Nell Gwyn on his father's side and Bernal Osborne, half Sephardic Jew and half Anglo-Irish protestant ascendancy, on his mother's. But his eccentricity probably came to him from his paternal grandmother, the Duchess *née* Elizabeth Catherine Gubbins, since it's she whom he shared with his batty half-brother the 11th Duke. We're all aware of the early Victorian nanny-reproof: 'You silly Gubbins'. One imagines it was derived from the sad fate of the duchess's brother,

57

Charles Gubbins, who went off his rocker soon after the Regency. There is a tale of Duke 'Obby' that he was having an affaire with the delicious wife of a suspicious French nobleman. However, he was allowed to be taken by her to be shewn round Nôtre Dame, which he'd already reconnoitred. There can be few lovers shrewd enough to realise that a good place to seduce a willing lady is near the top of that cathedral's tower stairs, as the footsteps of any questing tourist climbing up can be heard well in advance. It was sad to learn from this book, however, that as Hereditary Grand Falconer of England he was allowed to wear his gold chain of office at George VI's Coronation, but at the last one wanted to bring a live falcon too, and when told he could only bring a stuffed one, stayed away. It was unimaginative, for once, of the Earl Marshal's Office. At my own wedding in the ruined mediaeval Chapel of Moncreiffe, my bride's page carried a live falcon (her family's crest) albeit hooded.

I had originally wanted a live falcon (also the Erroll crest) at my first wedding, held against my wishes at the 'smart' church of St Margaret's Westminster, so more like a cocktail party than a solemn religious ceremony, but my then bride's Sackville relations were too English to permit anything so Celtic and bizarre. However, one of our bridesmaids, now married to Ian Gilmour the MP, was a fetching descendant of Nell Gwyn. The descent came through her mother Mollie Lascelles, Duchess of Buccleuch, granddaughter of the 10th Duke of St Albans and certainly the grandest, most understanding and talented, also wittiest of all Charles II's living offspring of the Beauclerk stock. To watch the Duchess curtsy on a great ceremonial occasion is to liken her to a Spanish galleon under full sail dipping her colours in a royal salute. Evelyn Waugh once wrote that you don't usually meet dukes in other dukes' houses. This is true of some; but not of a house-party in that close-knit present-day family group where the Duchess's grandfather was Duke of St Albans; her son is Duke of Buccleuch & Queensberry; her daughter is Duchess of Northumberland; the Duke of Northumberland's sisters are Elizabeth, Duchess of Hamilton & Brandon, and the present Duchess of Sutherland; their late mother was daughter of the Duke of Richmond & Gordon; and their grandmother was daughter of the Duke of Argyll. Just to confuse the reader further with the Sutherland part of this ducal jigsaw, let's add that the attractive 24th Countess of Sutherland in her own right, present Chief of the Sutherland clan, is also an offshoot of Charles II's liaison with Nell Gwyn.

Topham Beauclerk, an old favourite of mine, rightfully gets a chapter of his own: what fun it would have been to have belonged to The Club with him and Dr Johnson and Sir Joshua Reynolds, followed by Burke and Garrick, Adam Smith and scribble-scribble-scribble Mr Gibbon. Indeed, what fun it must be still to belong to The Club at all. Oddly enough, it was at a little conversation-club which I founded in Edinburgh and called Puffin's that I first met one of the co-authors of this book, brought as a candidate for invitation to membership, which was immediately and very properly approved by our ferocious dictator: me. But it was as a paternal Dewar rather than a maternal Beauclerk that he was chosen – for we tend to the side of 'Scotch nonsense', as the late Lord Chamberlain Cromer described such ancient names as Cameron of Lochiel and Moncreiffe of that Ilk.

The frankness of the chapter on the present duke entitled 'The Belated Entrepreneur' shews how this incredibly resilient amalgam of royal energy, naughty rise from the stage to the palace, haughty 'Vere de Vere' courage *par excellence*, and shrewd common-sense combined with application to sheer dynamic work, are still directed to the maintenance of a ducal position that will enable the Beauclerk family to continue to fulfil those duties that our only pseudo-bolshie Britain still expects of its aristocracy: as even a 24th Ilk knows to his overburdened cost. We are all conditioned to these duties I suppose, like Pavlov's bow-wows, but at least more is expected of dukes than barts. My own latest invitation is rather different from the usual ones that want our unpaid support for some Good Cause. By chance, at the very moment of typing this ultimate paragraph, we've just been asked to dine by the present Duke and his charming Alpes Maritimes authoress wife: and must hope that they'll remember in reverse the Merry Monarch's dying injunction – 'Let not poor Nelly starve.'

Books & Bookmen, April 1975

Adopting his alter ego 'Dr R. I. K. Moncreiffe', I. M. subsequently submitted a rider to the above review:

I'm surprised that Sir Iain Moncreiffe of that Ilk omitted to mention one of today's leading scions of the Beauclerk stock.

For another of Nell Gwyn's present-day descendants is that fascinating thoroughbred Diana, Duchess of Newcastle – nicknamed 'hurtle-wurtle' in her maiden days as Lady Diana Stuart-*Wortley* for being the speediest dashing motor-bicycle despatch-rider in the Second World War – former MFH and the first women to hold an international jockey's licence: as well as being a leading authority on her remarkable ambassadress-ancestress Lady Mary Wortley-Montagu, who introduced vaccination from Constantinople in the reign of George I.

He also surprisingly omits among Nell Gwyn's talented issue today the children of the marriage of 'Obby' Duke of St Albans' sister to Lord Richard Cavendish, who include Mary, Countess of Crawford (her son Ld Balniel was a minister in the last sane Govt) and Elizabeth, Marchioness of Salisbury (whose husband made Mac the Knife with which to cut his, the benefactor's own, political throat) – Cecils and Lindsays, amongst the most civilised of our crumbling heritage – and also, a generation younger, Sir Iain's buddy Hugh Cavendish of Holker who has worked in and cherishes a centuries-old North Lancashire slate mine peopled by craftsmen from *Puck of Pook's Hill* that can make one single slate cut with years of wisdom rival in human quality the Cullinan diamond itself once cut. Dust to dust, carbon to carbon.

And in discussing the ancestry of Mr F. R. Howkins, Sir Iain really ought not to confuse Louise de Kerouaille, who brought the French duchy of Aubigny back to the Lennox Stuarts, with her brainy rival Barbara Villiers.

A Pride of Kings

Now, Aunt Helen had a daugher called Mrs Willie James, an Edwardian hostess with the mostest, and she begat my cousin Audrey who married a chap from Chicago called Marshall Field. He was a successful shopkeeper, or rather his father was.

This shop they had was the original model for Selfridge's (number nine 'bus from Harrod's it used to be before I became a Guards officer and wasn't allowed to travel by motor-omnibus, though luckily the Underground was too modern to have been proscribed). Unlike the puritanical English, who scowl at fascinating Marcia Williams [*Lady Falkender*] for taking successful risk in slag, the Americans enjoy the creation of new wealth. They also enjoy being able despite being only private persons to found new public things. Marshall Field founded the Field Museum of Natural History in Chicago. During the Depression the shop was rescued by the brilliant management of my fellow chief, McBain of McBain. When I went to Chicago at the time the Moon Men were getting their ticker-tape, McBain gave me F. W. Holiday's *The Great Orm of Loch Ness* (W. W. Norton, New York, 1969), with its theory that Nessie and family are vast boneless expansions of a prehistoric water-slug whose tiny fossils are found in Chicago and classified as the *nillimonstrum*. Then he took me to the Field Museum to see them, where the curator of fossil invertebrates disillusioned us by saying that no creature the size of Nessie could ever support its bulk out of water without a backbone: and we all know it comes ashore – a relation of mine called Hugh Fraser slew one in the heather in 1500.

Arnold McNaughton's monumental compilation *The Book of Kings: A Royal Genealogy* (Garnstone Press, 3 volumes), is thus the backbone of the skeleton needed to support our understanding of the Protestant royalty in Europe. It sets out, so far as he has found possible, the lawful descendants of King George I. This amounts to the sum total of our whole Royal Family (as opposed merely to those immediate members who by the Queen's command enjoy a special precedence among themselves which is, by the way, quite different from their public precedence). For, by the Act of Settlement, the throne is vested in the Protestant descendants of the Electress Sophia, the heiress of Elizabeth Stuart, the 'Winter Queen'); and the only children to leave descendants were George I and his sister, whose only child married George I's daughter.

So in this Age of Envy bubbling for nuclear warfare few hitherto unparalleled disasters could bring to the throne a most interesting assortment of ladies or gentlemen born thank goodness by the Grace of God (the so-called 'accident of birth') and not by those dead boars, bores or is it bears who are our masters at the TUC and wouldn't allow me join the Transport & General Workers' Union when I applied on the grounds of being a General Worker.

These volumes have a Foreword by our President of the Society of Genealogists who is, of course, Lord Mountbatten of Burma; though no more Burmese than Lord Dufferin and Ava. They reveal the ramifications of our present royalty, from such dynastic houses as Nassau and Radziwill to 'Flash' Ambler's three infants by his marriage to Princess Margaretha of Sweden. Catholic descendants with historic Austrian names like Hapsburg and grand Venetian names like the last now extinct Mocenigo are included, although they would of course have had to become Anglicans to succeed. We also learn that the present Prince of Wales is descended (through cousin marriages) seventeen times over from George I, and therefore 17 times from Mary Queen of Scots; which will please Prince Charles who has a special love for Scotland. This may mislead readers into supposing that the Royal Family is more in-bred than most. The Royal Families of Europe were like the inhabitants of a farflung village who inter-married each other most of the time. But this would, before modern transport, have been equally true of the labourers in any ordinary village: it's just that their inter-connected genealogies haven't usually been worked out.

To take but one example from among our potential Sovereigns: Mrs David Butter (wife of my Lord Lieutenant), whose grandfather was the

Grand Duke Michael of Russia. Nobody could call her too in-bred. Her family have imported into Scotland some exotically romantic blood, for she descends from both Czar Peter the Great and from his pillow, an enobled Ethiopian page called Hannibal (afterwards a General of Engineers). I seem to remember that Hannibal was a man of character who flogged his Greek wife daily in order to make her agree to a divorce. Myra Butter descends from him through the poet Pushkin, whose death in a duel deprived us of so much, for he translates so well into English that the original Russian must be like a glorious rushing waterfall.

Mr McNaughton's *Book of Kings* will be indispensable as a work of reference for genealogists and historians alike. People are links in a chain between their ancestors and their descendants, and can never be really understood except in the setting of this sort of tapestry tree of life, to cocktail the metaphor still further. This applied more especially to royal people, by virtue of the importance of their birth. Moreover, to be descended from George I is nowhere near the start. An Este from northern Italy in the direct male line, Guelphed for some centuries in Brunswick, he brought to the characters in this book female-line descents from such variegated personalities as El Cid of Spain, St Louis of France, Brian 'Boru' of Ireland, St Vladimir of Russia and Simon de Montfort. Nor was he himself quite the stuffy character of standardised generalisation. He was, for example, Godfather to the son of his hatter in Hanover, Herr Wagner, whom he brought to St James's and who was forefather of Sir Anthony Wagner, present Garter King of Arms, whose son is my own Godson. Readers may find this little bit of information a suitable ending to this review of what is almost a computer of special genealogical information about the wide-scattered and very numerous scions of the leading family in the world.

Books & Bookmen, June 1974

Royal Matriarch

A fish out of water is supported by its skeleton, but is not complete without flesh and blood. Of course a real fish like the sturgeon would need to be able to breathe open air as well: and only got included among *Fish Royal* in Edward II of England's statute because it was mistakenly thought to belong to the mammalian Dolphin family – probably protected through some now unascertained connection with the heralic 'beast' of the Dauphins of Viennois that (like the protected swans which must somehow link our royal house through the family of the

Crusader-King Godfrey of Bouillon to the Swan Knight) we haven't yet been able to track down. Unfortunately this harmless quaint conceit – since the Sovereign used the sturgeon to enrich the coffers of needy hospitals who sold it to restaurateurs to smoke for gourmets – was swept away amongst legal cobwebs by the new broom of Quintin Hailsham, while his daughter Frances Hogg was running a mobile discothèque with my son the electronics wizard Merlin, *Fish Royal* among the Gaels was salmon, which is why the Crown was able to raise revenue or reward service by the grant of salmon fishings just like land in Scotland: where salmon is the only legally reserved wild fish.

Theo Aronson's *Grandmama of Europe: the Crowned Descendants of Queen Victoria* (Cassell, 1974) puts the flesh and blood on some of the more important characters whose backbone I reviewed recently in Arnold McNaughton's *The Book of Kings* [*see above*]. But so numerous have the Great White Queen's crowned descendants been, that Mr Aronson has wisely confined himself in his well-researched, sympathetic and interesting book to intermingled biographies of her first descendeath – for those of some of their husbands' reigns were whether as Sovereign or Consort.

With their happy family pet-names and dates of birth and death – for those of some of their husbands' reigns were shorter, longer or even repetitive – these were, for reference back in this review:

wise and liberal 'Vicky' *alias* Victoria, German Empress (1840–1901); worldly and popular 'Bertie' *alias* Edward VII, our King-Emperor (1841–1910); romping 'Harry' *alias* Maud, Queen of Norway (1869–1938); misunderstood 'Sossie' *alias* Sophie, Queen of the Hellenes (1870–1932); tragic 'Alicky' *alias* Alexandra, Empress of All the Russias (1872–1918), known in her childhood as 'Princess Sunshine'; brainy yet romantick 'Missy' *alias* Marie, Queen of Rumania (1875–1938) – not to be confused with her cousin 'Mossy', Princess Margaret of Prussia; sad 'Ena' *alias* Victoria Eugenie, Queen of Spain (1887–1969); efficient Louise, Queen of Sweden (1889–1965); practical 'Mignon' *alias* Marie, Queen of Yugoslavia (1900–1961), also 'Paiky' to her friends; and the beautiful Ingrid, now widowed Queen of Denmark (born 1910, but looks much younger).

You will have to read the book to know who 'Ducky' and 'Dona' and 'Nando' and 'Moretta' were: I'm not telling.

The only time I met Queen Ingrid of Denmark was when she came to north-east Scotland to attend the wedding of her one-legged but staunchly kilted cousin 'Sandy' *alias* Alexander Arthur Alfonso David Maule Ramsay of Mar (grandson of Arthur, Duke of Connaught, who was Godson of the Iron Duke of Wellington – hence 'Arthur' – and third son of Queen Victoria) to Lord Saltoun's daughter and heiress, 'Flossie' *alias* Flora Fraser. It caused a great stir among the honest burgesses and friendly fisher-folk of the homely coastal town of Fraserburgh, fronting across the North Sea direct to Denmark: quite apart from the gathering of our own royal family who also arrived at the church to the locally unaccustomed sound of trumpets, before we all popped off for noggins at the Frasers' mediaeval castle nearby. Queen Ingrid combined fresh-complexioned beauty with simple dignity and regal friendliness. Sandy Ramsay tells me an instructive anecdote of his mother, the 'Princess Pat' of the Canadians' famous battle-regiment the PPCLI, who was selected to marry King Alfonso XIII of Spain, but decided she didn't want to. At that time, however, she was amused on getting into a conveyance with the courting king, when he turned to her and said: 'Patsy, if anyone throws a bomb into the carriage, remember to throw it back quick.'

He was all too right. In grimly grand Spanish style, his pregnant widowed mother's tummy had been ceremonially crowned, for whatever was inside her womb – boy or girl – was Sovereign of Spain. And Spain has rarely been easy on its Sovereigns. When, having failed to secure Princess Patricia of Connaught, he married another of Queen Victoria's grandchildren, Princess 'Ena' of Battenberg, a large bouquet of flowers was thrown in front of them from a window, just missing their carriage, but wounding the terrified horses and causing bloody havoc among 'the torn and bleeding bodies' in the crowd. For the bouquet had duly contained a bomb. The tragic wedding present Queen Ena herself brought him though neither of them knew it at the time, was haemophilia – transmitted from Queen Victoria to two of four of the Infants of Spain born of this marriage. Queen Ena had imparted it through her mother, Queen Victoria's daughter Princess Beatrice, widow of Prince Henry of Battenberg – a Battenberg prince *fought* for us in the First World War *knowing* he had haemophila. As a boy I was sometimes taken by my grandmother to visit Princess Beatrice. Stately she was and straightforward; but her signature in our Visitors' Book here in 1913 is rather unfortunately bang opposite a typical earthy Edwardian joke photograph of the back view of two tweedy gentlemen (one in a kilt) whose unconscious stance on top of the front steps at Moncreiffe makes it look as though they're relieving themselves after luncheon.

In 1941, King Alfonso died in exile in Rome, and in uniform with a black crêpe armband I was one of the ushers at his Requiem Mass far away in blitzed London. There was no nonsense about his being referred

ABOVE LEFT: I.M., Albany Herald, leading the procession at the Duke of Argyll's funeral, Inveraray, 1973.

ABOVE RIGHT: 'Puffin' Countess of Erroll, I.M's first wife, at Easter Moncreiffe, 1954. I.M. is looking through the window.

RIGHT: 'Lord of the Dance': I.M. dancing with the Queen at the Royal Scottish Country Dance Society's gathering at the Assembly Rooms, Edinburgh, 1973.

TOP: I.M., wearing his Afghan coat, on top of Moncreiffe Hill in Perthshire at the old Pict fort, 1967.

LEFT AND ABOVE: I.M. at Easter Moncreiffe in the Moncreiffe tartan: in kilt; in waistcoat and trousers, with O'Higgins, the Irish wolfhound.

to in the orders given to us officers of the Household Troops as 'ex-King Alfonso' as most of the Press did, for he had never abdicated. On the other hand, HM Government no longer recognised him as *de facto* Head of the Spanish State. So we simply called him 'King Alfonso XIII, KG'. Besides, he'd been educated for a short time at Harrow, where Harrovians tell one every boy took his turn to be able to say in after life that he'd 'kicked the King of Spain'. But of course the English public schools have been 'comprehensive' for centuries.

The best analysis of how Queen Victoria gave haemophilia to her descendants is probably that made by my bolshie kinsman, Professor J. B. S. Haldane (who was such an aggresive individualist styling himself a communist that the Soviets would probably have restrained him in a looney bin, but he emigrated to republican India instead), in the chapter called 'Blood Royal' in his *Keeping Cool* (Chatto & Windus, 1940). He includes genealogical table setting out the matter in its simplest form, and concludes: 'The gene must have originated by mutation and the most probable place and time where the mutation may have occurred was in the nucleus of a cell in one of the testicles of Edward, Duke of Kent [Queen Victoria's father], in the year 1818.'

(As an aside, it's impossible to get medical doctors – I write as a doctor of philosophy – to consider the possibility that a coincidence should be investigated until their made-up minds see good reason for it: when, of course, it no longer requires investigation. But readers of Dr Ida Macalpine's and Dr Richard Hunter's *Porphyria: A Royal Malady* – published by the BMA as an extract from the British Medical Journal 1968 – studying especially the genealogical tables, will note that the same Duke of Kent may probably have inherited mildly his father George III's porphyria: and it's worth considering why, when one hereditary malady *appears* to disappear, another *apparently* unconnected one immediately replaces it. Moreover, while staying with Lochiel, I once accidentally drenched with a hose – it was meant to be a mere sprinkle in a jesting battle – a late descendant of Queen Victoria who did have mild porphyria, but he *could* have got it from his mother who, although not descended from George III, was also a descendant of that almost undoubted porphyriac Mary Queen of Scots.)

Haemophilia is a helplessly numbing, then insuperably nerve-jarring tragedy for the parents of an otherwise healthy, bonny and intelligent boy. It means your blood don't clot, whether wounded on your skin or internally. Normally, in a family that has developed this inborn malady, an average half of the sons will have it and an average half of the daughters (women don't have it themselves) may transmit it. A man haemophiliac himself can only transmit it through his daughters: he can't give to his own sons, since it is sex-linked to the 'X' as opposed to the 'Y' chromosome. Thus it was with one of Queen Victoria's younger sons, Prince Leopold, who had it. He must have had great difficulty in surviving membership of Loder's *alias* the Christ Church Society, in my time the most happily inebriated dining club at Oxford (Max Beerbohm modelled *the Junta* of *Zuleika Dobson* on it), of which the Prime Minister Lord Rosebery said the proudest moment of his life was when he became president of Loder's and to which such other well-known soaks as the Viceroy Lord Halifax, Anthony Eden and Alec Douglas-Home have belonged, if my memory serves me right. At the end of our dinners, all the remaining port was poured into the vast games-trophy-type silver cup given us in the last century by Prince Leopold and passed round as a loving cup. When it reached the junior member, he had to finish all that was left before stopping and usually then passed out: the one in my time was a noble lord who is now a respectable don at Newcastle University. One tumble over that after-dinner table and Prince Leopold would have had it: it's not surprising that he barely survived his 30th birthday, even after he'd escaped from us. But through the ghoulish inevitability of genetics, two of his literally Victorian sisters transmitted haemophilia: and on the world scale the most important recipients were the royal house of Spain and the imperial house of Russia.

Leaving aside the point that we and Russia were fighting the First World War to support a gang of murderers (for some reason murder when political becomes more respectable when referred to as 'assassination', which shows how little the utterer has studied the *hashish-in* methods of the Old Man of the Mountains), Rasputin's chief offence seems to be that he was a rather scruffy and sexy man of peace who wanted to stop that lunatic War: perhaps the first in which millions of smashed human bodies were used to slake the propagandist lust of the Yellow Press. His merit was that his hypnotic talent as a healer could alleviate the hereditary tortures unwittingly conferred by Queen Victoria on Alicky's son, the little Czarevitch (I spell it thus because 'Tsar' or 'Czar' is simply 'Caesar'). Those who believe in euthanasia may kid themselves into thinking it was just as well those sufferings were ended at Ekaterinburg by good Left-Wing bullets and possibly bayonets.

But it's perhaps salutary to observe that the Left-Wing 'brotherhood of Man' is the brotherhood of Cain and Abel. When anybody except a fellow freemason calls me 'brother' I loosen my dirk in its scabbard and make sure the black stocking knife or *sgian dubh* is ready in reserve. For why do the very people who cry mercy for the Moors Murderers and oppose capital punishment, condone in their inner hearts the murder of a happily united imperial or royal family who have abdicated everything: and genuinely believe – for who would accuse a Left-Winger of insincerity – that it's socially OK (isn't that what 'socialism' is about) to 'execute' teenage Grand Duchesses?

There remains still [*1974*] the tragic question whether the wounded (*is it a bullet-wound from Ekaterinburg?*) and lonely old lady in the Black Forest is the Grand Duchess Anastasia ['*Anna Anderson', who married Dr John Manahan and later died in Virginia, USA* – ED]. My bizarre archaeologist friend, Prince Frederick of Saxe-Altenburg, is so convinced she is his cousin that he has investigated similar lost causes and now also believes Naundorf really was the Dauphin, the titular Louis XVII, warped as a child for the usual doctrinaire reasons by our lefty 'comrades' who wouldn't like some royal maniac to do it back to their own children. And did the Maid of Norway really die? In Scotland, we have the mysterious case of the slave-girl being auctioned on the German Baltic coast in the 13th century, who appealed in vain to some canny bawbee-saving passing Scots: 'Rescue me, for I am your Queen.' One of Prince Frederick's reasons for believing in the Black Forest Anastasia is that she knew of the close-kept secret visit of her uncle a *Hessian* prince to the Czar in a vain attempt to negotiate a separate peace between Germany and Russia in the First World War: a visit known only to a few secretive statesmen and the immediate royal familes in both countries. (It's just like that Victorian every-picture-must-tell-a-story painting of po-faced Roundheads asking an innocent little Cavalier boy 'when did you last see your father?'). For the mother of the murdered empress was Queen Victoria's saintly daughter Alice, Grand Duchess of *Hesse*, an excellent biography of whom by Gerard Noel entitled *Princess Alice: Queen Victoria's Forgotten Daughter* is shortly to be published by Constable [*1974*]. Luckily Princess Alice had died before the murder of her two daughters, and massacre at Ekaterinburg of her grandchildren.

But Ekaterinburg was not a manifestation of Russia. It was a manifestation of Revolution, when sadism is almost universally acceptable to extreme Left-Wingers: although it is not their monopoly, as witness in 1849 the centralising foreign conqueror General 'Hyena' Haynau (bastard of the German Landgrave of Hesse-Cassel) making naked Magyar girls run the gauntlet of his brutal and licentious soldiers' canes to and fro between two ranks in public until they fainted, for which he was later himself splendidly beaten up by Messrs Barclay & Perkins' draymen on a visit to their brewery in England. Despotic dynasts could be just as nasty as late as the 20th century: for example Sultan Abdul the Damned and the Armenian massacres so gruesomely depicted in Noel Barber's *Lords of the Golden Horn* (Macmillan, 1973).

But there was no cruel streak in the royalty sprung from Victoria and Albert. Nor are all Socialists libidinous blood-lusters: as witness the Scandinavian social democracies and our gentle civilised statesman Roy Jenkins and Mr Lee, present socialist premier of Singapore, perhaps the best Prime Minister in the world. Nevertheless, royalty and aristocracy, however gentle and dutiful, are regarded as fair game by revolutionaries in a very special way.

For example, it was not the Soviet Union that organised the murder of King Feisal of Iraq, whom I knew but slightly, and his uncle the Regent and Nuri the prime minister, my guests on Guard: I only spare you the horrors of the latter's death for lack of space. When the Iraqi royal family came out unarmed, a gallant revolutionary officer safe in his armoured tank machine-gunned the lot, including nannies and a tiny orphan child of no grand birth whose only offence deserving capital punishment was that she had been adopted by a princess. But the British left-wing Press went mad with joy. One journalist wrote it was the best day since the Fall of the Bastille. Do you remember what happened at the Fall of the Bastille, where the historians tell us that under Louis XVI 'food was good and abundant'? They murdered the kindly governor; and released seven prisoners (one at least asked to go back there and live in peace) of whom the principal was the liberated Marquis de Sade. The point is that bourgeois leftists – not the ordinary country people – don't regard royalty or its loyal folk as human: and all their talk of brotherhood or even 'equality' is humbug. So royalty must forever, it seems, be clay-pigeons used as targets set up on a pedestal – and aren't even allowed to show any feet of clay in the meantime.

As for the royal pedestal, Mr Aronson tells us about the husband of Queen Victoria's tomboyish granddaughter 'Harry' *alias* Maud: Prince Charles of Denmark, who rather reluctantly became King Haakon VII of Norway because he felt he had no right to his royal birth unless he was prepared to accept kingship itself when invited by a Norwegian plebiscite of more than five to one. His and Maud's Coronation, the once-and-only one Norway has known, is perhaps the most unused illustration in the book. The new 'King Haakon shocked King Edward's entourage by announcing his intention of travelling about the streets of his capital by tram. Only by moving amongst his subjects on the utmost simplicity would he be able, he reckoned, to win popularity and combat republicanism. Against any such notion, the British argued hotly. "I told him," claims Ponsonby [our Edward VII's Private Secretary], "that he must set on a pedestal and remain there".' Both were right in a way. The British have a knack for popular urban pageantry unrivalled in the world. The Norwegians are content with the simple beauty of their ice-quiet fjords and mountains. I met them a lot while General Staff Officer III (Plans) for Norway to deal with the ending of the War, by force if need be; was in the admiral's cabin aboard HMS *Renown* when we received the surrender of the German Navy from Norway ('Why are you late?' were the startling first words of Lord Perth's brother Vice-Admiral the Honble Rupert Drummond to the exhausted Nazis who had flown in at our summons); then was sent there in a destroyer – very sea-sick – as Military Liaison Officer between our Naval and Military Commanders-in-Chief; saw the attractive white wooden royal palace, Trondheim, where in 1905 on Queen Maud's first arrival 'not even in the royal apartments was there a lavatory'; and returned with that tiny sea-tiger Admiral McGrigor (afterwards First Sea Lord) in HM cruiser *Norfolk* in time to see off King Haakon, inspecting a splendid Guard of Honour of turkeys, *i.e.* the Royal Marines, before he boarded her on his sail homewards from exile. The inspection was marred by tiny shaggy Press photographers in grubby tweed suits capering along between the ranks taking close-ups of HM's face. I've often reflected since that, as Press photography is a reasonable and indeed proper method of sharing ceremonial with a wider public, there ought to be a choice of coloured uniforms for them to wear compulsorily (for those who show us up are bashful themselves) and thus help to beautify instead of defile the pageantry, and that a certain dignity of movement be enjoyed.

With Queen Maud's father 'Bertie' *alias* our King Emperor Edward VII, there was no nonsense about coming down from pedestals, even when travelling abroad allegedly *incognito* as the Duke of Lancaster. Mr Aronson observes that 'No capital in Europe – not the barbaric splendour of St Petersburg or the showy militarism of Berlin – could match the assured magnificence of King Edward VII's court. With the decorative and perennially youthful Queen Alexandra by his side, King Edward restored to the British monarchy a lustre that it has not known since the days of the Stuarts'. The Viennese of that date, with their proud grand 'imperial and royal' Austro-Hungarian 'Spanish' or 'Burgundian etiquette', might have tried to challenge Mr Aronson in favour of their elaborate and stately waltzing Court (despite the overwhelming smell of boot-polish), but they'd have certainly agreed with him about Berlin. They used to say:

> Es gibt nur eine Kaiserstadt,
> Es gibt nur ein Wien;
> Es gibt nur ein Raübernest,
> Und das heisst Berlin.

Mr Aronson is certainly right that Edward VII was meticulous about decorations. While dining with the Queen, I have myself been reasonably asked by HM about the neck-order I was wearing: for it was the jewel of St Andrew worn by officers of the Thistle, and only six such jewels exist. As as naval lieutenant the future 22nd Ilk was serving on board the royal yacht *Victoria and Albert* when he was given a mighty rocket by the admiral commanding, for having his dirk-belt buckled on upside down. A few minutes later Edward VII emerged, and to my uncle's delight gave the admiral a truly royal dressing-down for wearing the star of his KCVO upside down. But it's hard to believe Mr Aronson's story that the King reproved Harold Nicolson's father, then Ambassador in St Petersburg, for wearing our Order of Nova Scotia: and called it a 'bauble'. It's older than any other British gong except the Garter, and we always wear it with the more new-fangled 'decorations', sometimes without them (the 19th Ilk was painted in 1790 wearing his with a hunt coat). Perhaps 'Bertie' was quietly informed he'd made a mistake for once, and he or his son made amends, for a different neck-order was soon allowed to all ordinary baronets too [*not, infact, until 1929.* – ED] The 21st Ilk certainly wore his Nova Scotia badge all the years he was ADC to George V, and the 24th Ilk wears it in attendance on the Sovereign whether as a royal herald or as an Archer of the Queen's Body Guard for Scotland.

As Prince of Wales 'Bertie' was known to love the ladies, especially Lady Warwick, but he settled down in the end with the Honble Mrs George Keppel. I first met her as a boy when our butler Sunley came into the dining-room at Moncreiffe during luncheon and said: 'A message from Lord Mar and Kellie, milady, to say that Mrs Keppel is bringing the Dowager Ambassador with her to tea.' This led to much speculation among the grown-ups, who decided he must be Lord Hardinge of Penshurst, though he turned out to be Baron Cartier de Marchienne, then doyen of the Diplomatic Corps, a magnificent moustachioed head that properly mounted by Rowland Ward could well have adorned our big-game Head Hall. But I noticed the guests all took it for granted who 'Mrs Keppel' was. She combined incomparably tact with wit, worldly wisdom with command: as any discerning child could sense. Later, she invited me at the age of 19 to propose myself to stay with her in Italy, What a pity that I didn't somehow find an opportunity to go while on vacation from Heidelberg. My grandmother told me that when King Edward died, Mrs Keppel explained to a friend that she thought of travelling abroad and observed: 'Haven't you heard, there's a slump in Cassels and Keppels and a boom in Bibles and babies?'

Mrs Keppel (whom that deaf but ever-young angel Queen Alexandra took up to comfort Edward VII on his death-bed) was of course referring to the rather more Victoria-and-Albert morality of Queen Mary and George V. It's true that before his marriage the future George V had been in love, though without any impropriety, with the future Marquise d'Hautpoul de Seyre: though Mr Aronson don't call her that. He mentions her briefly, implying she was a sweet but unsuitable Cinderella, and refers to her as 'Julie Stoner'. She was unsuitable as a non-royal Papist like Mrs Fitzherbert, but in fact otherwise could scarcely have been of grander noble birth. She was the Honble Julia Stonor, whose forefather had been granted by King Edward II in 1329 licence to maintain six chaplains to celebrate divine service in the chapel at Stonor, and whose family is perhaps the only one in England to have kept the Mass going continuously (for a while secretly from a 'priest's hole' in their old manor at Stonor) all through the years of persecution from the Reformation to Catholic Emancipation; and whose later ancestor Sir John Stonor of Stonor fought in full armour at Crécy when the Black Prince won his spurs. Her father was brother of the celebrated shot and courtier Sir Harry Stonor, whose signature for 1884 we're also proud to have in our Visitors' Book here. Their elder brother was Francis Robert Stonor, Lord Camoys (a peerage created in 1883) and she was christened after her aunt Julia Peel, Countess of Jersey: for her own maternal grandfather was Sir Robert Peel the Prime Minister. No Cinderella she.

Even so, how *clever* and *wise* (these are disparate qualities hard to ride in tandem) was Queen Victoria in her ultimate choice of a bride for her eventual heir. For this country could hardly have done better to get instead, without religious and dynastic complications, Princess 'May' of Teck *alias* Queen Mary. We were once startled when attending our local kirk as children to hear the holy minister say: 'When we look at our own Queen Mary, with her vast bulk, as she lies on her side for her bottom to be scraped.' And were about to arise and do a Jenny Geddes with stools from the 'laird's loft', our upraised pew that gave us a tactical fighting advantage over the pulpit, when we realised the Rev was only referring to that enormous super-liner named after our then Gracious Queen. But Her Majesty herself had 'bottom' in the good English sense: come wind come weather.

Everybody must regret that Edward VII didn't get on with his touchy nephew 'Willie', the German Emperor William II *alias* 'Kaiser Bill' (Kaiser like Czar means Caesar): so much in need of understanding because of the inferiority complex derived from his withered arm. The emperor adored his grandmother Queen Victoria, and propped up her pillow, presumably with his other arm, on her deathbed. He had a love-hate relationship with his mother's country (it's perhaps worth considering why his empire was the 'Fatherland' while Aussies call us the 'Mother Country' whatever they may think of pommies, on whom they're inclined at present to 'go snakes', if you understand Barry Mackenzie's lingo). For instance, when he was made a British honorary Admiral, he exclaimed with joy that he could now wear the uniform of Nelson and St Vincent, and when he was made Honorary Colonel of the 1st Royal Drgoons he enthused 'at the idea that I now can wear beside the Naval uniform the traditional British "Redcoat".' (How many readers recollect that when Pearl Harbour was bombed the youngest Field-Marshal in the British Army was the Emperor of Japan?) But after the failure of the Jameson Raid, he sent a tactless telegram congratulating President Kruger: I don't know enough about Wilhelmstrasse politics, but have long suspected that odious blackmailer Baron Holstein (the destroyer of Count von Arnim and Prince Eulenburg) had a hand in him making this international *faux pas*. As a boy in my Harrods Boys' Dept dinner jacket I used to meet Sir Lionel Earle in my grandmother's house: he had lost an eye in the raid, and described watching from his prison window the scaffold the Boers were building to hang him on. Then the Emperor William made one of his customary somersaults, and on the outbreak of the Boer War sent to Windsor a plan of campaign for the British invention of 'concentration camps' and, of course, *ultimately* our losing Natal and Cape Colony to those expatriate Dutchmen who disenfranchised the 'Cape coloureds' from the votes we British had given them.

Mr Aronson obviously finds him tiresome, and refers to him as 'Wilhelm' rather than 'William', though he calls his likeable father 'Frederick' and not 'Friedrich'. In his recent book, *Our German Cousins*, John Mander tells us of Marx that the English Crown Princess of Prussia (*i.e.* 'Vicky', cleverest of Queen Victoria's children and the future Kaiser Bill's ma) had read *Das Kapital* when it appeared 'and sent a private spy to London to beard the sage in his den. The spy was impressed, but commented, "he is not the man who is going to make the revolution". It is curious [adds Mr Mander] to reflect that European Royalty and European Revolutionaries had at least one point in common: German was their *lingua franca*'. It's an interesting idea but requires some criticism. The only time I saw Lenin he was lying stuffed in a glass case, so it wasn't possible to ask him what language he spoke at an *Internationale*. One imagines Engels spoke English when indulging in his favourite sport of fox-hunting. And Mr Aronson makes it clear enough that the *lingua franca* of Victorian-descended royalty was English as it still is. The Russian empress butchered at Ekaterinburg told Kerensky: 'I am English by education and English in my language.' Yet the British Ambassador in Paris in 1917 has some of her blood on his hands. When our Government suggested the imperial family should be given asylum by their ally France, our ambassador thwarted it by replying: 'The Empress is not only a Boche by birth but in sentiment *She did all she could to being about an understanding with Germany* [my italics, remember the Lansdowne letter's fate]. She is regarded as a criminal or a criminal lunatic and the ex-Emperor as a criminal from his weakness and submission to her promptings.' This was about Queen Victoria's granddaughter.

English too was the language in which Vicky normally expressed herself even after she became German Empress. Trained from childhood for the task of her father Prince Albert had set her and Queen Victoria of encouraging the liberalisation of a confraternal Anglo-Germany, and with all her brains and foresight, Vicky was thwarted by Bismarck ('that was a woman! One could do business with her!' Mr Aronson quotes the Iron Chancellor as exclaiming as he mopped his brow after a dreaded interview with her mother the Great White Queen in person) who never lived to see us therefore have to Blood our own Iron on his illiberal monster Frankenstein. But had Vicky's husband the liberal Emperor Frederick not perished so soon from the tumour on his throat, Western Civilisation might have been saved. We might still have progressed upwards (I mean in the right to that literally eccentric individualism which is political freedom, not in socially concentric material convenience and welfare which would have come anyway) instead of down the Gadarene slope of the two World Wars. What politicians call 'progress' is simply movement, and the retrograde herd always find it simpler to move downhill. The Empress Vicky couldn't have suffered more from being commonsense, independent-minded, moderate and above all English.

Yet when her son the Emperor William quarrelled constantly with her treating her so badly that she had her father's papers smuggled to England just before her husband's death (Willie in person with his hussars sealed off the palace too late to seize them) and later did the same with her own, Kaiser Bill actually wrote: 'That good stubborn English blood which will not give way is in both our veins.'

He was not responsible for the First World War and lost it by delaying mobilisation after the Russians had begun. But much of his *Ehr* (the English don't understand continental 'honour') was lost when he changed the name of his father Frederick's palace back from Friedrichskron to the Neues Palais, quite apart from his raving derivation of his German troops from the Huns when he told them to give no quarter in China. He treated his sister Sophie, Queen of Greece, as badly as he did his mother.

I believe the Emperor William to have been a decent Christian. But Xians love to squabble among themselves more than they love their neighbours – as witness Ulster or the Inquisition or the 'Wee Frees' in Inverness-shire (where a choirmaster was sacked for being seen entering a cinema: yet how could Our Lord have forbidden cinemas?). And when his sister Sophie was sincerely and devoutly converted to the Greek Orthodox Church, he banned her from visiting Germany for three years. 'Mad. Never Mind' was her comment in an open telegram to their imperial mother, and she ignored the ban.

In describing the Kaiser's ban on his sister, Sophie of Greece. Mr Aronson makes it clear that this was at least founded on his own *religious* bigotry. But this evokes various thoughts on the religious conduct of contemporary Christians to other Xians whose disagreeement with some of them is purely *political*. Are ordained Xians appointed to fat livings by leftist governments really all Christians to other Xians whose disagreement with some of them is purely *political*. Are ordained Xians appointed to fat livings by leftist governments really all Christians any more, or are they comfortable cynics like rationalist (it's now called 'humanist' by a supreme modern impertinence to the Renaissance scholars and artists) Archdeacon Puxley in James Elroy Flecker's delightful satire 'N'Jawk' (those of you who haven't read his collected prose have jolly well missed something)? The archdeacon didn't believe in God or immortality, and found it preposterous after death to find himself somersaulting through Space in pyjamas and bedsocks accompanied by an equally dead yet living poet wearing an undervest on their way to Judgement by the true god, N'Jawk, who had one large eye in the middle of its forehead. (Elroy was perceptive, for the Eye-Gods of Tell Brak in North Syria had not then been researched. I think; but perhaps he was thinking about mad Carruthers and the 'green-eyed god of Khatmandu'). The archdeacon was made into porridge, but the poet was handed over to eternal dalliance with beautiful Burmese ladies.

When in London on a Sunday, my wife and I go to communion at Westminster Abbey, both being Founder's Kin: St Edward the Confessor our ancestral uncle and Henry VII who founded the Chapel there our direct and lawful forefather, as he was Queen Sophie's and Queen Victoria's too. Nobody objects to openly convinced 'humanists'; it's their own business in the Free World if they choose to think themselves as transient as cabbages. But are we receiving the sacraments at the hands of a Red Dean and Chapter? Remember a paid-up communist ain't allowed to believe in the opiate of the people. Let the dean sue me if he dares, but Allende couldn't have been a communist party leader without being an atheist. I know Chile from end to end, from Peru to the Magellan Straits, and have even entered the cave on the Juan Fernandez islands where Alexander Selkirk *alias* Robinson Crusoe was monarch of all he surveyed. I remember happy placid Coypue hard by the Tolten river ferry in Araucanian redskin country, and the smiling face of Aladino the groom who loved his horses, all happiness wrecked by the jealousy of an incompetent but dogmatic potential tyrant: but let us not speak ill of the dead and simply content ourselves with observing that the road to Hell is paved with good intentions. As an Anglican my soul is equal to that of the Dean and has been endowed by Divine Providence with the necessary knowledge and experience to deliver him a holy rocket for encouraging an atheistical jamboree ('demonstrating' what but bad manners?) to desecrate the tomb of my children's ancestral first-cousin Cochrane the Dauntless, while forbidding the annual reverent laying of a wreath there by the Christian Chilean Navy in memory of their gallant and inventive Founder. This is not to deny the right of public demonstration to weirdoes or stockbrokers alike, so long as they keep off other people's holy ground. But Dr Ian Grimble was right on TV to say that it would never have happened had Cochrane (Lord Dundonald) had been buried at St Giles Cathedral in Edinburgh instead.

But Sophie's conversion to Greek Orthodoxy was as genuine as it was politic. After Sophie became Queen of the Hellenes, she and her husband did all they could to keep Greece neutrally out of the senseless First World War. She had no liking for her brother Kaiser Bill, speaking English with her family, calling England 'the most beloved country in the world' and exclaiming that 'My beloved England is the one place I love to be in most'. See then how we requited her. She felt that neither protecting the murderers of Francis Ferdinand (the Franco-Russian excuse for carnage) nor poor little Belgium (the alleged British excuse, though we'd known of the Schlieffen Plan for years) was any business of the Greeks. So the French and British violated Greek neutrality, landed troops, imposed a blockade; and used Venizelos to depose her and her husband and drag Greece into the loopy bloodshed. 'Can Belgium have suffered more at German hands?' she asked. Now, there is a very ancient ritual of slaying a black bull as the symbol of the enemy chief: indeed the Nguni Zulus did it as late as 1879, and Isandlwana was a great victory for them, but all they bagged thereafter by way of a chief was the Prince Imperial and the *induna* responsible was much upset when he learnt he'd slain the Bonaparte heir beloved of the Great White Queen. The black bull's head at the death-banquet features in Scottish mediaeval history at the political murder of the young Black Earl of Douglas in Edinburgh Castle and the defensive massacre of their Cummin hosts by the Mackintoshes. Readers of Sir James Frazer's *Garnered Sheaves* (London 1931) will recollect that on Xmas Day 1916 the Metropolitan of Athens solemnly excommunicated a black bull's head representing Venizelos and cast the first of many stones in the cursing of the man who had 'plotted against the King'. And the curse came about. In 1920 Venizelos was given the bum's rush and Queen Sophie and her husband were restored by a plebiscite in which they gained over ninety-eight per cent of the votes. Although they were later sent on their travels again, the monarchy was restored yet again after her death.

Soon after the restoration she, Queen Victoria's granddaughter who had called England 'the most beloved country in the world', was promptly and publicly cut by her old acquaintance Lord Granville, the British envoy; who should have had the guts to defy our Foreign Office's non-recognition of the Restoration as (like my children) he was a descendant of fearless Sir Richard Grenville of *The Revenge*. Before that, when Sophie had been in exile in Switzerland, her two British governesses had been forced to leave her for fear of losing their passports.

And this brings us to the astonishingly discriminating and undiplomatic bad manners cultivated by some British diplomatists in bullying zeal, always towards countries that can't hit back. When in Moscow in 1946, a Very Important member of HM Foreign Service complained to me about the impertinence of our recent ex-enemies the Finns being the first legation to give a white-tie party there since the War and said he was going in a dinner-jacket: while I shuddered at the callous but overwhelming reasons that had made us abet Stalin's aggression against the innocent Finns a few months after we had been training a picked ski-battalion of so-called Scots Guardsmen, including everybody from Eric Hatry to a Rothschild, to go to their aid. British calculated diplomatic rudeness reached the rock-bottom of ridicule the other day when the Lions rugby football team was banned by a socialist lady politician from attending the multi-racial parties given by our embassy in Capetown (tho' ping-pong teams are not shunned by our diplomats in China because of genocide by torture in Thibet). The same day we read how young left-wing intruding reformers in southern Africa 'grabbed an elderly village headman and forced his two wives to watch while he was slowly beaten to death. The wives were then raped and beaten.' If I know anything of sexual sadists, the ladies were stript and whipt *before* rather than after being raped. Many men enjoy prolonging an attractive captive's submission to their mastery, by making her plead and cry out as they wallop her naked juddering bottulphs so that it appears as though she were having an unwilling orgasm with a giant (what our radical friends might call her 'divine discontent'): but they wouldn't feel in the mood *after* the eventual culminating rape, when – as I understand it – they tend to relax. The same journal included a photograph of the Socialist lady in question, who looked very attractive. If she really thinks whipping and rape a more valid left-wing political argument than multi-racial fraternisation behind the Diamond Curtain, it would be surprising, almost discourteous, if a long queue of male comrades weren't turned-on to stand in every sense of the word to the Left of the sweet charmer and see as much of her as possible – again, in every sense of the word – in such a gargantuan travesty of slap-and-tickle.

But it's doubtful old-fashioned royalty or aristocrats like Queen Victoria or Lord Lansdowne could have envisaged such a method of politics. And it's no good revolutionary fascists or lefties alike saying 'there's a war on'. Mercenaries are now much in disfavour with the consensus, unless they're pagan Gurkhas thousands of miles from their home let loose on Xmas Eve by a United Irelander in aggressive war against particularist black Christians defending their own Katanga homeland. But my favourite mercenary forefather the Swedish Field-Marshal Sandy Leslie, 1st Earl of Leven, the 'old, little, crooked souldier' of the Thirty Years War, issued a proclamation forbidding outrages on women and adding that 'murther is no less intollerable in the time of War than in the time of Peace'. In the mercenary Highland regiment raised for the same war by another of my forefathers, the Mackay chief Lord Reay, a private who'd made a pass at the pretty daughter of the German farmer on whom he was billetted was executed but allowed to command his own firing squad. In Queen Victoria's reign a good example of a mercenary was her loyal subject General 'Chinese' Gordon of the Sudan. And Lord Sydenham wrote: 'The right to kill unresisting non-combatants has never been recognised.' This is the fundamental difference, to generalise: Revolutionaries rule by propaganda and Fear, constitutional Royalty reigns by love and Awe.

To return to Queen Sophie, 'the cruelly misunderstood daughter of a cruelly misunderstood mother', the reason for Venizelos's enmity towards her and her husband in 1916 was that they didn't share his pipe-dream that now was the time *in practice* for the Greeks to regain Constantinople. Nor was it. For Constantinople was certainly one of Czarist Russia's war aims. But the royal family had all along sympathised *in principle* with the Pan-Hellenistic ideal of a revived Byzantine Empire. That is why her father-in-law King George I (afterwards murdered at the moment he was proposing to retire in favour of his son) had christened her future husband 'Constantine'. Mr Aronson writes of Constantine's signature 'Constantine b' (The b meaning King, always followed the royal name). Yet, to many ... this scrawled B looked more like IB, which in Greek numerals stood for XII. The last Emperor of Byzantium had been Constantine XI; had the new King, inadvertently or intentionally, signed himself 'Constantine XII' Now this is puzzling. I have Palaeologue blood myself from far back, just before that family attained the purple; and am quite sure the last Palaeologos emperor who went down to death in battle in 1453 when Byzantium was conquered by Sultan Mehmet was Constantine XII himself? Sophie's husband 'Tino' would have been Constantine XIII, sometimes a lucky number in royal circles for very ancient sacral reasons. Tino's father King George had been a Prince of Denmark before he accepted the Greek throne, which is why our Prince Phillip is of Danish origin. But unlike his subjects he also had many descents from Byzantine emperors, especially the Comnenoi and Angeloi. I was astonished some years ago, when staying at our Embassy in Athens, to talk to a Greek prince who had no idea of all his Byzantine blood. So it seems likely that Kings George and Constantine were equally uninformed about their own grand local ancestry. This is where the publicists of apparently alien Sovereigns so often fall down on their job. For historic genealogy is the fundamental principle of dynastic royalty.

Similarly, very few Swedes realise that their Bernadotte dynasty now descends, through a princess of Baden, from the Vasas who reigned in Sweden at her apogee, and through them from the old viking Swedish kings of saga-time as far back as the dawn beteen myth and history still represented by the vast grave-mounds of the pagan Ynglingar sacrificial Peace-Kings at Uppsala. We know the names of every link in the genetic chain between Ingialdr, last of the Peace-Kings, who lived in the 600s AD, and Carl Gustaf, present King of Sweden. Nevertheless the Swedes, who loved the husband of Louise Mountbatten, Queen of Sweden as a dear old scholar of great cultural distinction and a devoted democrat, think simply of the Bernadottes as a new royal house unlinked to Swedish history.

There is indeed a certain Napoleonic flavour about the Swedish Court. Some years ago I stayed to shoot his cock pheasants with Baron Rutger von Essen at Skokloster, the most famous country *slott* in Sweden – it's rather like Drumlanrig in style and was illustrated on their stamps – which he had inherited through the premier Counts Brahe from its founder, Admiral and Field-Marshal Count Wrangel, a contemporary of Oliver Cromwell. The bedrooms still opened out of each other in the 17th century way; and to get out of his bedroom the present Fouché, Duc d'Otrante, a reserve officer of the Swedish household cavalry, had to pass through my bedroom; whereafter we both had to pass through the bedroom of a married couple who luckily hadn't turned up, before reaching the stair landing. That's why our four-poster beds were heavily curtained. But a large proportion of the Swedish aristocracy and other leading families are of Scots origin, as witness such of my buddies as Count Archibald Douglas and General Malcolm Murray. In their hygienic welfare state the Swedes have set up a model which deserves, however, a few criticisms. It's sad that the system of taxation makes it wise to mortgage one's house up to the hilt. Having exhausted equality of opportunity, they've now turned to its opposite, equality *tout court*; and in bureaucratic pursuit of this fetish have abolished the *fidelcommiss* system under which certain historic homes were retained intact by primogeniture, even though the younger sons begged their Government not to change the law in their favour. So, although Skokloster was already open to the public, the von Essens have since had to leave their quarters in the old castle and live in the park. Yet the public who visit historic homes anywhere in the civilised world are thrilled to know the original family is still in residence, if only in a few rooms. For it brings everything to life, just as Woburn would be less fun were it merely a museum. I know this from experience, having written the guide-books for two palaces and a country house, besides short histories for visitors to a number of castles, in Scotland. Again, many young people in bars in Stockholm asked me what was the point of a politically powerless royal family that didn't provide them with pageantry.

None of these points, however, would have bothered Queen Louise of Sweden. The great-granddaughter of Queen Victoria through the marriage of Princess Victoria of Hesse to our own brilliant First Sea Lord Prince Louis of Battenberg *alias* Marquess of Milford Haven, Queen Louise was the sister of our Supremo Earl Mountbatten of Burma. Thus she was also the present Prince of Wales's great-aunt, and it is through his Battenberg mother that our royal consort Prince Philip is a great-great-grandson of his predecessor Prince Albert the consort of Queen Victoria.

Of the crowned descendants of Queen Victoria, Louise Mountbatten, Queen of Sweden was as practical as she was down-to-earth. For Queen Louise's forefathers in the direct male line had a flair for being forward-looking soldier-statesmen. The Mountbattens *alias* Battenbergs are themselves a morganatic branch of the Brabantine landgraves and Grand Dukes of Hesse, who had been the most powerful ruling house in mediaeval Belgium before their branch moved over to Hesse through an heiress. In the 12th century, Duke Reginar 'Long-Neck' of Upper Lorraine was already reforming the monasteries of which he was hereditary abbot. Perhaps the most famous of this remarkable line was the Landgrave Philip of Hesse who signed the original Protest from which the word protestant is derived. He was the soldier-statesman who negotiated the Schmalkaldic League and led its armies to defeat the imperial catholic forces. He founded Marburg University, and used up-to-date heavy artillery to put down Franz von Sickingen, the last of the 'free kights' who were in effect robber barons. He was even wilier than his contemporary Henry VIII, for he got Luther and Melancthon to write an apologia declaring that bigamy was not prohibited by Holy Writ especially in the case of princes where dynastic marriages were politic, and thereafter bred regularly by both his wives; but keeping the succession for the sons of his first and dynastic marriage. Springing from such a dynamic stock, that had always regarded royal birth as entailing duty rather than privilege, it's not surprising that Queen Louise, both as a Battenberg princess and then as Lady Louise Mountbatten when the family name was Anglicised, had nursed the grisly wounded in a French military hospital for three years during the First World War. (It would have been nice if they'd taken the surname of Lovaine, that of an extinct branch of their family who had settled over here and became Peers of England by the 14th century). So the welfare state atmosphere of Swedish social democracy was particularly attuned to her character.

Mr Aronson conveys her naturalness and energy, also her vigour in scrapping obsolete formalities, reorganising the staff, modernising court etiquette, and quotes her biographer Margit Fjellman at a meeting with her: 'she radiated vitality and it flew into my mind that here was the dynamo on the heart of the Palace, the centre of a great machine'. Yet she had always been frail and it was in spite of a weak heart that she lived to be 76.

Very different was the flamboyant life of her Ruritanian cousin Marie, Queen of Romania, the 'Missy' who was daughter of Queen Victoria's second son Alfred, Duke of Edinburgh. Justly known as 'the Brains of the Balkans', she was an accomplished linguist, talented painter and imaginative gardener. The French Ambassador to St James's said, 'She has all the brain-power of a man, and all the allurement of a woman'. She loved the barbaric splendour of the Orient that centuries as satellites of the Sultan had brought to her semi-Byzantine country. No nonsense with her about coming off pedestals. When her son Carol wanted to marry a Romanian commoner, she opposed it with the words; 'It is for a ruler to remain above the people, a demi-god'. The devotion the troops 'offered Her Majesty was as to a goddess divine', wrote one observer, as the Queen rode to inspect them in a slightly theatrical uniform and fur busby. In the First World War, when her husband despite being a Hohenzollern had come out on the Allied side, she spent her tireless days in a nurse's white uniform 'organising, inspecting, encouraging and visiting the wounded . . . She became, in a way, the symbol of Romania's will to fight'. At a parlour game of epitaphs, a young Russian grand duke wrote on his slip about Queen Marie; 'A star danced when she was born'.

When she was dying, she received 'with open arms' in hospital someone who had caused her much distress. 'You see', she explained to her astonished daughter Illeana, 'there is so little left to me except to be kind'. Her heart was buried in a jewelled casket in her chapel at Bracic. It was hurriedly removed by a faithful ADC as the Bulgarians advanced in the Second World War. It was taken to the late Queen's castle of Bran. 'Here her daughter, Princess Illeana, placed it in a chapel carved out of the rock in the hillside'. Although now behind the Iron Curtain, it still rests on her beloved Romanian soil. Years later, I used to take part in the BBC TV Brains Trust with such varied people as John Betjeman and Marghanita Laski; and once appeared with the same Princess Illeana of Romania. Having been given claret at luncheon to prepare us for the ordeal, once the nerve-racking live interrogation before an invisible audience of millions was over, the one thing needed was a drink but all we got then was tea. The Princess offered me a lift to the airport and I offered her a drink there on arival. But when we got to the bar, it was closed. We had forgotten the Brains Trust was held only on British Sundays.

Queen Marie was also mother of Queen Marie of Yugoslavia, 'Mignon' to her family and 'Paiky' to her friends, according to Mr Aronson. When I had my last talk with her son King Peter of Yugoslavia, during a visit to Venice, we sat together in the Piazza San Marco, one of the most serene places among the Wonders of the World. I may be wrong, but he seemed to be bitterly reflecting that he might have saved his throne had the Allies allowed him to return to his country towards the end of the Second World War. Yet the Yugoslav dynasty's fate had already been sealed when gullible Roosevelt started to build the Iron Curtain for Stalin during the wartime summit conferences; after which Fitzroy Maclean made HM Government understand we had no choice but to support the *fait accompli* and trust Tito to be more

Yugoslav leader than Soviet satellite. Our Highland chum 'Fitz' is a wily Maclean of Ardgour, a territory conquered by his forefather (son of the Maclean chief slain in battle in 1411) in a surprise massacre of the resident MacMasters; when the last fleeing MacMaster was murdered by his own ferryman seeking to curry some favour in the rising sun, Sir Fitzroy's ancestor slew him too, remarking that he wouldn't be much use if that was the way he served his masters in time of peril. On the other hand, my indignant coz Rowland Winn, now Ld St Oswald [died 1985], resigned from his liaison work with the Royal Yugoslav forces on the point of honour when he realised we had begun to desert their lost cause.

King Peter's mother Marie really had married into the wild Balkans. Her husband belonged to the tough Karageorgevich dynasty, and at the time of her marriage his father was King of Serbia. Their founder was a tough cookie called 'Black George', *Karageorge* from the Turkish form of his Serb nickname *Tsrni Dyordye*, an irascible brigand leader who slew his own father for trying to persuade him to flee and hanged his own brother for rape. In 1804 the Serbs elected him their Supremo in the struggle for freedom from the Turks and four years later they made him hereditary Hospodar of Serbia. Returning from exile by the Turks in 1817, he was murdered in his sleep on the orders of his successor, Milosh Obrenovich, who sent his head to the Sultan. The result was a Balkan blood-feud on the grandest scale. Karageorge's son was elected Reigning Prince of Serbia in 1842, deposing the then Obrenovich prince who in turn deposed him but was bumped off in due course.

The Obrenovichs were finally fixed in 1903; King Alexander Obrenovich and his love-Queen Draga hid for two hours that dreadful night in a secret alcove until the queen recognised a trusted senior officer of the Royal Guard and called to him from its window for help, whereupon he fired at her. Their Minister at St James's, Chedomille Mijatovich describes what followed in *A Royal Tragedy* (London, 1906) of which I possess a signed copy given to my great-uncle:

The enraged conspirators continued for a few seconds firing their revolvers at the Royal couple, bleeding and groaning on the floor. They then drew their swords, and began to slash them in all directions. The poor woman, Queen Draga, was especially the object of their revolting cruelty . . . They seemed to emulate the exploits of Jack-the-Ripper . . . They threw her into the garden. Another group of officers had followed with the body of Alexander, covered with terrible wounds, yet still groaning in agony. They raised him to throw him out of the window, but the fingers of the dying man convulsively caught the frame of the window, and held it fast. One of the officers took his sword, and cut off his fingers . . . Falling on the grass lawn of the garden, Alexander's body received such a shock that his right eye fell out of its socket! Still, he was not yet dead. Two hours their bodies naked, bleeding, and broken, were lying in the garden, in view of the soldiers! At four o'clock it began to rain.

Thus was Karageorge finally avenged, and Peter Karageorgevich became King in puddles of blood and rain.

It was this king's son Alexander Karageorgevich that Marie married, and her husband became Regent of Serbia in 1914. He was an acquaintance or rather 'pin-up' of my mother's in her 'teens. At the end of the First World War, which was deliberately provoked with Russian backing by the Serbian secret society called the 'Black Hand' run by Colonel 'Apis' Dimitrievich, the Pan-Serbs achieved their ambition of a united Southern Slavland, which is what 'Yugoslavia' means. In 1921 Alexander succeeded his father as its King, and after a few years he became its dictator as well. This was in an attempt to run differing beasts in one harness. Mr Aronson reminds us that 'The old names of the various states – Serbia, Croatia, Slovenia, Montenegro, Herzegovina, Bosnia, Macedonia and the Voivodina – were swept away, and a set of new provinces, making up a single country – Yugoslavia – were proclaimed . . . To conciliate the Croats, the Cyrillic script, so dear to the Serbs, was abolished to be replaced by the Latin script'. It never occurred to the Allied 'peace-makers', in their gloating carve-up of Austria-Hungary after the alleged War to end War, that the Croats for instance were more anxious to leave Hungary than to join Serbia; and that a Danubian Federation of autonomous states was the obvious solution. The Croats were civilised Catholics, the Serbs half-savage Orthodox, the leading Bosnians still Moslems, the Macedonians longing to remain part of their beloved Bulgaria.

Serbia was the strongest component and dominated the police. Sadly unequipped with the modern Space Age electric sexual tortures used by the republican French in Algeria and the dictators of banana republics elsewhere, the Serb police had to make do and mend in their duty to suppress IMRO, the Macedonian organisation of irredentists: Bulgars not Slavs. I have mislaid my copy of *Black Hand over Europe*, which reports the methods used and gives chaper and verse, including names and dates and a frank interview with the police chief. One *comitadji* had an angry cat forced down the front of his trousers, which were then belted on to keep the biting and scratching in the right place, and really got into an awful state before he was hanged, refusing to calm down. The girls were flogged, touched up with a hot iron if not 'amorous' enough, raped and then interrogated with 'the candle', which was lighted and then slowly thrust into their genitals, though cigarette lighters were sometimes used instead. But I'm quite certain King Alexander knew nothing of this. He was out to get rid of his 'Serb' image.

The difficulties were enormous, and still trouble Tito. In Bosnia the Moslems still classified themselves as 'Turks'. Because of their special Bogomil form of Christianity – which denied the divine birth of Christ, the coexistence of the Trinity and the validity of sacraments – their aristocratic *begs* led by forty-eight hereditary *kapetans* had readily adopted Islam after the Turkish conquest in the 6th century. Herzegovina, *i.e.* 'the Duchy' linked to Bosnia, was so called after the once-only Duke of St Sava in 1448. Montenegro, the 'Black Mountain', solved its religious and political problems in another way. In 1696 the *vladica* or bishop of Cetinje, Danilo Petrovich, became its hereditary ruler; the episcopal throne passing from uncle to nephew in the Petrovich dynasty until 1851, when a later Danilo Petrovich took the title of *gospodar* or reigning prince instead. The only King of Montenegro was his nephew, son of Mirko 'the Sword of Montenegro' who had routed the Turks. King Alexander of Yugoslavia's mother was a Petrovich, Princess Zorka of Montenegro (a truly Ruritanian name). So there he had grand historic local blood-links. In Serbia he at least sprang from 'Black George', but no-one in Serbia could trace themselves back to anyone – let alone the dynasts – before the Turkish conquest. Nor had he Croat blood, let alone Bulgarian, to sweeten his macédoine of peoples.

Curiously enough, my mother could have given him the lot, and they'ld have been of far more use to him than to me, skilfully used. My most recent Croat ancestress through my mother died in 1872 (her equally Croat mother being a Draskovich countess). Her father Count Iganz Festetics descended in the male line from a manumitted serf of the Bishop of Zagreb in the 16th century. By contrast in the female line she descended from the hero Count Zrinski, Ban of Coatia, who sallied forth from Szigetvás at the head of all his beleaguered garrison to die sword in hand against the hosts of Sulaiman the Magnificent, already secretly-dead in his tent amidst the Turkish camp, Through Zrinski's wife I descend from a sister of the Croat cardinal Utisenith killed in 1551. But Countess Zrinski also brought me unusual Serb blood. My forefather George Brankovich was popular Despot of Serbia 1427-1456, being killed in a duel at the age of 90. Through him, I spring from the much-maligned Vuk Brankovich; and from immortal-in-death 'Tsar Lazar' who slew the sultan but fell on that fatal 'field of the crows' at Kossovo in 1389 when Serbia went down under Turkish paramountcy; and from the Namanjich dynasty, including King Urosh-Stephen *Dushan* the Great who sought to partition the Byzantine Empire in alliance with the French king of Naples; which takes me back to Ljubomir, living in 1083, the first Great Zupan of Rascia and nucleus of the mediaeval Serbian monarchy. It's an irony of history that Serb folk-songs, while adoring Tsar Lazar, unfairly revile to this day Vuk Brankovich as a traitor because he didn't receive orders in time to turn the tide at Kossovo; whereas their epic hero *par excellence* is my ancestral first-cousin Prince Marko, who in fact joined the Turks afterwards and was killed fighting for them two years later. All this even gives me numerous Bulgar descents, as Urosh-Stephen's queen was daughter of Stracimir, Despot of Western Bulgaria, and Urosh-Stephen's mother was daughter of Smlec, Tsar of Bulgaria under Mongol supremacy.

Most people remember Bosnia only from its capital, Sarajevo, where the Archduke Francis Ferdinand's murder triggered the First World War. Mignon *alias* Marie's husband King Alexander was to meet with a similar fate elsewhere. On their way to France for a state visit in 1934, they visited a sleeping Montenegrin monastery with his cousin Prince Paul (a former member of Loder's). 'Then the boys did something they shouldn't have done', Mr Aronson quotes Queen Marie. 'They found two ropes and rang the monastery bells. The bell my husband rang was very rarely sounded. It had a peculiar tone . . . I am not superstitious . . . But afterwards we heard . . . that the bells the boys had rung each had a name. The bell my husband had rung was called "Death" and the bell Paul had rung was called "Life".' And Paul was soon the living Regent. On the way to Paris, King Alexander was gunned down while driving in state through cheering crowds by an assassin, hired in *Day of Jackal* style by a Croat organisation instructed by the Italians. The French Foreign Minister was quite unnecessarily also shot by the gunman, presumably for the capital offence of being in the royal motor car, and died complaining loudly.

Naturally I would take issue with Mr Aronson when he says Queen Victoria, from whose loins the principal characters in his book stemmed, 'would have no truck with what she looked upon as a wicked and worthless aristocracy'. He can hardly mean Lord Melbourne nor the successive Lords Lansdowne, nor Lord Derby 'the Rupert of Debate' nor her Prime Minister Lord Salisbury, nor 'the silent Lord Hartington' afterwards Duke of Devonshire. She stayed with the future Duke of Atholl, whose loan of Blair Castle inspired HM to acquire and rebuild Balmoral. She married her daughter to the Duke of Argyll (mis-spelt 'Argyle' in the tabular pedigree). One of her closest friends was the Lady Erroll who went to the Crimean War, and others were Lord Elgin and the late Duke of Portland. Her personal staff, like General Grey and Sir Henry Ponsonby, were drawn from historic families. And he is mistaken in supposing that the Prime Minister Lord Rosebery was unsuitable by birth to marry her granddaughter Princess Victoria of Wales, whose sister afterwards married a more junior earl in Lord Fife. For all earls bear the style 'most noble and puissant prince' and are addressed as honorary cousins by the Sovereign. That is why Princess Alice was styled Countess of Athlone as well on marrying an earl, but Princess Maud became Lady Maud Carnegie on marrying an earl's son (though the heir) and Princess Patricia was made into Lady Patricia Ramsay on marrying an earl's brother; for the 'cousin' rule applied only to earls themselves.

However, Mr Aronson's book is full of insight, often put over by apt quotation. He gives us two thought-provoking quotes about poor Czar Nicholas II. Himself on his succession to the throne at the age of twenty-six; 'What is going to happen to me . . . to all of Russia? I am not prepared to be a Tsar. I never wanted to become one. I know nothing of the business of ruling'. Then Princess Victoria of Battenberg heard him say at Balmoral in the old Queen's reign that he envied a constitutional monarch, 'on whom the blame for all the mistakes made by his Ministers was never heaped'. Mr Aronson adds 'And indeed, if Nicky could have changed places with his cousin Georgie, there is little doubt that he, too, would have died peacefully in his bed after a successful reign'. And so, dear reader, to bed.

Books & Bookmen, September – November 1974

The First Mountbattens

In 1883 a young Lieutenant in the Royal Navy became engaged to his first cousin. Years later, he wrote, 'All the happiness of my life begins with that memorable day' Richard Hough's *Louis & Victoria* [Hutchinson, 1974] is a sensitive and thoroughly frank account of the lives of this happily married couple. It even tells us of his pre-marital affair with a famous beauty; being manly in every sense of the word and the most handsome naval officer of his time, he had had the luck and good sense to have it with 'the Jersey Lily'. And, though the book doesn't name the love-child of that escapade, everybody knows why Mr Hough tells us Basil Bartlett was able to write a play about it, since Sir Basil married the love-child's beautiful daughter (I first met the Bartletts on their honeymoon, and she is the only lady of such beauty to have a face of equal symmetry on both sides).

At the time of his engagement in 1883, the excited youth wrote of his betrothed in charmingly pre-Wodehouse English to a brother naval officer: 'She is such a lovely girl, as you know, and I am nearly off my chump altogether with feeling so jolly . . . I am in a deuce of a hurry and have such heaps of letters to write . . . Goodbye my dear old boy. Ever your affectionate old shipmate.' Many years later, a veteran statesman who had been First Lord of the Admiralty wrote of this same youth, by then our greatest naval organiser, trainer, tactician and strategist: 'He is the ablest officer the Navy possesses and, if his name had been Smith, he would ere now have filled various high offices to the great advantage of the country . . . a better Englishman does not exist or one whom I would more freely trust in any post in any emergency.'

But his name wasn't Smith. It was His Serene Highness Prince Louis of Battenberg, and his 'old shipmate' was the future King George V. The bride was their mutual cousin Princess Victoria of Hesse, granddaughter of Queen Victoria. Those who have seen the film *The Mouse That Roared* about the Duchy of Grand Fenwick's establishment of world peace by its unintentional capture of the 'Q'-Bomb, may wish that the social democratic Hessians were the selfless arbiters of our fate. For no family could have been more international in its outlook than that to which Prince Louis belonged.

Louis's family had moved across the Rhine to Hesse after marrying the Thuringian heiress in the 1200s but only after establishing a younger branch in England, the Percy Earls of Northumberland, to which Harry 'Hotspur' belonged. Louis's father, the dashing young General Prince Alexander of Hesse and the Rhine had eloped with and married morganatically the charming Countess Julia of Hauke, whose mother was of mixed French and Hungarian blood and whose father had been decorated in battle by Napoleon in person and years later been rough-hewn bloodily to death in front of his horrified wife and children by revolutionary sword blades while Minister of War in Russian Poland.

Because the marriage was morganatic, a countess to a dynastic prince, the children were given the name of Battenberg – later Anglicised to Mountbatten during the British xenophobia of 1917 – and at first the European dynasts were inclined to be stuffy about them. Queen Victoria soon put an end to that nonsense. The grandest Monarch in the world, she wrote of the marriage of her daughter Beatrice (whom I knew as a boy) to Louis's brother Henry of Battenberg, quoting her Foreign Secretary: the Queen of England thinks a person good enough for her daughter what have other people got to say?' This newly-named branch of one of Europe's most talented families burst like a star-shell to illuminate the world of European royalty and went on, to change the metaphor, to become a dynamo on its heart. Prince Louis's brothers were Sandro, Sovereign Prince of Bulgaria, the remarkable general who personally saves his adopted country at the victory of Slivnitza, and Henry who fathered Queen Ena of Spain and died for us in that utterly unnecessary war we forced on the proud Ashanti because a petty-minded bourgeois British official wanted to sit on their sacred Golden Stool. Princess Victoria's sisters were the ill-fated last Empress of All the Russias, our ally whom Lloyd George deliberately abandoned to a ghastly death because royalty are not included in the Welsh methodists' Brotherhood of Man, and Princess Henry of Prussia, whose husband was Kaiser Bill's brother and Grand Admiral of the German Fleet. Adding all this to Louis's French and Hungarian blood, with his wife Victoria half British, how much more Common Market could his background have been? Yet he chose to be English.

See then how England requited him. The first snag was that he was so popular with his wife's genial uncle Albert Edward, Prince of Wales that he was long in danger of being permanently side-tracked into some such role as Admiral commanding the Royal Yachts. Moreover, those who shout loudest for 'equality of opportunity' are furious when it turns out that the 'best people' are sometimes really the best people after all. Queen Victoria summed it up when she wrote: 'There is a *belief* that the Admiralty are afraid of promoting Officers who are Princes on account of the radical attacks of low papers and scurrilous ones.' The second snag was that Louis was a brilliant forward-looking perfectionist, and (although the soul of tact and much employed in unofficial diplomacy) was annoyingly always right when it came to the test. Czar Nicholas II had difficulty in convincing a Russian sea-captain that it really was his brother-in-law Louis who had invented the scientifically ingenious Battenberg Course Indicator.

The third snag was the one Lord Charles and his cronies used to ruin him: the 'accident of his birth' in Germany. Nevertheless, it was Prince Louis who risked his career by taking the decision Churchill had shirked of 'standing the Fleet fast' on a war footing on the fateful 26 July, 1914. Had Louis not been hounded out of command, I rather think Jutland would have been a far more decisive victory. However, Louis's farsighted strategy of distant blockade, which won us the War, was exciting neither to the death-or-glory Beresford boys nor to the cush-job journalists of the Yellow Press. So he was sacked at the moment we needed him most, turned out of a Prince into the 1st Marquess of Milford Haven – from Prince Jekyll into Lord Hyde, as he himself put it – but as a slight saving to our national honour made a Privy Councillor and at last an Admiral of the Fleet.

Richard Hough, the author of this work, has kept me awake for many hours. Every page is packed with interest. He has, moreover, had the advantage of having had audiences with the Queen herself, Prince Philip and indeed almost all the surviving members of both royal families. Also, their private papers have been made freely available to his untrammelled discretion. Here we have a concertina-ed Forsyte Saga drawn not only from real life, but from the harsh disciplined real life that is the Grimm background to popular Fairy-Tale.

Mr Hough's book is, however, not a glorified William Hickey prying into grand peoples' lives. It is the best account that will be written for a lifetime yet of two of Prince Philip's grandparents; the very flesh and blood that makes his son Prince Charles such a straightforwardly competent batsman against all comers.

[*Spectator*, 30 November 1974.]

Reflections of a Praetorian Guard

The Chief of the Clan Colquhoun was breakfasting with the 24th Ilk under a table-umbrella on a sun-warmed beach on the island of Penang. We were there to call on the Chief of the Clan Khoo, the largest and best organised *urban* clan in the world, of Chinese origin but whose Kong-si or centre is in Penang. Sir Ivar Colquhoun of Luss and I were suddenly accosted by an intelligent Malaysian journalist. Luss fled, as ever in peacetime though never in battle, and I was left: as always filled with that curiosity that prevents suicide before the denouement. Our expedition to South-East Asia had been disrupted (despite rattling good introductions from Lord Mountbatten and the Foreign Office) because we had been unaware of a Royal Visit, and all the nobs to whom we had plotted holding out our tongues for noggins were either busy conning the Ministry of Works for much-needed renovations in anticipation or else nervous wrecks afterwards wondering if they'd trod on some royal toe. There's no doubt a Royal Visit does a lot of good anywhere, pepping everybody up, and the Queen – one of the most attractive girls that ever was or will be – and her forthright Consort are tougher than most of their subjects.

The journalist asked the startling question: 'How many kings and queens have you ever met?' Now, how can one of the two – or three (the other two are of course both Bohemian princes) – Master Snobs of Europe answer such a question off the cuff, especially when wearing a cuff-less black-and-yellow batik dragon shirt and multi-coloured Thai shorts? Does it count to have shaken hands, giving that ungainly nod that is the special British method of bowing to royalty, while processing past the late King Gustav of Sweden at a Congress? To have been at school with Prince Rainier of Monaco, later celebrated for his popular marriage to the exquisite Grace Kelly (whom I suspect descends from ancient Irish kings); or to have been given luncheon at the sinister Castle of Vaduz by the reigning Prince of Liechtenstein while on my honeymoon? To have lost at that after-dinner game with Don Juan? Or to have had luncheon, as aide-de-camp to my Army Commander, with the present King Olaf of Norway; and years later, to have driven in a carriage dressed as the Knave of Hearts when HM was made a Knight of the Thistle on the first Norwegian royal visit to Scotland since the Queen's forefather and mine the Great Stewart repulsed King Haakon in 1263?

Were I allowed the fun of belonging to the William Hickey team instead of being an increasingly-impoverished self-financing historian ('capital gains tax' with inflation is a stealthy form of robbery for which the Tories will perish at the polls, and serve them right, nor will I ever save a golden sovereign nor a copper farthing again by my patron saint St Dotto). I suppose taking King Umberto to Pratt's or giving the late King George of Greece dinner at the Tower of London to watch the Ceremony of the Keys might count? At a later such dinner Cecil Beaton and Freddy Ashton watched the Ceremony while their motor cars were being locked into the Tower for the night, as although their host I can't drive a motor and hadn't thought of the problem. 'Try anything once', said the great Sir Frederick Ashton as he turned his back on me when Lady Dunsany recalled this dinner while 're-introducing' me to him at a luncheon for Dicky Buckle's famous Diaghilev Exhibition. Then I'm sure Hickey would be delighted that my grandfather's sister Harriet Moncreiffe, Lady Mordaunt, was the unwitting cause of Albert Edward, Prince of Wales's being called in all innocence but out of an honourable sense of gentlemanly duty to appear in Court in the witness box to defend her in that said Victoria *cause celèbre*: her divorce. But, still speaking of Edward VII, I must perhaps be the only survivor who went tiger-shooting with the Maharana of Udaipur in 1938 with Mrs George Keppel as a fellow-guest though not our fellow-shot. They put 18 elephants and 2,000 spearmen through the jungle, and the whole 'bandobast' was controlled by a white-bearded herald with the sort of elephant-tusk horn Roland blew too late at Roncesvalles. Also, what about attending the strange Orthodox christening of the Crown Prince, son of my acquaintance King Peter of Yugoslavia and his queen who had bitten me in the leg as a child, when in Westminster Abbey our own king as Godfather had to scurry round the font dressed as an Admiral of the Fleet, carrying the infant Highness in his arms and pursued by what looked like bearded archimandrites, while (according to our song-sheets) we renounced and 'spat at' the devil? The Slav music was beautiful.

Then there was a care-free dance given by the present reigning Grand Duke of Luxembourg, a former Irish Guards officer and one of the firmest friend this moaning country has the luck to possess. It was held at their Embassy when we all went to London to attend the then Princess Elizabeth's wedding to the *çi-devant* 'Lieutenant Philip Mountbatten', i.e. Prince Philip of Denmark soon to be Duke of Edinburgh but meanwhile renamed as nephew of the great royal Admiral of the Fleet. The indescribably attractive Queen Frederica of Greece (disliked by the rich Athenian bourgeois and wisely attacked by the Balkan communists for her spirited and talented support of the Hellenistic equivalent of *kulaks* i.e. the idea that a peasant can rise by his own family's endeavours instead of the patronage of a business or the Party) having lost at musical chairs was thrown sliding up and down from end to end of the ballroom by the late Lord Milford Haven and King Michael of Roumania. For when royal people get the rare chance to let their hair down, they do it straightforwardly like us: like romping children and not self-consciously like pompous 'grown-ups'. Goodness, I feel sorry for grown-ups: chairmen of companies, social democrats, civil servants – 'no longer servants and no longer civil' in Churchill's phrase – retired majors, *etc.* (I must declare an interest to defect as I was a Major in the Perthshire Home Guard, but jolly well saw to it that my second-in-command captain Lord Rollo, who is *nouveau* as his family only arrived here in 1370, did all the work).

Once I helped the Balkan brigadier, Fitzroy Maclean, when he had the late King of Nepal to stay on a State Visit. HM wore a dinner jacket but we all wore the kilt. Fitz wore lace with his, as did his other guests the Colquhoun and Campbell chiefs. Argyll and I were both wearing our Orders of Nova Scotia, according to a custom of doing so even when more newly-invented decorations are not officially worn. But I also stuck to the purely Perthshire custom of wearing a white tie and, during a silence, leant across the table and observed to His bewildered Majesty: 'Sir, you will wonder why the other three chiefs and chieftains are wearing lace. During the Middle Ages their ancestors were hereditary footmen to mine, so whenever Moncreiffe of that Ilk comes into the West, they wear lace in my honour.' My fellow chiefs were taken aback, but the King just thought I was nuts.

Mr U. R. Wright in August's [1973] *Books & Bookmen*, is worth partly re-quoting to make several points. He wrote:

I saw your contributor Sir Iain Moncreiffe of that Ilk on television dancing with the

Queen at a Scottish jamboree; later the same week another of your contributors, Tariq Ali, was on television shouting in the London march protesting against the official arrival of the Portuguese prime minister. Is it that you are trying to be all things to all men, or sitting on the fence?

He then enquires in a wily way for your opinion on Watergate. I will give him a Counsel's Opinion for free.

First, *Books & Bookmen* has broken through the consensus barrier, and doesn't just pay mere lip-service to 'freedom of the Press'. Sir Oswald Mosley is as free to express his unfashionable views as an ex-socialist (like Mussolini) as Tariq Ali is to put forward his fashionable objections to suppression in Southern Africa as opposed to unmentionable genocide in Tibet. I understand Tariq Ali, whom I have never had the honour of meeting, is a rich young man who has found a literally protestant role in life. But I've never heard that he was ever rude about our Queen, nor about the Duke of Braganza, head of Portuguese royalty.

Indeed, I would now be a Kenyan Asian myself but for a genuine 'accident' of birth. For my father was born in India and settled in Kenya. So the British passport bureaucrats, kind as they are, would have had to class me as a 'Kenyan Asian' (those folk betrayed) had my mother given birth in Nairobi instead of being taken short on top of a motor-omnibus in Hampton Court: the parish, not the palace, but the 'place of birth' still looks grand on my passport. A native Englishman, therefore, educated in Switzerland and Germany, if I hadn't been kidnapped at the age of four from Nakuru, I would doubtless have been brought up an East African of Asiatic parentage. Perhaps it wouldn't have been such a bad thing; all my babyhood friends were Nandi tribesmen and I love the whole Indian subcontinent next to my own country. When I was marooned in 1964 in Afghanistan it was the Pakistani and not the British amabassador who had me to stay. Australian in the direct female-line, I am only a Scotsman by choice, having bought Easter Moncreiffe from my ducal cousin whose mother would have been our heiress had my grandfather not been born as the 20th Ilk's tenth child.

But above all, I am a man of Queen Elizabeth. Before the War, a great-uncle offered to leave me a valuable ranch in Wyoming. It was implied it would entail becoming an American citizen. Rather than give up my allegiance to my then King-Emperor George VI, one of the greatest gentlemen the world will ever have seen, I therefore refused; much of an honour as it is to be a US citizen. Years later, I found the letter and it had contained no such stipulation. The ranch had passed meanwhile to the far more competent Porchester-Wallop polo-playing family of my great-aunt. So all turned out for the best. But if ever I had to choose again between my Sovereign and my country, I would always choose my Queen. And Tariq Ali hasn't insulted my Queen.

Secondly, Watergate provides various fascinating lessons. Electrically to record confidential conversations with visiting Prime Ministers is simply commonsense, provided the tapes are kept top secret. When my Ambassador interviewed that detestable sadist yet likeable humorist Stalin he had to record their conversations in writing from memory, which is obviously not so accurate in such world-shaking matters as 'tape'. Certainly socialist Russia is sensible enough to be the world's leader in bugging, and the Kremlin must be shaken with laughter just now. As for Watergate itself, our nannies were usually right that eavesdroppers seldom hear good of themselves. But as the Democratic party President Woodrow Wilson was the first to disrupt world diplomacy by insisting on 'open agreement openly arrived at', what was it the goody-goody Democrats didn't want the dirty Republicans to hear? Writing as a member of both the bench and the bar, I was horrified to watch on the telly the sort of hypothetical questions being put by that obviously publicity-conscious Senator Ervin, snuffling joyously like an untrained terrier every sniff of political scandal without considering what might snuff out the candle of the elected leader of the Free World. We all know how to distinguish between naughtiness and evil. Nevertheless, bugging is illegal in the USA.

And this leads to the question whether a Prime Minister should also be Head of State? Although that frantic genius Ludwig of Bavaria named his palace at Linderhof near the Ettal monastery *Meicost Ettal*, which my old friend Chips Channon pointed out was an absurd anagram of '*l'état c'est moi*', what the Roi Soleil actually said was '*le premier ministre de l'état c'est moi*': and look at the deluge into which France was eventually plunged. The civilised world never recovered from his Jacobin as opposed to Jacobite successors, and we have seen conscription and received the metric system as a punishment for toadying to them. But can anybody imagine Buckingham Palace bugging Transport House?

I am strongly opposed to monarchy. That is, in its proper Greek sense of 'Rule by One'; as Louis XIV would have had it. The most powerful monarchs of my time have been Hitler of socialist Germany and Stalin of socialist Russia; under both of whom I lived (in pre-war Heidelberg and post-war Moscow) though some of the American presidents have come near to being monarchs too. I am an anarchist in principle, again in its proper Greek sense of 'being bossed about by nobody and bossing nobody about': as happens among some primitive negrillo and negrito pygmies, for example. In practice, the imperfections of Nature –

especially Human Nature – render anarchy impossible in advanced societies, and so empirically I support aristocracy in its literal Greek sense of 'Rule by the Best' (e.g. myself), tempered by a limited democracy and with many checks and balances. In a complete single-chambered democracy, allied to no moral principle, it would only be logical for 51 per cent of the population to form a single party to rob, enslave and work to death the other forty-nine per cent; and then for a new 51 per cent to do the same and so on *ad infinitum* (if you want to know the Moncreiffe attitude, look up which side we were on when the decision was taken to bump off Riccio). After all, both Hitler and Stalin were democratically elected. But readers of *Books & Bookmen* who have forgotten most of their perfect Greek will perhaps accept that the word 'monarchy' in fouler if not Fowler English has come to mean a ceremonial royal Head of State: is indeed nowadays almost a synonym for 'royalty'. And it's in this sense it will be used here. Anything else would be pompous pedantry.

Nevertheless, the word 'monarch' has dangerous connotations when applied to royalty in general and modern royalty in particular. Many of the Monarchist League do believe in Rule by One, provided he be a king. I repeat, I do not agree. For that One (or his successors) must sooner or later make a mistake or, even if he doesn't, fall: as Louis Philippe did 'because France was bored'. Other people complain: what is the point of a king who has no power. They should read the late Thomas Mann's *Königliche Hoheit*, in which the reigning prince is called Hans and carries an untidy umbrella like most of his ordinary subjects, while the aristos all look like greyhounds and have Xian names like Dagobert and Bogumil. The answer to what a constitutional monarchy should be, therefore, is above all to be a non-political and classless focus of national unity, chosen from birth out of the historic nuclear family of the nation; not necessarily its senior but its most convenient member; and against whom nobody has ever had to decide to vote in some perplexing contest. Secondly, it is there to be advisory in statecraft after training since childhood and also to try to act as a buffer against an absolute dictatorship (i.e. a literal monarch); although the late King of Italy was obliged to fail in this task for many years, it was he who took the initiative at the end. Thirdly, it is to provide a colourful ceremonial stabilising link between a country's historic past and its ever-changing future: to make 'change and decay' apparently less painful – to be Vishnu the Preserver while Shiva the Destroyer breaks down organic material for the great Creator to re-create in novel form. The unifying force in a nation should be a common religion, but this has long been impossible. The alternative is an unelected hereditary Head of State.

The two greatest monarchies in the world are Britain and Japan. In both case they are over-populated islands lying in economically strategic ocean positions on opposite ends of the Eurasian land-mass. They have to live by their wits. The American tycoons are never sure whether their front is the Atlantic, with George III and me at Lloyd's, which leaves their behind exposed to Hirohito striking across the Pacific with his transistors and motor-bicycles, or *vice versa* Mr Bultitude. We and Japan are like dynamos. New ideas must be allowed to prevail if they are better than old ones. Nevertheless the old ones are sometimes better. So we live in a state of constant clash, and this politico-economic dialectic *must* forge success after fair disagreement. But to be a united nation there has to be some centre of agreement. Where there is an elected President, the very party that voted against him will be the one taking over in a time of crisis and disunity. When in the loo of an airport in Chile, nearly ten years ago, I crossed from the graffiti the words VV COMMUNISMO and substituted the more sensible VV EL REY IMPERADOR DON JUAN: which would have saved Allende's life but have annoyed my wolfhound who is named after Don Bernardo O'Higgins, 'liberator' of Chile. Royalty satisfies the now-recognised need for a national Parent Figure without that figure becoming Big Brother. So the answer in both Britain and Japan is that ever-living monarchy which phoenix-like embodies the ever-changing spirit of our peoples.

It is in question whether the third most important monarchy in the world is Canada or Sweden, and after that whether Australia is a more important monarchy than the Netherlands. But the Canadians have the advantage of being the only monarchy in the drab New World and having their great red-coated tradition of the *Royal* Canadian Mounted Police (a style whose attemptd abolition was violently resisted out there), who performed invincible exploits in the *Boys Own Paper* I used to read secretly by torchlight under the bedclothes. And to whose territory were those redskin refugee women and children desperately trying to escape when they were massacred by the robust republican cavalry? To the protection of Queen Victoria, over the border into Canada. Moreover, most Americans long to meet or at least to see the Queen of Canada, finding an emptiness about their own Head of State system. How many US citizens can name the present President of Paraguay or Uruguay, but haven't heard of Queen Elizabeth? As for their own bewitched attempt at a semi-royal family: 'Kit' Kennedy, sister of their murdered President, once cut a dance with me when her father was Ambassador in London before the War, and it's astonishing how one recollects the turbulations of one's youth so much more than those of yestere'en.

In Sweden, students of both sexes at bars complained to me that they were bored with the idea of a 'Scandinavian monarch in his shirt-sleeves with two telephones ringing or on a bicycle' and wanted more colour and ceremonial. Nor is it a coincidence that, apart from the special case of Switzerland, the stablest countries of Europe are the north-western monarchies, Britain, Sweden, Norway, Denmark, Holland, Belgium and Luxembourg, whereas the most unstable this side of the Iron Curtain are France, Germany and the Mediterranean republics. Every Italian and West German has heard of our Queen Elizabeth, but how many British subjects can name the Presidents of Italy and West Germany? I bet you more people could tell you of which tiny country Grace Kelly is the Princess than could tell you the maiden names of any six President's wives: however powerful the republics in question.

Incidentally, writing of dreary republics, I don't incline to the view that most British socialialists are opposed to our Royal Family: quite the reverse, in my experience, and Willie Hamilton is the exception that proves the rule. In fact, a purely ceremonial Head of State chosen from a truly royal family and paid to do the job (so long as he kept out of politics altogether) doesn't seem to me to be incompatible even with communism. When I attended our ambassador to the Kremlin in Stalin's time to present HE's letters of credence, it was to Mr Shvernik as Head of State that we presented them. How many of our readers have heard of Mr Shvernik? How much more romantic for us and the Russians had we presented those credentials to a royal descendant of Prince Igor or Peter the Great. The Soviets have a great sense of their historic past, as witness the removal for aesthetic reasons of the later silver encrustations that hid the beautiful autumn beech-leaf coloured background of Rublev's fifteenth-century icons at Sagorsk, and their complete restoration of the imperial palace at Tsarskoye Selo after its smashing by the Nazis.

Curiously enough – since monarchy has replaced religions as the modern unifying force – 'the earliest religion of which we have any certain knowledge', according to that crusty bastard Plantagenet but undoubtedly learned President of the Royal Anthropological Institute, the late Lord Raglan, was that of sacral *royalty*. In this, apparently still the most satisfying emotional means of uniting a free people, the Head of State, though not necessarily the effective ruler, incarnates that part of the supreme godhead that is the nation's mascot – you can take that literally or figuratively according to your personal disbeliefs – and I was in attendance at the Coronation when we prayed that our newly-anointed Queen should be specially endued with the Divine Spirit. Excluding *nouveaux rois* like the late King Farouk and the otherwise admirable Shah of Persia (whose papa unfortunately made a house-law excluding from the succession any prince who married into the previous imperial family, no great shakes themselves for they reached their nadir not long after Nadir Shah pinched the peacock throne from the Great Mogul, whereas our Duchess of Gloucester [Princess Alice] descends from Mithradate), most real royal families spring from sacral kings or queens who embodied through a special ritual the lucky spirit of their people in ancient times.

To sum up, we all have an emotional need for Something or Somebody upon whom we can concentrate the focus of our feeling for our nation ultimately as a whole. However much we may squabble among ourselves, this feeling cannot be satisfied by an elected head of state, because if he is our personal choice he must necessarily be the very target of our fellow citizens when a squabble comes to the boiling-point. Emotionally, therefore, in Britain as with Japan we have evolved what is probably the most civilised, though it may appear illogical, but is obviously the most nearly perfect human answer to this problem. Anybody who denigrates this is apparently more concerned with showing off, in personal and provocative argument, than advancing human happiness. Such a person can only be unhappy, for although he may have been talked himself (through some genuinely uncertain don at Oxbridge) into believing he is sincere, he is only being disruptive of the greatest civilisation the World has yet seen. Such a prude is merely a priest of that unintentionally diabolical out-dated 18th century belief that 'Progress derives from Divine Discontent'. That's why you've got 50p instead of half-a-gold-sovereign in your pocket. I personally just want to make everybody as happy as I can. And in an immensely more useful role, so does the Queen.

A 17th century writer puts it all in a nutshell. 'Yet if His Majesty, our sovereign lord, Should of himself's accord Friendly himself invite. And say "I'll be your guest tomorrow night", How should we stir ourselves, call and command All hands to work! Let no man idle stand! Thus if a king were coming, we do; And 'twere good reason too; for 'tis a duteous thing To show all honour to an earthly king . . . But at the coming of the King of Heaven. All's set and six and seven: We wallow in our sin, Christ cannot find a chamber in the inn'.

The kindest and greatest Sovereign in this world would surely have found a chamber at her Buckingham Palace if only HM had been warned of poor Mr Noor Husain the 77-year-old Pakistani carpenter who made HM two beds (sent by an airline mistake to Karachi) and having been robbed in Turkey was only allowed by our immigration authorities to peer for ten minutes through the railings of Buckingham Palace. Why should it not have been otherwise, and why wasn't a very peremptory order issued. If I'd belonged to the effective division of the Royal Household someone would now be in the civilian equivalent of close arrest, awaiting court martial, for not properly informing the Palace about that poor old Pakistani.

President Truman in his forthcoming memoirs summarises the Royal Family's problem (yet he only got a few years but they're born with life sentence): 'If you can't keep the two separate, yourself and the Presidency, you're in all kinds of trouble'. Perhaps the attitude of the bulk of the Queen's subjects is best symbolised in a remark that was intended to be allegorical, since no loyal subject could want the necessity to arise. But when the late Lord Halifax's son, afterwards killed in action in Egypt, was dining as President of Loder's at 'the House' at Oxford, somebody asked him how he would best like to die. The reply was: 'Sword in hand on the steps of Buckingham Palace'.

Books & Bookmen, 1973/74

The Jubilee Spirit of Britannia

As I bowled along backwards in the Russian Sociable with Two Bay Horses through the streets of Glasgow, the crowds were cheering more happily than ever before in my lifetime. Like at the Coronation a quarter of a century ago, I was disguised for the Silver Jubilee in my heraldic tabard as the Knave of Hearts. My uniform trousers badly needed letting out at the waist, and I had been fortified beforehand with my usual stirrup-cup of binding kaolin morph for the long ceremony. But the coincidence of marriage had made it for me a Happy Family as well as a national occasion. Ahead of us was the Balmoral Sociable with Two Bay Horses (in which Queen Victoria had crossed the Alps with John Brown), containing my wife's stepfather the gigantic Hereditary Bearer of the Royal Banner of Scotland, the *lyon rampant* flaming out above him. Awaiting us at the cathedral, in kilt and eagle's feathers, was my son, in his uniquely Scottish title of the Master of Erroll, representing his mother as Hereditary Lord High Constable of Scotland. Before and aft were the glittering breastplates and plumes of the Household Cavalry: while massed children to right of us, children to left of us cried "Smile!" This is always rather a dilemma when on duty.

We and our colleagues displayed a meticulously assembled pageant of Scottish history. But we were among the merest ornaments to adorn the occasion, there as *hors d'oeuvres* to please the crowds, not to impress them. We were less than their equals, for we were present only as peculiarly Scottish historic servants of their Hereditary Representative, the Head of their whole national Family. And as she came into view with Prince Philip in the third carriage, a Semi-State Landau with Four Grey Horses, the cheers rose to a deep roar of sheer Glaswegian football joy. For it was with the Queen and her husband that the people had come to identify themselves, to claim and to acclaim. She was their fairy tale made tangible.

A week later, we stood in the tiny chapel of the Order of the Thistle. With the possible exception of the Garter cloak in which Annigoni crystallised her spirit for us, the Queen (with her perfect complexion that few photographs can convey) looks at her most beautiful in her dark green velvet Thistle robes. Her immediate presence always makes a new Knight's oath startlingly moving; an electric current of loyalty encircles our blaze of colour. But it was especially so when Prince Charles himself was installed, and his voice was broadcast and recorded for ever in the traditional words as he swore: 'I shall never bear treason about in my heart against our Sovereign Lady The Queen, but shall discover the same to her. So defend me God'.

Next day, as we waited in the Throne Room at Holyroodhouse to attend her in another carriage procession to the Opening of the General Assembly of the Church of Scotland, she appeared among us again in a diamond tiara and dress of shimmering innocence, and swept on radiant to captivate the grave leading elders of the Kirk. She then changed into everyday clothes to go walkabout among the ordinary folk who love her so much better than the intellectuals, who pretend to believe in democracy, think they ought to. It's the contrast that has turned for a while the pumpkin and white mice into the State Coach and Greys for them, and then turns it back again to remind them that it's a fellow kindly human being behind the enchanted mask. Even Podgorny or Scheel in all their glory could not compare with her in giving happily and thoughtfully to the people what they actually want.

There's an interesting lesson to be learnt from all this. For, although carefully incorporating the essentials of such ancient Scottish ceremonial as the pre-Union 'Riding of the Parliament' – the present Standard Bearer, for example, uniquely still holds charters from both Wallace and Bruce to his forefather whom the English hanged in 1306 for carrying the *lyon* banner in battle – this popular pageantry in Scotland is not a quaint survival waiting to be slowly suffocated by those ageing Fabians who haven't yet realised it's themselves that time is outmoding. It is, instead, the first flowering of a Scottish royal renaissance.

Some years ago, I was leaning on my bows as an Archer of the Queen's Body Guard at a Royal Garden Party in the grounds of the

Palace of Holyroodhouse, into whose spreading chestnut trees my ill-aimed practice arrows have oft sunk by mistake. Two American guests were exclaiming at the beauty of our age-old traditions, and lamenting they had nothing like it in the States. Even if I hadn't been on duty, it might have been a wee bit tactless to point out that we'd only been the Body Guard since 1822 (ten years after the British burnt the White House), and were hardly ever required for ceremonial before the 20th century. No Sovereign even bothered to set foot in Scotland between 1651 and 1822; we spent two centuries squabbling among ourselves in a backwater, until the kindly genius of Scott put us back on the European map. What little ceremonial survived, from before the Union, had attached itself to the temporary Lord High Commissioner to the annual General Assembly of the Church of Scotland.

Queen Victoria, the greatest and last of the House of Hanover, loved the Highlands but shunned public appearances. It's the House of Windsor who have taken Scotland to their heart; and it's perhaps no coincidence that Prince Charles, whose most romantic title is Lord of the Isles and who makes no secret of his special affection for the rugged North, descends from Mary Queen of Scots 17 times over; that is, by eight separate blood lines through King George V and Queen Mary, also nine more through Prince Philip, all from that immortally tragic heiress of the Royal House of Stuart.

Between the Wars, with his much-loved Scottish consort the only Lady of the Order ever, the late King George VI, one of the innovators of the tartan smoking jacket on Deeside, revived the regular installation of Knights of the Thistle. But it's to the Queen herself that we owe most. Not only has she already paid more Royal Visits to Edinburgh than any other Sovereign since her ancestor King James VI went South in 1603, but she is also the second since the Reformation to attend in person from time to time the Opening of the General Assembly. Nor has the colour of our Scottish renaissance put the English majority public to any great expense. The Archer Body Guard buy their own uniforms and give their services for free, as do the High Constables of Holyroodhouse in their blue coats and blackcock feathers. The Queen has quietly re-asserted for the Scots our claim to a full share in royal pageantry; and the tremendous personal triumph of her Silver Jubilee Visit to Scotland shows how perceptive she has been of our emotional desire to prevent our historic identity from being swamped in an increasingly Euro-American cultural uniformity.

However, all this royal glamour would serve little purpose in the vast community of our industrial island, were the people not all able to behold it, more than most actual participants can unless it's canned, through the magic of television. National royal ceremonial was long limited to such Londoners as could watch the Colour Trooping or the State Opening of Parliament. Nowadays, the ability to share in it through TV is in itself one of the main reasons for the ever-broadening popular base of our monarchy. Indeed, the proportion of her people having a television set has already risen from one in 66 to one in three during her reign.

We used to hear a lot about Scandinavian royalty on bicycles. When I was last in Sweden, many of the younger total strangers with whom I fell into conversation as usual at public bars and on trains complained that they got too much 'shirt-sleeves' and not enough pageantry from their monarchy; that there was no longer any contrast, no 'dressing-up', almost nothing but everyday sameness.

Nevertheless, great ceremonial must be kept for comparatively rare splendid occasions, lest familiarity breeds blaséness. The Queen and her advisers are adept in their timing; what seems old hat to the 30-year-old is nostalgic to the elderly and a fresh astonishment to the child. I've therefore dwelt at some length on Scottish royal pageantry only because this is one of my functions. It is, however, wise to stress that ceremonial in general could seem perhaps to make the monarchy rather remote, were it not set against the happy backdrop of equally public easy informality that has been the greatest change of this reign. For the pomposo presentation party, the Queen has substituted what she rightly much prefers, the popular walkabout.

The changes developed during the present reign naturally form the subject in this Jubilee Year of a number of books. Among these are the Penguin Special on *The Queen* [Allen Lane/Penguin, 1977]. My schoolfellow Peregrine Worsthorne's 'The Case for the Monarchy' in it could hardly be bettered. All the same, the Penguin Special is out of balance in that the only article on the Queen as Sovereign of 11 independent nations, let alone as Head of the Commonwealth, is on 'The Queen as Queen of Australia' by the minority republican Donald Horne. This is rather like getting a spokeswoman for Lesbian Nation to represent New Zealand, or submerging the role of Queen of Canada, as one of our livelier Sunday newspapers did in the unfortunate 'Confessions of Mrs Trudeau . . . the full story behind her sensational abdication as Canada's First Lady.' Although the Queen would perhaps be represented more appropriately by a Regent rather than a Governor-General in each of her realms, the importance of separating political election from the royal magic role becomes daily more obvious.

'You have the Queen', an American once said, 'We have only the Flag', In this sense Queen embodies the spirit of Britannia, as in a far lesser way consecrated Colours enshrine the spirit of a Regiment. Neither Chairman Mao nor the Kremlin could explain to their well-disciplined people's democracies why their fellow ruler Nixon was dethroned for bugging dissents; but try to imagine Buckingham Palace bugging Transport House.

Changing fashion is dead as the dodo tomorrow: and our monarchy should adapt only slowly and carefully, as is indeed its policy. I took part in 'You The Jury' BBC debate in May [1977] as witness with Lady Longford in support of Nicky Fairbairn's proposition that the Monarchy should remain the same unchanged for the next 25 years which, although obviously a proposition potentially loaded against us, we carried by a majority of two-thirds despite the oratory of its rather rum opposer Tony Howard, editor of the anti-Jubilee *New Statesman*. He had the disadvantage of having as his first witness a professional financial snooper who had a monumental chip on his shoulder that the Queen didn't have to pay income tax; I hope the Queen's advisers will take note that a large majority of the audience were opposed to any such: for it's of the utmost importance to us all that the sovereign should be completely independent of the caprice of politicians in the last resort. Nor had Mr Howard liked our pointing out that we could pay the whole Civil List for ten years if the MP's would merely forego the cost of their new Car Park. Indeed, after all this fuss, it turns out that the whole cost of the Monarchy is much less than one packet of cigarettes per head of the total population. Mr Howard's other witness was more objective; basically neutral, and perhaps fitter to be a juryman than an advocate. He was Mr Robert Lacey.

[*Books & Bookmen*, July 1977]

Our Sovereign Lady

Before the ram's horns sounded, an advance proof copy of Robert Lacey's *Majesty* [Hutchinson, 1977] arrived here with the irresistibly tempting caption: 'All the material in this proof is strictly confidential and should not be communicated to any other person. Unless the recipient agrees to be bound by this condition this proof must be returned *unread* to the publisher.'

Nothing could have been better devised to ensure that this essentially respectable book was immediately scanned with the furtive fervour normally reserved for some scandalous breach of trust. It was as though *The Times* had arrived in a *Private Eye* wrapper. This is the sort of psychological approach which captures the rat-like attention of the meanest grown-up while it also captivates the child in us. For years I've wanted to acquire a good plastic skeleton to hang in a bedroom wardrobe, and then say to a guest 'There's only one thing. *Please* don't open that door. We've got rather a skeleton in the cupboard'. So I felt Mr Lacey's publicity machine deserved to succeed. And it has.

He has told us what we would wish or need to know about the Queen in her public capacity and family background, and has managed to write around her private personality in such a way as to allow people a very human peek without too much 'what the butler saw' stuff. Jean Rook, who described the book with insight and acumen in her jolly forthright way that sometimes reminds me of the late Nancy Mitford, wrote of *Majesty*:

I am fascinated to know that the Queen is a Weight Watcher, loves '*Kojak*', personally cuts up the corgis' meat, owns a bright orange jumper, works at her desk with her shoes off, and is still very fond of Lord Snowdon . . . Along with the fact that Elizabeth dearly loves her sister, and was cut-up by her separation. And that, if you're invited to stay the weekend with her, the Queen will expect you to eat fish paste sandwiches and play charades. To enjoy long, muddy walks, for which she provides you with wellies.

This is 'writing around' Her Majesty's private personality without intruding on that ultimate intimate but literally innate royal mystique which is the most civilised method of embodying a head of state ever devised.

It may be worth examining a differing newspaper review of *Majesty*, one which presents the opposite of my own opinion, by Margaret Forster:

'As a serious attempt . . . to describe the woman who wears the crown it is a failure all the more maddening because it could so easily have been a success. That it is not is due more to the obduracy of Queen Elizabeth II than to the inadequacy of Robert Lacey. Her hostility to journalists, her absolute terror of any kind of interview, her misguided conviction that to talk to any of the media would be like Samson having his hair shorn, result only in the gulf between herself and the people she is reputed to love and serve so well widening every year . . . O dearest Queen, bare your heart to us (or R. Lacey), and what liberation might be thine!'

A moment's reflection will shew what unsound advice this is. The Queen has only to mention that she is sympathetic towards devolution but was crowned Queen of the United Kingdom to set off a howl of rage from the wilder shores of the SNP that led their leader, before he had time to back-pedal, to lose innumerable votes by referring to us loyal Scot as possibly having to choose between our Queen and our public. Supposing she said cats gave her the creeps? That fishing is more cruel than fox-hunting? That one of her Cabinet ministers had halitosis? or that she finds sensible socialists just as loyal but less pushing than flamboyant 'monarchists'? Casual asides in the course of a long and tedious interview purporting to be about something else, elicited by apparently innocent question – & – answer, and possibly given a deliberate twist in the reported phrase. People who don't have to fill ceremonial roles don't sufficiently distinguish betwen the *persona* or mask of the function, with the need to maintain its dignity in public, and the essentially private character of its dutiful wearer, which is no business of theirs.

More than 30 years ago, my own first encounter with Press methods now seems innocuous enough. Mr Lacey tells us of 'the private dances that King George VI started giving in Buckingham Palace for his daughters after VE Day at the end of the Second World War, and of 'clumps of young Guards officers' invited by the King for 'entertaining and escorting' them. I was one of those Guards officers, and belonged also to what was known as 'the Choir'. We joined the princesses in weekly evenings of Elizabethan and other part-songs in the round drawing room at Buckingham Palace, led by the tuning-fork of Dr Harris the organist from Windsor; all the refreshing peace of 'My love's an arbutus on the Borders of Lene' after the buzz-bombs that had first greeted our weary return from the exhausting shell-fire of Italy. We drank sherry or orange squash with them; we danced with them at parties; I shewed them how to do strathspeys and foursome reels; and they came to my first wedding. We all thought Princess Elizabeth an absolute honey; very much on-the-spot and down-to-earth yet immensely attractive then as now, and emanating already that aura of radiant goodness which no photograph can capture.

The one thing we did not do was to repeat their Royal Highnesses' conversation, nor discuss them with strangers. After dining early one night at 'Buck House', Princess Elizabeth's dinner party went on to a theatre. During the interval I went to the loo, full of people as always at such a moment. A stranger entered beside me and asked casually; 'Enjoying the play?' to which I replied 'Yes', buttoning up my blue uniform's flies. Next day, a newspaper reported that 'Captain Iain Moncreiffe of the Scots Guards, one of Princess Elizabeth's party at the theatre last night, tells me that she was thoroughly enjoying herself', or words to that effect. It was my first ingenuous encounter with the embarrassing and potentially misleading Press system of turning a casual private question-&-answer into a public personal statement and then embellishing it. I felt hot-and-cold all over; and suddenly took in that the life of the Royal Family must seem one long betrayal of confidence even when none had occurred. It all seems so trivial now. But it didn't to me at the time; and I quite understood when they felt let down by 'Crawfie'.

A generation later, things have greatly changed for the worse. It's not just the mass reiteration of deliberate half-truths. It's become commonplace with some of the media to arrive with a false story already invented, and then try by every wile to put it willy-nilly into the victim's mouth. 'Refused to comment' can be given as misleading a twist as 'denied the rumour'. I could cite several examples from personal experience. Democracy, we are told, has a right and indeed a need to be informed. By the same token, we ought perhaps to have a remedy at law against being deliberately or negligently misinformed.

Thus, in Ascot Week the public were told untruthfully under a large portrait of an attractive princess and front page headlines:

Official: PRINCE CHARLES IS TO MARRY PRINCESS MARIE ASTRID OF LUXEMBOURG. The formal engagement will be announced from Buckingham Palace next Monday. The couple's difference of religion – she is a Roman Catholic – will be overcome by a novel constitutional arrangement . . . The Queen and Prince Philip have assented to this procedure, which also has the approval of Church leaders . . . A close friend said last night: 'They fell for each other at that first meeting.'

Now, although a devout Anglican myself, I could think of nothing more suitable than such a match, I've never met the princess in question, but have known her talented father the Grand Duke for many years, and know of no happier nor more sensible family background. In these oecumenical days, when the Christian ethic itself is menanced by dialectical materialism – the only missionary religion there will ever have been that knowns not God – the outdated parochial C of E restriction on any British royal heir's marriage to a Catholic should be removed in any case by parliament as offensive to loyal Catholics, even if HRH doesn't wish to marry one. Indeed nobody save a token Pastor Glass objected to Scotland's cardinal archbishop reading the lesson at the Queen's presbyterian Jubilee Service of Thanksgiving in Glasgow; the very home of Celtic *v* Rangers. But that Press crack from 'a close friend' of Prince Charles seemed a bit too reminiscent of some other front page news a couple of years ago, about which I did know at first hand.

Sprawled across another front page, with a large photograph of a girl in a tartan sash, I learnt of:

'LADY ALEX: A NEW GIRL IN THE LIFE OF CHARLES. The 26-year-old prince was at Lady Alexandra's coming-out ball in London earlier this week. Guests said they appeared to be 'very close'. One guest said: 'Prince Charles kissed Lady Alexandra as soon as he arrived and hardly left her side all evening. Everyone thinks there is romance in the air . . .' The prince has taken Lady Alexandra to London restaurants and she is believed to have been invited to Balmoral in August when he is on leave from the Navy.'

Now, Alexandra is my daughter, then recently returned from Cracow

University behind the Iron Curtain. I gave a crowded cocktail party for her *début*, not a dance. When the Prince of Wales did us the honour of attending, I would naturally have preferred to discuss some recent researches with HRH myself, but it didn't seem an appropriate moment. So Alexandra was presented to the prince, *whom she had never met before*; and they made conversation for two or three minutes. Prince Charles then talked politely to other guests for about an hour before leaving; *and that was the last they saw of each other*. If this is what the Press can make of a very minor private occasion when none of them was even present, what on earth might some equally unscrupulous journalist not make out of a grand personal interview with the Queen herself?

Even Mr Lacey isn't entirely free from a Fabian habit much to be frowned on. This is the parrot-repetition by journalists and commentators of routine "surprise" that we "still" have a Royal Family in this Day & Age, coupled with patronising but fatuous remarks that it may very likely continue for the foreseeable future. There are more monarchies than republics in free Europe, and to-day is nothing more special than the latest of ever-receding yesterdays. Indeed to be a dry republican is to miss something in life, to lack a feeling for romance. This attitude goes with a standard intellectual Pavlov-dog reaction about the National Anthem being a boring tune. But intelligent people remember that Beethoven envied us our National Anthem; and Yehudi Menuhin, in his recent autobiography, tells us how much the 'unaggressive nobility of the chorale' appeals to him. I much enjoyed it, by the way, when delightful Italian musicians at St Andrews in this Silver Jubilee year, with harpsichord and a cello, and two violins, played variations in the style of Bach on Handel's theme of 'God Save the King'.

Indeed, John Grigg (the *çi-devant* Ld Altrincham) suggests in his *Spectator* review that a close reading of *Majesty* shews Mr Lacey to be ambivalent about the Queen and even more so about the monarchy. But I don't think Mr Lacey has really been trying to run with the hare and hunt with the hounds in his efforts to be objective.

All the same, Mr Lacey might have worded the rather offensive close of his book differently, had he been able to observe how the reaction of some of the more trendy media during these Jubilee months had been a source of innocent merriment. Starting off to pay what they had convinced each other within their narrow consensus was formal lip-service to an 'anachronism' (another of their parrot words), they were genuinely astonished to find that to the vast and usually silent general public it wasn't lip-service at all, but that our love and loyalty is the real thing. There was a brief rearguard action, when self-proclaimed 'republican at heart' George Gale and a great national newspaper, by what could hardly have been coincidence, both simultaneously tried to come up with the idea that we were really 'celebrating ourselves'. This didn't last more than a couple of days, and by the time the bonfires were lit we were able to feel that at last the Queen, always so modest for herself though proud on our behalf for her office, the greatest Crown in the world, really realised how much we love her for herself.

The Queen is at once our talisman, our ultimate protector and the head of our national family. The nuclear royal family is the basis of kingship; the family around whom countries and nations grew, as from Wessex to England, and from England to Britain, and from Britain to the Commonwealth. Indeed, the very word 'king' is derived from Old Norse 'konungr', meaning Offspring of The Kindred; latest scion of the blood royal. And it is as *The Family* writ large that we see the Queen and Prince Philip and Prince Charles today. Churchill spoke for us all when he described Her Majesty as the lady whom we respect because she is our Queen, and whom we love because she is herself.

Books & Bookmen, August 1977

III

The Master Snob

The Hereditary principle

In 1968 the House of Lords was threatened with wholesale reform designed to eradicate the hereditary element (a measure subsequently defeated by the unlikely combination of Messrs Enoch Powell and Michael Foot). I.M. produced this apologia for the system:

'I knew a lord once, but he died'. Writing as the Master Snob, I feel sad whenever I hear that wistful plaint. The world shouldn't be filled with people like ants, all conforming and brainwashed and dressed alike. It should be full of variety, with people like tropical birds to add to its infinite kaleidoscope. How dull it would be if we all had numbers instead of names, to avert 'social inequality': if there were no MacGillycuddy of the Reeks, no Marquess of Cholmondeley, no Knight of Glin, no Wali of Swat, nor even the biggest tease of all, our own [1968] Westminster MP, Mr John Smith. Writing as the 24th Ilk, I know how much ragging we have to stand nowadays. But that is as it should be. We are not there to show off, but to add to the fun.

Asked by a Danish journalist why I preferred to be called Sir Iain as opposed to Dr Moncreiffe, I replied that it would be boasting to call myself Doctor, since I had earned the doctorate myself – but as a Baronet I was only a living memorial to a greater man, the first Sir Thomas (a back-room boy on the grandest Scottish 17th century scale). Similarly, the continuing existence of a Duke of Wellington is our most resplendent living war memorial.

The whole thing springs rightly from the Fountain of Honour. Earls were originally genuine cousins of the Sovereign, and so dressed up similarly with little crowns ('coronets') and velvet robes to help in our national pageantry. When the Queen made Attlee an earl she was making him an honorary member of the family, a 'well-beloved Cousin'. Other peers copy earls, and we barts have to make do with neck badges.

People link Peerage with Parliament too much. Men were created Irish peers specially to prevent them from sitting in the House of Lords, nor did peeresses in their own right have any seat until lately. All the same, because it is topical, I suppose I must discuss the hereditary principle from the political point of view. For, in an age of technocratic change and 'gritty purposive government', it is too readily dismissed as an irrelevant anachronism and as an obstacle to the rightful domination of the numerical majority.

Yet absolute power vested in a numerical majority can corrupt that majority just as much as it can corrupt a single ruler. Allied to no moral principle, it could some day seem logical for 51 per cent of the electorate to enslave the remainder. So, in civilised Western Europe, wise compromises have been evolved whereby the enthusiasm of democracy is tempered by senatorial safeguards and the neutralising force of a constitutional monarchy. In the days of their greatness and wisdom, the British solved both these problems in the same way: through the hereditary principle.

It should be clearly understood that, in this context, the hereditary principle does not require hereditary talent. Some ancient Greeks selected men for office by casting lots: but this was only practical in tiny city states where the free citizens were financially independent. We cast the lot of birth, within a group of families chosen by history. The object is to produce a completely independent person, of a family that is at least average in ability (the average for the country would perhaps be about stationmaster level), and who has if possible private means (so that he is a free man, for that is the only way to be free) and been bred to a sense of responsibility. And if democracy means the mass of the people getting what they want, then the hereditary principle is not at all undemocratic. For, in This Day & Age, most of the people continue to adore the Queen and to love a lord.

As usual, the people are right. Most stable democracries in civilised Western Europe – Norway, Denmark, Sweden, Holland, Belgium, Luxembourg – have an hereditary sovereign as head of state: of course, those excitable Latins chop and change. An elected but nominal president is a dead bore in a country effectively governed by its Chancellor or Prime Minister. He just isn't romantic; and in times of rapid change, those who are coming into power are the very people who voted against the distinguished old buffer, so there is nobody above politics to hold the nation together.

It isn't nationally relevant, though interesting personally, that Winston Churchill descended from Simon de Montfort and William of Orange, from Mithradates and from a brother of St Thomas Aquinas, also (through the Jeromes) from several million Red Indians. But it's very relevant that the Queen and Prince Philip both descend from Alfred the Great and Harold and William the Conqueror, from King Duncan and Robert Bruce and Mary Queen of Scots, above all from Queen Victoria, and that the present Prince of Wales descends from Old King Coel and Rhodri Mawr and Llewelyn the Great. For, in our national history, they act as living links between the past and the future. The Queen is also the present focus of national unity, precisely because nobody has ever had to take sides to vote for or against her.

To turn to the House of Lords, it is similarly because they haven't had to commit themselves to anybody, that the hereditary peers form our principal body of independent thinkers and speakers with a nation-wide platform. More than half of them are not in receipt of any party whip; 736 are there by inheritance, enough to man an entire battalion from commanding officer (Lord Carrington) to drummer-boy (Lord Foley?). They are a well-chosen mixed bunch. About a third of them are real aristocrats, in that their predecessors actually wore coats of arms over their armour in the days of tournaments. Another third represent the capable families who helped to establish us in our halcyon days, between Elizabeth I and Queen Victoria. The remainder are mostly of middle-class or working-class origin.

Taken all in all, they're the best group of independents, with a built-in cautious approach to unnecessary new laws, that we're likely to get. It isn't really their job to attend unless they feel they have something to say; the life peers and regular attenders are ample for normal business. If the Upper House tends to be conservative with a small 'c', that is as it should be, for it is intended to be a brake on the Lower House; not its rival. A radical second chamber is almost a contradiction in terms – for how, then, is it a safeguard for the minorities? But, with no written constitution, many of us would feel safer if somebody (other than the paid professional Commons) had the power to oblige governments to go to the country for a fresh 'mandate' when they find it their duty to break their major pledges to the electorate.

All the same, the White Paper proposals are not nearly as half-baked as they've been made out in the debates. Roughly speaking, they are that the Prime Minister of the day (he used to be called the Cabinet) can force through the Second Chamber any legislation he likes, provided only it isn't opposed by the votes of (a) the whole Opposition, themselves political nominees within the consensus, together with (b) most of the mandarins nominated by the bureaucracy, to be known as cross-benchers. So the only check on legislation by the executive is to be the retired executive, and then only for six months. Since we've already given up our liberties to them, and can never recover them in your time or mine, we might as well face realities; the White Paper gives logical expression to real power, and the dreaded placemen will at least be made free men (probably too late) by the grant of private means.

In such a context, in the interests of all non-conformist, we must insist on retaining independent *voice* as opposed to the useless irritant of independent vote. The White Paper's greatest defect is that it proposes to exclude from its 'two-tier' system the voice of *future* hereditary peers, and thus gradually to deprive the House of all its young men and most of its last free speakers. There will, in a generation's time, be nobody like the late Duke of Bedford or the present Lord Colville of Culross.

Most outside speakers today, whether they realise it or not, depend for their careers on conforming. The Establishment imperceptibly merges into the consensus, which in turn has managed almost all the mass-media since the rapid suppression of the free wireless. Radios Caroline and Scotland would have been much wiser to have had some minority party political broadcasts, say for the Liberals and the SNP, in order to bring the real issue of free speech into the open. What use is a soap box in Hyde Park when trying to inform an electorate of over 50 million. Soon only the hacks and the mandarins will be left in Parliament; and (doubtless to the amusement of Lords Balogh and Kaldor, imbued with a sense of our present great national practical joke) the voice of Russell and Cecil, Cavendish and Stanley, will no longer be heard in the land – unless, of course, they abandon all their other local duties to become county absentees as well-whipped Westminster professional politicians. On this single point of future peers having no voice, the whole scheme, in my opinion, should founder.

But, in stressing that the hereditary principle does not require hereditary talent, I've perhaps implied that the peerage families as a whole are not more talented than the average. This is, of course, far from the case, and I suspect is the real reason why they're under attack. This Day & Age is the Age of Envy. The best, we are told, is the enemy of the good; and certainly there is much hatred of excellence today. What school is most attacked? Eton. What regiments are most attacked? The Guards. Which House of Parliament is to be deformed? The Lords. But few people could name better schools, troops or Second Chambers anywhere in the world. (Guy Fawkes is the chap who'd attract most people's votes). And, although throughout all mankind no family is in fact any older than any other, the trouble about our so-called 'old families' is that they will tend to be talented beyond the average.

Readers of Galton's *Hereditary Genius* will realise that (apart from rare mutations) all talent is inherited, both physical and mental, and that they tend to go together. Happily for the rest of us, talented families often produce amusing eccentrics; so we are able to enjoy Lord Stanley of Alderley and 'Boofy' Arran, also the aptly named Lord Strange; nor would Lord Egremont wish to be exempted [*all now deceased* – ED]. If it's eccentric to win the Victoria Cross, the higher aristocracy out-rival the general population fantastically. Although it's only about a hundred years old, the grander peerage families tend to have won it almost as a matter of course. Men who could have been Premier Duke or Premier Earl of Scotland have won it. Even middle-class peerage families like Moynihan descend from a VC. Perhaps more surprisingly, since the George Cross has barely come of age, men who could have been Premier Duke or Premier Earl of England have won that, too.

The Lindsays (who naturally won the first military VC) may serve as examples of hereditary talent. Froissart called them polished, and they have produced poets and playwrights and lovers of art and architecture ever since the Middle Ages. Their head is Lord Crawford [*the 28th Earl, who died in 1975* – ED] and it is not 'privilege' but civilisation that has made him rival even Sir Colin Anderson in cultural chairmanship. Yet, in This Day & Age, the 27 [*now 26*] ducal families haven't been able to give us anything better by way of statesmen than Churchill (who might have been Duke of Marlborough) and no better philosopher than Bertrand Russell (a mere earl, but who might have been Duke of Bedford). And when we were fighting for national survival, the earls' families fobbed us off with Lord Caledon's brother, Field-Marshal Alexander.

Recently the Tory party, after a lot of talk about everybody having an equal chance to prove himself, sacked Sir Alec Douglas-Home (who has proved himself perhaps our leading statesman, as opposed to politician) because he was a 14th earl in disguise. This was ironic, for the Homes have had little to do with politics since they defeated and slew King James III in 1488 over an Inland Revenue dispute. The real reason for Sir Alec's inborn interest in public affairs is his descent from 'Radical Jack' Durham and Earl Grey, the Reform Bill Prime Minister, two of the leading left-wing statesmen of their day. Perhaps earnest men in the corridors of power will never get over the casual approach which the aristocracy pretends to bring to the problems of government. We all remember the deceptively able Victorian nobleman who entered his new Ministry, as Colonial Secretary, and inquired of his Permanent Under-Secretary: 'Tell me, Mr Merivale, where are the Colonies?' Mr Merivale took him literally as all too many people took Lord Randolph Churchill's 'damned dots', and still take Sir Alec's doing his sums with matches today.

Spectator, 6 December 1968

112

Commons Peers

In a review of The New Extinct Peerage 1884–1971 *by L. G. Pine (Heraldry Today, 1972), I.M. discussed the 'jabberwocky Peerage Act' of 1963, which, among other things, allowed peers to disclaim their titles for life.*

Seldom have we had a better example of the saying that a camel is a horse constructed by a Committee. The trouble was that the Joint Committee was composed of professional politicians who thought of peerage dignities only in selfish competitive terms as Peerages of Parliament. But Peerage is not necessarily anything to do with Parliament. Earls existed long before the first Parliament. Ladies were created Peers in their own right centuries before they were allowed to sit in the House of Lords. Irish peers can sit only in the Commons, and don't have to surrender their titles to do that. Unelected Scottish peers couldn't sit in either House before the 1963 Act. Standing for service in the House of Commons is performing a public duty, not assuming a privilege. Why should it be punishable by permanent deprivation of one's honoured name: and Lancashire lose their beloved 'Earl of Derby' for life if they choose him to represent one of their constituencies for a few years? The answer may perhaps be sought in Envy. A crusty Commons member of the Joint Committee complained that the people love a lord, and that it would be disastrous to have a lot of lords snapping up the best constituencies – a good comment on contemporary 'democracy', that the people can't elect whom they love. All that was needed in 1963 was to pass a short Act saying that peers could stand for election to the Commons, but could not vote in the Lords so long as they were serving in the Lower House.

My Kinsmen and I

Coming up for its 170th birthday, *Debrett's Peerage, Baronetage, Knightage & Companionage* [1972/73], couldn't be in better hands than those of its conscientious editor Patrick Montague-Smith [*retired 1980; died 1986*], who has a wide interest both in genealogy and in the niceties of precedence and custom that our French governesses used to call 'etiquette' (English governesses were different, concentrating on our leaving something on the platter for 'Miss Manners', following like night on day the nannies who had forced us to gobble it all up, even to the extent of bringing back unfinished breakfast porridge bowls cold, to be consumed forcibly at tea). People usually pretend to know all about this sort of thing already, but secretly they sometimes have to look up the odd point, even if it's only when somebody was born or where to seat a bishop in their *placement* at dinner. 'Honourables before Baronets', Bobby Corbett always observes as he hurries through doorways ahead of me – and *Debrett* is a good reminder to place the Honble *Mrs* Zuckerman, wife of a life peer's son, before *Lady* Bacon, wife of the Premier Baronet of England.

The main text of this vast and necessarily labyrinthine tome is heralded by its List of Contents, which the novice enquirer would be wise to invoke before entering string in hand. The book then opens with an explanation of those hydra-headed abbreviations commonly in use. From KG and MRTPI – Member Royal Town Planning Institute – to EFTA and UNRRA. At the end of the last war, the late Emerald Lady Cunard came to luncheon with me when I was Captain of the King's Guard. She made her usual entry at St James's Palace, *i.e.* an hour late, went straight up to another guest, and enquired. 'Ah, Colonel Codrington, what are you doing these days?' John Codrington of the Coldstream Guards (who is, of course, also in *Debrett*) replied that he was Military Assistant to General Urquhart and, on enquiry who that might be, replied, 'of Arnhem' – which readers will recall was our bloodiest air-borne battle. She teased him, apparently in bewilderment: 'ARNHEM, ARNHEM, I've never head of ARNHEM. I've heard of UNRRA'. The colonel smiled, but she got a rise out of my hero-conscious ensign, who actually took her seriously. When our troops had fought in Italy rather earlier, civil administration was run by AMGOT (... Allied Military Government Occupied Territories), pronounced 'Amgot', which turned out to be an exceedingly dirty word in Turkish. During the First Battle of Monte Camino, using valuable AMGOT bank-notes because I had no Army Form Z to put to paper's most delicate early morning use on that shell-wracked mountain, I reflected on the *mot de Cambronne*. So much for Abbreviations. Almost the only good thing about that noisy maniac Hitler, who was undoubtedly not suitable *Debrett* material, was that he detested the proliferation of bastard words coined from initial letters or their syllables; or so I was informed while a General Staff Officer at the KME.

The abbreviations are followed by a list of 'Clubs Referred to in the Work, with the Addresses of the Club Houses'. It's spitefully gratifying that the Eccentric Club is omitted, as while on my way back to our St James's flat from a convivial evening spent at White's and Pratt's, the hall porter of the Eccentric surprisingly chased me of all people out when asked in passing for a look at their list of eccentric members. But it's sad the Royal and Ancient Golf Club at St Andrews, whose No. 1 and 2 special whiskies are so potent, is also omitted; for there in the Regency my great-great-grandfather, the 19th Ilk, then Captain of the Club, the gold medallist, won a bet with his partner that he would propose to and be accepted by a pretty gal whom he had just noticed while on the course. She turned out to be a Miss Mackay, sprung from the family of Lord Redy, and when Sir David Moncreiffe died she married his sister's widower, the 2nd Earl of Bradford; we still have her Florentine work-box of gold and semi-precious stones. However, as the Founder of Puffin's, a tiny club in Edinburgh, it's gratifying that is is included.

Debrett's naturally includes Lord Londonderry's sister, Lady Annabel Birley [*now Goldsmith*], but hasn't yet gone so far as to club-list the fashionable night club named Annabel's after her. It's difficult for an old 400 member not to have a soft spot for such modish clubs. My near kinsman the late Lord Kinnoull married one of the three daughters of shrewd Mrs Meyrick, the 'Night-Club Queen' – her other two married the 6th Earl of Craven (a member of whose family, still-born with two heads, is bottled in the South Kensington Natural History Museum, according to their relation Dicky Buckle, but he was probably pulling my leg) and the 26th Lord de Clifford (the last peer to be tried by his peers before the Socialists brushed away the remnants of *Magna Carta*, being acquitted of what to my childhood reading seemed to be man's-laughter). Moreover, my grandfather's grandmother, an earlier Countess of Kinnoull, was the last surviving Lady Patroness of Almack's: perhaps the most distinguished and socially powerful night club there will ever have been. The Iron Duke of Wellington was turned away for trying to enter it *sans culottes*, wearing under-strapped trousers instead of knee-breeches.

This brings us to the Preface, which points out that by coincidence the recent Dukes of Wellington and Marlborough and Lord Nelson all died last year (the late Duke of Wellington was one of the most civilised men of our time). The thing about such historic peerages is, what more romantic war memorials can we have to our epic heroes, than living heirs of their own flesh and blood? How despicable can a nation of many, many millions get, than to spend parliamentary time to do away altogether with the niggardly inflation-debased over-taxed pension our relieved forefathers had voted to install our sea-saviour's representatives in Trafalgar House, that modest shade of Blenheim Palace; which in its turn is only still saved for our mean self-respect by American marriages? But for Nelson, we'd have gone into a Napoleonic Common Market on much inferior terms. To continue this theme through Nazi schemes for an even worse Common Market for us, it always seems a pity that Churchill didn't become Duke of Dover, to carry on another such living war memorial; though doubtless to the disclaiming dismay of his would-be parliamentary successors.

Perhaps the most controversial part of the Preface is that in which the editor advances the argument that, precisely since Edward VIII abdicated because our law does not recognise morganatic marriage, it was and is unconstitutional to deny HRH the Duke of Windsor's wife the style of Royal Highness [*wrongfully denied up to death in 1986* – ED]. He points out that George III's sister-in-law HRH the Duchess of Gloucester was the illegitimate daughter of a milliner. As a matter of observation, there is a great deal of ignorance in high quarters, as well as among quite knowledgeable writers on ceremonial, about nobiliary matters. For instance, it was quite ridiculous to argue that the Duke of Edinburgh had to be specially granted the style of 'Prince'. *All* British dukes, marquesses and earls are princes already, as honorary cousins of the Sovereign. The Duke of Norfolk, the Marquess of Lothian and the Earl of Derby are all equally princes. It's their most formal style, proclaimed by the herald in attendance in the old days of regular State funerals for high-ranking peers, and used on certain other grand occasions. To quote, I suspect, that authoritative King of Arms the late Sir Bernard Burke (see *Burke's Peerage*, 1939 edn, pp 3-4): a duke 'is officially addressed by the Crown as "Our right trusty and right entirely beloved Cousin". A duke is likewise entitled, upon some occasions, "Most High, Potent and Noble Prince". A marquess is . . . "Our right trusty and entirely beloved Cousin". He bears also the title, upon some occasion, of "Most Noble and Puissant Prince".' An earl is . . . "Our right trusty and right well-beloved Cousin". He bears also, upon some occasions, the title of "Most Noble and Puissant Prince".' Indeed, since the War, a charter of the ruined castle of Slains was granted to my first wife as 'the Most Noble and Puissant Princess, Diana Denyse, Countess of Erroll'. So the Duke of Edinburgh *as such* was automatically a Prince already, quite apart from being also made a Royal Highness.

The reason why people have come to think that 'prince' means 'royal', is that our only princes with no other title are those immediate male-line cadets of the royal family who have not yet received peerages, such as Prince Henry before he became Duke of Gloucester. The reason why Princess Alice was called Countess of Athlone, and Princess Louise was called Duchess of Argyll, was precisely because they were married to peers of princely rank, an earldom and a dukedom. Formerly it was usual for a royal princess to renounce her rank and be given a different

116

precedence on marrying somebody who was not an earl or higher peer, the honorary 'cousinhood of the Sovereign', as in the cases of Princess Maud, who became Lady Maud Carnegie on marrying an earl's son, and the Canadians adored 'Princess Patsy', who became Lady Patricia Ramsay on marrying an earl's brother. Princess Margaret's husband was logically made an earl when she retained her rank, for what value would the honorary 'cousinhood' offered retiring Prime Ministers be, if the Sovereign's own brother-in-law wasn't made an earl. These matters are better understood abroad, where there are many non-royal princes ranked below ordinary dukes. Indeed, the mediatised Count of Pappenheim is in Part II of the neo-*Gotha*, whereas Prince Bismarck is only in Part III.

The Preface is followed by a list of Life Peers and Law Lords. Life Peerage has always seemed a sensible idea, and there were at least 29 Life Peers created by Stuart times. Leaving out promotions, as from Viscount Hereford to be Earl of Essex, I doubt Queen Elizabeth I created more than about eight new hereditary peerages in her 45 years' reign. However, when Queen Victoria tried to stem the flow and, for a test case, created an elderly bachelor a Life Peer as Lord Wensleydale, she was cheesed off by being told by a suicidal House of Lords that once he'd sat, it must become an hereditary peerage. It's one thing to retain hereditary peerages for such English families as the Howards and Cavendishes, Cecils and Stanleys, Fitzmaurices and Russells, or Scottish families like the Murrays and Lindsays, Drummonds and Ramsays, who have all proved themselves in statecraft generation after generation throughout the centuries. But it was ridiculous to honour biennially with *hereditary* titles the sort of people our politico-bureaucracy thinks fit to be kicked up to represent the Establishment's consensus in the Upper House.

We have a sufficient number of hereditary peers by now to keep the House of Lords from becoming a mere body of elderly life mandarins. On the other hand, it would be a great pity were a tiny elegant boot not to be kept in the hereditary door. Mr Heath would do a kindness to history if he were to create just one hereditary peer during his term of office. The old Scottish system of honouring a whole clan by conferring an hereditary peerage on its Chief might afford such an opportunity, especially where the Chief had very many thousands of loyal clansmen at home and in America, Canada and the Antipodes, was already an hereditary Baronet and a Jacobite titular Peer, and had achieved the distinctions of the Order of the Thistle and a Life Peerage. Such a person could be found in the present Lord Chamberlain [*Lord Maclean, who retired as Lord Chamberlain at the end of 1984* – ED].

The whole of civilisation is based on *inheritance*, and in building yet higher on inheritance; primogeniture conserving it, and the chips on the shoulders of younger sons and the emulation of other families keeping up its momentum. Thus the *family* is the stimulus for nearly all who are neither dedicated fanatics, nor purely selfish. Primitive peoples like those in New Guinea, burn a man's hut and smash his utensils when he dies, which leaves each successive generation in egalitarian stagnation on Square One. Death duties are the modern equivalent. As an hereditary baronet myself, it ought to seem gratifying at first sight that the original 17th century royal promise not to create any new baronetcies – so that as any old baronetcy died out we would become more and more select – is at last being honoured by modern Prime Ministers. But it's being done for the wrong consensus-type purpose. It's the essence of civilisation that new families who prove themselves should have the chance to catch up if they can. One of the reasons why I am no longer a Conservative is that they've lost faith in their principles and just ape the Socialists, who want to apply the solutions advanced in 1860 for the problems of 1820, in order to solve the problems of 1931; yet this is 1973. The great advantage of the British hereditary system has always been our acceptance of new talented families. *Debrett* mustn't become an impenetrable closed shop like the Swedish nobility, sterilised under the boring sanitary Socialism there. So, few baronets would probably object to an occasional but very rare and distinguished addition to their number, by way of commemorating some such hereditary genius as that of the Huxleys or the Feet, or rather Foots.

After the list of Life Peers, there follows in meticulous reference-work succession; Life Peeresses; Hereditary Peeresses in their own right (of which Lady Erroll, mother of my children, is the senior, although her earldom was only created in 1452 while the exquisite Lady Sutherland's earldom dates from about 1235, through the literally intriguing anomalies of our Scottish 'Decreet of Ranking' in James VI's reign); Peers who are Minors (it seemex cruel that the Earl Marshal's Office were adamant that Lord Hereford, the *only* Viscount in the Peerage of England, was not allowed to do homage at the Queen's Coronation for all the lesser viscounts, although he was *nearly* 22 at the time – my own Coronation problems were different, an allergic itch like a million midges under my tabard, coupled with an urge to strike that dwarf-like Scotophobe bully the late Norroy King of Arms [*Sir Gerald Woods Wollaston* – ED] with my batôn, that only the Queen's sacred presence on Holy Ground enabled me to resist); the Order of Succession, rather ghoulishly giving the first two dozen heirs after the Prince of Wales; the Royal Households, a medley of unpaid but honoured luminaries from the Hereditary Grand Almoner to the Royal Chaplains, together with those necessarily under-paid (for we are mean to our Queen) and infinitely-maligned, tactful but firm courtiers who make our royal arrangements the envy of every republican president's staff, and who are rewarded by the ignorant public referring to them as 'hangers-on'; HM Officers of Arms (with us, these properly form part of the Scottish Royal Household, but in England it may have become different when a separate College of Arms was established by King Richard 'Crouchback'); a Diplomatic Section (the Zoo, as we used to call each other when I was Private Secretary to the British Ambassador in Moscow), giving Her Britannic Majesty's representatives abroad, and the heads of missions acredited to the Court of St James's from overseas; a Guide to the wearing of Orders, &c; Foreign and Commonwealth Orders; the Table of General Precedence, also Precedence in Scotland (thank goodness neither form of precedence in Britain bears too much relation to real importance, unlike communist countries, else one would always have to trail along behind the insufferably slicker chap who regularly pipped one to the post in every job); 'Forms of Addressing Persons of Title', which has a quaint old-fashioned but courteous ring; Peerages that have become Extinct, Dormant, Abeyant or Disclaimed in the last year (don't forget that a peer can only disclaim for himself and his wife, the precedence and courtesy titles of his children remaining unaffected unless they so wish it, else a nonentity could disclaim just to spite his family – but a child born more than nine months after the Disclaiming would not be the child of a peer – and while Sir Alec Douglas-Home's son chose to give up being styled Lord Dunglass, he might at least call himself 'Master of Home', a real and not a courtesy title that belongs to him of right as heir to the latent earldom); an article on the Sovereign, Royal Family, Peerage, Baronetage and Other Dignities and Ranks; the list of Royal Warrant Holders (one learns that Sleepeezie Ltd are patronised by restless royalty, and that the Household's Lucozade comes from Beecham Products); Antique Dealers; Eating Out (a surprise to find in *Debrett*); also a Wine and Spirit Section, followed rather ominously by last year's Obituary.

The main body of the work at last emerges. This is built out of the social-anthropological passage-rite dates and official positions of the Royal Family; of Peers with their living relations and a brief account of their predecessors; the same for Baronets; the official list of Chiefs of Scottish Names and Clans (the general public often think chiefs are confined to the tribal leaders of our shaggier mountain-folk, but the word is originally Norman-French and the historic Bruces and Hays still have their chiefs); and finally concise biographies of all living Knights and Companions of Orders of Chivalry. One of the most useful titbits is the inclusion of *addresses*. Only the hereditary Knight of Glin is omitted. He was originally the Black Knight. Later, he was known as the Knight of the Valley, thus of the Glen, corrupted to 'Glin'. The omission may be because Glin is in Eire, although the present Knight's knowledge is devoted to work in the V & A Museum [*an authority on the arts, the Knight is now Christie's representative in Ireland* – ED] The Green Knight, now the hereditary Knight of Kerry, is of course included anyway as he is also Sir George Fitzgerald Bart. Alas, unlike *Burke, Debrett* separates the peers from us baronets as sheep from goats, and we Ruddigory Barts are not best pleased at this.

Yet through constant intermarriage the peerage and baronetage are inextricably intermingled (this is not so true of the grander dukes themselves; my mother-in-law comes of a ducal family, Buccleuch, who descend since the late 17th century by intermarriage from at least 20 other ducal families, such as Norfolk, Portland, Argyll and Bedford, though the present Duke of Buccleuch does include the Moncreiffe of that Ilk baronets among his *seize quartiers*). The great thing about being a Master Snob is to enjoy it, instead of slinking about as if you were ashamed of it, so my own family will be sacrificed as examples, to their hot-and-cold embarrassment. My far from diffident cousin, Lord Bath, whose grandmother was a Moncreiffe, keeps sleepy lions to amuse tourists prowling round his Elizabethan stately home at Longleat. My other cousin, Sir John Muir, Bart, has that Safari Park with even giraffes for tourists outside his Scots baronial *schloss* at Blair Drummond. To take also, therefore, others of my own *Debrett* relations, for instance, my grandfather was a son of the auburn-haired Sir Thomas Moncreiffe of that Ilk, 7th Baronet and 20th Laird, by his marriage to the 11th Earl of Kinnoull's daughter, Lady Louisa Hay. They called it the wedding of carrots to hay. Old Lord Kinnoull went a bit barking in his old age; they say he used to pop out of his London house in his dressing-gown to chalk rude *graffiti* on doorways; he was, of course, both Lord Lyon King of Arms and Lord Lieutenant of Perthshire at the time. It's of this Lady Louisa Moncreiffe that Anita Leslie, in *Edwardians in Love*, relates that she advised a debutante daughter 'Never comment on a likeness'. This may be because one of them, my great-aunt Harriet Moncreiffe, who married Sir Charles Mordaunt, 10th Bart, became mentally deranged after puerpural fever when her daughter was born. Nobody could then be divorced for madness, and the subsequent disagreeable Court proceedings by the desperate Sir Charles, in which Lord Cole and a baronet called Sir Frederick Johnstone were cited, became a sad Victorian *cause célèbre* because the Prince of Wales himself appeared in the witness box to deny that he had tampered with Aunt Harriet; his kindly letters to her proving completely innocuous. Her mother, Lady Louisa Moncreiffe herself, had eight daughters and eight sons. When the last of them was due, some ass asked whether she wanted a little boy or a little girl. 'I don't care if it's a parrot', she snapped (Sir Thomas doubtless off repopulating the village) and out popped Uncle Johnnie Moncreiffe, whose ashes are buried in the roofless mediaeval Chapel of Moncreiffe under his initials JAM, but who won a DCM as a Sergeant and an MC, mention in despatches and French *croix de guerre* with palm as a Major, and lived up to *Debrett's* standards by marrying a daughter of the 1st Duke of Westminster.

His sister were top Victorian beauties who also all naturally stayed married within *Debrett*. The youngest, Aunt May Moncreiffe (who was playing as a child at Glamis when one of the Bowes-Lyon children accidently fell against a catch that opened a secret door, perhaps to the hidden stairs leading to the Monster's den, and they were hurried from the room or so her daughter assured me) married the hot-tempered but house-and-garden artist Sir Basil Montgomery, 5th Bart, who owned Kinross House, one of the two or perhaps three most beautiful *Châteaux* in Scotland besides the famous trout fishing in Lochleven. But to take only the three eldest: Aunt Louisa Moncreiffe married the Gaelic-speaking 7th Duke of Atholl, the only nobleman in Britain allowed an albeit colourful and kilted private army of his own. The next, Aunt Helen Moncreiffe, married Sir Charles Forbes, Newe 4th Bart, and her grandson's men still parade heavily-armed with 'Dandy' Wallace's equally well-armed men for the annual March of the Forbes Men with plenty of whisky behind pipers to the annual Lonach Gathering on Donside, a mountains' watershed north of Balmoral on Deeside. Lord Frederic Hamilton in his inimitable memoirs, gives Aunt Helen's 'cameo-cut' beauty top marks of all. Through her, my eccentric cousins include that adventurous descendant of St Thomas More, the Andaluz *aficionado* Lord St Oswald [*died 1984*], so often parachuted with an unusual soft-bone ailment that broke 'em (his) behind enemy lines from Albania to Indo-China, and whose ancestral house-carpenter was the boy Chippendale, much of whose early and later work he therefore possesses. But the laurels of beauty were given to the third daughter, Aunt Georgie Moncreiffe, wife of the 1st Earl of Dudley who had £1,000 a day, which in golden sovereigns and little tax was enough to jog along with in those days. Some even said she was the most beautiful woman in Europe, and when she appeared outside Dudley House in Park Lane with the beautiful fated-for-assassination Empress of Austria, crowds stood on chairs in the park to see them. The Shah of Persia is said to have seen her at a Court Ball and wanted to buy her, but was told Lord Dudley could buy Persia; which was probably true before oil had been discovered at Abadan. Anita Leslie's book tells us that Aunt Georgie gave a 'midnight supper' to the elated Prince of Wales after his famous Derby win with Persimmon in 1896. But she wasn't merely social. The First World War official report said of her: 'The history of women's work for the Red Cross in this country provides, so far as we are aware, no similar example of equally-sustained labour producing results of the same value'.

Incidentally, Aunt Georgie leads us to a little-known aspect of the higher peerage that doesn't appear in *Debrett*. That is the custom of giving an eldest son a nickname derived from his courtesy title. Thus, Aunt Georgie's son was called 'Eddie', not because he was Xianed 'Edward' (he was William) but because his courtesy title was Viscount Ednam: he grew up to be Governor-General of Australia. Again, my first wife's predecessor, the 20th Earl of Erroll, who commanded the Blues, was known as 'Kil' from having been Lord Kilmarnock. His galloper, wounded by being thrown from his horse and landing on his sword-hilt at Queen Victoria's Diamond Jubilee, was that veteran *bimbashi* from the battle of Omdurman, my cousin 'Bardie' as Marquess of Tullibardine: afterwards 8th Duke of Atholl, he personally raised and commanded the Scottish Horse in two wars (as a boy, I remember his dinner-gong was a piper playing up and then down the antler-avenued Long Passage at Blair Castle). The 11th Marquess of Tweeddale was also very kind to me as a boy. His nickname was 'Giff' because he'd been Earl of Gifford. The state rooms of his wonderful Robert Adam house were the haunt of live goats (the family crest), although one of his daughters, 'Peanut', emerged at debutante dances with a small green snake called Freddie Bartholomew snuling up her startled partner's arm from an ill-shut handbag. Similarly, Cousin 'Weymie' Bath, the 5th Marquess, was originally Viscount Weymouth. He kept up the old tradition of wearing the Garter round knee-breeches whenever a fellow Knight of the Garter came to dinner. Nowadays, the nickname custom is kept up by such as 'Sunny' Duke of Marlborough, formerly Earl of Sunderland (whose pretty first wife, like the actress Georgina Ward, is sprung from beautiful Aunt Georgie Moncreiffe's marriage to Lord Dudley); also by the Earl of Carnarvon's heir 'Porchie', Lord Porchester (married to a Wyoming rancher-family granddaughter of the late Countess of Portsmouth whose sister married my pioneer rancher great-uncle Malcolm Moncreiffe, a friend of 'Buffalo Bill'), also by the Earl of Warwick's heir 'Brookie', Lord Brooke [*who has now succeeded to the Earldom* – ED].

Nevertheless, it is *Debrett* that gives us the skeleton on which the bones of so much national as well as social history can be fleshed. To delve deeper it is necessary to go to *Burke's Peerage* but that is not a hardy annual [*last published edition 1970* – ED]. Nevertheless, *Debrett* gives us the clues if we will follow them. It's good that modern thought and legislation has removed from innocent offspring the stigma of illegitimacy. So we can rejoice to find in *Debrett* the several ducal scions, such as Richmond and Buccleuch, who continue the Royal House of Stuart through Charles II; the Earl of Munster, who through William IV continues the House of Hanover that in turn sprang from the ancient Italian Lombard rulers of Este; the Mountbatten peers, who came to us by way of Hesse and Brabant, ultimately from the dominant house in Belgium at the end of the Dark Ages; and perhaps above all the Duke of Beaufort, a true hot-tempered in the saddle, gentle mannered out of the saddle, Plantagenet still with us.

But the majority of gentlemen in *Debrett* don't bear titles, though they are cadets of those who do. Humphrey Lyttelton, Ludovic Kennedy and P.G. Wodehouse are all in *Debrett*; if you remember to look them up under (Lyttelton) Viscount Cobham (Kennedy) Marquess of Ailsa and (Wodehouse) Earl of Kimberley. And all the while, if you delve into these apparently dust-covered family statistics, you'll unearth many a pleasurably eerie skull, especially if your view of British social Society is panoptic. Thus, should you visit the House of Lords out of curiosity, you'll see on the Government Front Bench my elder son's Godfather, the Premier Baron of England. He is Charles Stourton, Lord Mowbray, Segrave and Stourton, and a Lord-in-Waiting, but occasionally gets letters from firms addressed to 'Messrs Mowbray, Segrave & Stourton, Ltd'. This genial but conscientious peer disguises himself as Bertie Wooster, and goes so far as to have a black patch over the eye that was shot out by the Boche in battle when he was an officer of the Grenadier Guards. Appropriately the first officers on that scene were the Duke of Rutland and a son of Lord Kemsley, sending for the doctor while Charles Stourton was demanding a priest instead. For his family have never changed from Catholicism, despite the centuries of persecution. But the quiet continuity in which our national family history flows on past even major set-backs is perhaps summarised by *Debrett's* entry about his ancestor Charles, 8th Lord Stourton; 'Was executed March 16 1557, at Salisbury, in a halter of silk, for murdering two men named Hartgill'.

Books & Bookmen, 1973

Correct Form

I was in Salt Lake City when I was interviewed by successive telephone calls on the American wireless. Questioner after questioner asked, 'What does *Sir* Moncreiffe think about . . . ?' until the studio bell rang and a voice said 'Mr Moncreiffe; I do call you "Mr" don't I?' I thought 'less of that' and caught him out with a reply: 'Well, you could call me *Mr* as I'm a Master of Arts, but you can call me *Dr* if you prefer.'

New titles are more fun than they would be in an entirely non-hereditary system like that of the American senators, because they equate the new to the old in a continuous flow of history. A new snobbery is being encouraged whereby some peers' eldest sons think themselves so grand that they won't use their courtesy titles (this is a friendly dig at Lord Silchester) [*alias Mr Thomas Pakenham, son and heir of Lord Longford* – ED]. It's different when a real function is involved, like the peerages of Sir Max Aitken [*now resumed by his son Maxwell, 3rd Lord Beaverbrook* – ED] or Mr Victor Montagu (an MP as Viscount Hinchingbrooke, but disclaimed the Earldom of Sandwich when he succeeded his father), where they choose to remain free of the Upper House. My late cousin, who shared this house with me, used to call himself normally Lord James Stewart Murray and only be Duke of Atholl when functioning as such, for he said to be Duke of Atholl and live at Easter Moncreiffe would be like being King of Bulgaria and living at Nice.

The custom of putting letters after people's names has only arisen in comparatively modern times, but has proliferated as our enormous increase of population – and the rewarding of service to the economy and not just to the State – has led to a great expansion of our Orders of Chivalry and higher honours, together with the multiplication of degrees and appointments. Since these letters are but abbreviations, we can write them as we please. However, custom has evolved certain standard abbreviations, and most people seek guidance about present conventions. Officially and in business it's polite to get all that lettering right; for what's the use of earning all those gongs if the poor fellow can't use them?

Unconventional abbreviations can be misleading. For instance, whenever Henry Douglas-Home [*the BBC 'Birdman' who died in 1980* – ED] writes to me he puts the letters 'BF' after my name. I always take it that they stand for Brave Fellow.

We have only two hereditary knights, the Knight of Kerry who is the Green Knight, and the Knight of Glin who is the Black Knight;. for the

White Knight has gone amissing these many years. It may therefore seem rather unnecessary to need to know the correct way of addressing them. However, I was asked this very question by the barman of one of my clubs which one of the two hereditary knights had just joined. The correct answer, which is given in this book, is just 'Knight'. So, if staying at Glin Castle, you will know to say 'Good-night, Knight'.

I myself also have to put up with being laughed at for having such a quaint name as Moncreiffe of that Ilk, which simply means 'Moncreiffe of that same', and which we have used since the Middle Ages because it gives other people such fun.

Like most of you, I'm a keen reader of gossip columns. The only thing is, it's hard really to believe the latest rumour about one's friends' private lives when the gossip writer evidently knows them so little as to be unable to get their names right. Anybody who refers to Lady Mary de Vere as 'Lady de Vere' or to Lady Montmorency as 'Lady Mary Montmorency' can't know much about them really. So all columnists *must* get their bosses to buy *Debrett's Correct Form* for them, so that they can add verisimilitude to otherwise bald and unconvincing stories.

From I.M.'s Introduction to *Debrett's Correct Form* Edited by Patrick Montague-Smith (Debrett's Peerage, 2nd edn, 1976).

Modern Manners

My own attitude has always been simple. As a child, I was taught that the good fairy Do-As-*You*-Would-Be-Done-By should be emulated. But adult observation soon reinforced the lessons of history that the fairy was slightly mistaken; a zealous 'do-gooder' who 'knows best' often causes people present inconvenience 'for their own good', distressing them now for some future pie in the sky they may not prefer. The true spirit to emulate is that of Do-As-*They*-Would-Be-Done-By, whether one agrees with them or not.

Confucius felt that if there was a correct mode of behaviour prescribed for every possible situation, the everyday stress and grind of human contacts would as it were be oiled to everybody's benefit. Survivals from such former codes can be fun, such as the custom in Guards Officers' Messes of wearing one's uniform cap at meals derived from the pre-1914 custom of a man wearing his hat in his own house or club but not in other people's.

To me, manners should be natural. The object is to put everyody at their ease, whatever their age or rank. This has sometimes to be played by ear and needs tactful observation, as even Queen Victoria discovered; she was served first and as soon as she put down her knife and fork everybody's plate was removed. Nobody told the Queen that everyone had not finished, until one dinner at Windsor Lord Hartington called to the footman to bring him back his plate, whereupon Her Majesty enquired into and stopped the custom.

From I.M.'s Preface to *Debrett's Etiquette and Modern Manners* edited by Elsie Burch Donald (Debrett's Peerage, 1980).

If It's Me, It's U

It was pitch dark. We were cold, wet and uncomfortable. I had been blown up by a shell, punctured a bit by shrapnel, ignominiously crushed by a dislodged boulder, and could only limp at a crawl while my soldier servant Guardsman Fraser carried my equipment. So I had remained behind on the mountainside at midnight with our patrol officer Dicky Buckle and his rear party, who were laying mines on the goat track to cover the Brigade's withdrawal. We weren't sure how close the enemy were on our heels. It was the end of the first (unsuccessful) battle of Monte Camino, now a battle honour on the Colours. We were the last on 'the Hill', a fine moment, we felt, in regimental history. Naturally, therefore, we were discussing heraldry.

Having established the basic fact that the Buckles were fairly *nouveau*, springing from an Elizabethan burgher who was Lord Mayor of London, we had got on to considering the 94 quarterings that Dicky had inherited on his mother's side. These were quite impressive. I recollect that we had reached the exact point when he said:

'I quarter Hoo'.

'Who?' I replied, mishearing him in mental transliteration.

'Hoo'.

'Yes, but who?'

'Hoo', Dicky went on hooting like an owl.

Suddenly it dawned on me that he meant the simple *argent & sable* coat of the mediaeval Lord Hoo of Hoo, an unpopular Knight of the Garter much derided in song by the revolting peasantry at the time of Jack Cade's rebellion. This exact moment remains fixed in my mind, as we were recalled to our rather macabre modern surroundings by a loud explosion followed by yells mingled with oaths. One of the mines we'd just laid had claimed their first victim.

Now, politeness apart, the true U reaction to the information that Dicky quartered the arms of this obscure mediaeval peer would either be boredom or interest. So too would doubtless be the reaction of most ordinary people. But a standard non-U reaction would be to resent him and feel he needed 'taking down a peg' for 'showing off'. The middle classes, perhaps sensing some outflanking Jones, would raise their plaintive bleat: 'Who does he think he is?' I well remember a peer, giving a public lecture about his stately home, mentioning (for it was relevant) that he descended from King Charles II. The non-U female next to me turned in typical misunderstanding to express her shock at such conceit. Her Pavlov-bitch comment ended resentfully: 'I *descend* – Period'.

This is a succinct form of the standard non-U crack, when any forebears are mentioned that 'we all descend from Adam'. The funny thing about most of the people who make it, is that few of them realise it's actually true. Biologists, when prodded hard enough, have to admit that every man who has ever lived since the world began has inherited his 'Y' chromosome (the genetic factor that makes him a man) from the same single humanoid being, just one person who lived at a particular moment long, long ago – however he in turn was evolved. The biologists dislike admitting this even more, when it's pointed out that we had a convenient name for this being even before my *coz* Darwin postulated him. For *adam* is simply a very ancient Mesopotamian word meaning Man.

In Adam, therefore, we have the embryo gentleman. But just as from the original equidae there evolved race-horses and cobs and cart-horses for different purposes, so too it has been with mankind – though fortunately we are continually crossbred.

Meanwhile, a moment's reflection will show that even had we all remained in an egalitarian Garden of Eden like lilies of the field, toiling not nor spinning, some of you would have evolved into nature's gentle men, and other of us into natural boors. For, whenever the brotherhood of man is most loudly proclaimed today, one would have to be pretty tone-deaf not to hear the primaeval voice of Cain.

This jealousy of our more fortunate or distinguished brethren, and especially of their children, is the deepest stain that marks out the present day as the Age of Envy. It's rather ungentlemanly, to say the least: and hardly brotherly love.

Owing to the crossbreeding that has kept mankind inter-related throughout the aeons, we've all had forefathers of every rank whether we can trace them or not. The most recent serf from whom I can personally trace my descent was freed by the Bishop of Zagreb in 1552: the most recent king from whom I can do the same died exactly ten years earlier. We shouldn't look down on those rude forefathers of the hamlet, without whose romps in the hay we could never have been born. But it ill becomes us also not to look up to the achievements of those grander forebears who led our nations upwards, and who evolved polite codes of conduct – courtesy means the manners of the Court – that weren't always honoured only in the breach. Nevertheless, 'the boast of heraldry' aptly sums up the poet's distaste for overdoing it.

In fact, therefore, everybody has as many ancestors as everybody else. No family is older than any other. We weren't each evolved separately like Pooh-Bah from some different personal amoeba or primordial protoplasm. It's simply that some families have maintained a known position, and their doings have been recorded longer than those of others. The Sackvilles of Buckhurst, for example, are the only Norman family who can actually prove that they were *not* at the battle of Hastings. But 'the 14th Mr Wilson' (to recall the 14th Earl of Home's famous retort when quizzed about a fellow Prime Minister) cannot prove that his direct male line ancestor wasn't one of the leaders in that battle. All the same, most people assume that descents that can't be established aren't likely to be distinguished.

As a result, U people in England – except among the tiny group of interbred ancient Catholic families like the Stourtons and Berkeleys – have an unease of discussing family history unless quite sure they are among themselves. They don't want inadvertently to make some middle-class worthy of uncertain pedigree, who might chance to be present, feel out of it. On the Continent, indeed, grand pedigrees and family histories tend to be limited to a fairly well-defined aristocratic group. But in England, precisely because the division between U and non-U is so blurred, and can so easily be crossed, delicacy imposes discretion.

In Scotland, of course, there is no such inhibition about discussing ancestry. This is for two reasons. First, we are so small a country that everybody can know who everybody else is, and there's neither need nor opportunity to pretend. But secondly, and this is a Good Thing, our noble clannish traditions are divided vertically between Names, not horizontally between classes. Campbells or Grahams may be dukes or dustmen, but they all share Roots, have their own special tartan and historic tradition. Moreover this is often demonstrable in practice as well as in principle. For instance, my late wife, as Countess of Erroll in her own right, was Chief of the Hays and thoroughly imbued with Hay tradition. But so equally was Mr Hay, the (unpaid) cox of the Fraserburgh lifeboat. He told me that when he joined the Royal Navy as an ordinary seaman, his father had reminded him that his forefathers had served before the mast in every generation since before Trafalgar and that, while ever mindful of the traditions of the Service, he must

I.M. with Hermione, and O'Higgins, in front of Easter Moncreiffe.

TOP: I.M. with Kisty Lady Hesketh, Robert and Janie Jarman at Easter Moncreiffe, 1984.

BELOW: I.M. in the hall at Easter Moncreiffe, with Shaun, the Irish wolfhound, 1969.

never forget that he was a Hay and always live up to the great traditions of his Name. His first nautical ancestor had been an impoverished 18th century cadet of the Hays of Rannes, and I could trace his line back without difficulty to a Hay baron of the 13th century. Here *noblesse oblige* was visibly at work in its most classless Scottish sense. Such collective nobiliary tradition is nowadays expressed particularly through the numerous and flourishing clan societies.

To revert to the contrast between the English and the Continental ideas of U, great confusion arises because a foreigner uses the word 'noble' to mean an *untitled* gentleman of known ancestry, whereas the English use the same word to mean only a Peer of the Realm and his immediate titled relations. Few English people therefore understand what is meant when it's explained that Napoleon Bonaparte was a noble by birth. Toqueville (by the way, my French friends have always told me it's non-U to refer to anybody as 'de' unless you use a prefix, *e.g.* you can refer to Monsieur de Monbrison, Amaury de Monbrison, or plain Monbrison, but never just to 'de Monbrison') observed that, as the position of a French untitled noble was fixed and unchangeable, they could know whom they pleased; but as the position of an English gentleman was judged rather by his way of life, Englishmen were anxious to avoid meeting the wrong sort of people and getting ranked with them by association.

On the Continent, apart from the Church, the upper class of noble gentlemen were expected to serve the Crown, for instance in the Army or Navy or in diplomacy, rather than engage in commerce for their own benefit; and indeed were only modestly paid but long freed from taxation as a result. Originally the knightly families holding manorial estates, the immemorial *uradel*, they were reinforced over the centuries by statesmen, by commanders in war (the *noblesse d'épée*) and by parliamentarians and judges (the *noblesse de la robe*). However, the great cities of Italy and the Empire produced patrician families of equivalent status; and grand banking families like the Medici and the Fuggers attained princely rank. But always the concept existed abroad of the legally identifiable gentleman.

In England, similar considerations applied only to the extent that in my youth, if a gentleman already had enough money, he was expected on the whole to enter the armed services or the Diplomatic Service for modest pay, otherwise the Church or the Law, and only commerce on the grand scale, with a bias in that case in favour of merchant banking. And there was always too the Empire, to go out and govern. But trade followed the flag. Though Napoleon was mauled by what he called the English leopards, he summed them up in his famous epigram as 'a nation

129

of shopkeepers'. It is of the essence, however, that the English are romantic shopkeepers, at their best in war. So the English gentleman came to differ widely from his Continental counterpart, although every gentleman was still a potential officer in war or a potential justice of the peace, in that he was not demeaned by engaging in commerce for his own benefit – so long as he behaved like a gentleman. And in time, an able man could rise to become a gentleman by his way of life. For though it's no longer birth alone that counts, still less is it wealth alone, but rather certain indefinable attitudes of mind that go with the gentlemanly concept.

On the other hand, it would be idle to pretend that birth and at least a modicum of wealth are not a head start. If it wasn't so, there would soon be nothing much to emulate. Obviously excellent heredity combined with excellent environment tends to give good results. Without an élite, or if the élite had been deliberately held back by egalitarianism, we would never have left the caves. When a man dies in primitive New Guinea, his hut is burned and his cooking pots smashed, because his children already have huts and cooking pots of their own; as it were primitive council houses. By this 100 per cent Capital Transfer Tax they are safely held back to the lowest common denominator even more firmly than we are going to be after a generation or two of (say) 60 per cent CTT. Meanwhile, however, we still have some gentlemen of ancient birth with the freedom to speak their minds that goes with private means.

Within these limits there's great scope for teasing. If the Duke of Westminster, head of the house of Grosvenor, is a multi-millionaire grandee of impeccable Norman lineage, it's possible to trump him by producing a Scrope. The head of the equally ancient Norman house of Scrope is the squire of Danby. But in 1385 their positions were reversed. Sir Robert Grosvenor was a simple Cheshire knight. Lord Scrope was Lord High Chancellor of England. They came up here to bash us Scots, and started a rival row instead because they found themselves both wearing the same coat of arms: *Azure a bend Or* (a golden diagonal band on a blue field). The celebrated case of Scrope *v.* Grosvenor in the Court of Chivalry went on for five years. Everybody sided with the great Lord Scrope against this obscure Grosvenor knight. It was pointed out that although one of them, a Chief Justice, had been put into a legal career (*'mis a la ley'*), the Scropes had been *'graundes gentilhommes et de noblez'* since the Conquest. The poet Chaucer, Harry 'Hotspur' and Henry of Bolingbroke (afterwards King Henry IV), all gave evidence for the Scropes.

Eventually the Lord High Constable gave judgement in favour of Lord

Scrope. When Grosvenor appealed to King Richard II, he was told he had lost and must change his coat-of-arms to a wheatsheaf (now well known to clients of the National Westminster Bank). The Grosvenors never forgot their lost *bend Or*, and after the 1st Duke of Westminster won the Derby in 1880 with his racehorse Bend Or, his grandson and heir was nicknamed 'Bend Or'. As 'Bend Or' Westminster he was recommended for a Victoria Cross in the First World War.

Meanwhile, the Scropes had refused to change their religion at the Reformation, so had been banned for centuries as Roman Catholics from all office and preferment, and their peerages had gone into abeyance among co-heiresses. The head of the family is still lord of the manor of Danby, which they inherited during the Wars of the Roses. He is Major Scrope and the Duke of Westminster is the Duke of Westminster, yet in the inner U world he still commands a special respect. People no longer wear coats-of-arms over their armour. But the Scropes still have the last laugh. They wear a special family tie: blue with diagonal gold bands – *Azure a bend Or*. Lady Leonora Grosvenor [*now the Countess of Lichfield* – ED] and Miss Diana Scrope have both stayed with me at Easter Moncreiffe simultaneously without a fracas. But Victor Grosvenor of the Life Guards, definitely a Hon. out of Nancy Mitford's Hons cupboard, has given me a standing order to find a very small Scrope for him to bash.

This brings us to Nancy Mitford's original article on 'The English Aristocracy' in *Noblesse Oblige*, and Evelyn Waugh's 'Open Letter' in reply to it, that caused such a furore in the 1950s. The fuss was primarily because it drew attention to Professor Alan Ross's work as a philologist, in which, as a professional observer, he had noted the linguistic demarcation of upper-class English, for which he coined the abbreviation U as opposed to non-U. This work, while of natural interest to his fellow philologists, was perhaps rather embarrassing when publicised socially through no fault of his. It only made U people self-conscious when talking naturally in the way to which they'd always been accustomed, and could obviously hurt or at least irritate non-U people.

It's rather like our perennial problem in Scotland. Most, but not all, U people in Scotland speak in the accent, use the expressions, and behave in the ways, described as U by Professor Ross. They don't do this by affectation, but because it's the way their parents talked before them. The Scottish aristocracy have in fact always tended to speak the language of the political centre. My own forebears have almost certainly lived here at Moncreiffe since Pictish times, although we only assumed the surname from our lands some seven or eight centuries ago. By the end of the Dark Ages they spoke Gaelic (Moncreiffe is the Old Gaelic place-name *Monadh Craoibhe*), then at the Court of St Margaret perhaps briefly Anglo-Saxon. During the Scottish War of Independence in the twelve and thirteen-hundreds they spoke Norman-French. (Whatever languages they spoke to their followers – Welsh or Northumbrian or Gaelic – if Wallace and Bruce met they talked to each other in Norman-French). From the 15th century onwards my forefathers spake Court Scots; but after the Union, with the move of the political centre from Edinburgh to London, they gradually came to speak what Professor Ross defines as U English.

This is, of course, nothing like the accent or mode of speech of the Elizabethan English courtiers, which doubtless survives in some of the Southern States of the USA. It has, instead, been evolved collectively by the U British since the Union. People aren't surprised that Lord Devon doesn't nowadays speak broad Devonshire, nor the Duke of Norfolk with a Norfolk accent, yet they are somewhat surprised that Lord Glasgow doesn't use a glottal stop and say 'Hoots mon'. On the other hand, the situation would doubtless change naturally once again after a generation of Home Rule.

I myself, however, don't want to get involved in any embarrassing U-pontifications, except to support the well-known quip: 'If it's me it's U'. This is a modern version of the famous remark by a 16th century highland chief misplaced by his host: 'Wherever Macdonald is sitting, that is the head of the table'. Earlier in this book, Professor Ross has brought readers up-to-date with U speech today, and the other contributors have described U life so much better than the What the Butler Saw sort of peeps we get from non-U playwrights and novelists. Lord Harewood in particular serves to remind us that most U people work just as hard as most other classes, differing principally only perhaps in outlook, and of course rather harder than those who have the 'right' to strike. The principal workaday U feature, I rather think, is that off duty all ages tend to converse naturally and associate in their homes and clubs without undue regard to age or position, whereas the urban middle classes tend to move in the same age group and income group from the cradle to the grave. I noticed this especially when I was ADC to a U general and attaché to a U ambassador. But it's only the gossip columnists who pretend that aristocratic life is one unending holiday – which is no doubt what many of their readers (vicariously but mistakenly) would like their own lives to be.

When she was preparing her celebrated article on 'The English Aristocracy', Mrs Peter Rodd, better known as Nancy Mitford, asked me if I would help her over points of fact, as she was in Paris most of the time. Her questions shewed a desire to be thorough. She wanted to know how many peers had been divorced? About one in eight. How many living peers had done well in the War? She obviously meant any war: Lord Dunmore, for example, had won his Victoria Cross in 1897 but was still alive. Taking all living peers of all ages, apart from peeresses in their own right and minors, nearly a quarter had either been mentioned in despatches or decorated in battle. How many peers were Roman Catholics? I telephoned to Lord Mowbray. He asked if I included Irish peers; we settled for members of the House of Lords only; he looked in the Catholic Director; the answer was 47. How many peers were patrons of livings? I hadn't the foggiest idea. And so on.

Perhaps her most interesting question was, how many peers really belonged to old families? This was interesting because I was surprised by the answer as it unfolded. For I discovered that well over a third of our hereditary peerage still belonged to families that had borne arms in the direct male line since the Middle Ages. So I was rather pleased when Evelyn Waugh, in his excellent Open Letter to Nancy Mitford, wrote: 'You say that 382 peers have arms granted before 1485 *and have inherited them in the male line* . . . The statement staggers me'. But then I was distinctly miffed, if that's the right word, when he went on to suggest that her adviser had overlooked the passage of old names through heiresses to new husbands' families: 'I think you should have questioned your pursuivant more closely before accepting his figures'. I didn't know him well enough in those days to ask him not to teach his grandmother to suck eggs, and indeed always had a special respect for his brilliance as an observer of contemporary life. But I did know enough, for example, to realise that the ancestor of the present Noel Earls of Gainsborough in 1485 was not a Noel, but the Red Douglas in person, or that in the male lion Lord Eglinton is a Wintoun and not a Montgomerie, or that Lord De La Warr is a West and not a Sackville. The real reason for the surprisingly high number is that, almost without exception, the peers of Scotland help to swell this pre-1485 category.

Eventually, Nancy Mitford sent me her typescript. She didn't, nevertheless, accept any of my criticisms of it, some of which followed the lines of Evelyn Waugh's later Open Letter. She seemed to me to compound the different muddled misusages of the words 'noble' and 'aristocrat'; and then to link them to the ridiculous notion that they applied only and automatically to all peers. She set so much store by the courtesy style of Hon., dependent on the title conferred on her grandfather in 1902, as though she was very nouveau *noblesse de la robe*; when all the time she was immemorially *uradel*, descended in the direct male line from the mediaeval Mitfords of Mitford (what the

Austrians would call *zu* Mitford and the Scots Mitford of that Ilk) whose beautifully simple coat was, and is, *Argent a fesse between three moles Sable*. Her forefather, Sir John Mitford of Mitford, was Knight of the Shire for Northumberland in 1369, and a later Mitford of Mitford fell at the battle of Towton in the Wars of the Roses. How could she have thought that her old mediaeval aristocratic family were made into aristocrats by getting a bit of paper from Edward VII? Sir Percy Blakeney would have turned in his grave.

Evelyn Waugh put the true situation snob-wise very well: 'the basic principle of English social life is that *everyone* (everyone, that is to say, who comes to the front door) *thinks he is a gentleman*. There is a second principle of almost equal importance: *everyone draws the line of demarcation immediately below his own heels*'. This is a typically English version of Field-Marshal Prince Windisch-Grätz's famous crack that *der Mensch beginnt beim Baron*: mankind begins with barons. But there is another aspet, summed up in its negative form in the martial offence of 'conduct unbecoming an officer and a gentleman'. It's positive form should not, in my opinion, simply follow that of the good fairy Do-as-you-would-be-done-by in *The Water Babies*. For this can give *carte blanche* to fanatically self-righteous opinionated do-gooders, upsetting people 'for their own good'. As Dicky Buckle himself once put it to me, a gentleman should not take pleasure in class distinctions, but should rather seek to ignore them. He should of course lay more emphasis on kindness – for instance, he shouldn't ostentatiously stick to U-shibboleths when drinking with or greeted by non-U speakers who say 'cheers' or 'pleased to meet you', but should try to respond courteously in like manner. Of course it rather goes against the grain.

Of course, too, the nobility and gentry who formed the old aristocracy didn't always live up to their ideals. As Sir George Sitwell pointed out, one of the earliest recorded gents was 'Robert Erdeswyke of Stafford, gentilman', who in 1414 was charged with 'procuring the murder of one Thomas Page, who was cut to pieces while on his knees begging for his life'. But their ideals were there as a shining example all the same. Everybody understands what is, or rather ought to be, meant by one's word of honour as a *gentleman*. Nobody would have accused Hitler or Stalin of being gentlemen. Nor would anybody describe them as noble characters. Yet the word *noble* has so often denoted 'of lofty character or ideals' that that's got into the dictionary as one of its meanings. Of course there's always the danger of the gentleman becoming the genteel man. However, 'truly noble' or 'a perfect gentleman' still mean something less unattractive than 'a complete boor'. *Aristocracy* is from the Greek words 'aristos' meaning 'best' and 'kratia' meaning rule, though the best people can so easily become the Best People. It's of course impossible to have both quality and equality, which latter is the opposite of equality of opportunity. But true quality can stagnate into the Quality. Courtesy – I repeat, the manners of a Court – and Chivalry, the code of the *chevaliers*, cannot but be a Good Thing, much to be encouraged in the young as one gets older (though note that one shouldn't treat people 'cavalierly' oneself). Though birth counts for less nowadays, most people would still rather behave as though they were 'well-bred' than 'ill-bred'. As we become increasingly classless financially, the English concept that a gentleman is recognised by his code of conduct and manner of life must make it possible for more and more people to be gentlemen because they have chosen to be, and so are.

But don't take all this too seriously. Gents should never appear too keen in public, nor lose their sense of humour. Naturally they are accustomed to excel, but equally to appear to do it with ease and not too openly. Fine models of gentlemen are to be found in the kindly heroes of P. G. Wodehouse or in the subtle good-humoured concealed character and remarkable but apparently effortless achievements of the Scarlet Pimpernel. For a debonair gentleman – we can alas no longer say a gay, debonair cavalier – so often conceals the skilled professional behind an apparently amateur façade.

Nancy Mitford went in for the occasional quiet tease herself. Her broad thesis was that in U speech a novel French word shouldn't normally be used when an old English one will do, *e.g.* she preferred 'napkin' to 'serviette'. Into the novel French 'refained' category she had wrongly consigned the word mirror, which in fact came over with the Conqueror. When she visited us in Scotland, I pointed out in vain that Shakespeare used the words 'mirror' and 'looking glass' in the same passage. At last, I wrote to her in Paris to play my trump card. My children's ancestral uncle, Sir Alexander Boyd, beheaded in 1469 after kidnapping the boy king, James III while instructing him in knightly exercises, was known to his contemporaries (long before the French governesses of the industrial revolution's *nouveaux riches*) as 'a Mirror of Chivalry'. How was I to describe him to my sons?

She sent back a postcard: 'Did they really call him that? How vulgar of them.'

From *Debrett's U & Non-U Revisited*, edited by
Richard Buckle (1978)

Are Aristocrats People?

Andrew Sinclair complains in *The Last of the Best: The Aristocracy of Europe in the Twentieth Century* (Weidenfeld & Nicholson, 1969) that our aristocrats (it's never quite clear whether he means titled folk or gentlemen) 'never have co-operated with each other against the pressures of society'; by which I hope he doesn't mean ganging up against the rest of the People. This is because the aristocracy are not only people, like everybody else in Britain, but probably the most independent-minded group among the People. Dr Sinclair doesn't quite see them as real people, but (as Arthur Koestler did in his earlier books) depicts from two-dimensionally, like those irritating toy soldiers that are flat instead of moulded in the round.

His political views seem immediately evident from his use of such words as *bourgeois* (for middle-class), *rentier* (for a man freed by independent means), 'lord it over' (for run the show), 'myth' (for a view he doesn't share) and 'anachronism' (meaning a pious hope that something will 'wither away', except perhaps a marxist state). This combination leads to the suspicion that he hasn't yet had time to rethink, by his own independent critical thought, many of the continental ideas emotionally instilled into him at Cambridge during his adolescence.

Peasants (who tend to be two-dimensional too) are always starving, though no doubt they sometimes were. Blood-sports are bloodthirsty, which is true. It's wrong to execute murderers but left-wing intellectuals tend to be gleeful when even the best-natured aristocrats are 'executed' horribly with their little children (think of their mixed joy at the blood-bath when a mob liberated the Marquis de Sade from the Bastille). Sure enough, Dr Sinclair writes cheerfully about 1945, when in East Prussia they 'killed the doomed aristocratic game at point-blank range like hares in a hunt, driven on to the guns by the closing ring of *hungry* beaters' (cannibals, we presume?).

It is often a fault in reviewers to assume that errors of fact disprove the arguments in whose support they are advanced. It does not necessarily invalidate the point that stags (although woodland beasts in Central Europe) can menace crops, that it *should* have been in Czech Bohemia and not in Magyar Hungary that the stags of the Schwarzenbergs, Kolowrats and Liechtensteins gobbled up the corn of the peasants – starving as usual (how did these supermen survive?) – although the quotation cited by the author then moves the location even more mysteriously to the Ukraine.

Then, we are told that 'Venice, which remained independent rather longer than the rest, kept its lesser titles, so that a Venetian count is now worth a Genoese marquis'. Now, independent Venice had no hereditary titles save Patrician, and it was not until her annexation by Austria that the great families like Mocenigo and Morosini which had given past Doges to Venice were created Austrian counts. But the point still stands; a Venetian Patrician of a dogeal family is certainly worth his opposite number in Genoa. Daisy, Princess of Pless, is cited as an example of a German lady shocked by English ladies declaring openly that they had lovers. Yet Daisy Pless was an Englishwoman, whose family have been peers from before the Wars of the Roses and whose forefather fought at Crécy. Though this doesn't mean that the Germans wouldn't also have been shocked.

Again the Duke of Buccleuch's 'moderately distant' lineage goes back in the direct male line through four kings (if you count Darnley as one) to a Breton noble living a generation before the Norman Conquest, while Prince Esterházy's earliest proved forefather married well in the 16th century, and the Duke's 'fairly good' state includes Boughton and Drumlanrig which are quite as grand as Frakno: but without these after-dinner type embellishements the well-known tale cited of the Duke having 5,000 sheep and the Prince 5,000 shepherds still makes the author's point. And we all know about those Bostonian swells the Cabots speaking only to God, but it's as unnecessary as improbable to suggest that they have any older proved lineage than, say, Sir Francis Beaumont, whose forefather was Count of Brienne in 954, or Lord Mountbatten, whose ancestor was ruler of much of Belgium and abducted Charlemagne's greatgranddaughter in 846. The author's points are still true: the Cabots are what we call an 'old family' and he doesn't mind their aristocratic power because they are (so boringly) untitled.

A pedant could nag on indefinitely. Who on earth told Dr Sinclair that the Hohenzollerns, Electors of Brandenburg and Arch-Chamberlains of the Holy Roman Empire (as well as being Kings of Prussia outside it), belonged to the German 'low' aristocracy: by which he appears to mean Part III of the *Fürstliche Haüser* in the neo-*Gotha*, and all volumes below that? Which great families from 'Central and Eastern Europe' had 'escape funds abroad'? Most of my friends exiled from behind the Iron Curtain are working their way back from penury. Is it necessary in English to call Princess Irmgard of Bavaria 'Irmgard Princess von Bayern'; and wouldn't it be more relevant in a serious study to explain that she belongs to what has long been (and still is) one of the most talented (and therefore occasionally battiest) families there will ever have been, than to write of her horses and to comment 'In modern times, the dream of aristocratic excellence has been transferred from the human to the beast'?

All in all, the author's best work is perhaps the essay that forms the final chapter. But his most valuable contribution to popular thought about aristocracy is the sensible way in which he includes the Jews throughout the book. From the downfall of their mighty Khaza Empire almost until modern times, few members of this remarkably gifted amalgam of races were able (for staunchly religious reasons) to take their proper place among the titled aristocracy of Christendom. Luckily for western civilisation, the religious obstacle was removed in the last century. Our three Cohen peers and two Cohen baronets (who demonstrate perhaps the most ancient pedigree in the world, though not its links) belong to an aristocratic stock that has been in England for some time. But the recent tragedies of the continent have brought this country a great further influx of some of the best inherited brains in the world; we've had nothing like it since the Huguenots (*e.g.* our Portal viscount and baronet). It's to be hoped that our aristocracy will soon also assimilate the best of the newer arrivals, through both peerage and marriage.

Indeed, the author is a little unfair when he rightly praises our existing Jewish aristocracy for selective breeding, but condemns other aristocrats in general for doing the contrary, without in fact making any analysis of the true situation. He quotes Princess Catherine Radziwill, who was my mother's godmother and Cecil Rhodes's girl friend, as reporting of five great Austrian families that they 'constitute one large family.' Well, then, to take (for breeding purposes) only one of those named: the Schwarzenbergs have been one of the ablest families in Europe for four centuries. For example, Prince Schwarzenberg was the field-marshal who defeated Napoleon in person (himself quite a talented soldier) at the battle of Leipzig; Prince Felix Schwarzenberg was the Prime Minister who put Austria together again after the 1848 troubles; the present Prince Johannes Schwarzenberg was until recently Austrian Ambassador in London. Again, Lord O'Neill is quoted by the author as not taking these things too seriously, but the existence of his cousin Sir Con O'Neill (thought by some to have been a better diplomatist even than Mr George Brown his 'comrade' at the Foreign Office) and of his uncle Captain Terence O'Neill (the firm but tactful Premier of Ulster) [*now Lord O'Neill of the Maine*], demonstrates that he hasn't so far needed to. Such breeding stocks seem to be almost keeping up with the Joneses (who have, however, scooped this particular pool!).

Throughout the book, one thread, holds all together. Sometimes the author equates aristocracy with titles, sometimes not, but it's the title he dislikes. His crack about members of Pop 'lording it in peacock dress over the rest' almost suggests that he got this chip because some huge Lord Fauntleroy in a flowery waistcoat was rather beastly to him when he was a fag at Eton. He ought to cheer up and be a sensible snob like most of us, thinking titles no more than a bit of fun: even sometimes Romantick.

However, all this carping is rather unfair for Dr Sinclair does like a bit of fun. It was a mistake to read the book the first time as though it were meant to be a serious work of scholarship. On re-reading the book as a gossip column, it's most enjoyable. The illustrations too, are of the glossy magazine type. We are not shown great aristocratic statesmen like Lords Lansdowne and Halifax or Prince Hohenlohe-Schillingsfürst at work, but other aristocrats shooting, playing polo or dancing, or simply looking silly (Lady Angela St Clair Erskine *bis*): as if aristocratic life was one unending hearty holiday – which is no doubt what many readers (vicariously but mistakenly) would like their own lives to be.

Spectator, 25 April 1969

Club Crawl

Anthony Lejeune has given us what I for one have wanted for a long time – indeed once contemplated writing myself – a racy yet scholarly account of *The Gentlemen's Clubs of London* [Macdonald & Jane's, 1979]. We are taken on an engrossing tour of over 50 London clubs, famous haunts like the Travellers' and the Garrick, the Athenaeum and MCC, mostly surviving, yet themselves the dwindling but vigorous remnant of a far larger number, many of which he tells us about in his introduction. Of the clubs opened up for us, the oldest is White's, whose primacy has been maintained from the start, in the 17th century – for a long time Brooks's, founded about 80 years later, had a rule that a member who joined any other club, *except White's*, was struck off the books – and the youngest that the author describes was founded in 1955 as the Number Ten Club, but is already defunct.

The nucleus of the premier club began to form among the fashionable young regular customers who went to drink cocoa at White's Chocolate House, founded in 1693 on the site of what is now Boodle's in St James's Street. These sociable habitués eventually took over to the extent of excluding the general public, and clubbed themselves together. Already, by the reign of Queen Anne, my sensible forefather Harley, her chief minister, complained to Swift that 'at White's in St James's Street, young noblemen were fleeced by fashionable gamblers and profligates', and (we are told in Perry Colson's *White's*) 'every time Swift passed White's he used to shake his fist and curse it soundly'. Meanwhile, before the end of the 17th century, White's had moved across the street, and then back again in 1753 to its present position in 'the great house' at the top of St James's Street, where the famous bow window was built in place of the old entrance in 1811, just in time for Beau Brummell and the Regency dandies, who according to Gronow knew it as 'the bay window', to make it perhaps the most famous club window in the world. When in London, I often sit there of an afternoon gazing out, but drinking tea instead of cocoa, and munching buttered toast spread with 'gentleman's relish'.

Of the modern clubs, the author rightly calls Buck's 'the only London club to have been founded since the First World War which ranks, in social prestige and elegance, with the best of the St James's Street clubs; and like them, it is named after its founder. Captain Herbert Buckmaster and some other young officers of the Blues decided – the time, he recalled afterwards, was October 1918 and the place a war-stricken village called Guillemont – that, when they got back to England, 'they would start a club'. Although in the Foot Guards myself, when I joined Buck's over 30 years ago Rule One was still that members were to be 'officers of the Household Cavalry and their friends'.

My own original introduction to London club life came unexpectedly in 1937. One of my closest friends at Stowe was George Rodney, afterwards killed in the War. We were drawn together by a love of family continuity and traditional ways, and perhaps also a feeling of possible future alienation from the hub of what was then still the Empire. I was being brought up for the Diplomatic Service, which meant in those days a lifetime *en poste* abroad. George's father, Lord Rodney, had commuted for a lump sum the hereditary pension of £2,000 a year settled in 1793 by a grateful nation on the great Admiral's successors in the peerage, and had used it to buy a ranch in Alberta. So George too envisaged a lifetime in Canada. But we both wanted to preserve a foothold, as it were, near the Court of St James's.

One day George hit on the solution, and asked me what club I was down for, as he understood it took so long to get into any of them that we ought to have been put up at birth. On enquiry next holidays, I referred to Cousin Archie, the family clubman, who had left 'the House' at Oxford in 1879 to join the 2nd Life Guards as the result of a sudden vacancy caused by the Zulu War. He replied that I was a bit young for the Marlborough, but being rather bookish would be suited by the

Carlton: that a family friend who had been at Harrow in the 'Seventies with my grandfather would therefore put me up, and that he himself would second me. Thinking nothing would happen for many years, I was astounded to receive a missive from the Carlton Club while still aged 17. It ran: 'You have been proposed for this club by Lord Ernest Hamilton and seconded by Sir George Arthur, Bart, MVO, and were this day elected a member. Your attention is drawn to Rule IV, a copy of which is enclosed.' This said one had to be a member of the Conservative and Unionist Party. These startling lines are still engraved on my mind, for the missive continued 'The entrance fee is 40 guineas and the annual subscription is 17 guineas. We would therefore be grateful to receive your cheque for 57 guineas'.

Such untold wealth was beyond Aladdin's cave to my schoolboy pocket money of a pound or two, but my equally startled family, although not best pleased, paid up as Cousin Archie (Sir George Arthur) had taken so much trouble. It turned out that when my name had come up for election, one of the committee had remarked that nobody had been elected at the age of 17 before. But Lord Clanwilliam, the chairman, had pointed out that the next candidate on the list was Sir Derek Keppel, who was 73, and had added: 'This gives them an average age of 45, surely very suitable for a member'. It was, however, one thing to be elected, but quite another to convince Bonar, the hall porter, that I wasn't joking when I turned up at the front door in my Harrods boys' department blue suit. In those days, as it was the confidential home of the Conservative party, only members were allowed into the main clubhouse in Pall Mall, while all guests, male or female, were sent round to the new annexe behind, in Carlton House Terrace, that had once been my Aunt Georgie Dudley's house. The porter tried hard to send me round there, until the secretary arrived to convince him that this schoolboy really was a member. My age didn't seem odd to Cousin Archie, as his contemporary, my grandfather, had joined White's at the age of 18 and been a member for seven years before dying aged 25.

Anthony Lejeune tells us of the Carlton Club that 'in October 1940 the building was destroyed by German bombs; only by great good luck were Harold Macmillan, Quintin Hogg and other Conservative notables, who were in the club at the time, not killed'. I had been in the club myself that afternoon, and went round next day to find that the bomb had gone slap through the chair in the library in which I'd earlier been sitting. We then moved to new premises, taking over Arthur's former clubhouse in St James's Street, where the club still is.

At 21, I joined the Guards' Club, now merged with the Cavalry Club. At 22 I found myself also a member of Boodle's with its fine 18th century saloon, and of Brooks's with its famous Great Subscription Room which contains 'the gaming table with a slice cut out to give room for Charles James Fox's tummy'. Next year I was elected to Pratt's where members dine together convivially at a communal table in the candlelit basement. It belongs to the Duke of Devonshire, but its most famous proprietor was Willie Walsh, afterwards 4th Lord Ormathwaite, maternal grandson of its founder, the Duke of Beaufort. I was delighted to find here among the hippopotamus jaws and stuffed platypus, a cartoon of my great-grandfather Sir Thomas Moncreiffe, who was one of the earliest members.

Sir Thomas, although a member of White's, was also a founder member of the Turf Club. When I myself joined the Turf in 1945, towards the end of the War, the club was still on its original site at the corner of Clarges Street and Piccadilly. Entering in uniform, I said to Stringer, the hall porter, 'My name is Captain Moncreiffe, and I'm a new member'. 'Any relation to Captain Ronald Moncreiffe?' he enquired. I replied in some surprise that a great-uncle of that name had been in the Siege of Mafeking but had died of drink soon after the Boer War. To my greater astonishment, Stringer observed; 'I knew him well when he was a member here in the 'Nineties'. Stringer was a worthy predecessor at the Turf of Grace, now [1979] the doyen of hall porters in succession to Newman of Brooks's.

Every club has its own character, and the same people are in some way transmuted when you meet them in different clubs. Some people regard clubs solely as a convenience, to leave luggage, cash a cheque or have not too expensive a meal. But true clubmen find in their club an extended family, and one, moreover, in which one can choose one's relations. It's like maintaining a *pied-à-terre* in London with servants whom one knows well, and what my wife calls a permanent cocktail party of one's friends. To me, every club is like belonging to yet another fascinating family according to one's mood. That is, perhaps, why club mergers are so rarely completely successful, each of the partners losing some essence of their original character.

I have always thought that clubs shouldn't wait to see who wants to join, and then grumble, but should rather consider who they would like to join and then encourage them to be put up. So, when I became a member of the Committee of the Turf Club 20 years ago, I thought out what suitable young members we ought to have and then persuaded them to be put up. It's necessary to consider first, whether a candidate belongs broadly to the category from which a club is drawn, in order to preserve its special character, and only then whether he would also be congenial as a fellow member. While writing this review, I came on some correspondence of that epoch expressing to the Secretary my misgivings at having proposed or seconded as many as half-a-dozen candidates at a single election; but got the reassuring reply that our then president, 'the Duke of Norfolk says it is quite all right as long as they are your candidates'. In the club is a book showing all the members since its foundation in 1864, together with their proposers and seconders. It's thus possible, by looking up one's proposer's proposer's proposer and seconder's proposer's seconder and so on back to founder members, to trace one's own club lineage, so to speak. Some years ago, I spent some hours browsing in that book and came to the conclusion that I was a club ancestor, as it were, of about a third of the then members. Anyhow, the Turf has now perhaps the best young membership in London.

Anthony Lejeune writes in his introduction that it's conventionally the proper thing to resign if your candidate is blackballed. This may be so in the less exclusive clubs, but would have created an impossible situation in the aristocratic clubs in the old days of cliques. Looking through the Turf Club candidates' books in Victorian times, when blackballing was intense, I found that although my great-grandfather Sir Thomas Moncreiffe was a founder member, two of his sons-in-law were blackballed. One was the Duke of Atholl, who had 200,000 acres and a private army yet was pilled as long as 'C & O', obviously Lord Cork and Orrery, was chairman; but put up again and immediately elected as soon as 'W' succeeded him. The other was Lord Dudley, who had an income of a thousand golden sovereigns a day but evidently had some enemies in the club. He was blackballed one autumn, but promptly put up again in the spring by Admiral Rous himself, then the undisputed autocrat of the racing world, *i.e.* the actual Turf, and elected at once. Meanwhile nobody had resigned.

Another custom that has arisen through the widening of what used to be called Society, is that of enlisting 'signatures in support' beyond those of the proposer and seconder. This used to apply only to the sort of American-style club in which businessmen move slowly in their own age-group and income-group from the cradle to the grave. But some of even the best clubs now require sometimes as many as 20 such signatures, which leads to a lot of undignified lobbying, not always pushed hardest on behalf of the more suitable candidates. For my part, it would seem wiser on the whole to have a really good Committee who made it their business to know who the candidates were, and select those most suitable to fill any vacancies, as we do in the Royal Caledonian Hunt. Thirty years ago in the Turf Club, for instance, it was particularly frowned on if anybody but the proposer and seconder signed the page. At the Beefsteak alone, that luncheon conversation club with its single

143

table, *two* seconders were required when I joined in 1946. But it had been different, of course, at Oxbridge. At either university one's whole 'life' there lasted only three years, and it was necessary to ascertain a candidate's standing rapidly by the number of signatures that indicated his popularity; as, for example, when I was a member of the Grid at Oxford. And it was probably from Oxbridge, by way of the wartime generation who returned there while sometimes already belonging to London clubs, that the custom spread to London itself. However, the greatest change of all during my club life has been the gradual introduction of the bar, often strongly opposed at the time but now the welcome hub of every club.

The future of clubs is of course bound up with the conquest of inflation. Seventeen years ago I founded a tiny club in Edinburgh called Puffin's. It wasn't intended to be a substitute for the New Club, which is a proper club with morning rooms and bedrooms like the Cavalry or Brooks's, but a luncheon or dining club with a single table and general conversation like the Beefsteak or Pratt's. The idea was to cast back along the lines on which clubs had come, and become parasites on an existing public establishment, as the embryo clubmen in White's Chocolate House had been. The idea was to be exactly as if we had clubbed together and taken a private room with a communal table in a restaurant for a single meal, except that we clubbed together and for a fiver each rented them annually for the whole year, each member paying the restaurant for such meals as he actually had. The club still exists, and we still each put a fiver a year into the kitty, but nowadays this enables us only to retain a private room with a communal table for luncheon on Wednesdays. However, the principle is established, and works; and could be expanded in the same form in London if a good restaurant with a private room could be found, though the subscription would obviously have to be more than a fiver.

Meanwhile, Anthony Lejeune has done a thoroughly good job, and has produced for us a happily readable, yet definitive general work on one of England's greatest contributions to civilised life; the gentleman's Club, which originated in London and has spread throughout the world. But it's still at its best in London.

Books & Bookmen, 1979

Puffin's still continues under the chairmanship of I.M.'s elder son, the Earl of Erroll. One of the few great clubs not to have I.M. as a member was the Drones, an institution which he would certainly have adorned. Below he pays his own tribute to its creator:

I.M. attired in his Yucata

ABOVE: The Prince of Lippe's snap of I.M. at a shooting party on Moncreiffe Hill.

RIGHT: I.M. and a trophy.

The Master

When I was at Stowe our English tutor was that remarkable falconer-pacifist-huntsman T. H. White, who wrote *The Sword in the Stone* and *The Ill-Made Knight*. One morning, Tim White came into our beautiful Georgian classroom and announced; 'G.K.Chesterton died yesterday. P.G.Wodehouse is now the greatest living master of the English language'. He then read out a number of passages to show the skill with which Wodehouse could 'turn a phrase', as he put it, 'better than any other writer'.

A light of joyous kindly fun radiated from P. G. W.'s inimitable works. They were worth myriad hours yawning in a pew, playing the sermon-game to pass devout time, as a voice from some pulpit tried to tell us what he could tell us better. For his works were truly parables, though he was too modest to notice it. With him, the nominally inferior wise uphold and protect the apparently superior weak (instead of 'taking them down a peg' or 'wiping the smile off their faces'); like Jeeves with Bertie Wooster, in a world where all is good-humour and everybody is happy in the end. Above all, he was an un-selfconscious influence for Good in this Age of Envy, an evil feeling self-righteously feeding upon itself that was so alien he could never really believe it existed.

His books were brilliant sketches in typescript of his own saintly jester personality, as I found (for we never met) when we had occasion to correspond some years ago: *e.g.*

. . . Do you remember Ellaline Terriss? Was married to Seymour Hicks. In 1906 I had a job at their theatre writing lyrics and encore verses and we became great friends. She is celebrating her hundredth birthday on April 13 and wants me to be there. I certainly intend to come, if I am fit enough. I keep thinking how amazing it is that she will soon be a hundred, and then I suddenly remember that it won't be long before I'm that myself!..Last night I finished a new Jeeves novel, and it looks pretty good, though as usual with my stuff a bit on the short side. I have now got to go through it and try to lengthen some of the scenes.

In 1945 I was an usher at the wedding in St George's Chapel at Windsor Castle of the head of his family, Sir John Wodehouse, 4th Earl of Kimberley, 6th Lord Wodehouse and 11th Baronet; but never got round to sending a wedding present and, as he's since been married four times [*now six altogether* – ED] feel it's a bit late now. His lordship's armorial 'supporters are two *wodehouses*, the quaint heraldic jargon for wild men of the woods. He has four sons. Were a fatal accident to have befallen them all together last year, which God forbid, the two family peerages would have become extinct. But the family that sprang from Sir

'Bertram de Wodehouse [shades of Bertie Wooster], a Norfolk knight who fought with distinction against the Scots under Edward I' in the 1200s, and that could produce that fruity tar Vice-Admiral of the White the Honble Philip Wodehouse (1773–1838), would not have been so easily stumped. For the Wodehouse baronetcy, created among the very first when the Order of Baronets was instituted in 1611, would have continued in the branch to which P. G. W. belonged, and he would have been eighth in succession, coming immediately after his own nephew and great-nephew.

So it was no accident that the late Sir Pelham Grenville Wodehouse was like a 'very perfect gentle knight' out of the Age of Chivalry. Having continued the family Scottie-bashing in 1461, his direct forefather, Sir Edward Wodehouse, donned his uncomfortable plate-armour to ride out again with his men for the White Rose and was knighted by King Edward IV on the decisive battlefield of Tewkesbury. Through grand marriages, the Wodehouse baronets brought to our late beloved writer much romantic blood. Sir Thomas Wodehouse, 2nd Bart, married a great-granddaughter of Lady Mary Boleyn, sister of Queen Anne Boleyn who got the chopper. Sir Philip Wodehouse, 3rd Bart, married a granddaughter of Lord William Howard, son of the 4th Duke of Norfolk (axed for having designs on Mary Queen of Scots), himself son of the equally beheaded poet Ld Surrey whose father was the victor of Flodden Field, Scotland's greatest military disaster. Through these Howards, long the premier noble house of England, P. G. Wodehouse descended from many strange folk; devious Byzantine emperors and hard-riding Magyar and hot-tempered Plantagenet kings and grim Russian grand princes, from the Cid and blue-blooded de Veres and Harry Hotspur, also (by way of the sinister Orsini, hence Popes for uncles) from Simon de Montfort. Tragic Lady Jane Grey, headless too, sovereign Queen of England for a few reluctant days, was his ancestral first cousin; St Thomas Aquinas his ancestral uncle.

There were writers among his forebears too: such as Geoffrey de Villehardouin (died circa 1213) 'the first vernacular historian of France, and perhaps of modern Europe, who possesses literary merit', the chronicler of the Fourth Crusade in which he himself had taken part. A remoter forefather of P. G. W. was King Alfred the Great (born 849 and still going strong in folk cake-lore;), 'eminently a national writer' who translated books into Anglo-Saxon and to whom we owe it 'that the habit of writing in English never died out'. And also through the Dukes of Norfolk (if, as I believe, the Arden-Whaleborough-Moleyns connection is correct), he was the ancestral fifth cousin of Shakespeare.

Talking of Shakespeare, did Wodehouse write Bacon? For, through the marriage of P. G. W.'s forefather Sir Armine Wodehouse, 5th Bart (died 1777), to Letitia Bacon, daughter and co-heiress of Sir Edmund Bacon, 6th Batt, the great Sir Francis Bacon was his ancestral uncle. Perhaps, however, the question should really be, did the ghost of uncle Bacon have a hand in typing Wodehouse?

Books & Bookmen, 1975

IV

Hark the Herald

The Renascence of Heraldry

I have a gentle Turkish friend called Nuri Bey Arlasez. He has the finest collection of Ottoman embroideries in the world. If you visit him in his native Istanbul, he will take you first to see a mosque. Then he will take you to see another mosque. Then a third. After the fourth, you may begin to feel that when you've seen one, you've seen the lot. But after the fifth or sixth, you suddenly realise the beauty of their difference. Thus mosques designed by Sinan have a different quality from other mosques, for instance; and there are subtle differences of ineffable serenity among the varied mosques of the great Sinan himself.

So it is with heraldry. Sometimes, as zealous heraldists at a congress drag each other from tombstone to tombstone, you may feel that when you've seen one shield of arms, you've seen the lot. This is especially so, when the coats of arms aren't coloured. For the essence of heraldry is Colour. Moreover, it's a constant surprise to me that great masters of stage costume of the calibre of Bakst (though I cite him as an example of greatness, not of this particular error) nearly always get the simplest rule of heraldry wrong: that is, that colour must not be displayed on colour, nor metal on metal. Yet a moment's daub with a paintbrush will reveal that a red lyon won't shew up well at a distance on a blue field, nor a golden lyon on a silver one. Nor should two people appear on stage wearing the same distinctive coat of arms or bearing the same distinctive shield, else the whole purpose of heraldry – the ability to distinguish the distinguishable distinguished by their distinguishable distinguished distinctions – is lost. Hence the rules of heraldry.

Nobody is *compelled* to use a coat of arms or crest. But by the same token, nobody ought to *want* to use a bogus crest, let alone somebody else's. Yet a surprisingly large number of clubmen who should know better yap away indignantly whenever expert heralds suggest that, if they're going to insist on using arms, they should get them right. Curiously enough, however, the tremendous upsurge of interest in

148

heraldry since the Second World War makes such a solecism far less likely nowadays. This renascence of heraldry is perhaps due to a combination of the new affluence, and the population explosion, with the rebellion of the individual human cog against the impersonal conurban industrial machine; with the resultant yearning for Roots. New roots, too, are in ever-increasing demand where old ones can't readily be unearthed. So the College of Arms in London and Lyon Court in Edinburgh are becoming accustomed to granting or recording in a decade as many coats of arms as they were formerly used to in a century.

Books & Bookmen, 1978

Swans and Tygers

Thank goodness we can still sing, as even non-angelic heralds do, 'here's a health to the Queen'. For, without guiltily trying to fend off the Sin of Despair, we can no longer continue with the joyous toasts 'and a lasting Peace, to Faction an End, to Wealth – Increase'.

Those of you who have read *The Fox's Prophecy*, as I did first in 1941 though it was in print by 1871, or the uncannily exact predictions of the 'Brahan Seer', will know what to think of a lasting Peace and an end to Faction. As for the toast 'To Wealth – Increase'; it's uncertain whether people who have spent their lives building up a good library in their homes, instead of smoking, will be allowed to keep it if it turns out to bring the value of their other possessions within that demagogic Claw of Envy – a wealth tax coupled with deliberate inflation – let alone hand it past capital gains tax to an intelligent and therefore by definition 'unequal' or 'élitist' successor. All the same, we must either emigrate – we were all immigrants hither once upon a time from elsewhere, whether Celts or Teutons or Slavs, Jews or cheerful Blackamors – or carry on as long as Western civilisation can.

The herald has played many roles although, contrary to popular belief, he never blows his own trumpet. This misconception has arisen from the age-old custom of drawing attention to him by music when he puts on his 'mask' or with us 'tabard' and speaks incarnate with His Master's Voice – it might be absurdly misconstrued if I wrote that Lyon speaks with his mistress's voice – so that Shakespeare always stage-directs 'enter Herald with Trumpet'. A Trumpet was an attendant on the herald, rather as an Ensign carries the 'ensign' or Colour and Ancient Pistol wasn't a dotard but a military officer strong enough to carry an earlier form of flag called the 'ancient'. Nowadays we heralds

149

call our Trumpets 'state trumpeters', though in the Foot Guards we perversely call our buglers 'drummers' (one got so used to the Blitz-sirens being followed immediately by the command: 'Drummer! Sound the Alarm'). This connection between heralds and state music is with good reason as linked as is music to religious ceremonial. For both spring from the same proto-historic source in the ritual of sacral royalty.

Now, the late Ld Raglan, whom I knew as the peppery President of the Royal Anthropological Institute, wrote in his introduction to A. M. Hocart's *The Life Giving Myth* [London 1952]: 'the worship of the divine king is the earliest religion of which we have any certain knowledge'. The eagle on European emperors' tabards, and the fleur-de-lys on those of the kings of France, alike derived ultimately from the same source as the falcon and lotus of Horus, that part of the divine spirit ritually incarnate in each Pharaoh; as was the eagle in the Zeus-born Greek king and Indra-born Hindu kings and the raven in the Odin-born kings of Scandinavia. This holy spirit has long been baptised into all Xians, symbolised by the dove in their bosoms. But a magical echo from the dawn of civilised imagination is heard at the Coronation, before the anointing, when the archbishop prays for our Sovereign to be specially endued with the Divine Spirit. The whole basic dawn religion's inauguration ritual is analysed into 26 theoretical requirements by Professor Hocart in his master-work *Kingship* [London, 1927], and he finds a number of these in the royal inaugurations of Vedic India and Ancient Egypt and as far afield as modern Fiji. One could add a few more requirements, such as the poetic chanting of the royal genealogy as in 7th century Iceland or its proclamation by the king-of-arms as in 17th century Scotland. And more than 60 kingdoms from Africa could be added to Hocart's list, by applying its tests to those kingships analysed in Tor Irstam's *The King of Ganda* [Uppsala, 1944] – based on the realm of the Kabaka of Buganda, the last of whom was my friend King Freddie at whose state funeral, in the Royal Hut that is the most remarkable survival of Central African architecture, we were President Amin's guests, whereafter we attended Freddie's son Prince Ronnie's inauguration as the first *Sabataka* instead. Nobody is likely to be surprised at the interest of heralds in these moving ceremonies.

But as the living king becomes considered more separate from the incarnate spark of the divine spirit – though still the people's lucky mascot – the function of the herald-priest is divided. The priest remains the mouthpiece of invisible divinity, while the herald continues the mouthpiece of the visible king. All the same in yet another work, *Kings & Councillors* [Cairo, 1936], Professor Hocart demonstrated that the two offices 'are homologues', and 'that the Greek equivalent of the brahman is the *Rerux* or herald'. The priestly kindred who officiated at Pharaoh's inauguration showed their *personae* (literally, not rudely) by wearing masks such as that of a falcon's head to symbolise Horus. The nearest equivalent to survive into the modern coronation rite is perhaps the tabard with the royal beast or beasts worn by the heralds who form an essential feature in it. Their names remind us that a lion, a unicorn and a red dragon took part in our present Queen's crowning upon the Stone of Destiny.

People are puzzled by heralds' names, and talk mistakenly about *the* Somerset Herald as though he were a local newspaper. He is a herald called Somerset, herald his office and Somerset his new name, as in 1593 such a monk as John 9th Ld Forbes might be given the new name of Brother Archangel on entering the Capuchin Order: in the College of Arms he is Mr Somerset not Colonel Dennys [*Colonel Dennys is now Arundel Herald Extraordinary; the post of Somerset Herald is held today [1986] by Mr Thomas Woodcock* – ED]. Time was when the telephone here used to ring and an unmistakable old Court Scots voice quavered 'Lyon speaking, is that you, Unicorn?'. Mediaeval heralds were baptised with their new name in wine out of a silver cup, which they kept for their fee; and my first wife [*the Countess of Erroll, died 1978*] maintained this custom when as hereditary Lord High Constable of Scotland she named a new Slains Pursuivant, the private officer-of-arms who wears her tabard. The chalice is the symbol of the herald, just as it has been the symbol of the priest from the temples of ancient China to modern Greenland's icy mountains, twin symbols that shimmer back through the centuries of decent respect to unite in some primordial Holy Grail. Similarly, a tabarded herald's person is still so sacred that to strike him is treason; and he was such an inviolable envoy between Sovereigns that a great part of his job was spent in diplomatic work yet in Tudor times. And so our greatest heralds themselves wear a crown and bear the title of King: an *archon basileus* or *rex sacrorum* indeed.

Sir Anthony Wagner's *Pedigree and Progress: Essays in the Genealogical Interpretation of History* [Phillimore, 1975] has been eagerly, indeed anxiously, awaited by genealogical historians. It has often been pointed out that he is the greatest scholar at the College of Arms since Camden was appointed Clarenceux in 1597. Writing as a Scots herald, geared to an unhappily justified suspicion of English heralds as anti-Celtic Fringe 'patriots for the English empire'. I would rate Sir Anthony even higher; if only because he has been willing to munch over and digest the immeasurably greater amount of printed material nowadays available from other countries as well as having more of the original English sources to wash it all down. As he tells us himself, his interest in Armory, popularly called Heraldry, was a by-product of his early and continuing absorption in Genealogy. Many genealogists are primarily interested in their own family; and useful work they do, for there is often more for the historian to learn from the particular details of an individual kindred's ups and downs and real way of life than from the sweeping generalisations that necessrily distort the information he derives from some other general historian's attempted outline in *précis*-view of a whole class or period. Sir Anthony, now at the genealogical summit of all England as Garter Principal King of Arms [*he retired as Garter in 1978 and is now Clarenceux King of Arms* – ED] has always been interested in everybody's genealogy, perhaps even more in that of peasant than of prince for the quest is harder since the records are fewer, and he is as much opposed to the snobbish as to the inverted snob's attitude to pedigree.

A great part of his tremendous book is devoted to the class-bridging results to be obtained by the detailed study of inter-linking marriage connections at selected periods. When in 1966 the Crown Princess of the Netherlands married Claus von Amsberg, the British Press misinformed us that of course he was 'not noble'. Doubting their word as usual, I checked in the *Adelige Häuser* of the neo-*Gotha* and, sure enough, there he was in B vol iv (1959), of a family duly ennobled since 1795. But, when the equivalent happened in this country, for Captain Mark Phillips is certainly a gentleman, a newspaper told us that 'the horse is nobler than the bicycle' but failed to note that his very surname is a hybrid for 'Son of the Horse-Lover'. The dashing captain's male-line can be traced back through cavalry landowners, and 19th century ordinary coal-miners rising at last to the rank of colliery manager, to a lime-burner born about 1725. We needn't worry that his grandmother was daughter of a solicitor with the VD, as this stands for Volunteer Decoration. But the captain's grandfather owned Oldbury Grange, and his cavalry uncle, Lt-Col Anthony Phillips, DSO, married a sister of the late Duke of Norfolk, premier nobleman of England. So Garter's social fluidity is there all right.

Though Sir Anthony doesn't use him as an example, on his mother's side Captain Phillips shares innumerable ancestors with Princess Anne through their common forefather Richard Wrottesley of Wrottesley (1457–1621), whose wife descended by way of an aunt of the Shepherd Lord from Harry 'Hotspur' – appropriately enough for the equestrian royal couple today – and ultimately from King Edward III. (Did you ever know that merry young blade, the late Honble Richard 'Wrotters' Wrottesley who used to enliven county Galway with I LOVE WROTTERS blazoned on his T-shirt?) Now, I myself join Captain Phillips' ancestry during the Wars of the Roses as I descend from the Shepherd Lord himself. *He* really did incarnate social fluidity. His grandpop, the 7th Lord Clifford (who gave life to Captain Phillips & Princess Anne and this reviewer alike), had been slain in the opening battle of the Wars of the Roses and his pa, slain as a cruel Lancastrian peer in defeat at Towton fight, was very specially hated by the Yorkists as 'the Butcher' who had personally hacked the head from the Duke of York's corpse and presented it, decked with a paper crown, to the Lancastrian queen. So his seven-year-old son Henry was smuggled away from the vengeance of the White Rose and brought up a simple star-gazing shepherd lad on a Cumbrian moorland farm, where nobody knew he was anything else. After the final triumph of the Red Rose at Bosworth, a distinguished cavalcade rode up to the remote farm and astonished his fellow farm-hands by bowing low to the shepherd boy and telling him he was now the 9th Lord Clifford, most powerful magnate in Cumberland and Hereditary Sheriff of Westmorland. Remembering his lowly, lonely life on the starlit moors, the Shepherd Lord built himself a tower whence to study astronomy when not taken up with the affairs of State.

Sir Anthony Wagner doesn't go out of his way in his book, to combine armory, what is popularly called heraldry, with his genealogical researches. But he discusses such use in his second chapter, 'Heraldry and the Historian'. And he compresses for us his work on *The Swan Badge and the Swan Knight* (published in *Archaeologia*, vol xcviii, 1959). This turns on 'the series of swans with golden collars and chains, borne as crests, badges and supporters' by a number of mediaeval families, including the Bohun Earls of Hereford and the Courtenay Earls of Devon, the Valois Counts of Angoulême, the Kings of Portugal, the Gonzaga Dukes of Mantua, and the Hohenzollern Margraves of Brandenburg, who even founded an Order of the Swan in 1433. 'The explanation is a descent shared by all of them from kinsmen of Godfrey of Bouillon [the crusader conqueror of Jerusalem in 1099], whom legend made the grandson of the Swan Knight'. One feels that our Queen's delightful maintenance of a Keeper of the Swans and swan-upping must fit into this innocently somewhere, but neither Garter nor I can think *exactly* how (we've corresponded about it) since She doesn't descend from King Stephen who was certainly of the swan kindred, though She does belong to it through Eleanor of Castile (metamorphosed into 'Elephant and Castle' from the chess *rukh* or charioteer travelling West with the game from Persia in that guise) whose husband King Edward I held the famous Feast of the Swans in 1306, when he swore 'before God and the Swans' to avenge Bruce's slaying of the Red Cummin, and whose grandson Edward III wore the motto 'Hay, Hay, the Wythe Swan, by Godes soule I am thy man'.

Sir Anthony's Swan Knight pedigrees, including Godfrey of Bouillon himself, all start with the marriage of Ld Mountbatten's direct male-line forefather to the daughter of Charles, Duke of Lower Lorraine (died 994). And here we enter on mysteries deeper than Garter's caution will take us. For *Lohengrin* means 'Lotharingian Garin' or Garin of Lorraine: the Garin le Loherain who has his own *chanson de geste* derived by the twelfth-century trouvères from an earlier Frankish age, which Paul Paris in *Li Romans de Garin le Loherain* (Paris 1833) thought was the third quarter of the 700s. There are French and German versions of the swan legend, but both emanate from the Frankish centre-ground of Lorraine. It may be noted that in the West Frankish (French) versions the swan knight is called Helias, that Helios was an ancient synonym for Sol, the sun-god also called Apollo, whose bird was the swan; and let's not forget Leda. In the East Frankish (German) versions Lohengrin's swan guide is his brother, attached to him in this swan-guise by the loss of his golden chain. In his over-simplified *The Hero* (London 1936) Ld Raglan believed heroic myth to be a Robin Hood-type survival of the spoken part of pre-Christian mystery plays, originally enacted as in Ancient Egypt by high-born representatives of the god-spirits thus mimed: from Ancient Greece to my old acquaintance Arthur Waley's Noh-play Japan (where my wife and I watched one in awe) the dramatic stage in *sacred ground*. Of my late pen-pal Tom Lethbridge's interesting speculations in *Gogmagog* (London 1957), I tend to accept his belief that one's historic ancestress 'Lady Godiva', *i.e.* Countess Godgifu of Mercia referred to above by Wagner as also an ancestral grandma of the Queen, ragged her rather 'square' husband (who died 1057) by taking the principal part in a Xian-tolerated annual folk-pageant based on a pagan Celtic ritual New Moon ceremony, in which the moon-goddess' role was played nude at night by a 'fine lady upon a white horse' with bells on her fingers and bells on her toes to scare off evil spirits like that naughty Mr Foot showing his hairy Heel. There are other instances of this ritual, and an earlier scholar has drawn attention to the probable connection between Lady Godiva and the White Horse of Uffington. So in the antecedents of the Swan Knight's kindred we *may* be looking for a sort of ballet-cross between Leda and *Swan Lake* in a pagan ritual mystery play, Xianised into a Godiva-type festival pageant with family actors (we are reminded of Oberammergau) whose grandest hereditary participants eventually had long delegated the 'mask' but retained the tradition of descent from the Swan Knight. This, however, is impure speculation and has no place in Garter's careful book.

He does, however, draw our attention briefly to one of the most potentially exciting fields of genealogical speculation at present under research, in 'The Jewish Kings or Princes of Narbonne'. The problem was discovered not by a genealogist but by an historian, in Arthur Zuckerman's *A Jewish Princedom in Feudal France 768–900* (Columbian University Press, 1972). Work on the subject from the genealogical point of view has since been undertaken by Professor David Kelley (sometime of Harvard, now of Calgary University), who has made a special study of the *chansons de geste* as well as the historical documentation relating to this perid, the era when the dying paladin Roland blew his great ivory horn at Roncesvalles. Like Mr Zukerman, Professor Kelley has the task of identifying men who often bore simultaneously a Hebrew, an Aramaic and a Frankish name, and whose religion was to some extent interchangeable.

What's already known is that the Jews in exile in Asia were ruled under the Persian and later the Arab empires by 'Princes of the Captivity' called 'Exilarchs', with a genealogy claiming descent by at least the second century from the Royal House of David, probably with justification because on it was based their acceptance. Their marbled palace was in Babylon, and they had sufficient palanquined prestige for a seventh century exilarch to marry a Persian imperial Sassanid princess whose sister was wife of the Caliph. In 759 the Jews of Narbonne are said to have helped the Frankish king to drive the Arabs out of Septimania on the Spanish border in return for autonomy under a Jewish king of their royal house. Mighty Charlemagne, Captain Phillips' well-known ancestor, who soon succeeded to the Frankish throne, sent an embassy to the fabled Caliph Haroun al-Rashid, within whose empire Babylon lay. Keeping to the point, Garter don't tell us that a gift sent in return by that caliph of the Arabian Nights was a clock in which 'as the hour struck, a number of horsemen (varying with the number of hours) issued from a door which opened suddenly, and as soon as the sound subsided they re-entered the door, which closed behind them'; perhaps the original inspiration that led to such horologues as the delightful public *Glockenspiel* of Charlemagne's talented Frankish descendants the Wittelsbachs in comparatively modern Munich. But Caliph Haroun also sent the Jewish prince Makhir of the House of David to found a dynasty of exilarchs in Narbonne, whose heir as late as the fourteenth century was referred to as the 'so-called Jewish king of Narbonne' and used an armorial seal charged with what appears to be the Lion of Judah.

The second half of the 700s was indeed the very moment for the Jews of Narbonne to attain this ambition. The Prophet's actual Fatimid descendants (who today include the Kings of Jordan and Morocco and the retired third King of Malaysia) were in temporary eclipse, and the key branches of his world-shattering *Quaraish* kindred were the unpredictable Ummayad caliphs at Damascus and the inscrutable black-robed Abbasids who overthew them in a horror man-hunt in 750 and transferred the caliphate to Baghdad. The Abbasids took over the vast Arab empire from the borders of China to the Atlantic coast of Morocco – 'we have marched from the Indus to Spain' sing the soldiers in Flecker's *Hassan* – all save southern France and Spain itself, where a separate realm that eventually became the rival Caliphate of Cordova was established by the good Ummayad Caliph Hisham's fleeing grandson, whose great mosque is now the strange cathedral there. (From him, through the lords of Lara and Pedro the Cruel, all the royal families of Europe *perhaps* descend in the female line, and many of us with them, but that's another story. One of a traveller's genealogical excitements, as with some presidential Kennedy revisiting Killarney, is to be able to 'identify with' and *know*, say in Sicily that one descends from the emperor Frederick II 'Stupor Mundi' and the Norman kings who built those stupendous churches in Palermo or in India that one's host's family provided great Akhbar's mother. So when, exhausted at Babylon, I took a £30 taxi from Baghdad and crossed for a thousand kilometres over the burning Arabian Desert road to become, through Ld Lovat's valued introduction, King Hussein's guest in Amman, I visited the excavated winter palace with its tessellated mosaic floors near Jericho of this very Caliph Hisham, once the most powerful ruler in the world, reflecting that he may have been my forefather and anyway his agnate was still my host there). Thus the Muslims of Baghdad and Cordova were at daggers drawn in the late 700s, when the Caliph sent the Davidic prince Makhir to hold the Jews of Septimania under the Franks against the Saracens of Spain.

We next come to an even more startling probability, summarised in Garter's book; 'Zuckerman goes on to propose a further ingenious identification . . . of Makhir with Theuderic' (*i.e.* those were his Hebrew and Frankish names) 'father of St William, Marquess of Septimania, 796–806, the father of Bernard, Marquess of Septimania (d 844), whose daughter is said to have married Vougrin (d 866) . . . Count of Angoulême'. From him most of the high aristocracy of Europe and innumerable other people in all walks of life are descended in the female line, and *if* the theory is accepted, would thus spring too from the Royal

House of David. 'Professor Kelley regards the identify of Makhir and Theuderic as virtually certain'.

But even more certain in Garter's 'Bridges to Antiquity' chapter, is the incredible blood-line that streams from Pharnabazus, King of Iberia in the Caucasus, born in the lifetime of Alexander the Great, down to Queen Elizabeth II. Sir Anthony is, as usual, cautious enough to write 'possible'. But I, too, have followed for years the researches of our mutual friend and mentor, Pr Cyril Toumanoff – Pr stands here equally for professor and prince – who is the greatest living authority on early Caucasian history and genealogy. Exiled in childhood from Astrakhan to America, he now has chambers as a Professed Knight in the smallest state in the world, far smaller than Monaco which is nearly the size of Hyde Park: the extra-territorial palace of the sovereign Knights of Malta within Rome. And I think the case has been established beyond all reasonable doubt, except that the names of some intervening generations are lost. This descent comes by way of the Parthian dynasty of Arsacids who were Great Kings of Persia or Shahs of Iran from the second century BC. So, when Prince Philip left Persepolis after attending the present Shah of Iran's 2,500th celebration of the Persian empire in 1971, he could reasonably (but perhaps tactlessly) have delivered the Parthian shot that it was his own known forefather, and not necessrily the Shah's, who had reigned there well over 3,000 years ago.

Those Parthian great-kings of Iran originally ruled horsey Scyths, and I have a coin of Mithradates II with the obverse showing our distinguished relation with his high-velocity bow: remember how they gave you that parting arrow when you were mug enough to think they were galloping away. This dynasty had a younger branch who were put in as kings of subject Armenia – our Queen's forefather Vologaeses IV was King of Armenia 180–191 before he took over the Persian empire 191–207 – and the descent passed through the grandest Caucasian families until it reached the Artsruni kings of Vaspurakan. Their realm was around Lake Van, in what is now eastern Turkey; but when I tried to go there from Byzantium last year to see the island church our Dark Age forebear had erected, we were turned back by several feet of snow as, believe it or not, Turkey is colder than Scotland in February. But it's here we track that antique, yet ever phoenix, lineage through Khachi'k Artsruni prince of T'ornavan in 1042 (a name that evokes one's chidhood awe at the Oriental-style illustrations in Edmund Dulac's fairy book) whose grandson had the doubtfully Christian name of Prince 'Abulgharib' Artsruni and was Byzantine governor of Tarsus. Through him, without difficulty, the Persian turquoise blood reaches the Lusignans, crusader kings of Cyprus, from whose genealogically invaluable heiress, Anne de Lusignan, Duchess of Savoy, my ancestral grandma our Queen and Prince Philip both descend through Mary Queen of Scots.

So, too, does Lady Wagner, though Garter is typically English and don't tell us this – a Scotsman would bang on about it all the time, you may have noticed. The reason is probably that Scots clannish divisions are *vertical* between Names, *i.e.* a genealogical Campbell can be a dustman or duke in Argyll but equally enjoy tales of massacring Macdonalds, whereas in England they're more *horizontal* along the ebb and flow of classes and people fear family historical interest may seem a boring boast. Yet pedigrees should always be of general interest as recording the continuity & change of DNA in living reality as opposed to dogmatic politico-historical generalisation. And that is what Garter's book helps us to understand.

The Lusignans, cited above as Crusader kings, bring us now to Rodney Dennys's *The Heraldic Imagination* [Barrie & Jenkins, 1975], a splendidly illustrated book of beauty and colour hard to describe in musty print, but gloating lovely to possess. For he uses as the initial W of one chapter the German form of heraldic *Melusine*, tutelary watch-doggess (for she's no bitch) of the House of Lusignan: a crowned mermaid holding the upward curving ends of her tails with each hand. This is an affront to our truly legendary ancestress, those of us who have Lusignan blood, as Somerset Herald observes. For Melusine was a serpent-fairy, the spirit of some water-spring in the old pagan days of Shinto-like communion with Nature. Ordinarily she was a beautiful lady, but on Saturdays she was a fair woman 'unto the navell' but a silver-and-blue serpent beneath the waist. In the mountain Castle of Bran in Transylvania, once the summer home of another of Melusine's legendary progeny, Queen Marie of Romania, I saw last year a painting on wood that looked late mediaeval Italian and bore the royal arms of Jerusalem and Lusignan. It's the picture I'd most like to possess; a sort of beautiful strip-cartoon of Count Raymond meeting her happy in the woods beside her fountain; of their grand marriage on his promise never to see her on a Saturday; of his horror, on breaking his word, at seeing her in her true guise; and the sepent-fairy's immediate flight from a window of the castle of Lusignan, 'uttering a loud cry of anguish'. Together they had built the castle of Lusignan, from which Melusine's decendants took their name, and we are told that 'thence forward the death of a member of the house of Lusignan was heralded by the cries of the fairy serpent. "*Pousser des cris de Mélusine*" is still a popular saying'.

It's *imagination* that raises the human spirit – as opposed to its cold calculating brain – above the beasts, whether lion or tiger, rabbit or even wyvern. Think how displeased we life members of the Loch Ness Phenomenon Investigation Bureau are that doubt has clouded our symposium on giving *Nessiteras Rhombopteryx* its lovely new name; so much more scientific-sounding than harpy, griffin or pterodactyl. The dragon is no folk-memory of a dinosaur, but a world diffused imaginative icon of the sacral king. Besides his royal Lion, symbolising his spiritual husbandy of Earth – the king's beast included his imperial Sky Bird, symbolising the life-giving power of Sun (how else was DNA first activated?), his sacred Serpent, symbolising virility and the life-giving power of Water – and later the Dragon, made up from all three. This dragon has been a symbol of sacral royalty ever since; from the early Nile-Euphrates dawn kingships and the venerated emblem of the Chinese imperial family (I forget the correct number of its claws), past the purple dragon standard of the Byzantine emperors, to the dragon-ship prows of the Norse sea-kings. Our forefather King Harold fell at Hastings under the Dragon Standard of Wessex and the dragon is still one of the Queen's Beasts today.

So the lion becomes stylised as a *lyon* and the tiger is a *tyger*. The lupine red Tyger in the arms of Thomas Sybell (painted in 1531) is snarling anxiously at its own likeness in a looking-glass – for the late Nancy Rodd would never let us call it what it is, a hand-mirror – and the author explains that the tyger's 'celerity is such that one cannot easily escape the beast, even on the swiftest horse, and the only ruse is to throw down mirrors behind one, "and the moder foloweth and fyndeth the mirrours in the waye, and loketh on theym and seeth her owne shadowe and ymage therin, and weneth that she seeth her children therin; and is longe occupied therefore to delyver her chyldren oute of the glasse; and so the hunter hath time and space for to scape"'. He tells us also of the mantyger, a tyger with a human head (just as the riddle of the Sphinx was that it was Pharaoh's own face on his regal lion body) that was the peacetime beast of the Lords Hastings, afterwards Earls of Huntingdon. They maintained their own Tyger Pursuivant and it would be a happy thing if the present Ld Huntingdon, after consultation with Garter, were to appoint some scholarly heraldist to that office today. They tell me Ld Huntingdon is a socialist, and thank goodness heraldry is a-political. The first time I met Mrs Harold Wilson [*now Lady Wilson of Rievaulx*] was when she opened an exhibition of modern heraldic art. Blake's tiger, tiger burning bright could bring the glory of human imagination even yet to lighten the darkness of those Satanic mills.

Heraldry is meant to be a blaze of blending colour, precious metal and rich fur; its flamboyant language that of splendiferous fun. 'Tis never quite

159

the same in pedants' monochrome books or when merely scratched by engraver on spoons, though there is a system of lines & dots that if used can revive the true colours for the initiate. Its jargon is apt to bore after the first quaintness of Saracenic French has been savoured. Yet the technique is needed, 'up to a point, Lord Copper', if accurate descriptions are to be sufficiently Tacitus-wise telegraphic.

Colonel Dennys has come on a track I've worked over for many years, the difference between shield-device and geometric flag of the same colours at the dawn of heraldry, but has done so independently, as the context implies that he hasn't read my 'Double Coats at the Dawn of Scottish and Northumbrian Heraldry'.

The joy of this book may be summed up in his picture of the mid-12th century matrix of the seal of *Raimund de Montdragon*, most romantic of names, a Provençal baron. The obverse bears two dragons combatant which 'are, of course, two-legged, but their bodies appear to be feathered and their tails end in small Dragon's heads; their human heads have beards composed of serpents which each dragon is holding with one foot. The reverse of the seal has a delightful picture of Raimund on his knees swearing fealty to his lady, which is very much in the contemporary spirit of the troubadours and the Courts of Love'.

Books & Bookmen, February-March, 1976

Double Coats

It is not proposed that this paper could be a work of exact and finite scholarship, but rather to put forward some speculative ideas about the kindred of the Scottish royal house (so closely connected with Northumberland) at the dawn of heraldry, which may be of use in affording clues to historians, genealogists and heraldists who come after me.

Some years ago the distinguished Bohemian heraldist, Charles, Prince of Schwarzenberg, drew my attention to the existence soon after the dawn of heraldry, in the 12th and 13th centuries, of a number of cases of two separate coats of arms being borne simultaneously by the same noble. Where they appear, the one has a device such as an eagle or lion, the other is a geometrical pattern or ordinary; and usually the colours are the same in each case.

It is not to the point to consider here the rarer case where the geometrical colours *differ* from those of the device, for this would include arms of office or allegiance, such as the shield gold with a lion azure assumed by both the

Counts of Solms-Königsberg and the Lores of Waldstein and Watenburg while in the service of the Kings of Bohemia; also the use by a nobleman of two differently inherited ancestral coats before the days of quartering; and the national crosses used as livery badge-flags by many kings, such as the St George's Cross of Merry England, the 'red cloth' of Dannebrog of Denmark, and the 'blue blanket' or St Andrew's Cross of Scotland.

Of the dual coats that have a device and alternatively a partition of the same colours, Otto Hupp tells us in his *Wider die Schwarngister*! . . . (1918) that:

Down to the beginning of the 13th century the only seals to be found are those of persons of high and the highest rank. Now it is precisely with these that, already in the earliest period, we often find two armorial ensigns in use; a beast or some other charge, and a partition. So far as I know, Gustav A. Seyler was the first to put forward an explanation of this odd phenomenon. In his *Geschichte der Heraldik* . . . he writes: 'The coexistence of armorial and arbitrary shield ornament that turns into armorial bearings, and the competition of banner and shield as bearers of armorial ensigns, explain the frequent appearance of two such ensigns for one family'. I believe we can now see somewhat further. . . . For such a charge as the lion to be displayed so large as to let a troop of horsemen be known thereby, demands a much larger ensign than would have been practical for use. So one took instead a small pennon, that showed the lion coat's colours in the form of a partition . . . Should anybody think this too theoretical, let him look at the lance-pennons of modern cavalry and ask himself whether these would fulfil their purpose if, instead of the simple colours-partition, they contained the full State coat?

Seyler gives numerous examples of the use of double coats of the dawn of heraldry in the Holy Roman Empire *Geschichte der Heraldik*. I have not presumed to go into the question in England generally, except that the hitherto unexplained Percy lion coat and separate Percy fusil coat in the same colours (now quartered together) seem an obvious example. In a stained-glass window at Chartres Chathedral, Amaury de Montfort, Count of Evreux and Earl of Gloucester (1199) bears a shield of gules a lion with two tails silver, and a banner per pale indented gules and silver. The arms of his famous cousin Simon de Montfort, Earl of Leicester (slain 1265) were the exact reverse; silver a lion with two tails gules, and alternatively per pale indented silver and gules.

SCOTLAND AND NORTHUMBERLAND

We have now come to the North Country in Britain. I have no doubt whatsoever that heraldry dawned in Scotland during the reign of the pro-Norman King David the Saint (1124–115), whose family also held the Earldom of Northumberland at that period (1139–1157). The Scottish royal family at that time were Gaels in the male line, and the royal *derbh-fine* or 'true family' were all the descendants in the direct male line of King David's great-grandfather Crinan, hereditary Abbot of

Dunkeld (of the Kindred of St Columba, scions of Niall of the Nine Hostages, the pagan sacral King of Ireland living at Tara in AD 400).

Until King David's time it had been the custom for brothers or even cousins to succeed to the throne before sons, and indeed for the heir to try to slay his predecessor. King David himself was the *youngest* son of St Margaret, and several descendants certainly existed of elder branches of Abbot Crinan's 'true family'. There also existed younger branches. But the whole of Abbot Crinan's 'true family' descended either from his elder son, King Duncan (slain by Macbeth 1040), or from his younger son, Naldred, Regent of the Cumbrians (the realm from the Lennox to Carlisle), who had married a daughter of the dynastic Earl of Northumberland. When heraldry dawned two generations later, the colours of the House of Duncan were gold and gules, and the colours of the House of Maldred were silver and gules.

HOUSE OF DUNCAN (MACDUFF)

I have argued in *The Highland Clans* [Barrie & Jenkins, revised edition, 1982] why I believe Gillemichael mac Duff, Earl of Fife 'by the Grace of God', living circa 1133, to have been paternal grandson of King David's elder brother Aethelred, the last hereditary Abbot of Dunkeld and first Earl of Fife. My opinion is therefore that, at the dawn of heraldry, the Clan MacDuff were the senior branch of the royal family to have supported King David; and that their grand Arms of gold a lion gules were chosen as the basic family coat, which King David himself chivalrously 'differenced' by adding the famous royal treasure, the fleur-de-lys having been since Ancient Egyptian times a symbol of the living king.

The Earls of Fife as Chiefs of the Clan McDuff used two coats; the one gold a lion gules, the other paly of six, presumably of the same colours. Both coats appear on their seals by the 13th century, but I suspect were in use much earlier. Their lion coat was 'differenced' with a riband sable on the arms of their cadets the hereditary Abbots (later Lord) of Abernethy. Their paly coat was 'differenced' by changing the colours to gold and sable on the arms of their other cadets, the Earls of Atholl of the Strathbogie ('Strabolgi') branch of the Clan MacDuff. The coat of Cameron of Lochiel is simply the paly Fife coat (which appears on the 13th century seal of the Monastery of Scone as three palets) turned onto its side. Since the parish of Cameron formed part of the demesne lands of the Earls of Fife; since Duncan, Earl of Fife (1154–1204), had a younger brother Adam; and as Adam of Cameron witnessed a charter in the Tay area early in the 13th century; I don't think we need go much further for the origin of the Camerons, especially as they were of baronial rank.

Other branches of the Clan MacDuff, holding baronial estates in Fife itself, have puzzled genealogists hitherto by appearing to have two separate coats. Wemyss appears with a fret counter-changed per pale (presumably gold and gules) as well as with the red lion on gold. Spens appears with various fretty coats as well as with what appears to be the Abernethy lion 'differenced' with three Quincy mascles on the riband (now a bend). In his famous *De Verborum Significatione*, my forefather Sir John Skene, Lord Curriehill, tells us that Spens was entitled to claim the unique privileges of the 'Law of the Clan MacDuff', but this may have been through the female line; the relationship had to be 'within nine degrees', and circa 1420 a number of lairds who were certainly not in the male line of Fife invoked these privileges as 'sib to Makduff Earll of Fyffe' after they liquidated an unpopular Sheriff of the Mearns and drank the soup they had made of him. Thus the obviously Clan MacDuff coat of Scott of Balweary in Fife (gold three lion's heads gules) may have derived from the Scott marriage to the heiress of the family of Syras (the place now called Ceres) who were MacDuff cadets. The old coat of Fernie of that Ilk (also in Fife) is obviously the same, 'differenced' by the addition of a fess azure. I have suggested in *The Highland Clans* that the similar coat of gold three lion's heads gules born by Gordon, afterwards Marquis of Huntly, ostensibly as a quartering for the Lordship of Badenoch, was based on some relationship to the Clan MacDuff coupled with King Robert Bruce's known practice of giving forfeited lands to supporters of his own who were related to the former owners; 120 square miles of forfeited MacDuff (Strathbogie) land having been given to the Gordon chief, for instance.

Reasons for believing the powerful Mackintosh chiefs, far away in Inverness-shire, who also quarter the red lion on gold, to be genuine cadets of the MacDuff earls of Fife have also been given in *The Highland Clans*. The Mackintosh cadets, including Farquharson of Invercauld, Shaw of Tordarroch, MacThomas of Finegand, and the Principal Chief of the Creek Nation (a redskin of grand Highland lineage), all quarter the MacDuff red lion on gold too.

HOUSE OF DUNCAN (ROYAL BRANCH)

I now turn to the immediate Royal House sprung from King David himself, who was also Earl of Huntingdon (a detached portion of Northumberland). The paly arms of gold and red traditionally ascribed to Northumberland will have arisen as the natural second coat of David the Saint's son Henry, King Designate of Scots but also more effectively Earl of Northumberland, who predeceased his father in 1152. The coat of paly gold and gules a bend sable (obviously Northumberland 'differenced') was that of his (the King-Designate's) youngest grandson John the Scot, Earl of Huntingdon and Chester, who died in 1237.

A study of the interestingly varied English arms of Basset in Joseph Foster's *Some Feudal Coats of Arms* (London, 1902) shows that piles were used in the thirteenth century as a 'difference' for palets. And the arms of the Lords of Brechin, descended from Henry of Brechin who was natural brother of John the Scot Earl of Huntingdon, were gold three piles gules. So much for the colours of the House of Duncan.

HOUSE OF MALDRED

We now come to the colours of the House of Maldred, to which I believe my own family belong. It can be reasonably accepted that he was ancestor of Dundas of Dundas (silver a lion) and thus of the present Dunbar baronets, and of the mighty English house of Nevill of Raby who later held the Dukedom of Bedford, Marquessate of Montagu, and Earldoms of Westmorland, Salisbury, Warwick, Kent and Northumberland, and who bore gules a saltire silver.

Maldred's female-line descendants, the Moubrays of Barnbougle (whose own Norman baronial male line, by a coincidence that may have suggested the marriage, already bore gules a blanch lion, which however they significantly *crowned* gold in Scotland) inherited from him not only the Queensferry but also considerable estates near Perth that were contiguous with those of the Ruthvens, afterwards Earls of Gowrie. These Ruthvens were also overlords of the great mountainous district of Crawford that had been part of Maldred's domain in the Strathclyde district of Cumbria. It is perhaps therefore not surprising to find the Ruthvens bearing paly of six silver and gules, which one was looking out for as the obvious second coat of so powerful a house as that of Maldred. So the origin of the prominent Ruthven forefather, Thor Sweyn's-son, who witnessed royal charters between 1127 and 1150, is probably to be sought in Maldred's progency.

It may next be noted that the nearest neighbours of the Ruthvens and Moubrays in Perthshire were the thanes of Logie, a thane or *toisech* being the appanaged chief of a branch of a dynastic stock. Their strange chevronny coat reminds me of the Wemyss coat referred to above, but is however in the colours of the House of Maldred. In 1364 King David II himself married the beautiful Drummond window of the then Thane of Logie, who was undoubtedly of baronial rank from his family's position in Parliament.

164

Great estates too were held in Bernicia, both Northumberland and Lothian, by the family of Gray or Grey, which produced the Scots Lords Gray, the Reform Bill Prime Minister Earl Grey and the 1914 Foreign Secretary. An analysis of the layout of their estates shows them to have lain mainly around the Northumbrian seat of power at Bamburgh. Maldred's son Gospatrick was Earl of Northumberland before becoming Earl of Dunbar; and the Gray arms of Gules a lion within a bordure engrailed silver could hardly be anything other than a 'differenced' form of the first coat of Dunbar.

For some fascinating reason, not yet tracked down, the Dunbars later added to their own coat a silver bordure charged with red roses. This puts one in mind of the baronial family of Hepburn, afterwards Earls of Bothwell, whose early stronghold was near Dunbar; who favoured the Christian name of Patrick so much used by the Dunbars; and who took their name from the lands of Hebburn in the Northumbrian parish of Chillingham, where the Greys had a famous castle that still exists with its mediaeval tilting ground. The Hepburn coat is clearly a version of the Dunbar coat, and also in the colours of the House of Maldred; gules on a chevron silver two red lions pulling at a red rose.

Those roses and the colours, together with the Nevill saltire now put us in mind of the arms of the Earls of Lennox: silver a saltire betwen four roses gules. Since their ancestor Arkill was a prominent Northumbrian thegn who had a son called Cospatrick (characteristic of the House of Maldred) it may be that we should revise Miss Ethel Stokes's brilliant article on 'Lennox' in *The Complete Peerage*, volume VII, and accept the earlier views of the editor of the *Cart. de Levenax* and of Sir William Fraser that they sprung from Arkill's male line. But I am not too sure, as arms were often adopted by female-line relations at the dawn of heraldry. So I incline to Miss Stokes right in supposing that the Earls of Lennox descended from an *heiress* of the line of Arkill, but would suggest that Arkill was a grandson of Maldred.

Taking Dunbar and Ruthven as the lion and paly silver and gules double coats, equivalent to the lion and paly gold and gules double coats of the Clan MacDuff and of our royal house in Scotland and Northumberland, it seems worth looking for a coat *silver with bargules* or *vice versa* within the area of the red-and-white lion coats on the lines of the Fife-turned-onto-its-side Cameron equation suggested above. The sphere of influence of Maldred's descendants extended from the Tyne to the Tay, with scattered cadets from Durham to the Clyde.

Now, recent research indicates a strong possibility that the distinguished Washington family, who gave her first President to the United States of America, may also have sprung from the House of

Maldred. Their family 'stars and stripes' are certainly in the right colours: silver two bars (and in chief three molets) gules. The family seem to have originated in the right district with the right rank of birth: William was granted Washington in county Durham in about 1180. His son, Walter I of Washington, was of sufficient local importance for his lion seal of about 1203 to survive. Morever, their early seals have a separate *device* from the more *geometrical* 'stars and stripes.' This – as might be expected – was a lion, which Jenyn's Ordinary shows to have been gules a lion silver, with over all a bend gobonny silver and azure. This, in that area at that time, is obviously (like the coat of Gray) a 'differenced' form of the early coat of Dunbar. Sir Walter III of Washington bore this lion coat in 1318, and Sir Walter IV of Washington sealed with the 'stars and stripes' in 1346.

It has always been believed by Scottish genealogists that the Earls of Home are a younger branch of the Earls of Dunbar, from whom of course they certainly descend in the female line, and that their arms of vert a lion silver are simply an early 'differencing' by tincture on the original Dunbar coat of gules a lion silver. The matter is discussed in Sir James Balfour Paul's *Scots Peerage*. Certainly the traditional account requires revision, but it should also be borne in mind that the Scots nobles usually gave the best jobs to close kinsmen if they could, and that Aldan of Home, the first recorded ancestor, had the plum job of Steward of the Earldom of Dunbar in the twelfth century.

Moreover, the earliest known example in colour of the arms of the lairds of Dunglas (*i.e.* the Homes of that Ilk, afterwards Earls of Home), is that illustrated in the *Armorial de Berry* (circa 1450–1455). This shows the second and third quarterings (for Home) as gules a lion silver – the original Dunbar coat before the assumption of the border of roses. However, in the first and fourth Home of Dunglas quarters, Berry shows the papingoes of the Pepdie heiress of Dunglas as sable instead of the usual vert. All the same, Berry's armorial heightens the possibility that at some stage the Homes may have formed a combined single coat (for quartering was still rare at the time of their marriage to the Pepdie heiress in the second half of the fourteenth century) and differenced Dunbar by changing the original field of gules to the Pepdie tincture of vert, while retaining the silver lion of Dunbar.

Finally, we come to Moncreiffe of that Ilk: silver a lion gules and a chief ermine. A chief ermine was a cadet 'difference' in the dawn of heraldry, as witness the arms of the Lords of Kerry (Fitzmaurice, now Marquess of Lansdowne), which are silver a saltire gules and a chief ermine, and who are twelfth-century male-line cadets of the Earls of Kildare (FitzGerald, now Duke of Leinster) whose arms are silver a saltire gaules. Moncreiffe itself is sandwiched between the former Dundas estates of Fingask and Dunbarney, and the arms of Dundas (known descendants of the House of Maldred) are silver a lion gules.

So there is little doubt that we too spring from Maldred, probably in the male line, though it is not absolutely certain there was not possibly an heiress in the 12th century when heraldry was fluid. That we were in a position not to adopt any 'arms of allegiance' is apparent from the marriage of my forefather, Sir Mathew of Moncreiffe, to the sister of one of the Regents of Scotland (sacked in 1255 because Henry III of England thought him too dangerous), and because a chief ermine would not then have been a sufficient 'difference' for anybody but a genuine cadet, since the red lion was the King's own device.

HERALDIC CONFIRMATION OF HILL-FORT'S LONG TENURE

This is perhaps of special genealogical interest, for Moncreiffe (*Monadh Craoibhe*) was the principal stronghold in this part of the world of Pictish kings, who first appear in history in AD 269 and whose line of succession was matrilinear. In the ninth century King Kenneth mac Alpin, their effective heir in the female line, had a *coup d'état* nearby that carried the succession into the male line of royal Scots. Then in AD 1034 Moncreiffe was part of the inheritance of the royal heiress Bethoc who had maried Crinan, hereditary Abbot of Dunkeld. As it was by then a disused prehistoric drystone fortress, it had long been abandoned for practical purposes but obviously formed part of the lands assigned to her younger son, the Regent Maldred, since his Moubray descendants were overlords of the whole area around it. In that case, *if* I am right about the heraldic and other circumstantial evidence, my family has been here (albeit as cadets of cadets of cadets and in the *female line*) since at least AD 269, and probably much longer.

SUMMARY

To revert to my main theme, and whether or not these speculations are right in detail, there seems little doubt that scholars should not only plot the geograpical location of family estates in the 12th and 13th centuries to see with what other families they lay contiguous (especially where this occurs with the same two families in more than one area), because land was the only heritable investment available in those days and there was a duty in Gaelic society for the head of the family to provide for all members of the 'true family' – and their subsequent branches – out of the original family lands. In Scotland, unlike some other countries, this was often done by subinfeudation under the head of the family or branch. But in this context heraldists should more especially consider the possibility of an original double coat, where one family appear using *geometrically* the same colours as their neighbour's *beast*: and therefore the possibility that both were branches of the same original stock before the firm establishment of surnames in Scotland. The same of course explains the use at different times of widely different coats, geometrical or beastly, by different proved members of the same surname.

The Armorial, December 1970

The Ravaillac Dagger and the Gowrie House Affair

My lecture is devoted to the dagger taken from Ravaillac, the assassin of King Henri IV of France, by the future Maréchal de La Force, a Captain of the King's Guard who was officially off duty, but who was accompanying the king in the royal *carrosse* at that fatal moment in Paris on Friday 14th May 1610; and who gave the order for Ravaillac to be tortured at the preliminary investigation that very day.

As Queen Marie de Medicis could not bear to look on the weapon that had slain her husband, the maréchal's family of Caumont La Force preserved the dagger at the Château de la Force near Bergerac in Perigord. Latapie, inspector of manufactures in Guyenne, reported that he saw it there in 1785 and that it was still kept in a *cassette* of which the intendant had the key, evidently in the duc's *cabinet de travail*.

The Château de la Force was demolished in 1793 by French Revolutionaries (a painting of the Château survives on a grandfather clock in the possession of the Duke of Northumberland's brother Lord Richard Percy, a connection by marriage of the Caumont de La Force family). At the same time the Ravaillac dagger was taken away by the representative Lakanal and deposited in the archives of the *mairie* of Bergerac. In 1808, however, it was handed back by the *sous-préfet* of Bergerac to M. de Caumont who reclaimed it for the La Force family; as can be seen from a report made in 1809 by M. Couderc, the *procureur impérial* at Bergerac, in response to an enquiry by the local historian M. Souffron, judge at Libourne. Since the dagger was restored to the very duke from whom it had been taken 15 years before, he could hardly have failed to recognise his own unique possession. The matter is dealt with very carefully in an appendix by M. Jouanel, the eminent conservateur des Archives municipales de Bergerac, to the Duc de La Force's biography of *Le Meréchal de La Force* (Paris, 1950). Further careful examination of the facts has also convinced me that no other weapon is the genuine Ravaillac dagger.

Even under the most excruciating tortures, Ravaillac was unable to say from whom he had obtained the knife: but could only tell his interrogators that he had stolen it from a stranger in a hostelry near the Quinze-Vingts (Rue Saint-Honoré) in Paris. Doubtless owing to the elaborate heraldic golden inlay on the blade, the interrogators obviously believed that he had been put up to the assassination by some foreign nobleman whose arms they evidently did not recognise.

The present Duc de La Force consulted me about the heraldry on the dagger, and I saw to my astonishment that it could only have belonged to one man. Indeed, this dagger is more murderous than had been hitherto suspected. For it had already been used in two other historic killings by the man who really owned it.

This man was John Ramsay. As Page of Honour to King James VI, he was in attendance on the king on his tragic visit to Gowrie House in Perth in August 1600. Curiously enough, he was talking to the then Moncreiffe of that Ilk's younger brother, John Moncreiffe of Easter Moncreiffe, at the very moment when they both heard the king cry out for help. The Laird of Easter Moncreiffe did nothing, because he was the Earl of Gowrie's friend; however, he was later knighted, perhaps for keeping his mouth shut. But John Ramsay (a favourite minion who had been doubtless keeping a jealous eye open) ran up an otherwise unnoticed turnpyke stair to the king's assistance, and found him struggling with Gowrie's attractive brother, the Master of Ruthven, whose head the king was holding down. The king shouted 'strike him low, for he wears a secret mail doublet' (actually, the king called it a 'pyne doublet'). Ramsay drew his 'dagger or *couteau de chasse*' (for the court had been stag hunting on its way to Perth) and mortally wounded the Master. He then went out into the gallery and killed the Master's elder brother, the Earl of Gowrie, who had drawn two swords from one scabbard in the Italian manner, and hurried to his brother's rescue, but had dropped the points in consternation on a false cry that the king had been slain. The whole mysterious proceedings are known to Scottish history as 'the Gowrie House Affair'. I have for some years been collaborating with [Christian] Lady Hesketh in order to try and solve the mystery.

The young Earl of Gowrie, recently returned from the University of Padua, belonged to an intensely political family closely linked to the Kirk of Scotland. The Earl's father had already kidnapped King James VI eighteen years before, and his grandfather Lord Ruthven had been the ringleader at the murder of Riccio in the presence of Mary Queen of

Scots when she was pregnant with the unborn king. It is our opinion that the young Earl of Gowrie indeed intended to kidnap the king, using his very handsome younger brother the Master of Ruthven as bait – for the king was a well-known homosexual – and take him down the Tay and then by sea to the Gowrie castle of Dirleton many miles away on the coast near North Berwick. The plot was foiled by King James's courtiers, and especially by jealous young John Ramsay, the current favourite. But it was impossible to give a public explanation why the king had allowed himself to be taken upstairs by the good-looking Master, locking the gallery door behind them. Hence the mystery, and the tale about the Master having captured a Jesuit carrying a 'crock of gold' which the embarrassed king improvised but nobody believed. The use of that hunting knife brought Ramsay fame and wealth, and he would certainly have treasured it. He was rewarded on the spot with an estate and a knighthood, and in 1606 promoted to be Viscount of Haddington.

His weapon is a characteristic 'dudgeon dagger' of the type illustrated in John Wallace's *Scottish Swords & Dirks* (London, 1970). Mr Vesey Norman, Master of the Armouries at the Tower of London, considers that the completeness of the Ravaillac Dagger with its scabbard and equipment makes it unique in its own already rare type, and that it 'is in fact the only one with a history'. Its sheath contains a bodkin (presumably for removing stones from horse's shoes), as also two little 'bye-knives' to which the date 1600 has been added in gold. There have also been added to the diamond-shaped quadrangular dagger itself the golden letters I^{S}R (the 'S' being raised centrally above the other two), the normal Scottish mode in those days when giving titled initials, for 'Sir John Ramsay' (Thus a 17th-century armorial stone at Old Slains has I^{E}E for 'John, Earl of Erroll'.)

King James had further rewarded Sir John Ramsay in 1600 with augmentation to his Arms. The Ramsay family coat is a black eagle on silver (differenced in his case with a silver crescent on the breast, being a second son) but now changed to a double-headed eagle instead, presumably in oblique allusion to that in the heraldic Achievement of the City of Perth where the Affair took place. The other augmentations were: the right to use the royal unicorn supporters (from the Scottish Royal Arms, but uncrowned), the motto HAEC DEXTERA VINDEX PRINCIPIS ET PATRIAE, and the right to impale with his own Arms a coat of augmentation, showing an arm holding an erect sword piercing a man's heart and supporting on the point an imperial crown. This new shield, with its supporters and motto, appears on the dagger blade, also added in gold.

In later life, he sometimes reversed the impaled coats; and he also used an antelope as one of his supporters, retaining the unicorn for the other; but I suspect that this was when he became the English Earl of Holdernesse in 1620, by which time the dagger was already in the possession of the Caumont La Force family. It may be of interest that he was then also accorded the 'privilege of bearing the Sword of State before the King every 5th of August, a thanksgiving day appointed for the preservation of the King's life in the Gowrie Conspiracy'.

Sir John Ramsay was created Viscount of Haddington in Scotland in 1606, when a golden 'H' and coronet were obviously hammered into the deadly dagger's blade much more crudely. But the other inscriptions must have been added earlier (presumably in 1600, immediately after the Gowrie House Affair) else his initials would have been ɪᵛʜ and not ɪˢʀ, following the contemporary Scottish practice. Lord Haddington was probably in France between 1606 and 1610, for he was constantly having what could only be described as lover's tiffs with the king and in the habit of retiring to the Continent after getting involved with enemies at court.

It seems impossible to resist the conclusion that this was the hunting knife which he had used on the Ruthven brothers in Gowrie House in 1600. He must have been very sad to have lost so prized and historic a possession. I wonder if he ever guessed that Ravaillac had used it too.

It is certainly an astonishing coincidence that in its brief ten years of active life from 1600 to 1610 this murderous poignard, intended for hunting, should have been responsible for the most important killings in Scotland and also the assassination of the first Bourbon king of France. Yet its heraldry, though unnoticed for the last 365 years, has marked it out for ever.

From I.M.'s paper at the XIII International Congress
of Genealogical and Heraldic Sciences, 1976

V

Spirit of Caledonia

The Royal House of Scotland

The history of the foundation and consolidation of Scotland, as a very special country with a strong identity of her own, is the story of our continuing royal family. For Scotland is made up of many peoples, and it was our royal family who moulded them into one country which despite its mixed racial origins has ever since maintained its separate identity from the rest of Britain.

So it's impossible for a Scotsman abroad to say 'Yes' when asked by a foreigner 'Are you English?' My English friends seem to think this mere pedantry, and stare incomprehendingly when asked how *they* would reply to the question 'Are you Scottish?' Yet their attitude has this merit, that they are taught so little about us at school that they tend to have an open mind on Scotland.

Now, the Scots do not have an open mind about themselves. Most Scots are riddled with preconceptions that increasingly become misconceptions about their country's past: whether trendy left-wing, like much of our current historical 'scholarship', or starry romantick, like the Victorian novelists. During the long years when our Royal Family temporarily abandoned us – no sovereign, except for the Old Chevalier, set foot in Scotland for nearly two centuries, between 1651 and 1822 – Scotland became in many respects a land of nasty, petty squabbling, lowlander against highlander, clan against clan. I could still get a rise out of very many of my Scottish readers *if* I were to say for instance, that one of the most civilising influences on Scotland as a whole during much of that period was the dominance of the Campbells (note, equally, that I haven't said it one way or the other).

It was perhaps the great and good Sir Walter Scott, above all, who gave Scotland back her self-respect. By his romances, which achieved European stature, he not only put Scotland back on the international map: he converted what had been squalid feuds into romantic episodes, changing real hatreds into what social anthropologists call 'joking relationships'. As a result of the Moncreiffes slaying a Jardine in 1578, for example, I was the guest of honour a couple of years ago at the Jardine Gathering. At the same time, Scott endeavoured also to reconcile the Highlands with the Lowlands: and to some extent canalised the tartan tradition to this end. Although originally highland, the use of tartan had spread to the lowlands before the Union with England, and by Sir Walter's time was already becoming the hallmark of Scots in foreign eyes. In this great task of pouring oil on fresh waters rather than old flames, Sir Walter was magnificently assisted by the understanding and generosity of King George IV, whose famous visit to Edinburgh in 1822 was particularly addressed to reconciliation with the highlanders – he even had the good sense to ask very particularly for Glenlivet whisky. – and who restored the actual presence of the monarchy to Scotland.

Of course, there can be too much of a good thing – even, alas, of Glenlivet – and there has been in recent years a reaction against what is known as 'tartan tosh'. Certainly, some of the tartan gimmicks for tourists are embarrasing, as is the garb of some Scottish football fans who, however, are only thoroughly enjoying themselves in identifying with their country. But I find the standard snide sniping by smart writers at King George IV himself for wearing highland dress mildly irritating as well as ungrateful: but for him, and his niece Queen Victoria, not just the Highlands but all Scotland might have continued to be a mere backwater called North Britain.

There is always something stimulating – a feeling of invigoration and renewal – about the presence among us of the royal house that gives unity and purpose to the nation: the Queen as Chief of Chiefs is the head of the whole family of Scots scattered throughout the world, even in countries where she is not also their Sovereign. The Royal Family is the nuclear family around which Scotland grew like a snowball.

Scotland has always had the same royal family. It shouldn't be, but is, constantly necessary to emphasise this point, which has been obscured by the historians' convenient use of dynastic names to form as it were punctuation marks in the long chronicle of our national story.

Thus we learn of what happened under the House of Kenneth mac Alpin, the House of Atholl (or Dunkeld), the Houses of Balliol, Bruce, Stewart and Stuart, Hanover, Saxony and now Windsor: as though these surnames denote different royal families. They certainly denote different male lines, but our throne passes through women, and most people don't regard our royal family as having become a different one because the throne passed through Queen Victoria, for instance. Very few people think of Prince Charles as not belonging to the Queen's family: yet the historians' standard dynastic classification would make the Duke of Gloucester appear her nearest kin, and Prince Charles found a new branch of the House of Denmark.

Old names like Fergus and Kenneth mac Alpin and Alexander I may seem to many readers far more shadowy then George III or James VI or even Robert Bruce. But they were all flesh and blood, of the same royal kindred as today, real people who left a real mark on the making of our nation. What is strange, however, is the way that the different races over whom the royal ancestors ruled should have been so welded together as to form a peculiarly Scottish nation that was never assimilated by the English. Although we have now been British for two and three-quarters centuries – longer than the United States have existed – we have retained a national consciousness within the framework of the United Kingdom that is quite different from that of, say, Virginia within the United States. Yet Scots is simply a form of the English language, and the great province of the Lothians was part of England until after the battle of Carham in 1018, while Edinburgh has still been an English city only 60 years before that.

Moreover, the Hebrides, including Skye and Mull and even Kintyre, were part of *Norway* until 1266. It was easier to sail from Norway to Kintyre than to ride there through bog and forest from Perth or Dunfermline. When my forefather Sir Mathew of Moncreiffe was living here under the shade of Moncreiffe Hill in the reign of Alexander II, he would have said he was voyaging to Norway, as indeed was true, if he had travelled to Skye to stay at Dunvegan with his contemporary the Norse prince Leod, ancestor of the MacLeods, or to Islay to visit his other contemporary the Norwegian local King Donald, progenitor of the Macdonalds. Now, the time between 1266 and the English Conquest of Scotland in 1296 is only 30 years: about the same as the interval between the death of King George VI and now. Furthermore, the Scottish royal house was deeply divided between its Balliol & Cummin *v.* Bruce branches. Yet Angus Macdonald of Islay and his so recently Norwegian Islesmen were among the staunchest supporters of Scotland's nationhood under Robert the Bruce. And the heroes of Bruce's patriotic army included, besides Gaelic chiefs like Campbell and Lennox, nobles of Flemish origin like Douglas and Murray, of Breton origin like the Stewarts, and Norman origin like the Hays and Bruce himself. Even Wallace means 'the Welshman'. It seems extraordinary that our inventive nation could be forged out of such mixed elements in so short a time. I put the achievement down to the tactlessness of Edward I of England, the Hammer of the Scots. He hammered us into an enduring nation in no time at all.

So it was that, unlike the kingdoms of Wessex and Mercia and

Northumbria and even Cornwall, the realm of England never assimilated the realm of Scotland; although our own royal house had assimilated Caledonia of the Picts and Strathclyde of the Britons and Argyll (*Earr a' Chaideal*, the Frontier of the Gaels) and even the Western Isles; England failed to take her chance to assimilate Scotland. Perhaps it would have succeeded had the Maid of Norway, King Alexander III's granddaughter and heiress to our throne, lived to marry her fiancé the future Edward II, and there therefore would have been no War of Independence. In the end, as everyone knows, a Welsh earl having conquered the English in 1485 and clinched that throne by marrying the Plantagenet heiress, their daughter eventually brought the throne of England to the Scottish royal family, who have held it ever since. It is by virtue of her Stuart royal blood that our Queen reigns over the whole United Kingdom.

Nevertheless, it isn't always realised that England and Scotland remained completely separate countries until 1707. They were still as separate as Canada is from Australia now. Sometimes England was at war with France when Scotland was not. Thus, in the North, Charles II was styled 'King of Scotland, England, France and Ireland' and not, as James VI and I had wished: 'King of Great Britain'.

And up here, the Queen still has her own ceremonial Scottish Royal Household, though she is accompanied for practical purposes by members of her ordinary Household wherever she may be in the worldwide Commonwealth of which she is the Head. The Scottish Royal Household provides us colourful ceremonial with characteristically Scots economy. But all this beautiful though inexpensive ceremonial, in which we are able to mingle our hopeful present with our colourful future, would be meaningless if the Sovereign were never there to be its focal flame. The Lord Lyon as King of Arms may be called the custodian of the Spirit of Caledonia, but that spirit itself is metaphorically embodied in the Queen herself, with her radiant aura of goodness that is the true outward expression of inner majesty. And the Queen has paid more special Royal Visits to Scotland, quite apart from private visits to Balmoral, than any other Sovereign since her shrewd Stuart forefather James VI set out in 1603 to become, as he himself put it, King James the First of Great Britain: and to be placed at last on what was literally his rightful family seat, the Stone of Destiny.

From I.M.'s *Introduction to Debrett's Royal Scotland*
by Jean Goodman (Debrett's Peerage Ltd, 1983).

The Massacre of Glencoe

Bloody massacres are a commonplace of Scottish history: whether of alien English garrisons like the 'Douglas Larder' or the recapture of Ferniehurst (when the Kerrs, enraged by local rape, bought English prisoners from our French auxiliaries to use for target practice), or the extermination of inconvenient landed predecessors, as when the Macleans surprised and conquered Ardgour from the MacMasters and the last surviving MacMaster fled to the Corran ferry – but the ferryman refused to help him, seeking to curry favour with the victorious Macleans, so Donald Maclean slew them both, remarking that if the ferryman was willing to betray his late masters in need, he would be of no use to him. Why then was the Massacre of Glencoe the most notorious in all our history?

It wasn't because it was an act of treachery. That too, was a commonplace in Highland history. Thus the military historian Stewart of Garth recalls the occasion when his 15th-century forefather agreed to meet the Macivor chieftain unaccompanied in Glenlyon, to settle a blood feud amicably. Just in case, he hid his men around him, telling them that he would give a danger signal by shewing the red lining of his plaid. At the conference, Macivor suddenly whistled: and up started his own concealed warriors whom he called 'my roes that are frisking about the rocks'. Garth turned his plaid, saying: 'Then it is time for me to call my hounds'. In the resulting affray the Macivors were slaughtered without mercy. A similar tale of Lochiel meeting the Earl of Atholl 'alone', and each treacherously (or prudently) signalling up hidden clansmen, had a happier ending when the two agreed instead of fighting, and sealed the compact by throwing a sword into what is still the Loch of the Sword. Then there is the well-known Caithness tale of a reconciliation meeting of twelve horsemen from each side: 24 Keiths came, two on each horse, and slew the twelve mounted Gunns, although they sought sactuary in a chapel. So it was not treachery alone that made Glencoe so special.

Nor was it because a few women and children perished in diabolical horror amid the bloodied snow in Glencoe. Men from a MacLeod galley forced by bad weather to Clanranald's isle of Eigg were accused by the islanders of rape and the survivors, castrated, were set adrift in a rudderless boat that drifted back to Skye. The avenging MacLeod war-party searched the isle of Eigg for three days before discovering the *entire* Clanranald population of the island hiding in an enormous cave which I know well. The MacLeods diverted the water-course that concealed the cave, and then lit a fire in its mouth that sucked out all the air (like the ghastly Allied fire-bombs on Dresden in the Second World War) and suffocated every man, woman and child: there were toys among the then still unburied bones when the late Sir Reginald MacLeod of MacLeod slept a night in the dread cave to see if it was haunted. Again, the Campbells as a clan were far more effectively beastly to the Lamonts in 1646 than the mixed group of soldiers in Argyll's & Hill's Regiments were to the Glencoe folk nearly half a century later: the tree, upon which 36 Lamonts were half-hanged by the Campbells before being taken down and buried alive, soon afterwards mysteriously shrivelled up and there is contemporary evidence that for years a red substance like blood exuded from its roots; of the Lamont survivors, many were murdered later as prisoners, while for the girls and perhaps a few boys, who were kept captive for another eight days, their fate was even worse, as a Victorian would have put it. Yet this massacre is scarce remembered today.

The element that so marked out the Massacre of Glencoe was that it was done 'under trust', after living daily among and making friends with the victims. Such conduct had otherwise been unknown among our countrymen until our own lifetime. Few realise the treacherous circumstances in which British officers and men spent a fortnight palling up with the crew, spying out the layout, and then at 3 a.m. on 3 July 1940 forcibly seized the French submarine *Surcouf*, which had specially escaped from the Germans to take refuge with us at Plymouth: when the friendly French crew resisted in astonishment, our marines shot the gunnery officer in the shoulder, tried to bayonet the French doctor who came to his aid, and bayoneted a French sailor to death. And the slimy treachery has only recently been unmasked that involved Scottish officers and troops in making friends with the trusting Cossacks in Italy after the Second World War was over, before dishonourably tricking their officers away and then sending them all (many we knew well had never been Soviet citizens) – women and children too bayoneted into the concentration camp delivery trains, except for those who managed to commit suicide – to be handed over to certain torture and death or slavery under Stalin. Here was a modern 'Slaughter under Trust', unparalleled since Glencoe, but easier as most of it was done in the style of Pontius Pilate, leaving most of the eventual torture and murder to be done out of British sight.

But the point is this: both the Victims of Yalta and the inhabitants of Glencoe suffered such two-faced barbarity because their new 'friends' were professional soldiers acting on imperceptibly worsening orders, with little time at the last moment, when the full horror was disclosed, to make up their minds whether to ruin their own families and careers to save their personal honour. That's why I have always believed officers, and indeed people in any form of authority, should have enough private means to afford to resign: they don't always need to resign since they can speak their minds. At Culloden, General Hawley ordered one of his staff officers to shoot a wounded Fraser. 'My commission is at your disposal, but I will not shoot that man,' replied the future General Wolfe, who was later to die in the arms of a faithful Fraser officer at the taking of Quebec. To me, the two heroes of Glencoe were Lieutenants Francis Farquhar and Gilbert Kennedy, who were sent back under close arrest to await court martial for refusing to take part in the massacre: but whose subsequent careers no historian has thought worth telling us about.

And here we come to another point. It was by chance that the Company Commander most closely involved was a Campbell: he might equally have been Captain Drummond, and if Major Duncanson and Colonel Hamilton had arrived on time according to plan, they would have got the 'credit' for the Massacre. Campbell of Glenlyon only got his sickening orders at the last moment, and although he had been ruined by the Macdonalds, whose fault it was he had had to become a soldier at all at his age, it must be noticed that higher military authority were so little confident in his willingness to carry them out that the very order contains a threat to his livelihood should he disobey. And the very moment the great Campbell lords, Argyll and Breadalbane, who had been all for getting rid of the marauding Glencoe men by ordinary military action, and for cutting off their escape, learnt the way in which it had been carried out by soldiers actually billeted in the glen under trust, they hastened to dissociate themselves from this shockingly un-Highland aspect of the affair.

Because of the long feud between the Clan Donald and the Campbells, it has been natural to play up Glenlyon's part. Both clans had their roots in ancient royalty going back to pagan times. The bulk of the mainland possessions in Argyll of their common ancestor, King Somerled (slain in 1164), had passed through MacDougall and Stewart heiresses to the Campbells; while the bulk of King Somerled's territory in the Isles had passed to his male-line descendants the Macdonalds. Both had struggled to maintain or extend their own share. *Mac Iain Abrach*, as the Glencoe chieftain was called, belonged to an illegitimate branch of the original Macdonald royal house. It was as though a branch of ducal FitzRoys descended from King Charles II and Barbara Villiers lived on farms in a great English vale under their head, the Duke of Grafton. The difference was simply the poverty of the soil, not the grandeur of the lineage.

Moreover, every king of the ancient Gaels had been obliged, as part of his qualifications, to carry out a successful *creach* or cattle raid; and at this tradition the gigantic, mustachioed Glencoe chieftain of 1692 had excelled like his forebears. But their neighbours had taken it in good part: instead of lodge gates, Major Stewart of Ardvorlich still has a group of boulders that mark the graves of marauding Glencoe MacDonalds caught by the Stewarts and slain on the spot. They had had a sporting chance and lost.

Indeed, Macdonald of Castleton, who is himself a Chieftain of the old royal house of the Isles and has also written an excellent history of Clan Donald, shews great restraint in making it clear that the *method* – as opposed to one of the ultimate reasons – for the Massacre of Glencoe was no doing of the Campbells as a whole: Campbell of Ardkinglas and his Campbell sheriff clerk had both tried to save Glencoe from the start.

The blame for the way in which the professional soldiers behaved at Glencoe must therefore cling like a stinking fungus, not to clan feuds, but to the usual villain in military matters of this sort: to the politician who initiated the orders and saw to it that any future Army promotion depended on their being carried out ruthlessly. This arch-villain was the Master of Stair, that master fiend who sat beside a warm fire in Kensington Palace either callously indifferent or else gloating over the thought of women and children whom he had never met dying far away of exposure in the mountain blizzards: his explicit orders having been 'to maul them in the long cold nights . . . for human constitutions cannot endure to be long out of houses'.

It's strange how little journalists bother to get things right, although they poke into everybody's privacy on the grounds that the public 'has the right to know'. Only yesterday I read in a daily newspaper: 'The nine of diamonds is the Curse of Scotland – some say because the Duke of Cumberland wrote the orders on the back of it for the massacre of a Jacobite clan in 1745'. Butcher Cumberland wrote no such orders. In the 17th century every nobleman's coat-of-arms was seen daily by the public, painted on the doors of his carriage. Any heraldist knows still, and I am Albany Herald, that the Arms of Stair are nine diamonds (technically lozenges) on a cross saltire. The Nine of Diamonds was the armorial device of the Master of Stair, the evil genius behind the Massacre.

Times change. The present Lord Stair, a kind-hearted officer who commanded my old regiment, the Scots Guards, is now also Captain-General of the Queen's Body Guard for Scotland (the Royal Company of Archers); and as I sit in Archer mess uniform at royal Body Guard dinners, a piper whose pipe-banner bears the captain-general's

Stair coat-of-arms with its Nine of Diamonds plays round the table. As I sit there, pondering that the Curse of Scotland is encircling the port as both go round the table, I reflect that a Glencoe clansman – Ellice McDonald, Jr – is now the equally peaceful High Commissioner, Clan Donald USA.

Nevertheless, the very name Glencoe became a byword for indiscriminately barbarous massacre almost at once. When the Jacobites occupied Edinburgh in 1745, the Hanoverian General Guest held out in the Castle, occasionally bombarding the innocent city at random with his cannon; and sometimes allowing out raiding parties of his brutal and licentious soldiery to 'put off their Regimentals, disguise themselves in other habits, & come out in the night time, to rob or steal in remote parts of the City & return to the Castle with the booty:' The General was accordingly sent a remonstrance: 'To slay the righteous & wicked promiscuously, to *Glenco* poor women & children, to murder his Majesty's good subjects, only for the diversion of his troops . . . are so repugnant to humanity' (my italics). But the honourable way, by contrast, in which the Glencoe men claimed the right to guard Lord Stair's property from harm in 1745, is related in *Slaughter Under Trust* by Macdonald of Castleton (1982).

It only remains for me to say how pleased I was, while staying at Inveraray Castle with the late *Mac Cailein Mor*, to be shewn by the Duke the Exchequer order for the payment of compensation to the surviving victims of the Massacre: it was signed by the then permanent head of the Scottish Treasury, Sir Thomas Moncreiffe of that Ilk.

From I.M.'s *unpublished* Foreword to *Slaughter Under Trust*
by Macdonald of Castleton (1982).

Modern Mythology

It's always a pleasure to read anything written by John Prebble [*The Lion in the North: One Thousand Years of Scotlands History*; Secker & Warburg, 1972] – more especially when it's dedicated to my bolshie friend James Robertson Justice, who appointed me his Assessor when he was Lord Rector of Edinburgh University, *i.e.* his deputy as the undergraduates' representative on the University Court (goodness, some of those professors can out-rival the Mafia blindfold when they apply their minds to something, but they do it with silken cords).

Mr Prebble's flashes of insight are conveyed in dazzling phrases. 'There is a darkness now over much of the knowledge we would have, ill-lit by legend and myth, a black mantle upon which shine the jewelled names of seventy Pictish kings and the red-gold of their battles'. But I would take issue with him when he called the Picts 'a lost race'. We still live here in the shadow of Moncreiffe Hill by virtue of our female-line descent from the ancient Pictish royal house whose stronghold was on its summit – encircled by their capital at Scone, their holy place at Abernethy and their palace at Forteviot.

The truth of the matter is that the Picts followed a system well-known to social anthropologists, by which a 'true family' consists of the joint descendants of a great-grandparent, and the head of the family is its eldest unblemished member who is not senile. The Gaels followed the same system, and that's why it's nonsense to talk of cousins being 'usurpers' before primogeniture was introduced much later. The difference between the Scots (Gaels from Ireland) and the Picts (a Gaulish-British chariot-horsey aristocracy inter-mingled with an earlier non-Aryan speaking population) was simply that the Gaels based their 'true family' on the male line from their common great-grandfather, while the Picts belonged in the direct female line to that of their common great-grandmother. Thus Picts belonged to their mother's mother's mother's family. So Pictish appanages and their realm passed not to sons but to sisters' sons. The ladies literally kept the family hearth. This system could be studied today among the Bemba of Zambia, or until recently among the Nayar of Southern India.

Albany was not originally the most delightful complex of comfortable chambers in the world. It was what is now modern Scotland north of the rivers Forth and Clyde. Mr Prebble takes as his founder-hero my forefather Kenneth mac Alpin, already King of Scots, who united the Picts and Scots by a successful takeover bid when he thoughtfully assassinated the Pictish nobles who disagreed with his claim to their throne, while they were his guests at a banquet a few miles hence. But he undoubtedly had Pictish royal blood: the only question was whether his claim had been the best. Obviously it became so, after the literal liquidation of the total opposition (they were drunk when murdered). Kenneth altered the succession laws so that the appanages and the realm passed in the male line unless there was no son. After that, it was only necessary to marry the Pictish ladies whose hearths dominated great estates to husbands who were Gaels and the Pictish nation as such – but not its blood – quietly disappeared: merging into the Scots. Yet our Queen thus still reigns here, where I'm writing this, ultimately by virtue of her ancient Pictish royal blood.

The Picts of Albany left many beautifully-carved stones behind, and as Albany Herald I will always be grateful to Messrs George Rainbird, who

181

have organised the format and illustrations of this book, for depicting one I had overlooked. It shows two bearded Pictish spearmen with plain-edged tunics, their square shields each charged with the same device, following a taller leader with a fringed tunic, a diadem around his brow and certainly a grander (because longer) hair-style, and bearing basically the same device on his shield but with many grander embellishments to distinguish it from those of his folowers. This is *incredibly* early evidence of a local proto-heraldry that already distinguished between what we would call personal Arms and followers' Badges. By the way, Mr Prebble is mistaken in thinking a banneret a flag, he was a high military officer; mediaeval lances were 'pennoned' not 'bannered'; and heralds do not blow their own trumpets. This last idea arose through my kinsman Will Shakespeare's 'Enter Herald with Trumpet': *i.e.* accompanied by what we nowadays call a trumpeter.

However, this book is really intended to begin where the Picts left off, and gives us a light general account of Scottish history from Kenneth's *coup d'état* up to the Crimean War. Its jewelled journalism is our magnet, leading to loss of sleep because the pace of the News is kept up throughout.

There are two main criticisms. The book's full of Modern Standard Scottish Myth, *i.e.* generalised half-truths, beautifully expressed; and it contains innumerable minor inaccuracies.

One myth is that our mediaeval castles were built to keep down the common Celtic folk; and that hereditary jurisdictions led to oppression. In fact, any student of the late Professor Croft Dickinson's work on Baron Courts and Sheriff Courts will know that the castles were built as centres of law and order for the protection of the ordinary people whose loyal support was required to defend them. In any case, even had they been bloody-minded, the lairds couldn't afford to hire mercenaries. The only baron I ever heard of being murdered by his own dependants – and never forget how truculent any Scot can be when put upon – was 'the Bad Lord Soulis' of Liddesdale, boiled alive in a cauldron (another literal liquidation) on the Nine Stane Rig: an event so unusual between a laird and his ain folk as to be still spoken of although it happened more than 700 years ago. We ourselves possessed powers of life and death here until 1747, and a feudal baron like Sir John Moncreiffe of Easter Moncreiffe an advocate, held courts as Sheriff Deputy of Perth from 1594. Now, I am also feudal baron of Easter Moncreiffe and an advocate, and sit in Court, wigged and gowned albeit in my kilt, as Honorary Sheriff of Perth and Angus; and can give you up to two years imprisonment if you deserve it. Why should Sir John have been less just than me? Yet the press headlined my latest sentence as 'JUSTICE

TEMPERED WITH MERCY' (all I really said was 'Buzz off, you nit, and don't bother me again').

Another myth is that the bulk of our nobility were *conscious* 'Normans', and pure opportunists in the Wars of Independence. It has all arisen emotionally in recent years from that silly crack about Kind Hearts and Coronets: somebody with 'Norman blood' like Lord Crawford ought to complain to the Race Relations Board. To call Bruce, holding the earldom of Carrick by descent from the ancient Gaelic-speaking princes of Galloway, a 'Norman' would be like referring to Reginald Bosanquet as 'that Huguenot newscaster'. Doubtless the Bruces had spent perhaps five generations near Cherbourg on their way from Norway to Yorkshire. The MacLeods, of similar stock, went more directly from Norway to the Hebrides, yet nobody calls them 'Northmen' which is precisely what 'Norman' means. And when the great King Robert rose in armour to re-establish our nationhood, his family had ruled the dale of the Annan for as long a from the Fall of the Bastille until now. Nor should any effective leaders of a Resistance Movement in a completely conquered country (as we were under Edward I, of England, the 'Hammer of the Scots') show their hands too soon. The Scots nobles didn't, and have received by way of obituaries parrot-repeated cunning half-truths from modern class-conscious writers; as if you'd been the Maire of Lille secretly working for the French Resistance, but officially carrying out Nazi orders, and then shot dead into infamy by bolshie historians of the Liberation who had never fired a shot themselves anyway. Our 'great lords', as this book calls them, bided their time until they could strike hard: which is precisely what Bruce and Hay, Murray and Lindsay, Campbell and Douglas, Stewart and Macdonald, did.

There are standard myths for each century, but there's scarcely space to discuss them at sufficient length in this review. The minor inaccuracies are too numerous also to be corrected here. But, in general, they are points of detail that do not affect the wider points that are being correctly made. For example there were no Vikings for the Gaels to 'dispute with' in the fifth century: but there very much were a couple of centuries later. Again, when he describes King Edward Bruce's abortive expedition to Ireland, the O'Briens of Munster and the O'Carrols of Oriel are referred to as 'Ulster clans', which would be rather like calling the Scotts of Buccleuch an 'Inverness-shire clan'. But this doesn't alter the wider point that Edward Bruce's main support did come from Ulster. Then Mr Prebble writes of the ringleader of Riccio's assassins (as usual, a forefather of mine) as 'Patrick, Earl of Ruthven, a grim old spectre'. In fact, he was not an earl, but Patrick Lord Ruthven, and was probably in his forties. But this doesn't alter the book's wider point: that the Ruthven peer of the day led the assassins, and as he had risen from a bed of 'flu he was certainly a grim spectre.

My favourite cousin, Lord George Murray, is described as 'a brave mercenary': but his only military service was as a Regular ensign in the 1st Royals before he deserted at the age of 20 to join in the '15 Rising, fought again as a Jacobite in the '19 Rising, and was their supreme guerrilla leader in 1745. I have always attributed this 'mercenary' legend to the ridiculous characterisation of Lord George as a crusty old military bore in the film where David Niven acted as Bonnie Prince Charlie. We are told that Oliver Cromwell 'supped with Argyll and Warriston in the Canongate, and there the squinted-eye Highland chief, the manic lawyer, and the God-tormented English yeoman settled the troublesome affairs of Scotland'. The phrase throws the fantastic scene into sinister but practical candlelight with great skill. My wife's ancestor Argyll and my own forefather Warriston (both executed at the Restoration) are summed-up with brevity and truth. But could anybody – except for effect – describe my unfavourite cousin Cromwell, a country gentleman who became an MP at 29 and JP at 30, was a nephew to two knights and grandson of another, as a yeoman?

And here we come to the crux. A half-truth can be half true, and popular. Mr Prebble writes with journalistic speed for a general public. But if he had to check every petty detail to make it a reference book for scholars, it would take too long before it could ever go to Press. Moreover, the scholars have their reference books already. His real object is to get the general effect right. He is painting an Impressionist picture for us. And so, occasionally he deliberately changes things a little tiny bit to give that impression without footnote-type pedantry, as it were.

Consider: 'Godfrey MacDonald of Sleat, fourth Baron of the Isles, was a humane man and deeply regretted the evictions his debts demanded. He did what he could to help his starving people during the famines, and it was thus an irony that the most bitterly remembered clearance in the Isles took place on his lands'. There is much compressed into this, and the impression given is correct. Lord Macdonald was a kind man in the hands of a consortium of mainland creditors after the unexpected collapse of the local economy. He was also the heir of the mediaeval Lords of the Isles. What does it then matter that he spelt Macdonald with a large 'D' (printer's or typist's error?) or that he was not fourth 'Baron of the Isles', but Baron Macdonald of Slate in the peerage of Ireland? The effect Mr Prebble has achieved has informed the general reader without tedious explanation of historic anomalies that

184

have nothing to do with the context. Moreover, note that, although keeping well within popular feeling about these horrors, he is characteristically just and honourable to the poor Chief as well.

Incidentally, I wish Mr Prebble would write a book on the lairds who did *not* clear, and why their glens are empty too: reminding us of the problems of the population explosion and that the population of the Crofting Counties, even Sutherland, was greater *after* the Clearances than *before* them. But Stewart of Garth's acid comments, on the overbreeding caused by insecurity of tenure and the need for children eventually to look after one in those days before old age pensions, strike an even balance between us twain.

Also, I disagree slightly with the book's account of Flodden, and hope for an opportunity to tell him how the late Sir John McEwen of Marchmont explained what then became obvious when he took me over the battleground. As the author of that brilliant battle-book on Culloden, Mr Prebble might well be induced to turn his mind and hand next to Flodden, our other major national disaster.

Mr Prebble may be fundamentally a publicist, but he is both sensitive and intuitive, never deliberately mean, and combines sympathy for hardship with admiration for gallantry. His flashes of genius illuminate our nation's story. T. S. Eliot wrote of Kipling's verse that verse and poetry should not be confused, but that good verse rises to poetry in places. Mr Prebble's poetic saga of Scots contemporary folk myth (though laced with much scholarly research) is not intended to be verse for pedants, and we have had nothing as good as it since Scott's *Tales of a Grandfather*.

Books & Bookmen, April 1972

Highland Games

It's ironic that the man who said 'the noblest prospect which a Scotchman ever sees, is the high road that leads him to England' should perhaps be best remembered, apart from his row with Lord Chesterfield over the *Dictionary*, through his Scots baronial amanuensis Boswell and for their journey together through northern North Britain 300 years ago. Their successors reveal to us their own happy journey today [*The Highland Jaunt* by Paul Johnson and George Gale, Collins, 1973].

Messrs Johnson and Gale infect us with the self-conscious light-hearted gaiety of a couple of office-freed, proud and prominent editors on a trip (if that be not nowadays a libellous imputation) round the other great Johnson's Scotland. I write 'self-conscious', because it's a very cunning task to lay bare what almost amount to selections from a diary without picking and preening and then pruning the preening and then picking again. However, I knew Evelyn Waugh only slightly, Chips Channon and Harold Nicolson well, and – except perhaps in the last, always discreet, case – the lesson to be learnt from the publication of their diaries is to do the picking oneself. This is what the writers of this book have done; and any nakedness in what they've laid bare is as they would wish it.

For instance, it's not clear what this book ought to have to do with *British* politics and prejudices in general. Yet the book is full of slick generalisations based on fashionable cant, Mr Johnson: 'I yield to none in my dislike for . . . the landed aristocracy.' If he revisits Scotland, Mr Johnson may find he has to yield to my auld acquaintance Willie Hamilton, who has his public image to maintain in an ex-Communist constituency and doesn't like fellow-Socialists snatching the bread out of his mouth. One wonders what Paul Johnson knows of these strange well-bred animals. How many British 'landed aristocrats', from the Duke of Northumberland to Cameron of Lochiel, has Mr Johnson met, let alone arranged to stay with and observe their Estate Office work in order to study in depth the problems of their job? He would, it may be assumed, never boast so sweepingly: 'I yield to none in my dislike for . . . crofters': an interesting body of folk he appears to know personally almost as little. Again, Mr Gale is for blowing off a wind of change throughout Britain, and is 'a republican by instinct'. It's to be supposed that he strives so hard for our good that one day we'll no longer be a police state like our fellow monarchies of Holland or Denmark but a happy republic like Hungary or Czechoslovakia. Freed from our tyrannous Queen, we'll be able to bow down at last to President Vic Feather or Jo Grimond. Enough of this buffoonery: to return to the book, we learn that Mr Gale's recreations are 'looking, brooding, disputing and roasting beef'. Here, *looking* is to the point.

For it would be a mistake to dismiss this book as mere light entertainment. The book is divided into two parts: *Paul Johnson's Narrative* and *George Gale's Narrative*. It's hardly necessary to inform our readers that Paul Johnson was editor of the *New Statesman* and that George Gale is editor of *The Spectator* [*until 1973*] both positions reached only by a talented flair for controversy. So two very shrewd observers have entered Scotland in a relaxed mood but, nevertheless, may be presumed seldom to have missed a trick.

No sooner are they over the Border, than they discover that a *mortsafe* is 'a cast-iron frame to protect graves from bodysnatchers'.

Now, this is an eye-opener to me, who's never seen the wood for the trees and hadn't known they weren't needed by the english (Mr Johnson insists on spelling Gael 'gael'. *e.g.* 'Scotch gael') This shows how far Scottish enterprise was ahead of the Southrons even in the heyday of furtive anatomy, and brings the sudden realisation that Burke and Hare were, of course, Scotch phenomena. Again, it's news to this member of the Queen's Body Guard for Scotland (the Royal Company of Archers), their second worst shot with a bow until Admiral Sir Angus Cunninghame Grahame retired from the butts – the admiral once managed to land an arrow accidentally on the roof of Holyroodhouse – that the *papingo* as an archery 'mark' or target was unheard of in England, although the most conspicuous one today is probably that of the *Gilde des Arches de Saint Sebastien* at Bruges, where our King Charles II was a member while in exile. It is refreshingly discerning too of Mr Johnson to describe Dunrobin as 'not unlike the extraordinary palaces built by mad King Ludwig of Bavaria'. And it's possible we are more kindred spirits than this bitter book would make believe, for my manifold Mackay forefathers would have shared his views about what to do with that statue on Ben Bhraggie. It's a pity he doesn't seem to have read John Lister-Kaye's *The White Island*, for it would have increased his enjoyment: but he may have done so, for his description of my late friend Gavin Maxwell as 'resourceful and determined' is apt. Nevertheless, the book is marred – though not irrevocably – by continual harping on bogies seen in a glass darkly. In this, Mr Gale is much less vicious than Mr Johnson, which makes his narrative easier to read the first time – though Mr Johnson's, stripped of its acid drops at a second reading, has much to interest.

Unfortunately, from the moment Mr Johnson is kindly helped by Mr Gale to shoulder his portable chip across the Border, his ready wit is turned to castigate his shadowy black beasts. 'This is the territory of the rich Border lairds, who send their sons to Eton and sit in the Cabinet.' The context shows the writers entered by Gretna, but in all the west Border I can't think of a single laird who's sat in a Cabinet during my lifetime, unless, of course, he's referring to Alec Douglas-Home, who lives on the other side of Scotland and who, everybody knows, is only a natural born statesman because of his English mother: a Lambton descended from 'Radical Jack' Durham and the equally radical Earl Grey who as Prime Minister forced through the Great Reform Bill. Perhaps in England one swallow makes a summer. Moreover, it's so easy, so damaging, so unkind and so thoughtfully untrue a thing, to imply as he does that the people on the estates of these 'rich border lairds' live in 'evident poverty'. Perhaps Mr Johnson might first visit, to take but three examples across the Border, the Buccleuch, Lothian and Home estates and talk to those who dwell there.

Indeed, one suddenly realises that his shrewd powers of observation are blinkered by the preconceptions of urban journalism. News has to be news, and so written as much as possible in advance. Thus the facts sometimes get fitted to the preconception, and a visit may be made to the spot itself only in order subconsciously to 'put the spot' on the chosen spot. There was much amusement during Sir Alec's historic by-election in West Perthshire, when a London journalist arrived at *Kinross* and wrote for a national daily that he was sitting on the banks of the Lake of Menteith 'where Mary Queen of Scots had been a prisoner' and that he was surrounded by innumerable lairds' retainers – he particularly specified 'footmen' – who would all subserviently vote Conservative (he meant Unionist, the local brand of Tory). I belong to no political party, but suppose Trades Unionists don't understand our secret ballot. The report could only have been pre-written in London. We disentangled our whisky-soaked brains to think of *any* footman – most of our friends were lucky to fawn on an *au pair* girl – but had little difficulty in recognising the distant Lake of Menteith as our own nearby *Lochleven*, whence my wife's foremother Mary Stuart was indeed rescued by my forefathers, the boy George Douglas and Lord Seton. Similarly, I once found an uninvited journalist in the hall here, who told me he was on his way to interview 'Timmy', who turned out to be my school-contemporary and neighbour the late Lord Strathmore, because he was 'the first Lord Strathmore ever to become engaged to a commoner'. I told him that, if by 'commoner' he meant someone not titled, apart from Lord Strathmore's mother and one fruitless marriage in 1850, no Earl of Strathmore had married anybody who wasn't a commoner since 1725. Feeling sorry for him, I gave him some then unpublished gen on the Monster of Glamis: a 'scoop' for him, in fact. Next Sunday, his silly rag ignored the monster story, to my relief, but had a headline about it being 'the first time an Earl of Strathmore had ever got engaged to a commoner'.

This book is a garner-house of such stuff, though it's uncertain it should be ranked as a treasured curiosity like the down-to-earth works of the poet McGonagall, who also visited the West Highlands and left us verses like:

And this is beautiful Oban, where the tourist seldom stays above a night,
A place that fills the lover of the picturesque with delight;
And let all the people that to Oban go
View it in its native loveliness, and it will drive away all woe.

Mr Johnson has a weird fetish about bonnets. He even invents a grotesque Constable MacTouchbonnet, suggests that one can get 18 months in Scotland for poaching a salmon, and tells us the lairds 'can no longer force the Highlanders to touch their bonnets'. What is one to make of this? Normally the only people to wear bonnets in the Highlands, apart from American tourists, are the lairds themselves, and they do it seldom. Perhaps we are to suppose that the Highlanders were required to touch the laird's own bonnet, presumably to cure him of scrofula – for all true Highlanders have a royal descent somewhere in back of them. But I do know they would much resent Mr Johnson's condescension in calling the beloved homeland of these proud if wily folk 'an area of servility'. Doubtless he has misunderstood the mutual greetings of ordinary country courtesy. One is in a journalists' world set apart from reality.

Still on the same tack, we learn pontifically of the Hydro-Board, not that its first chairman was Lord Airlie, chief of the mighty Ogilvys, but that 'it is hated by most of the lairds, *for it operates to the good of all*' (my italics). How many lairds did the writer consult, and were they really so unworldly as to admit to him such universal malevolence? The rummest thing of all is that it emerges the writer has never consciously seen let alone met a laird: the creatures he hates as much as Hitler hated the Jews are chimera, it seems. For he describes a typical party of English middle-class shooting-tenants in Strath Naver and thinks them typical of the Highland 'upper class', whom he wouldn't notice if he passed them: 'brand-new posh car', he says of another alleged specimen, which shows what I mean. Yet he and Mr Gale stayed at the end of their jaunt with a genuine example, *Mac Shimi's* brother Hugh Fraser who was President of the Union when we were at Oxford together, at Eileen Aigas: the river island where my ancestress the Dowager Lady Lovat was held prisoner after Simon Fraser had raped her. Perhaps Lady Antonia distracted Mr Johnson's attention from his host's Highland upper-class brand mark.

On arrival in the Highlands, our authors patronised the delightfully elegant 18th century town of Inveraray, built by my wife's ancestral uncle the then Duke of Argyll. They removed the chip off Mr Johnson's shoulder for a moment to give my old friend Ian Lindsay the architect, alas now dead, a pat on his shoulder for his restoration work there. Mr Johnson goes on immediately to tell us about the Ministry of Works' grant and the 'democratic taxpayer' (talking of 'disputing', this gives rise to the question whether it wouldn't be more truly 'democratic', in the sense of government by consent, if surtax had had to be voted by a Parliament including representative surtax-payers, and indeed the highest taxpayers were specially represented *as such* in the Japanese Diet devised by Ito Hirobumi in their first modern Constitution). But there's never a word about the National Trust for Scotland, who planned the restoration of Inveraray, where the old town belongs to them, and who conserve it today with the help of voluntary funds. We would willingly take the Cash and let the Credit go, if Mr Johnson will join our Trust.

Then we are asked silly questions, not for the first but believe me not for the last time. 'Why do they call gardens "policies"? What is political about a garden?' Well, if only he could get his absorbingly one-track urban politics out of mind and relax, 'policies' are not politicians' bear-gardens but the polished improvements creating a polite area in which civilised lairds can in their turn relax strolling pensively around their homes before turning over the outlying fields to the utilitarian purpose of grinding the sweated faces of the bleeding poor by cultivating food for everyone to eat. While on the subject of gardens, we come on this baffling *non sequitur* about the unforgettable beauty of Poole we hacked from nothing on the Atlantic Coast and tended into radiance by a nineteenth-century cousin of my first wife: 'Osgood Mackenzie, who *despite the fact that he was a laird and sportsman*, was also a gardener' (my italics). After much reflection – thinking over renaissance Glenesk, 17th century Pittenweem, Lochleven as restored by my Uncle Basil, Drummond, Dunrobin, Crarac, Gigha, Stonfield, Colonsay and many others – I can think of only one exquisite garden in all Scotland that was *not* the creation of a laird: that gem at Branklyn in Perth itself. The English 'common man', like his fellow Scot, often keeps a beautiful little garden; but this has no obvious connection with his watching soccer on the goggle-box or belonging to the local anglers' club. So it's hard to understand what 'despite' can possibly mean except Mr Johnson's 'spite' welling up. To raise a completely different point of disorder: it is *not* 'a matter for argument whether Loch Lomond is in the Highlands'. Tell that to the ghost of that bullying cateran Rob Roy, or to the present Chief of the Clan Colquhoun. It's no more left the Highlands than Dover has left England. If this book were to fall into the hands of some misguided tourist, he would indeed be mis-guided.

We are asked of the Caledonian Forest that once covered enormous tracts of the Highlands, 'Is it true, as local tradition maintains, that the Vikings burnt it down?' No, it isn't. Vast areas were denuded by man during the population explosion during the seventeen- and eighteen-hundreds. We are told 'it is known, *or at any rate believed*, that a Spanish galleon' (my italics) sank in Tobermory Bay after the wreck of the Armada, and that 'the lairds', those ubiquitous villians of neo-Johnsonian myth, 'ferret' for her (with water-rats, one supposes). It is not 'believed' that she sank there. It is known. The great ship caused grave worry to Queen Elizabeth I because the Spaniards remained for some time, aiding the Maclean chief as hired mercenaries against Macdonald of Islay, and the Queen feared attacks on her own communications with Ireland. We learn from the English State papers that her govenment (then headed by my sensible forefather Burghley) hired a spy called Smollett to arrange for the galleon's distruction. But it's reasonable for Mr Johnson to have reported the firm local tradition that a Maclean hostage called Grey Donald blew her up, for this may have been the way of it in practice (Mr Johnson has been given the traditional tale a bit wrong). The Maclean chief (about whom Mr Gale is very nice, having beheld him kilted in a bar not sharing Mr Johnson's aristophobia, to coin a word with a splendidly apt true meaning), who is the present Lord Chamberlain and was my first Company Commander in the Scots Guards, won't have the story otherwise, and disdains the modern-discovered evidence about Smollett. No lairds 'ferret' for her, since as Mr Johnson himself points out she belongs by charter to the Duke of Argyll for salvage purposes. By the way, the printer has omitted a few words in a short version given by Mr Gale of some of the Campbell chief's titles, so that he gets called rather romantically by mistake 'Marquess of the Great Seal of Scotland' instead of Marquess of Kintyre and Lorne, Keeper of the Great Seal of Scotland.

It's difficult to write about the Clearances without emotion. I disapprove of them as much as Mr Johnson does, but for essentially different reasons. The Clearances were typical and radical left-wing planning for other people's 'own good'. Mr Johnson has read 'John Prebble's magnificent and fierce book, *The Highland Clearances* (1963) but his comments show once again that he is emotionally incapable of studying the problem. Whatever one may think about the justly hated Patrick Sellar's conduct in Sutherland, which eventually earned him the sack, 'genocide' is at first sight an exaggerated word to use for resettlement in coping with a population explosion. In 1801, before the Sutherland Clearances, the local population was 23,117; in 1831, at their height, it had risen to 25,518; and by 1851, when they were over, it had risen again to 25,793: the highest point ever reached in the history of that county. In another sense, though, Mr Johnson is right, for its native culture had been destroyed in the name of 'progress'. Mr Johnson could have found the same thing in a much more ferocious guise in the Ukraine, had he served with me in Russia in the days of his fellow-socialist Stalin.

To go back to Mr Johnson's answers to his own rhetorical questions. 'Why should Applecross be a centre of religious fervour? So far as I have been able to discover, it was not visited by St Colomba (*sic*). It was not the ancient site of a monastery'. Indeed it was, the most important monastery in the far North in the Dark Ages, founded from Ireland in 673 by my ancestral seventh cousin St Maelrubha. I am a proud Gael, of the Kindred of St Columba: neither gael nor Colomba, as Mr Johnson would have it, King Alexander III, who belonged to our Kindred, set on the obverse and counter-seal of his Privy Seal in the 1200s our punning motto *esto prudents ut serpeas et simplex sircut columba* ('be wise as the serpent and gentle as the dove'). It's childishly tempting to think up some similar pun based on Gael and Gale, but actually Mr Gale comes much nearer the truth, marred only by comment. He tells us about Applecross that:

according to McLaren, 'In AD 671 Maelrabha (*sic*), an Irish monk from Bangor, founded a monastery in this place . . .' The preciseness of the dates which guide books chuck around always amuses. The knowledge of places and dates of the seventh century is scanty indeed . . . 'An Irish monk from Bangor' creates a quite false impression, for in no useful sense was there Irishness in the seventh century and in no sense was there Bangor, and only in our senses were there years called 671 and people named as monks.

This shows that he hasn't had time to make any realistic study of Irish history at that period. There was an *ard-ri* or High King of Ireland from at least the fifth century, and we know their names, lives and dates from the various careful chronicles kept by the monks established in every part of Ireland in that and the following century. Moreover, these annals can be checked against each other, to verify dates. It was Ireland that kept alight the torch of Christian civilisation throughout the Dark Age western Europe. My kinsman Maelrubha was born about 642, a member of the royal house of Cenel Eoghain in Northern Ireland. His mother was sister of St Comgall, abbot of Bangor (in what is now County Down), which had been founded as far back as 558 and where there were three thousand monks. St Maelrubha became a monk at Bangor, but crossed over to Scotland in 671 (the date erroneously given by MacLaren for his foundation of Applecross, which took place two years later). Traces of his missionary activities can be found in twenty-one places, and he died on 27 August, 722 at the age of eighty. As a Fellow of the Society of Antiquaries of Scotland, I can recommend to the writers of *The Highland Jaunt* that for their second edition [*there wasn't one*] they have recourse to Dr William Reeves' S 'Maelrubha, his History and Churches', published in our Proceedings for 1861.

No chip mars the breezy flow of Mr Gale's narrative, and as for his being a republican he could in a sense have had his cake and eaten it in free Scotland. In 1548 my ancestral uncle Peter Moncreiffe, whose elder brother had been killed fighting the English at Pinkie, resigned his succession to the lands of Easter Rynd (a mile hence on the other side of

Moncreiffe Hill) to his own younger brother because he was unfit for military tenure: '*et ibedem palam exposuit se membris impotentem, inhabilem et debilem, ad serviendum Supremae Dominae Reginae. Reipublicae, et nobis domino Superiori*' ('and there showed himself to be impotent and too feeble in his limbs to serve our Sovereign Lady the Queen, the Republic and our Lord Superior'). So it isn't necessary with Mr Gale to parry wild swipes in order to protect the truth. A couple of corrections may suffice, the first probably a printer's error. No Scotsman could write 'Avertarff' for Abertarff, long the home of the now extinct illegitimate descendants of the line of the 'Old Fox' Simon Lord Lovat who was beheaded on Tower Hill. The letters 'b' and 'v' may often be interchangeable linguistically (Sebastopol, Sevastapol) but the Celtic word *aber* meaning 'mouth' is not. Abertarff means the mouth of a raging stream: literally *tarbh*, a bull. The only place in the Highlands I can think of beginning with 'aver' is Avernish by Lochalsh, but that is from the Old Norse *hafre naes*, oats promontory. Secondly, he has been told very nearly but not quite the form about our most sacred island, Iona. 'I, Y, pronounced Ee: the isle called by the shortest name for island, I. Iula, mis-transcribed into Iona, lovely mellifluous accident'. In fact, Y, the word meaning island and the original name for Iona as *the* sacred island, is pronouced rather like the first letter of the alphabet: as Eriskay or Mingulay in the Hebrides and Lindsey in Lincolnshire or the numerous eyots or aits in English rivers. Nor is Iona a mis-transcription of *Iula*, but rather of Ioua, the monkish Latin for that island. But Mr Gale is quite right about 'Iona' being a lovely mellifluous accident, and many girls bear this name nowadays, including the Colquhoun chief's attractive daughter who is the new Duchess of Argyll.

Having noted a few minor errors, it must be said that on re-reading the book becomes more readable. Once used to ignoring Paul Johnson's dogmatic bitterness, that has led him into some erratic sweeping generalisations it becomes possible to observe and admire his perception in matters he understands. And throughout Mr Gale blows on us a refreshing new wind with endearing rumbustiousness, so that one wishes one had been with them or at least met them on their spree. To give an itinerary of their jaunt with comments would amount to rewriting the book. But I wish I had been there to tell them more about what they were seeing. They passed a ruined castle with a stone house inside it (modernised, not modern) where they supposed a laird to live. From the description, this must have been the royal castle of Dunstaffnage, of which the Duke of Argyll is Hereditary Keeper, and the stone house only contains a room or two in which the Hereditary Captain (Campbell of Dunstaffnage himself, who lives in a small house some way away) has to sleep three nights a year. Mr Johnson sketched a stark, strong ruined castle at the head of Lochawe. This was what Sir Walter Scott called 'Kilchurn and its towers' in his song 'MacGregor's Gathering'. My MacGregor cousins taught me as a boy to eat the old staple diet porridge standing up, ready to run for it lest they be raided by Campbells. For Kilchurn was the 15th-century strongpoint from which my grim forefathers the Campbells of Glenorchy set out on their four hundred-year campaign to dominate a hundred miles of Breadalbane in a straight line. They succeeded. All is gone away again now, save the ruins of Kilchurn alone. The descendant of the men they harried and outlawed, hanged or beheaded, has more land in Scotland than they. He is Sir Gregor MacGregor of MacGregor now [1973] commanding the Scots Guards in scarlet tunic and bearskin cap, but those dreadful hunted days are still remembered in his title of Chief of the Children of the Mist.

To conclude, pompous people mustn't seek here a neo-Johnsonian narrative. The new Johnson has been enjoying a holiday, and so can we with him and Mr Gale in this revealing book. We must remember they are not statistical historians writing a guide book, or even doing a sort of H. V. Morton. Like the page to my ancestral uncle St Wenceslas in the carol, they are joyfully treading in the dinted sods of their scrofulous master the great Doctor – not 'by feathers green across Casbeen' tracking a literary phoenix, but just for a lark.

Books & Bookmen, June 1973

Alistair MacLean's Scotland

I Recommend *Alistair MacLean Introduces Scotland* (Andre Deutsch), but not its dust-cover. This is a book intended to provide a mature guide for serious visitors to Scotland: readable, not earnest, but knowledgeable. And this it is. But what tempts the intelligent traveller from Japan or Santiago to open the book in the bookshop? A reproduction of my wife's ancestral uncle the Duke of Gordon, to whom 'The Bluebells of Scotland' that I was taught as a child to strum on the piano was dedicated, when he went to war in all his tartan glory with his eagle's feathers and mighty horn as Cock of the North? Or of Raeburn's raffish portrait of The MacNab, from whom (The Macnab, not the Distillers who now own it) several girls in the district around Killin 'got the bad disorder': or perhaps some romantic sea-girt castle like The Macneil of Barra's astonishing stronghold at Kisimul? No, we have instead on the dustcover the delightful smile of what looks like a pretty Finnish air-hostess, such as would drive me to the nearest bookstall to buy *Penthouse* instead.

The book opens with Alistair MacLean's (he ought to spell his name with a small 'l' like his chief, the Lord Chamberlain [*retired 1984*] since it doesn't mean Son of Lean but Son of the Devotee of St John) personal introduction to Scotland, written with the perception of a tax-exile in Switzerland which I understand so well, having been a health-exile there myself more than 40 years ago. Switzerland is a far more beautiful country than can be imagined only by those who go there to ski in the lovely snow-covered Alpine mountains. In the Spring the meadows are covered with wild flowers the way England's are lush with grass. But there's nae place like hame, with its nettles & brambles & wasps & barbed wire: all so suitable to the kilt (under which, by the way, I can assure you one wears nothing). Alistair MacLean's main points are astute with that half-truth that is always more unbearable than the truth: as when a thief is accused of a burglary he hasn't commited. He writes: 'I fear that with religion as with nostalgia the element of hypocrisy is never far from the surface.' So I'm glad that he qualifies this: 'I defy anyone, even the most dedicated pacifist possessed of the most genuine abhorrence of every conceivable form of warfare, to visit the Shrine in Edinburgh, surely the most beautiful in the world, and come away unmoved.' For the driving force behind the then controversial creation of that war memorial in the Castle was my Cousin 'Bardie' Tullibardine, 8th Duke of Atholl, a majestic yet naughty hero-figure to me as a child. His Tudor blood came through in that force, turned Highland.

There follow chapters which I will not dare to criticise in detail except for two – as there are three doors into this room, and only two dirks in it and I can't keep my back to my front. Take my word for it, though, they're a' richt.

A few comments, however, may be useful asides. Alistair MacLean asks what, in the famous tune, renamed by Andy Stewart 'The Scottish Soldier', the Scottish soldier is doing in 'the green hills of Tyrol'. The answer is, that that was the original name of the Piedmontese march adapted for the bagpipes by a highland pipe-major who heard it when some Sardine troops were sent cynically by Cavour to their deaths alongside us in the Crimean War.

It's nice of Alastair Dunnett, the book's editor, to write a couple of pages about my fascinating Bulgarian great-aunt Nada Lady Muir as an ambassador like her father, but actually she had only just been appointed First Secretary in Washington when Uncle Kay got her to stand beside him on a carpet in London, suggested they should share it for life, and whisked her off to be the international yet Scottish intoxicatingly cosmopolitan châtelaine of Blair Drummond (no safari part there in those days) in startled Perthshire. Sipping gritty Turkish coffee with some Bruce scion, as a child, we could listen to Greeks in one corner and Russian exiles in another arguing in French about Albania, a strange reminder that Albany is an auld name for our ane countrie.

Two chapters therefore have alone been singled out. The first is 'the Law of Scotland', written by one Nicholas Fairbairn. I know the villain well. He lives in a castle called Fordell not 50 miles away by motor car. I've stayed there and bumped my head too often on the low turret stairs. He is the F. E. Smith or Marshall Hall of modern Scotland – the sort of QC who, to the typical enquiry from the bench about George Robey made by Mr Justice *Darling*: 'Who is Mr Robey?' would reply: 'A low comedian, m'lud, the *darling* of the Music Halls.' So you must realise that Fairbairn of Fordell's views on 'the Law of Scotland' are as unlikely to go down well with the brass hats, I mean big wigs, as mine are. Nevertheless, as honorary Sheriff of Perth and Angus I must instruct you to pay no attention to anything subversive in his article. However, he writes nicely about my forefather Sir Thomas Craig, 16th-century author of 'the first Scottish institutional text' on law.

Finally, you must be warned against the arch-villain. I do not suppose those responsible for these reviews realised that they had delivered into my itching fingers a work that contained a bigotedly-biased chapter on Scottish history by that ink-spotted show-off Sir Iain Moncreiffe of that Ilk. It is time this obscurantist dodo understood that Liechtenstein and Monaco are over-taxed countries that can't compare with the happiness of the USA and the USSR; that 'particularism' went out with the musket; and that *Pictish* nationalism is (even with all that oil) too late to save his old-fashionedly happy homeland from *Scottish* nationalism, which would bring the blessing of all the exiled foreign professors and bureaucrats who inhabit the vast housing complex that links Glasgow with Edinburgh. If he don't like this criticism, let Sir Iain sue me if he dares. I happen to know that he draws from us deserving taxpayers only £140 a year as a wounded Captain's 20% disability pension, and so is financially and physically unable to carry out this critic's advice to take a running jump at himself.

Books & Bookmen, 1972

The Isles

Many of us have a special feeling for islands, probably because they can only hold a limited and thus homely community. Indeed, I regard Monaco and Liechtenstein as sort of earthbound islands. Everybody knows everybody else, theft is almost impossible (Monte Carlo excluded), and the Sea gives a feeling of moat-like protection: really unjustified because, as on Colonsay twice and St Kilda once, there's no escape if a horrible raider lands with cunning or in superior force. How dare we complain that the Channel Isles don't share the burden of our Defence taxation, when we declared war on their behalf without consulting them, and then abandoned them to Hitler's well-known mercy? I myself love the Isle of Man, of which my Stanley forefathers, the Earls of Derby, were Kings and then sovereign Lords: but am neither rich enough to afford a holiday cottage there nor poor enough yet to have to be literally radical here and retreat thither altogether.

St Kilda is the ultimate habitable isle beyond the Outer Hebrides, far out in the stormy Atlantic. The islanders' remote chief was MacLeod of MacLeod, who lived far away in Skye near the mainland; they worshipped him from afar as a kind of tribal deity', and they thought he owned 'what seemed to them all the countries of the world'. But they ran their own affairs through the 'St Kilda parliament' to which all grown men belonged. As for Westminster, they never voted for any candidate there, 'and the benefits of taxation never reached their shores'.

In the 17th century they still 'could not really believe that it was possible to express oneself by making black marks on a white piece of paper'. But by the last quarter of the 19th-century they had established the celebrated 'St Kilda Post'. Their toy-sized 'mailboat' was inscribed PLEASE OPEN with a hot wire on the wood. It held within a bottle, water-proofed with grease and containing the letter with a stamp. A float made of an inflated sheep's bladder with a small red flag was attached to the hull. Launched into the sea, as many as two-thirds arrived on the coasts of Scotland or Norway, to be forwarded. Dame Flora MacLeod of MacLeod [*now deceased*] still preserves one of these 'mailboats' at Dunvegan Castle. For nearly five years they had a wireless transmitter, presented to them by the millionaire Selfridge of Selfridge's in London, but it was destroyed by gunfire when the innocuous islanders were shelled in 1918 by a German U-Boat.

In this Arcady, 'if a family lost a sheep, whether by accident or disease, the loss was indemnified . . . by one of the wealthier families, who took it in turns to compensate such losses'. But the inevitable

197

intrusion of the Stranger, with strange diseases and stranger techniques, eventually brought Death to their Arcady – as surely as the coming of the cannibals to happy Easter Island or that of the fur-traders who brought measles to slay the Eskimo. This 'separate culture . . . had more in common with a tribe of African bushmen than the inhabitants of their own capital cities of Edinburgh and London'. Twice the community was nearly extinguished. In 1723 it was so ravaged by smallpox from another MacLeod island that a fowling expedition returned to find only four adults and 26 children still alive, too weak to have buried the corpses of their tiny nation. There is an earlier story that two fiendish robbers from the Lewis blocked the gullible islanders inside their church and burnt them all, except for one old woman who smelt the charred human flesh and hid in a cave. She was able to creep out and speak about this naughtiness when MacLeod's Steward arrived on his annual visit; whereupon he fixed the robbers in an interesting way (read the book if you want to find out how) and eventually refounded the community.

But even the Steward's visits always brought infection, for the islanders were so isolated that they had little immunity. Those were the days when they fled from strangers, not from fear of violence but from dread of disease. However, the failure of their bird economy towards the end of the Victorian era, when the demand for their puffin-feather-mattress-and-gannet-lamp-oil products fell away, led to their feeble reliance on tweed – and to their welcoming strangers in the mask of tourists (as I write this: one Greek, one Turk, one Australian, one Prussian princess, Victor Hugo's great-grandson, one Scottish lord and two pretty girls of Italian-English descent are camping in tents on my lawn on their way there; almost two generations too late to help). Even so, the St Kildans were no longer self-supporting. When Mary Gillies died of appendicitis in 1930 because they couldn't get her to the mainland in time, they lost their Spirit, *i.e.* literally gave up the Ghost. Staunchly behind the times to the last, they petitioned 'Her' Majesty's Government to be removed, and left for ever. On the last sad day 'the island dogs, objecting even louder than their would-be protectors', were taken and drowned in the sea. But, ecology prevailing already, the cats were left to prey on the mice.

Since then, people who've stayed for a certain period on St Kilda, where the Army now has a missile tracking station, are entitled to wear a special tie powdered with puffins, the local seabird: 'tam-o'-nories' we called them in Old Scots, when my forefather King James V used to sail round the Bass Rock picking them off with a primitive gun to be scoffed up at the royal table. Being myself autocratic Founder of a club called

Puffin's in Edinburgh, I much covet this tie. We heralds are unmoved by the current trend against the wearing of ties; though it's an understandable inverted snobbish reaction to the stifling Old School Tie dominance of pre-War days, and I'd agree that *meaningless* ties combine discomfort with their lack of meaning.

But I've another personal reason for being interested in St Kilda: the strange tale of Lady Grange's hideous fate, in which my own near kinsfolk were deeply implicated, related in this book. Daughter of a murderer (hanged only after his right hand had been hacked off, flesh and bone), she had married a learned judge, brother of 'Bobbing John' the Earl of Mar who led and lost the 1715 Jacobite Rising; and was ancestress of the present Lord Mar and Kellie who is Godfather of my son as I am of his. Shrewing her husband, she threatened to betray his table-talk of Jacobite plots. So, in 1732 my cousin Lord Lovat (who had already raped my ancestress, the Dowager Lady Lovat, his highlanders cutting her stays while his piper drowned her screams) promptly sent a gang of Fraser clansmen to kidnap Lady Grange from Edinburgh, knocking out some of her teeth in the struggle. After a couple of years hidden in the power of Macdonald of Macdonald, she attempted escape and was handed over to my equally unscrupulous cousin MacLeod of MacLeod.

This politic MacLeod chief, whose portrait wearing trews and plaid painted in the attitude of Apollo Belvedere by Allan Ramsay is celebrated among tartan connoisseurs, was brought up as a boy here at Easter Moncrciffe: some extra rooms being added to the 1599 part of the house by the 14th Moncreiffe of that Ilk for Lady MacLeod's convenience. MacLeod sent the helpless Lady Grange as his secret captive to St Kilda. The islanders couldn't speak English, there were no books and little whisky, she spent long sleepless nights wandering by long sea-breakers; and she went mad. After seven years a smuggled message at last reached the mainland, but the rescue party got to St Kilda too late, and she died MacLeod's lunatic prisoner in Skye. The irony is that MacLeod eventually supported the Hanoverians when the crunch came in 1745, reckoning rightly that Prince Charles Edward was a dud bet (the St Kildans simply heard that their distant godlike chief had won a war against 'a great woman', presumably the Scarlet Woman of Popery). Moreover, the 'Old Fox' Lord Lovat, who had been a Hanoverian in the '15 Rising and had had nothing to do with Lady Grange since his men's rough dentistry in 1732, was after all this needless bother literally 'axed' as a Jacobite on Tower Hill after the '45.

Alas, I've never been to St Kilda, though always hoping to be shipped thither by the National Trust for Scotland, to whom the 4th Marquis of

Bute bequeathed the empty island as a nature reserve after buying it in 1932 from Sir Reginald MacLeod of MacLeod. It's otherwise impossible to reach this *ultima thule* save by private boat or Army landing craft. However, I've observed the author of this book [*Island on the Edge of the World: Utopian St Kilda and It's Passing*; published by Tom Stacey, 1972] Charles *alias* Charles Edward Maclean, since his nowadays unfashionable Eton and Oxford days. He has since redeemed this seamy background by becoming in turn merchant seaman, cowboy, wandering minstrel and now freelance journalist. His family are foam-soaked in the lore of the Isles. His father, Sir Fitzroy Maclean, the Balkan Brigadier who was the first to understand Tito's coming role in Europe, belongs to one of the greatest Hebridean clans (they owned the 'Isles of the Sea') in constant contact with MacLeod – while his mother is sister of the present warlike Lord Lovat, whose roguish predecessor intiated the tragedy that led to wild demented Lady Grange's misery all those sad years ago in what was otherwise the Arcady of St Kilda.

The White Island by John Lister-Kaye (Longman, 1972) is another book about a Hebridean island, but without a separate community for sociological study and as near the mainland as can be. It is Eileen Bhan, the 'White Island', in Kyleakin, the 'Straits of Hakon', the sea-gap that narrowly separates misty Skye from Britain: Mackinnon from Mackenzie, who both once had Macdonald of the Isles for suzerain lord.

Here, by a now automatic light house, my dead friend Gavin Maxwell converted the two former light-keepers' attached cottages into one 'long, low, lime-whitened house crouched in the only really sheltered position'. He made this home civilised in his talented, introspective way. His desk had belonged to the poet Wordsworth. The watercolours of game-birds were by Thorburn. The jewelled Moroccan daggers were reminders of his book on The Glaoui, that Arabian Nights hero-monster of my youth (I haven't been to Morocco since the Spanish Civil War). The 'long room . . . was dominated at the far end by an enormous Michael Ayrton' of falling Icarus. This is a sharp jab to my sleepy nerves: years ago, I bought for four guineas a sketch called 'Mist Rising' by an unknown artist called Michael Ayrton. I prized it much for its subtle excellence: it adorned this house, but a friend mislaid it, and some thief enjoys it now.

On that little island, Gavin Maxwell decided to make a happy zoo, and summoned the author to his assistance to be curator and to help him in a new book on 'British wild mammals, all 125 of 'em including aliens'. The zoo got as far as bird of prey aviaries on a cliffside, grouse and black-game netted with almost invisible nylon in a large area of flat heather; but the heron enclosure was menaced by the escape nearby of cunning foxes, who eventually had to be slain, albeit with reluctance.

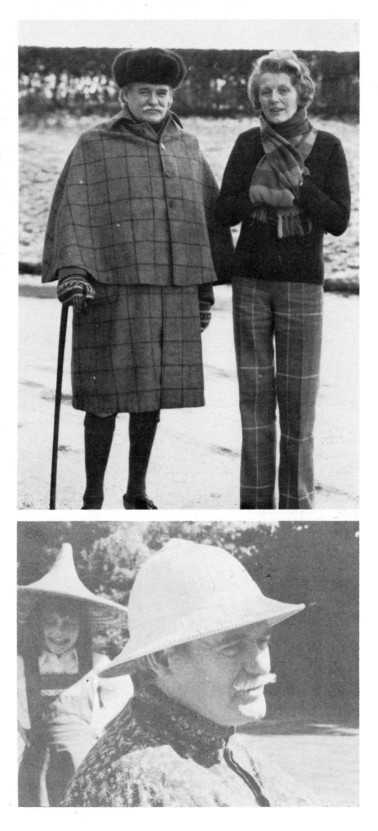

TOP: I.M., in Scots Guards cape, with Lady Lovat, 1976.

RIGHT: I.M., in solar topee (with Miranda Fox-Pitt).

OPPOSITE: I.M. on his travels: with the Blunden twins, Caroline and Jane, in China, 1978. Under the 'singing fountain' in the Belvedere Palace, Prague ('if you sit under it', said I.M., 'you can hear the bells ringing'), 1977; with Lord Dunsany in Denmark, and RIGHT on arrival at Cuzco, Peru 1969.

BELOW: I.M. with Chief Arogundade at the wedding of I.M's elder son, the Earl of Erroll, to Isabelle Hohler, 1982.

Mr Lister-Kaye discusses most sensibly the eithics of killing for sport. I myself have been head of two hunts, the Perth Hunt and the Royal Caledonian Hunt, though neither have actually hunted since the 18th century and a bicycle is kinder to my wounded back than a horse. I've shot tiger and panther, stags and capercailzies and even a cobra: yet, although I belong to the Shikar Club, I'm also an FZS and belong to our 'sister society' dedicated to paying for the preservation of Fauna throughout the Commonwealth (what we used to call the Empire). My Game Book, like Gavin Maxwell's – see his *The House of Elrig* – is in a sense my diary [*see* PART VII]. But we both loved wild animals.

The author understands this: that the hunter has a clean skill-relationship with his natural kill, and the urban dogooders reveal their social dislikes rather than real sympathy by concentrating emotionally on sabotaging supposedly 'upper-crust' fox-hunting rather than the hideous cruelty of a mammal struggling terrified and thirst-mad for a couple of days or more until it dies exhausted in an unattended snare set (as they do in my own land without my permission) by the county Vermin Control Officer or whatever they call the local ratcatcher nowadays. And the author's moving tale of how Jubilee the big brown rat converted a zoo colleague from attempted murder to affectionate liberation clinches this point: why is it consensusly OK to trap a rat but not politically acceptable to have a 'grouse-moor image'? Every grouse shot is food, but how many of you have eaten a rat?

This leads me to rag the author a bit unfairly. He writes convincingly (as if it were about the great Lord Curzon) of an unintentionally escaped heron:

its imperial haughty eye and august composure, suggest an extreme right-wing Conservatism, and absurd awareness of its own social superiority; yet, true to its human counterpart, the more it attempts to maintain its dignity in unfamiliar circumstances, the more ridiculous it looks.

This is rather too near the knuckle to expect a good review from the 24th Ilk, although I'm an anarchist in principle and a patriarchal empiricist in practice. But it seems not unreasonable to remind the author that his hero, Gavin Maxwell, had only two grandfathers; the one a Baronet who was a Knight of the Thistle, and the other a Duke who was a Knight of the Garter.

The projected zoo and book began to collapse after Gavin Maxwell knew he was dying. Although he dictated what was to have been a posthumous epilogue, there was no vast modern consortium to finance his foresight. He and I were in the Scots Guards together, it's nice to be told of the consoling help given to the stricken enterprise after its inspirer's death by Colin Mackenzie, of Kyle House on the mainland of

Skye. He too was a Scots Guards officer, who used to live in Robert Louis Stevenson's old house in Edinburgh and lost a leg in the First World War. He confided to me years ago that the ghost of the old leg is still attached to his nervous stystem; that it's maddeningly impossible to scratch an itch on an ankle that hasn't been there for more than half a century, and that the imaginary foot moves closer up to the real hip each year.

Mr Lister-Kaye instructs us valuably without pomposity. We learn why sea-gulls are better off with white under-bellies; of the harmless curiosity of a shark looking the size of a London 'bus; and of the horrors of do-gooders (my natural foes) 'mal-imprinting' pet animals or birds with their own kindly image and then releasing them, forever defenceless, into the nasty, brutish and short world of reality. It's not surprising that Gavin Maxwell had on that White Island a favourite otter called Teko, since he was writer of the otter's masterpiece *Ring of Bright Water*, to which Sir Robert McEwen of Marchmont contributed many of his delightful drawings. So it was appropriate that after his untimely death 'a carpet of flowers . . . was placed over the spot where Gavin's ashes were laid. It consisted of pinks with a single otter made of white carnations at its centre'.

To end more full of needed cheer: the author discovered from the sea an exciting polythene bag nostagically reminiscent of the 'St Kilda Post'. The paper inside hailed 'FEMALES BETWEEN THE AGES OF 16 AND 25 PLEASE CONTACT J. R. TAYLOR, TEL WRIGHTON 3215'.

Ascension by Duff Hart-Davis (Constable, 1972) is yet another island's story, but for a change not in the Hebrides. The author, however, has (like Charlie Maclean) cleansed himself of the current odour or odium of having been at Eton and Oxford and in the Coldstream Guards, by working as a deck-hand on a cargo ship along the coast of West Africa and then writing novels.

This thoughtfully-illustrated book describes a small volcanic island scarcely midway between Africa and Brazil, and therefore naturally one of the goddess Britannia's well-ruled protégées. It was once hateful to marooned mariners – a mute inglorious Robinson Crusoe's skull was discovered near the Devil's Riding School 'in the baking deserts of lava' – so that 'it became common practice for passing ships to fire a cannon into the rocks to rouse up any castaway who might be languishing there'. It's said that in 1726 the remains of a Dutch sailor, marooned for the nautically natural practice of sodomy, were found alongside the diary in which he had recorded his prolonged death in waterless agony.

Although the island is fundamentally indefensible, the Royal Marines took charge of it in 1815 to make sure 'General Bonaparte' (as the

Emperor Napoleon was named in their orders) didn't escape from St Helena, 800 miles away, of which Ascension is still officially a dependency. My uncle Sir Guy, the 22nd Ilk and a veteran submariner when not serving on the Royal Yacht, firmly instructed me in childhood to refer to Marines as 'turkeys' because the Royal Navy had never forgotten that Marines originally wore scarlet tunics; but I suspected there was a subconscious touch of guilty animosity because long ago the Marines used to guard the flogging naval officers from their press-ganged seamen. As a former Drill Adjutant of the Scots Guards myself, it can only be said that the Marines' drill is almost up to our required standards: which has never been reached, for we've never reached it ourselves.

The Marines ran Ascension until 1922, when its evident utility became obvious to Cable & Wireless Ltd, now its masters for more than a generation: except for the 'American Invasion' for an airstrip in 1942, when their pilots wending the wide Atlantic sang 'If we don't hit Ascension, our wives get a pension'. While the Marines held the rock, rum as it seems, Rum was their currency. For they were very bored, except perhaps in 1851 when an engine fitter called Peel had to be sent home to be tried for murdering Sergeant J. Perkins. And a private's wife had to be sent home too because she 'cut the man so severely in the hand with a knife whilst he was beating her . . . and in another quarrel they had he kicked her in the belly until the blood ran from her vagina'.

However, their duties included literally 'turning turtle'. The miserable turtles were turned upside down to make them helpless before their long live voyage to grace the soup of the great man whose name was marked on their fair white belly-shell. There was even a Captain of the Turtles. The sailors duly reported on these turtles' condition:

'I don't like the looks of Lord Melville this morning, sir'. The turtle list for 10 June, 1913 began: 'Right Hon Winston L. Spencer Churchill, MP, 6 quarts: Admiral HSH Prince Louis Athlone of Battenberg, 4½ quarts; Vice-Admiral Sir John R. Jellicoe, 4½ quarts . . .

During the last 26 years of the Marines' occupation, the head gardener was the dedicated Hedley Cronk, who made the mountain into the Green Mountain. Characteristically, since he was not a politician nor an intriguer but only a good man, he was retired prematurely on a pension of £100 a year. Today, his spiritual successor, Peter Critchley, keeps up the island's morale with dairy cows and breeding sows and 2,000 sheep, yet with only about 20 acres not too steep to be cultivated arably. His enemies are the wild donkeys left behind by the Marines. They do much damage, and he is considering replacing them with gazelles who would be more useful and more edible.

203

Last year a delegation of Scottish chiefs visited New York accompanied with bagpipes and wearing the kilt, also our wives carrying rare heather out of season. We were taken straight to the smartest night-club and introduced, in the general throng, to the celebrated Shepherd, the Man who Played Golf on the Moon. I told him I am a member of the Royal & Ancient Golf Club, and that in the Regency my great-great-grandfather, Sir David (then Captain of the Club), had seen a pretty girl on the golf-course at St Andrews and won a bet with his opponent that he would propose to her and be accepted. A few minutes after this conversation, someone offered to introduce me to the famous Armstrong, the Man on the Moon. Delighted to meet two astronauts in one evening, I was immediately led back to the good Shepherd. We kept poker faces: but realised we had been type-cast, a 'Scottish chief' and a 'Moon Man', and weren't really people at all. However, it's nice the scientists tell us that moon-rock has certain characteristics in common with Green Cheese – and our moon miracle owes much to the satellite and Moon spacecraft tracking-station now on Ascension Island.

Book & Bookmen, September 1972

Lochs

Being a life member of the Loch Ness Phenomenon Investigation Bureau (drunk, of course, at the time I joined), I can only say as a lawyer that if as many witnesses appeared in a criminal case somebody would have been convicted of being one of the phenomena. Moreover, Hugh Fraser, tenant of Glenconie, actually killed 'ane dragon' in the area in 1500.

In his second volume on *Scottish Lochs* (Constable), Tom Weir tells us about the mother of Osgood Mackenzie, and how Osgood created the beautiful gardens at Inverewe, where I first saw a handkerchief-tree (it looks just like a shrub growing Kleenex). He was, as might be expected, a cousin of my first wife's grandmother Lucy Mackenzie, Countess of Erroll, who died here at Easter Moncreiffe in the bedroom now named after her. Osgood's mother, Lady Mackenzie of the Gairloch, behaved splendidly during the potato famine, as Mr Weir informs us. She set all the able-bodied men in Gairloch to build a road for which she paid, thus enabling them to keep their pride and yet earn enough to live. She rode:

everywhere at this time of desperation, acting as doctor, building nine or ten schools in which the Gaelic language had to come first, and influencing people to pull down their insanitary dwellings and build new ones with timbers which she provided.

Mr Weir's mention of Loch Morie is nostalgic for me. I was walking up grouse in the heather there over pointers at the time the War broke out. One of the dogs, perhaps symbolically, froze, pointing at what turned out to be a toad.

Books & Bookmen

Edinburgh Cartoonist

'I KNOW NOTHING about art, but I do know what I like.' With many exceptions like Rublev and Breughel and Turner (thank goodness I still have some of the Dürer engravings bought by the 1st Baronet from Sir Peter Lely), I like portraits. So I would prefer a portrait by Martin of Sir Thomas Moncreiffe of that Ilk to a landscape by Landseer or a sacred subject by Botticelli, such as Venus (not known to be my ancestress for certain) rising from the sea. My main reason for liking Millais is that he was a friend of the family, put two of my Moncreiffe great-aunts' (Ladies Dudley and Forbes) into *Apple Blossoms* and depicted Sir Isumbras Crossing the Ford on the Moncreiffe estate. That, and as an historian, is why I'm a member of the Committee of the Scottish National Portrait Gallery, which has a 'richly splendid' portrait of my forefather Lord Seton, rescuer of Mary Queen of Scots; though when my wife called it that she flatly refused to add a little note to please me, saying I descended from him. All she did was to point out her own descent from the needlewoman whose work she was reviewing.

So I've known Kay's quaint cartoons since childhood, though our Paton copy of his *Original Portraits* (published 1837–8) perished in the library at my childhood home when the whole House of Moncreiffe, built in 1679 by the 14th Ilk, went on fire like a matchbox on a midnight in 1957: and my cousin the 23rd Ilk perished too in what I do hope so redoubtable a warrior would have regarded as his Viking funeral.

It's therefore puzzling to realise that Kay's work, which I've always taken for granted, is apparently so little known that the writers of this book [*John Kay of Edinburgh* by Hilary and Mary Evans; Impulse 1973] tell us 'Kay's work must be hunted for'. Kay was in an oblique way a sort of cross between an 18th-century Scots *Spy* cartoonist and Osbert Lancaster. His sketches bring the Edinburgh, indeed much of the Scotland, of those days to life. And his characters were characters indeed. They remind me most often of the present Nicholas Fairbairn of Fordell, QC, the best criminal lawyer in Scotland, and some of his clients and their judges.

Books & Bookmen, November 1973

Flying Moderator

At the age of about eleven I was sent for nearly a year to a literally revolting school in Switzerland. It was horrid to see a little Spanish girl aged eight being tortured by the mistresses (forcibly fed with tubes: put into a revolving cylindrical clothes-dryer with holes and told that if she moved it would start up and throw out all her blood) and to hear a young Pole called Serge Poznanski groaning all night in the next bedroom because Saint Nicolas (dressed up like our Santa Claus) had given him a sack in which he was made to sleep with the sleeves sewn up too short for his hands, to cure his nervous biting of his finger-nails (the 'saint' had also given the mistresses a cane to beat him with every Thursday night for a year). To near the point, there were only two English books in that French-speaking horror joint. One was Freeman Mitford's *Tales of Old Japan*, which made me such a samurai Nipponophile that I secretly learnt more Japanese than British history by the age of fifteen, and D. K. Broster's evocative *The Flight of the Heron*, a Jacobite romance which has ever since made the name of Lochiel sacred in my heart, and later forced me to apply all my skill as a lawyer (which is probably more than you think, hence PhD) to prove that my adorable Queen is the rightful Jacobite sovereign.

It's therefore only necessary to observe that the Very Reverend Andrew Herron's third chapter in his gentle and humorous autobiography *Record Apart* (Scottish Academic Press, 1974) is called 'The Flight of the Herron' to realise that his book deserves a favourable review.

Three years ago the author was elected to and held the grandest position in the Church of Scotland, that of Moderator of its General Assembly. A glance at the General Tables of Precedence printed at the beginning of the invaluable *Kelly's Handbook* [now superseded by *Debrett's Handbook*] will remind you that in Scotland the Moderator (like the Archbishops of Canterbury and York in England) is placed before the Prime Minister, and way ahead of mere dukes. The principal person who goes before him – indeed even before Prince Philip and Prince Charles – is the Lord High Commissioner, our nominal viceroy, who lucky chap is attended by people like me dressed up to look like Solomon in all our glory. But we get crammed into the tiny royal box overhead (surprise, surprise, I once had a hangover and was nearly sick down the neck of Mr Douglas, the then American Ambassador) for neither the Sovereign nor her Representative are technically allowed into the main Assembly itself. There Christ alone is King. And there the Moderator struggles to moderate.

Our local minister, a kindly man, once gave me a lift to Edinburgh, for I don't drive a motor car. He agreed that 'saint' simply means 'holy man', and that many statues are erected to crafty statesmen and bloody generals. So I asked why all the statues of holy men were deliberately destroyed by egged-on urban vandal loons at the Reformation, yet there was now a statue of the holy man John Knox bang outside the General Assembly itself? The author refers to that statue, and reflects on what Knox would have thought of the 'resplendent glory' of our procession, without considering the irony of that jolly good graven image.

Now that our Sovereign has given up Presentation Parties and levees are long gone, perhaps the grandest Court in the world is that held at Holyrood House by His Grace her Lord High Commissioner; and the author describes the proceedings with insight. It does a lot of good, for it gives Scotland an emotionally ceremonial centre that is by no means provincial and is nevertheless directly linked to her truly democratic Church.

Books & Bookmen, 1974

MacPuff

Before I was kidnapped at the age of four, I was fascinated by motor cars and knew all their names. Since then, for some reason that only a trick-cyclist could discover, I have shunned them. At Sandhurst, cunning was therefore needed to pass the Car Maintenance examination. I consulted Reggie Gordon-Lennox, a keen motorist: what on earth were the only twelve questions that could possibly be asked about the internal combustion engine?

I memorised his answers and diagrams, as some lunatic Egyptologist on Radio Luxembourg might try to solve the prophetic significance of the convolutions of the Great Pyramid. The correct unintelligible questions were duly posed, and I got very high marks. However, whenever I drove anybody in a military motor car, they all jumped out and walked: and I longed to leap out too. So I've never applied for a driving licence. It's a strange coincidence that an advertisement has just arrived asking 'COULD YOU AFFORD TO LOSE YOUR DRIVING LICENCE?'

Youthful enthusiasm for motor cars is usually followed by the ambition to become an engine driver. Lords Northesk and Garnock, among others, have achieved this amibition, and Lord Hesketh is acquiring a second-hand miniature railway for Knoydart: though Lord Teviot has to be content with driving a bus by way of a career [*he married his clippie and they are now distinguished genealogists* – ED]. This is perhaps why there was much less public sympathy for the railway strike than for the miners' strike – and why the David & Charles illustrated railway series have reached the convenient rank of Pan Books in paperback.

This fascination for trains needs no conveying to a devotee. Count Moltke won the Franco-Prussian War by his close study of railway time-tables. Years ago, in Boodle's, there was a member called Leveson-Gower who knew Bradshaw by heart. I could ask him how to get from Bristol to Ullapool on a Saturday, and he would produce the necessary connections out of his head. Those of you who have served in the British Army will be surprised to hear that this round peg was actually shoved into a round hole, by being put in charge of railway transport by the Lieutenant-General (who was naturally called 'the Major-General') Commanding the Brigade of Guards. A. J. Leveson-Gower's fellow enthusiasts will be bound to welcome this book [*The Highland Railway* by H. A. Vallance, revised by C. R. Clinker; published by Pan, 1972] to their libraries: and as a work of reference it will be essential to them.

The book carefully avoids discussion of the political and social effects of the Highland Railway. So, even if I dared, I'm unable to smell out the civil servants ('no longer servants and no longer civil', in Churchill's famous warning) whose persuasion of a hapless Tory Minister prematurely to disclose the Beeching Report on the eventual closure of vital stations on that railway cost enough seats to lose Sir Alec Douglas-Home his premiership. Luckily Frank Thomson tackled the enemy (and was himself destroyed) with his celebrated 'MacPuff' campaign that saved many Highland rail lines from closure.

For the Railway is the main artery of the Highlands, and the only *valid* justification for nationalising it should have been that fares and freight should now cost the same for any distance throughout this island, just like postage stamps. In the long run, without a railway, no amount of 'crofter access roads' will be of much use to our substituted motor transport, unless the North Sea brings up enough petrol to redeem what we lost to the Red *bloc* when we pulled Mad Mitch out of Aden.

Books & Bookmen, 1972

VI

South of Berwick

The Hapless Hapsburgs

The then youthful Emperor Francis Joseph had taken over the Hapsburg empire during the European crisis of 1848. It was a generation since Waterloo, just as we now have a generation that knew not the Hitler War. Then, as now, idealistic youth was spoiling for something to fight for. Then, as now, left-wing politicians saw their chance to stir up 'students': an idea which we have at last imported from the Continent – like those of milord professor Kaldor & milord Balogh, one of whom said at an Oxbridge conference, soon after the War in which I was wounded saving their livelihood and possibly their lives, that his object was 'the gradual euthanasia of the *rentier* (*i.e.* the doctrinaire elimination of those saved-up and usefully-invested private means that alone can give a family man the freedom to speak his mind and resign), presumably so that we can all be jolly State serfs together as has already been achieved in their happy homeland of Hungary. In 1848 we still had undergraduates, the Continent already had students. I've been both the one at Oxford and the other at Heidelberg. *Vox populi vox Dei* is paradoxically nowadays the slogan of a largely agnostic or atheist *authoritarian* Left. As a howling rent-a-crowd smashed the windows of wily Prince Metternich, who had preserved the balance of peace in Europe for 33 years, he observed 'That is what our Liberal friends would call the Voice of God' (he then slipped away disguised as a sailor, if I remember right). Since the dawn of *fraternité*, whenever a politician calls any of us 'brother' I recognise the voice of Cain.

But Field-Marshal Prince Windisch-Grätz parried their violence and riposted as firmly as any modern Soviet marshal in a satellite republic. While the bureaucrats dithered as usual, he acted immediately, without saddling them with responsibility which is always like trying to put a saddle on a cow. A sensible soldier he had remarked that '*Der Mensch beginnt beim Baron*' ('mankind begins with barons'): a truth as manifestly self-evident as the one slipped by those American slave-owners into their Declaration of Independence that 'all men are born free and equal'. Moreover his own wife had just been killed by a stray bullet fired in the fraternal cause of radicalism. The field-marshal found that a brisk bombardment of Prague stopped the rioting literally in a flash, and Bohemia with Austria were saved for the *schlamperei* of bureaucracy.

By the end of 1848 Francis Joseph's Prime Minister was the field-marshal's brother-in-law, Prince Felix Schwarzenberg, who also believed in firmness, pointing out that 'You can do anything with bayonets except sit on them'. However, although he belonged to the greatest and perhaps the most talented family in Bohemia (his uncle had defeated Napoleon at Leipzig), he didn't share his brother-in-law's class solidarity. According to Szemere, writing only three years later, my moderate cousin Count Lajos Batthyany, the first constitutional Prime Minister of Hungary, bled himself to death with a small concealed dagger at night when Schwarzenberg got him sentenced to be hanged after the Magyar nationalist rising of 1848–9. This appears to have been hushed up, as history books say he was merely *shot* which would not have driven a *Catholic* magnate to suicide. Like Conor Cruise O'Brien who on a Xmas Eve unleashed on our behalf kukri-armed aggressive foreign pagan mercenaries against black Christian homerulers dying on their own soil for their beloved homeland in the Katanga, the Prince thought Home Rule reactionary. It seemed to him an attempt to retrogress from Hapsburg supranationalism to local particularism.

I would have sought a constitutional confederation of Austria, Bohemia, Hungary and Croatia, and therefore have been opposed to the policies of the young emperor and his prime minister. But my maternal great-grandfather was an officer and a count, also an Imperial and Royal Chamberlain in Vienna; besides being a confidential agent for Francis Joseph's bother, the Emperor Maximilian of Mexico who was shot by a firing squad in a typical Hapsburg tragedy; and what ultimately is loyalty if, after giving your best counsel, you don't respect the decisions of the Sovereign to whom you are loyal? This was the classic position of the Gentle Lochiel in 1745. The head of steam building up in the nationalist kettle was reduced a bit through the *Ausgleich* with Hungary in 1867 that placated the fiery Magyars yet sacrificed the educated Croats. But it was *too late* when Francis Joseph's saintly successor the Emperor Charles tried to establish such confederal autonomies. At the end of the First World War, in which Charles from his accession had always sought peace more than any other European statesman, the Czechs and South Slavs blew the lid off the Hapsburg kettle. Though many Czechs now regret belonging to Yugo-Slavia, and the Czechs seem to think they've met with a worse fate than confederation with Austria (I met Jan Masaryk in Moscow and he talked good sense but that didn't save him from the latest Defenestration of Prague), the Hapsburgs sought to emulate our Dominion System too late. Yet Alec Douglas-Home's ancestor 'Radical Jack' Durham's world-changing report on Canada had been laid before our Mother of Parliaments nine years before Francis Joseph himself acceded to his motley thrones. As with friendly Siena in 1559, the Hapsburgs couldn't take 'Yes' for an answer. With them, it was all or nothing *Où sont les neiges d'antan?*

During the 19th century the abler young archdukes toyed with similar ideas: but they were politically impotent. When I dabbled in diplomacy, a British ambassador once told me how sad it was that the present generation of Hapsburgs are the most brilliant of all, yet even more impotent politically. But to return to the formative years of Francis Joseph's reign: Prince Felix Schwarzenberg's undoubtedly high intelligence made him despise alike what he considered the woolly Constitution-seeking aspirations of the various liberal-nationalist bourgeoisies and the 'dangerously' independent attitude of the higher aristocracy, whom he deprived of their local 'patrimonial jurisdictions' without compensation and whom *as a class* – though not individually – he effectively excluded from government. They were left with service in the army, the Church or diplomacy. Miss Cassels, in *Clash of Generations: A Hapsburg Family Drama in the Nineteenth Century* (John Murray, 1973) quotes my wife's great-granduncle Lord Frederic Hamilton as saying of the Austro-Hungarian high aristocracy that 'they did not trouble their intellect'. Schwarzenberg had seen to that: he didn't want them to.

So the Emperor, dressed daily in his simple workmanlike field-marshal's uniform, soldiered on alone at his desk for the rest of his life. He bore in person the daily burden of administering his variegated peoples: United Nations more forcibly united in real life than our sacred cow UNO. He also had the boredom to him (I would have enjoyed the pageantry) of having to turn up regularly for functions to keep the Court of Vienna a ceremonial melting-pot for his even more variegated 'First Society' of *intermarried* princes and counts who sprang from almost every European jumble. The exception *par excellence* was perhaps the marriage in 1894 of one of them, Count Coudenhove-Kalergi, sprung from mediaeval knightly Brabantine stock, to the delicious slant-eyed daughter of a Japanese samurai: their grandson told me that to their surprise Francis Joseph was unexpectedly friendly about it as her father had himself been a mediaeval knight in exotic armour until the dawn of *Meiji*. It somehow reminds one of the practical joker who toured

England lecturing as His Highness the Sanjak of Novi Bazar. The Court was *petit-point* ruffily starched with the elaborately civilised protocol of the Burgundian Etiquette, brought with Golden Fleece by the Hapsburgs from Brussels to Madrid, and thence crystallised into the scintillating hardness of a beautiful diamond as the Spanish Etiquette when they took it with the grey Lippizaner *haute école* horses on to Vienna. But although Miss Cassels' book opens with the 'First Society' at a *Hofball*, it's really about the even grander Hapsburg archdukes who were imprisoned by their conscientious Emperor in this gilded cage.

The Court Balls, and the even more exclusive Balls at Court, were a kaleidoscope of waltzing coloured uniforms and swinging dolmans: for those were the heydays of Johann Strauss. As an ensign in the Scots Guards at the Tower of London during the Blitz, my Company Commander was the present Sir Dudley Forwood who had been honorary attaché in Vienna. He introduced me to a Free French air force officer who was, of course, that tough cookie Prince Starhemberg, former Vice-Chancellor of Austria, foe of 'the Manitu' (Hitler's old nickname) but best known for the action of his private army the bourgeois-peasant *Heimat-Schutz* against the Marxist-proletarian *Schultzbund* through that cad Frey's doing. The Prince most courteously taught me to waltz: to stand bolt upright with one's partner as though both are one, to be able to rotate continually on the same spot, and never to focus one's eyes too near the swirl. Unfortunately he said gentlemen didn't reverse, and I've never yet been able to master this feat even to assist a giddy partner. Highland balls are picturesque and frenzied enough: and the 23rd Ilk and I once made up a party with the Archduke Robert to dance reels until dawn at the Oban Ball. But Viennese bands still break through the clouds of life in a dazzling sun-burst to inspire and invigorate us all with the most intoxicating ballroom music in the civilised world. Venturing with the Colquhoun chief to don our tartan jackets for a brilliantly uniformed ball in the Schwarzenberg Palais some years ago, I still remember flying through the air with the greatest of ease in an unforgettable *polonaise* with an energetic La Rochefoucauld: and all the horns of Elfland wildly blowing. Moreover, we had the advantage of escaping the stink of boot polish. Miss Cassels tells us it ruined the imperial balls with 'a strong and most disagreeable smell ... Army regulations included no provision for patent leather'.

In *Clash of Generations*, her consuming work on the demi-godlike tragedies that lit up the twilight *Götterdämmerung* of the greatest Hapsburgs in our Victorian era, Miss Cassels uses word-sketches as Osbert Lancaster illuminates our own times with lampoon-cartoons.

This is one of the best books my wife or I have read for many a night, although we differ as much as any two critical individuals must do in our literary choices.

Miss Cassels ends by a comparison between the 16th-century Emperor Charles V, who abdicated and rehearsed his own funeral when his physique broke under the burden of ruling from the Danube to Peru with sailing ships over an empire on which the sun then never set, and his weary descendant Francis Joseph, who somehow struggled on to the end, 'But he too was very tired.'

It's hard to recognise without a jerk 'Karl V' as the emperor whose biography was written by my old Stowe history tutor Bill McElwee in *The Reign of Charles V*. But Miss Cassels is writing about Austria, and is consistent in her decision to stick to the Austrian form of German names, only slipping into our spelling 'Hapsburg' once or twice. Thus she renders what we call 'Saxe-Coburg' as 'Sachsen-Coburg'; and indeed our form is ridiculous, since Saxe is merely the French for Saxony. We don't talk about Autriche-Hungary, nor of the King of Saxe or the Anglo-Saxes, so why don't we call Queen Victoria's consort Prince Albert of Saxony-Coburg?

Incidentally, Miss Cassels don't like the Saxe-Coburgs, having taken in aversion that Congo skulldugger Belgian Leopold and Foxy Ferdinand of Bulgaria. The fox's son King Boris had the royal taste for practical jokes, one of the rare ways in which they can relax. My Bulgarian great-aunt Nada Lady Muir told me that before a grand but unavoidable meal he would secretly sprinkle aniseed on a chair-leg of the most pompous guest and then leave his pet dogs to complete the jape. Her father, General Dimitri Stancioff, had been Prime Minister but more usually represented Bulgaria in every capital of importance and owed his Ruritanian-style uniform and martial rank of General to being an honorary colonel in the royal Guards: he was uncommonly kind to me as a boy and initiated me into Balkan affairs. The Saxe-Coburgs were the family of Crown Prince Rudolf's wife, to whom he gave gonorrhoea: an irony, since her first cousin Ferdinand of Saxe-Coburg was married to the sovereign Queen of Portugal whose father had reigned as Emperor of Brazil over the birthplace of rubber goods (Boswell records that in Dr Johnson's time he himself had to do it sheathed in leather 'armour' and caught the same affliction when he didn't). Her dislike of the Coburgs misleads Miss Cassels into writing that their 'blood was not very blue'. On the contrary, they can be traced father to son from a Count living in 892, and their direct male ancestor was also Prince Elector of Saxony in 1423, before Archdukes of Austria existed. Indeed, this is the male line of our present Queen.

Nevertheless, Miss Cassels's book is throughout a masterpiece of disciplined statement. Otherwise, so tangled a task must have led to anecdotal incoherence. This is what happens at Easter Moncreiffe, where few guests are tricked by Oscar Wilde's play into supposing that Moncreiffes believe in the Importance of being Ernest to such an extent as to keep our candle-lit after-dinner conversation to the point. So, since there is so little to criticise – except that she is surely wrong in describing the Emperor as 'tall'? and might perhaps have mentioned Bay Middleton as well as Count Charles Kinsky amongst the Empress' equestrian friends in England – this review will be subject to no such discipline.

For example, we are told of Heinrich Slatin's official duties in the aftermath of the Crown Prince's self-doom at Mayerling, without the irrelevant aside that he was brother of that Flashman of the Sudan, Baron Sir Rudolf von Slatin *Pasha*. In this bizarre context, it may be worth noting that the Slatins were originally Jews before becoming Catholics. From the downfall of the mighty steppe empire founded by my Khazar forefathers who adopted Judaism in the eighth century, the adherents of that religion had been so excluded from open power within Christendom that theirs was the last hereditary talent to be absorbed into the European community. By then they had become what Arthur Koestler has described as 'the exposed nerve-centre of Western civilisation'. The Hapsburgs deserve credit for rectifying this. By the 19th century my own renaissance Fugger [*see* EDITOR'S INTRODUCTION] and my wife's renaissance Medici banking ancestors had long vanished from the financial scene and been succeeded by the Barons Rothschild and that intriguing character Baron Hirsch, to whom the Crown Prince left a secret dying note, never betrayed.

My own nearest connection with Mayerling was to take the Crown Prince's granddaughter Stephanie Windisch-Grätz to the Four Hundred night-club. But I've always wondered whether Count Hoyos wasn't at least partly in the secret and expecting a suicide pact by cyanide instead of shooting, which would account for his not bringing himself to enter the fatal bedroom when he ordered the valet Loschek to break in and then immediately dashed off to take the poison story to Vienna. On the other hand, Miss Cassels has unearthed a Rothschild counter to my theory, and also notes a Viennese rumour that Hoyos 'had offered to Franz Joseph to spread the story that while out shooting he had accidentally killed Rudolf, and then leave the Monarchy for good'.

It was perhaps typical of the Hapsburg empire that the Austrian Prime Minister who then had to deal with the tragedy was an Irish peer with estates in Bohemia. The Crown Prince was a keen ornithologist but an obsessive shot, and should have entered himself in his own Game Book.

The Magyars mourned Rudolf most, Miss Cassels prints a moving telegram of condolence to the Emperor: 'The humble inhabitants of a small faraway village add their tears to the sea of sorrow. The Parish of Bögöz'.

Rudolf's cousin the Archduke Johann Salvator perished in the second of the tragedies examined in *Clash of Generations* – if you except Albrecht's daughter the young archduchess who, 'caught by her father smoking, set her dress on fire while trying to hide her cigarette and was burnt to death'. The Hapsburgs of that day were rather like Struwwelpeter trying to play Happy Families with inflammable cards. Johann Salvator belonged to the *Toskaner* branch of the Hapsburg-Lorraines who, inheriting Florence through the Medici heiress, had 'made Tuscany into a model state'. They were talented and sometimes eccentric, like those of us who are not slavish morons. Known as *Giani* as a boy, for his native tongue was Italian, Johann Salvator always loved the Mediterranean. Curiously enough, he shared this love of the sea with Rudolf. It was a cruelty of history that their Danube Monarchy became increasingly landlocked: and an undeserved Nemesis that they were eventually succeeded in Hungary by Horthy, an admiral without a port. Once I was sitting up discussing Tiberius with Lady Cunard after dinner when Duff Cooper came in and said the Peace Conference was delating Trieste but no good would come of it, for although it was obviously Austria that really needed a seaport it must, for practical reasons, be given to Italy or Yugo-Slavia.

Yet Johann Salvator was ready to sacrifice the Mediterranean for love of the Italy whose unity I've always thought almost as big a disaster as that of Germany. After his brother lost Tuscany, he observed: 'The Tuscans are Italians, the Italians wanted unity and the existence of the Grand Duchy was an obstacle to this: it was necessary for the Grand Duchy to be abolished. The people are not made for Princes' (he meant princes are bred to serve people). The present Dr Charles, Prince Schwarzenberg, a Czech at heart but a shrewd observer of Austro-Hungarian history, tells me that the difficulties of the Tuscan Hapsburgs 'were the consequences of the shock of their family being first required to be as Tuscan as possible, then exiled, then required to become Austrian but still being jeered at for being Italians'. Archduke Johann Salvator was probably the best Hapsburg to be a soldier since the Archduke Charles defeated great Napoleon. But to be a politico-military archduke without the power to discuss the needle-gun or the Danube basin was rather like having been an Ethiopian prince marooned with the other potential heirs to the throne on top of one of Thomas Pakenham's Mountains of Rasselas. The Archduke himself wrote of his own imperial rank as 'the utter vanity of being penned up with 70 relatives on an isolated peak'.

Miss Cassels's other character is that old stuff-pot Archduke Albrecht. It is impossible honourably to like him after his treatment of Benedek. Also all the gallant soldiers died at Sadowa because he couldn't be bothered to study railway time-tables and modern firearms like his Prussian opponent Count Moltke, that former Danish royal page and martial 'man of gold' who was besides a scholar of classical history. But he's also hoodwinked Miss Cassels into supposing the Hapsburg dynasty the oldest then surviving in Europe. 'The title of Archduke he asserted was older and therefore superior to that of any Grand Duke or Kurfürst.' I would have laughed to see him trying to go into dinner in front of the reigning Grand Duke of Hesse, let alone the head of a former electoral family still in possession of his State. It's as well he wasn't speaking English, as we didn't distinguish between German *Grossherzog* and Russian *Velikiy Knyaz* which the Germans rather illogically translated *Grossfürst* without calling cadets *Grossprinz* instead. For the heads of the House of Rurik had been Grand Dukes in Russia nine centuries before. The Hapsburgs had only confirmed to themselves in 1453 the imperial title of *Erzherzog* or Archduke of Austria which they had brazenly tried to assume by a deliberate *forgery* of 1358 (slapped down by the Emperor Charles IV who was not a Hapsburg) – although it's true that it was not until 1567 that Cosimo de Medici was created papal Grand Duke of Tuscany and became the first historical character to be called *Grossherzog* in German. However, Albrecht might have noticed that even in exile his equally Hapsburg-Lorraine cousin that Archduke Ferdinand, effective descendant of the Medici heiress, preferred to use the title of Grand Duke of Tuscany.

As for claiming his own cadet title of archduke to be older than *Kurfürst* or Prince Elector, even Albrecht must have known he was burbling through his cocked hat. The first Count of Hapsburg (*i.e.* Earl of Hawksborough) to mount any throne of any sort was elected by the then already existing Prince Electors in 1273: our forefather Rudolf I, King of the Romans, he was mean to minnesingers and our gramophone is blaring at this moment the sly contemporary paean *Der kuninc Rodolp* in which they sang his virtues only to mock his stinginess. Indeed, Albrecht's crack left him wide open to the retort he'ld have most disliked: that the direct male ancestor of the Hohenzollerns, who wrested the hegemony of the *Reich* from the Hapsburgs in 1866 was already Prince Elector of Brandenburg by 1417, when Albrecht's was only Duke of Lorraine. For in the 19th century Hapsburgs were only so named through descent in the female line from the Empress Maria

Theresa, the periodic rehash of whose dollars by those merchant-bankers Samuel Montagu is still [1973] currency in shaggy lion-skinned Ethiopia. And if dynasties may be reckoned in the female line, as is sensible if thrones have come that more certain way, Queen Victoria's Scots throne went back by family descent to the AD 400s. As for the male line, in Albrecht's lifetime the Sovereigns of France and Spain, Portugal and Naples, Parma and Brazil, had all belonged in the male line to the same dynasty as *le Roi Soleil* (whose only actively sovereign male-line scion is now that Irish Guards' able ex-officer the Grand Duke of Luxembourg) and Eudes, King of France in 888, which for dynastic antiquity beats both the Hapsburgs and the Lorraines hollow – even though the Lorraines do spring through two heiresses from the Carolingian emperors.

For my book *Blood Royal* (1956) I worked out that through cousin marriages the present Count of Paris descends at least over five million times from the Emperor Charlemagne who gave Western Europe some new semblance of unity. But so also must descend millions of times from Charlemagne the present Archduke Dr Otto, eminently commonsense head of the remarkable House of Hapsburg-Lorraine today. The real point is not whether they were the oldest, but that they are still the grandest family on the Continent. True admiration isn't dependent upon the ups and downs of fortune. More than any other house, they were advisedly chosen Holy Roman Emperors again and again until at last General Richardson's bisexual enigma Buonaparte caused them to throw their last card in that imperial game and become Emperors only of the lands of the shrewdly-married *felix* house of Austria. Are the bulk of their peoples happier now behind the Iron Curtain? Why do so many try to escape? And think of the burden the Hapsburgs bore.

Miss Cassels don't tell us the old Emperor's last words. He had handled daily and personally from 1848 to 1916 the ultimate details of diplomacy, defence and bureaucracy as the supreme patriarch of an empire speaking eleven different languages from Polish and Czech to Serbo-Croat and Italian. Nor does she give all the Emperor's official styles, some of them already then purely titular relics of long ago but nevertheless a romantick's treasure-chest perhaps worth proclaiming for the curiosity of readers, who are unlikely to hear them again: 'FRANCIS JOSEPH, BY THE GRACE OF GOD, EMPEROR OF AUSTRIA, King of Bohemia, Galicia, Lodomeria and Dalmatia, of Illyria, of Jerusalem, etc. Archduke of Austria, Grand Duke of Tuscany and Cracow, Duke of Lorraine, Salzburg, Styria, Carinthia, Carniola and of the Bukowina, Margrave of Moravia, Duke of Upper and Lower Silesia, of Modena, Parma, Piacenza and Guastalla, of Auschwitz and Zator, of Teschen, Frioul,

Ragusa and Zara, Princely Count of Hapsburg and the Tyrol of Kyburg, Goerz and Gradiska, Prince of Trent and Brixen, Margrave of Upper and Lower Lusatia and in Istria, Count of Hohenembs, Feldkirch, Brigance, Sonnenberg, etc. APOSTOLIC KING OF HUNGARY, King of Croatia, Slavonia, Rama, Servia and Bulgaria, Great Prince of Transylvania, Ispan of the Szeklers, IMPERIAL AND ROYAL MAJESTY'. The night of his death, this over-burdened monarch's last words were to his faithful valet: 'Wake me at half-past three. I have much to do.'

Books & Bookmen, April 1973

SPELLING LESSON

Following the publication of the above review in Books & Bookmen, *a Mr Charles Osborne, an Australian describing himself as 'Literature Director of the Arts Council of Great Britain' wrote to the Magazine saying:*

It surprises me that someone claiming to have Habsburg blood in his veins is unable to spell the family name.

I.M. replied as follows:

Although my native tongue should be Gaelic (Moncreiffe being *Monadh Craoibhe*: the Hill of the Sacred Bough, where my foremothers, the sisters of the Pictish kings, had their prehistoric stronghold), I was brought up to speak English – unlike the children of my great-uncle, the 7th Duke of Atholl, who wouldn't allow anybody to speak anything but Gaelic to them until they were five.

Now, my forefather, the Emperor Rudolf, was a Swiss and probably couldn't spell anyway. But I can assure Mr Osborne that the English spelling of Rudolf's surname is Hapsburg: 'Habsburg' is the German form I learnt as a scarless student at Heidelberg, while watching a sort of *son-et-lumière* of that 'ganz Arische poet', my cousin Shakespeare's Macbeth, in the Alte Schloss, with Goebbels in the ex-royal box there.

My wives both descend from the Emperor Ferdinand I as well, and they know how to write Hapsburg in English too.

Yours snobbishly,
IAIN MONCREIFFE OF THAT ILK

Blood is Thicker than Water

VLAD AND THE VAMPIRES

The Squeamish must not read this review. Gabriel Ronay has penned his acount of *The Dracula Myth* (W. H. Allen) in human blood clotted all too legibly. He is a Transylvanian exile who had to flee Hungary after the Russians dealt so grisly with the Rising there.

Puritans, however, will find in the book some nice nasty ideas about how to fix people who disagree with them. Time was, we are told, when after long deliberation the theologians under the Emperor Sigismund on the brink of the Reformation decreed unanimously that anyone who denied that a human being could transform himself into a were-wolf was guilty of heresy and should therefore be burnt at the stake. Think this out: have you ever been burnt even for a moment by somebody passing with an ill-held cigarette at a cocktail party? But it would be prudent of religious fanatics not to try anything so hot in an attempt to reform this reviewer: for I am a well-armed Scottish chief who maintains a giant bone-crushing wolf-hound plus other well-sited reserves, and can sentence you up to two years in the Sheriff Courts of two countries.

The book reminds us inexorably of the unmentionable thrust that drives sensuality into cruelty and, worse, can sublimate into tyranny. This pervading truth used to be swept under the moral carpet by our unworldly governesses, on behalf of our all-too worldly but hypocritical predecessors of the Victorian and Edwardian eras.

And what isn't blood-stained in this work, delves up the graveyard problem of the zombie-like un-dead. But it's not just a typescript for a horror Hammer Film. It is soundly based on much careful research, and puts forward new ideas as a result. It's even managed to teach me more about these horribly fascinating subjects.

I work to a background of music that eliminates distractions and soothes my wounded back, as a Buddhist monk meditates to his repetitive recitation of *Om mani padmi hum*: O Jewel of the Lotus Flower. It don't signify whether it's Mozart or Pop, so long as it ain't Shostakovich imitating the discords of modern machinery. But it's an uncanny coincidence that, at the precise moment my biro was first poised to review *The Dracula Myth*, the wireless BBC Radio 1 – that Establishment-shackled shade of good old free-speech Radio Caroline – should have stopped its useful background cacophony to jerk out some verses entitled *The Prayer of Dracula*. The unwelcome Count complained about being un-dead. It was like listening to a dud version of Tennyson's desperate plea on behalf of the immortal ex-mortal

Tithonus, eternally transfered into grasshopper-hood, to Aurora the dawn-goddess he had dared to love:

> Release me, and restore me to the ground;
> Thous seëst all things, thou wilt see my grave;
> Thou wilt renew thy beauty morn by morn;
> I earth in earth forget these empty courts,
> And thee returning on thy silvery wheels.

I cry every time I re-read it. The wireless immediately followed up Dracula's similar less well-expressed blubbing with some stuff about harpies (note that harpies are female, like Valkyries, for this will become relevant) and *bleeding* wounds.

In 1938 I was staying in a time-smoothed castle; known as 'Lennoxlove' since Charles II's adored 'La Belle Stuart', still Britannia on our coins and lang syne lovingly Duchess of Richmond and *Lennox*, left money to buy it for her cousin Lord Blantyre. There's yet a country dance called 'Lennoxlove to Blantyre'. Anyway, I shut a finger in a motor-car door, jumped about shouting 'Ow', and ran to put the blood under a cold tap. Hastening through the drawing room, I called out 'Look Uncle Ian what I've done'. He went ghostly pale and fled the room. My great-aunt, his wife, chided me: 'Didn't you realise Uncle Ian has never been able to stand the sight of blood?' Now, Uncle Ian was General Ian Hamilton, GCB, GCMG, Colonel-in-chief of the Gordon Highlanders who may have been the Gilbert-and-Sullivan pattern of 'a modern Major-General' because he was also a poet; but had fought in the Afghan War; been severely wounded at Majuba; got a brevet promotion for courage coupled with ability in the Nile Expedition and a higher brevet for gallantry in the Burmese War (from which we still have some loot in the family, which serves the Burmese right for playing me a dirty trick over a visa some years ago): commanded a tough brigade on the North-West Frontier and a flying column in the Boer War, being recommended for the VC; and ended up (supported by his friend Churchill but sabotaged by Kitchener) as Commander-in-Chief at blood-soaked Gallipoli, where he was so successful in withdrawing our shattered remnants from the unbeaten Turks that it's sometimes hailed as a great British victory like the Retreat from Mons or Dunkirk.

I can't stand the sight of blood either. Nothing would induce me to drink it. One of the points of this book is that genuine vampirism tends to be a *feminine* streak. It's different in battle. An officer forces himself not to notice; because he's physically frightened, also frightened of showing fear before his men, above all frightened of making the wrong tactical decisions. While Vesuvius eructated its lava-dust like a warm touchable London pea-soup fog around us, we surviving officers of the

Scots Guards groped to dine together after coming out of the Line. Our invincible patrol officer Dicky Buckle sang and danced with brave élan on a table. A raw ensign rather prompously (for I was a captain) asked 'How can you laugh when poor So-and-So is still warm in his grave?' I replied: 'You must either laugh or cry, and if you cry your nerve won't last long'. But women can stand bloodshed almost eagerly, which makes them ministering angels as nurses. It's probably something to do with the exciting termination of their virginity. So, although for us wounded soldiers it's unforgettable to be cared for by the Lady of the Lamp, other women should look out lest she turn into the Lady of Shalott. Blood brings their sympathy, yet blood is their curse.

The un-dead pose a nasty problem too. At 16 I was much struck by the works of Anton Wiertz, a post-Napoleonic painter whose hackle-raisers survive in this *musée* in a Brussels back-street. One was of a prematurely-buried cholera victim recovering from coma and trying to struggle from a badly-nailed coffin into the foot of which a loathsome rat is nibbling. I always laugh when being motored to Edinburgh past the obelisk *erected* to commemorate the foundation of the Secession Church of Scotland by my tribesman Moncreiff of Culfargie and Ebenezer Erskine. For little did their prissy kirk realise that an obelisk is literally an *erection*, of sacred pagan phallic origin. Ebenezer Erskine's wife (they told me as a child) apparently died; was buried; but dug up by professional body-snatchers who roused her from coma by tearing off a finger to steal her golden wedding ring; scared them stiff by suddenly sitting up; and then returned home. The reverend reformer was a bit startled when his supposed bereavement suddenly tapped on his candle-lit window with the torn-off finger, naturally still dressed in her winding-sheet. This brings us to Mr Ronay's classical and later Central European un-dead.

The *Sunday Express* has recently been discussing whether some dead spirits can materialise through a living medium. Certainly a jury trial would convict ghosts in general, because of the overwhelming circumstantial evidence. People forget that 'ghost' (as in 'the Holy Ghost') literally means 'spirit', as does the Arab word 'alcohol'. Then there are the questions whether ghosts are just photographs lurking in Space-Time; and Arthur Koestler in *The Roots of Coincidence* points out that we now believe that in some instances time now flows backwards or whether they can materialise by drawing heat-energy from their surroundings, whence that sudden cold that's been so often noticed when dogs raise their hackles and there's an apparition.

Certainly there are weird happenings that can't be supernatural but aren't yet explicable. Sir Arthur Grimble, in *A Pattern of Islands*, told how he passed a dead man making his way to the Place of the Dead on a remote Pacific island, without realising the limping man's funeral had already begun. Prince Henry of Liechtenstein told me that the families who had denounced so-called witches to be tortured and burnt by the wicked Count of Vaduz (deposed in 1684) in order to get a cut of blood-money out of the lands thus forfeited to him, were cursed by an Innocent Witch in her death-agonies to squat on their hunkers from death to Judgement Day in the bleak Lavena gully or *tobel* the prince pointed out high up in the mountains. The accursed families minded their doom so much that it had to be made a punishable offence in Liechtenstein to call anybody a 'gully-squatter' (*tobelhocker*). Early this century, an Austrian customs officer, who didn't know the uncanny tale, had to be smuggled out of Liechtenstein quickly because he had passed a *tobelhocker* woman on her way to the Lavena gully, and had casually mentioned it while the bells were still tolling for her burial at that very hour.

Mr Ronay tells us how a freedman of Hadrian records the dead girl Philinnion returning nightly to make love to Machates until her body was burnt by the city elders. This is reminiscent of the now-unobtainable novel *Ferelith* by my first wife's grandfather, the ambassadorial Lord Kilmarnock, in which a ghost has a child by the lady of a castle that was obviously modelled on the Erroll's sea-girt family home. We hear too that Gordon Honeycombe wrote a cosy night-bed book about a rotting corpse that follows his former mistress about and tries to make love to her. But Gabriel Ronay examines the traditional connection between the un-dead and a need for human blood: just as the Aztec priests tore out living human hearts daily to keep the Sun shining Nippon-wise upon their Mexican empire.

He suggests that the notorious vampire-terror in Eastern Europe during the 17th and 18th centuries resulted from the excommunication clash in the recaptured area betwen Catholic and Orthodox cemeteries after the Turkish menace was driven back. Although I did a year's course in Forensic Medicine, my knowledge isn't sufficient to know whether the author's medical suggesting may be right. He thinks that vampire-terror led to a sort of hysterical anaemia in those who believed themselves victims. To find the un-dead bloodsucking bodies, a maiden lad rode a black horse into the local graveyard, and when the horse shied away from a grave, it was opened and usually found to contain 'a sleek, fat corpse', often with fresh blood on it's fingernails. The authorities would then unearth other tombs of decomposed corpses around it, to make sure there was no preservation element in the soil (as in a catacomb). Mr Ronay tabulates what was done in 17 countries, from

Albania to Saxony, to deal with the un-dead corpse. Think how many bodies this involved. When (as in Albania, Rumania, Hungary and Russia) a stake was driven through its heart, it usually jerked and cried out, gushing fresh blood: the same happened when its head was hacked off (as in Greece and Croatia). Mr Ronay's theory is that they were really not dead at all, but simply suffering from catalepsy, and had their own blood on their finger-nails from having tried in vain to claw their way out on temporarily coming to. We are reminded of the Byzantine emperor, entombed alive by mistake for dead, who recovered but whose howls for help merely panicked the sentries into fleeing from so haunted a place (as a former Parade Adjutant, I'd have placed them all in close arrest for being so wet). When the imperial mausoleum was opened, he had died at last, though not before eating off one of his own arms in famished thirst.

I've no idea how a cataleptic can live in an almost airless grave some feet underground, but note that the scrupulous Court Records made by *Western* European bureacrats in *Eastern* Europe investigating the vampire epidemic at the beginning of the Age of Reason make it clear that some of the 'corpses' had remained uncorrupted for disturbingly long periods: 'over 30 years', 'over 16 years', *etc.* I suggest that any serious medical student interested in these hitherto unexplained matters, and who is prepared to accept at least some of the massive evidence to be true, should think out why the four following methods of dealing with allegedly un-dead 'corpses' were successful. (1) Poland: re-bury face downwards, ? rapid stifling. (2) Bulgaria chain them to the grave with wild roses, ? slow stifling. (3) Prussia: putting poppy-seed in grave, ? drugging to death with an opiate. And (4) shoving a lemon into its mouth, ? stifling if snoring un-dead's nose is blocked with snot as mine often is (Saxony). Anyway, any canny PhD student doing a successful thesis on these very real problems will earn the prejudiced scorn of the BMA, like so many innovators of medical progress before him. They still don't believe in Chinese acupunture, which has saved me and my family much pain and is understood throughout the civilisations of the far Orient, and as yet not all of them have the brains to accept (what I don't doubt) that my children's forefather George III inherited porphyria instead of madness through his Stuart blood.

And this brings us to blood and sadism, rather than the un-dead, who were never associated in Transylvania with vampirism. In completely separated chapters, unconscious of their blood-relationship, the author deals with the original Dracula and with Ivan the Terrible. He identifies satisfactorily Dracula as Vlad V 'the Impaler', voivode of Wallachia (murdered 1476), whose father had been nicknamed 'Dracul' (the

Dragon) and had borne 'a cross with a dragon on his escutcheon' that presumably related to his having been an ani-Hussite Christian ruler proud of belonging to the Holy Roman imperial Order of the Dragon. Professor Nandris and the author both agree that the suffix – *a* is the addition by Orthodox scribes of a Slavonic genitive into a Latin language to create a surname equivalent to 'son of Dracul' – as we might have said Macrackle (Mac Dhraicul) or the Norman-English might have put it FitzDragon. As 'Dragwyla, Vaivoda partium Transalpinorum', and in other spellings of the same name, Vlad V issued many documents.

He, the original Dracula, got his Roumanian nickname of 'the Impaler' because he liked picnicking among the stench of forests of people dying in lingering agony impaled alive on sharpened stakes: reminiscent of the similar horror-garden in Monsarrat's *The White Rajah*. There is a realistic woodcut of Dracula doing this, published only 24 years after his murder, though his best portrait looks awfully like me when younger. He impaled 25,000 men, women and children during one Bulgarian campaign alone. he had 'mothers with their children ... impaled together' and 'the breasts of young mothers cut off and their children stuffed in head first and then impaled together'. Dracula also forced 'mothers to eat their children and compelled husbands to eat their wives' (mine is a bit scrawny, so we prefer to call her 'slim'). Many folk the great voivode cooked alive. While centralising the government and illegally overthrowing local customary law in the way so much beloved of modern opponents of happy country ways that aren't logical to their desk-ridden 'brains', Dracula impaled 50 of the greatest nobles after giving them a banquet. Other nobles had their heads fed to crabs and then the glutted crabs served up as scoff to their relations. But this disgusting psychopath was hailed as a 'very severe but just prince. Thieves, liars and spongers he could not suffer.' Like the best-man at my wedding in our roofless mediaeval chapel, Dracula was a descendant in the direct male-line of Genghis Khan, who built hills of human skulls.

Genealogy is the tapestry in a treasure-hunters' chest that conceals yet can with knowledge of it reveal where lie hid the originals of so many jangling secrets. Thus, although the author has missed the connection, Dracula sprang from the same stock as the Tatar princess that was mother of Tsar Ivan the Terrible, who in much the same way illegally centralised Russia with incredible cruelty. The free city of Novgorod stood up for its lawful rights in 1570. It remembered the old Slav *vox populi vox Dei* maxim 'If the prince is bad, into the mud with him'. My kinsman Ivan captured it and tortured the *entire* population of more than 50,000 women, children and men to death between January and February, during the cold Russian winter.

Those blood-relations Dracula and Ivan had something else in common. They nailed displeasing foreign envoys' hats to their heads for not taking them off quickly enough. (The marbled Lord Elgin's answer to his envoys' murder by the Chinese, knowing the Oriental lack of care for human life but care for beautiful possessions, was his otherwise incomprehensible sack of the Summer Palace at Peking: from which I still possess some loot). Yet, when I worked for some months in Moscow, Ivan was depicted as a great 'unifying' (*i.e.* centralising) hero, and his Stalinesque abhominations as justified means towards a human ant-heap end. Indeed, it was obvious from the pictures in the Tretiakov Gallery and Eisenstein's epic films that Tsar Ivan 'the Dread' is still regarded as ranking with Peter the Great and Catherine the Great as the best Russian rulers before Lenin. About to set off to serve in our Muscovite embassy, I asked a recently returned diplomatist called Sir John Balfour what to read. He replied 'Arthur Koestler's *Darkness at Noon*'. This explained the basic philosophy why such apparent monsters should also have appeared to multitudes as benefactors.

It is of course hypocritical for learned scholars to criticise Dracula and Ivan, let alone 'the Blood Countess', so long as they praise imperial Rome. There the official government had captured foreign *ladies* stripped naked in public and then raped by trained animals before being eaten piece-meal at each rush by half-starved carnivores munching bits of them as they were dragged alive behind chariots at a smart pace in the circus arena for the entertainment of many thousand 'highly civilised' people. It was the TV part of the Welfare State that was great Rome – the 'bread' part being what we now give strikers' families. I understand sadism too well to think that a Moors Murderess can sincerely reform, much as she may want to. I suspect the Marquis de Sade was probably a kinsman of mine. But, working on this problem in the British Museum Library under the shade of the world-shattering Marx, and wearing a morning-coat on my way to Ascot, the most amusing ancestor I could find for myself in Sade's part of France was the *Baron de Bon Repos*, who built a canal with Colbert's backing from Marseilles to Bordeaux. Perhaps I'll have to go on identifying myself with that kindly chap Pelham Grenville Wodehouse.

But wait: a great part of this book is concerned with my ultimate grandma, a regular gal if ever there was one. She was Elisabeth Báthory, Countess Nádasdy, my own direct ancestress through 10 intervening generations on my mother's side. Although her father was George Báthory, Count of Szatmár, and her mother was a sister of Stephen Báthory, King of Poland and Prince of Transylvania, the author is mistaken in calling her complex character, the result of 'endless inter-marriage'. For none of her *seize quartiers* was the same person — the two Báthory branches had separated generations before.

She was a social lady of great beauty, charm and intelligence, spoke several languages, and was very well-read. The Emperor Maximilian attended her wedding; and her war-hero husband, an ambassador and general, was so strong he could throw two Turkish prisoners into the air simultaneously and catch them both with twin swords on their way down. The family were so rich that my forefather, their grandson (secretly tried and illegally beheaded in 1671) was known as 'the Hungarian Croesus'.

Above all, this attractive blue-stocking was especially generous to any impoverished peasantry on her family's vast estates. This was despite her knowing that in the Peasants' Revolt of 1514, her great-grandfather the Lord Treasurer Stephen Thelegdy, leader of the conservative Magyar magnates and former Ambassador to France, had been hanged naked from a tree and St Sebastianed to death with arrows by revolting peasantry (not his own). By the way, my ancestral first cousin John Szapolyai, voivode of Transylvania, fixed that revolt by riding north with his yeomanry. The eight peasant leaders to survive a fortnight's starvation were let loose publicly on their ringleader, Dózsa, who was seated on a red-hot throne wearing a red-hot iron crown and a sizzling sceptre thrust into his hand. While his famished followers tore and devoured the cooking flesh from his body, all the stoic Dozsa observed was: 'These are hounds of my own training'. It's therefore a genealogical irony that my descent from Elisabeth Báthory and Stephen Thelegdy and cousinhood to John Szapolyai should come to me through the 19th century Countess Amalie Festeties, whose family sprang from a Croat *serf* liberated as late as the 16th century. How many Scotsmen can establish so recent descent from a serf as I can ? The English record is obviously Elmhirst of Elmhirst, but they were liberated in the 14th century: one of them, the Air Marshal, has had the good sense to marry my mother-in-law's sister [*grandmother of HRH The Princess Andrew, Duchess of York* — ED], so we really are a servile family.

The only thing is, after Elisabeth Báthory's beloved husband's sudden death, possibly from appendicitis, she went just a wee bit schizophrenic. The trouble is that no medical historians (such as Doctors MacAlpine and Hunter who wrote that work of brilliant insight *The Royal Malady*) have applied themselves to her case. So it's left to Hammer Films, who dubbed her 'Countess Dracula' in last year's cinematograph about her. Although a devout Calvinist notwithstanding her relationship to Cardinal Báthory, she started attending secret midnight sacrifices of white horses under sacred oak trees. 'Moncreiffe' means the 'Hill of the

Sacred Bough' and my heraldic badge is oak around mistletoe. Remember Frazer's *The Golden Bough* and the white horses of Apollo's Sun-chariot. Note that one of His Grace of Norfolk's immemorial heraldic 'beasts' as Earl of Arundel is a white horse holding an oak-sprig in its mouth. Reflect that Dracula's Tartar forebears used to impale white horses alive as sacrifices to the Sun. It seems clear that Elisabeth Báthory's Calvinism ws of the 'elect' Predetermination-as-opposed-to-Free-Will type of religion made so frighteningly clear in John Buchan's *Witchwood*. Koestler has demonstrated that the two are compatible through the random difference between probability and certainty, in one of his rather Manichee works on the eternal inherent conflict between G(o)od and (D)evil. The Countess also had a superstitious faith in a powerful incantation writ on parchment, just as most of us have lucky mascots.

But after that, ancestral grandma went a bit far in her desire to remain ageless. Yet, because she had a genuinely dual personality, her social friends didn't notice for several years. She may have read works akin to Malory's *Morte d'Arthur*, which the author quotes with Sherlock Holmes zeal: where 60 'good maidens' all of 'King's blood' were successively martyred of their own free will in the hope that their blood would save a 'sick lady'. The Pharaohs tried this cure for leprosy. Constantine the Great, of whom there's a coin here in the remains of our robbed collection, refused a medicinal dip in innocent children's blood, and made do with Holy Water. I brought some back from the river Jordan to baptise my son. Anyway, my foremother preferred blood, and became like a nastier *She* from Rider Haggard. We are told why the blood had to be innocent of Eden's knowledge. Almost daily, at four o'clock in the morning, betwixt night and morn, she bathed in virgin's blood. This was to ward off wrinkles.

After she learnt the girls must be noble, some 50 gentlewomen were included in her total. She preferred 17-year-old blondes with particularly enticing cleavages, it seems. But my ancestral grandma went a bit *too* far. She had to get the blood through torture. Sometimes the girls 'were forced to eat their own flesh roasted on fire'. The sleepy Austin friars next-door to her Vienna house, in an early protest for 'noise-abatement', were so insolent as to throw pots and pans against her august windows. This was because of the caterwauling of the young ladies who were forced naked into a cylindrical narrow cage lined with long metal spikes and hoisted up on a pulley. Then they were prodded with a burning iron until they spiked themselves to death jumping to, also fro.

When at last another forefather of mine, the Lord Palatine of

Hungary, took notice of her 'pastimes', he rode with a formidable escort to her castle of Csejthe, which rises like a land-girt St Michael's Mount from the wooded Slovakian plain. There he found enough evidence to put everybody in close arrest. Guided by terrified servants through a labyrinth of secret passages, my ancestral grandpa burst into my ancestral grandma's torture chamber. There he found girls too late to save, whose breast-less fate with burnt genitals you must read the book to recoil from. The clockwork machinery of the Iron Maiden was still wound up for long hours of work.

A poor view was taken of grandma's activities. Lord Longford wasn't there to help her. Those of her servants, who'd known but not reported her quirks, were strangled then burnt. Those who'd abetted her had their fingers torn out by red-hot pincers before being burnt alive. But my ancestral grandpa, the Lord Palatine Count Thurzo, wouldn't have her brought to trial; despite the king's being angry at her having tried to poison His Majesty and having invoked 99 magical cats to nibble out his heart. The Lord Palatine was more powerful than the king. He took the unusually modern view for 1610 that she was a nut case, and anyway she was his cousin. He hid away in one of his own castles the trial papers from which we know all these sad things, instead of filing the documents officially. They were only discovered by chance in a garret there in the 1720s by Father Turoczy.

Elisabeth Báthory wasn't even mentioned by name at the trial. She was just referred to obliquely as 'a blood-thirsty, blood-sucking Godless woman caught in the act at Csejthe Castle'. Instead, she was immured in her bedroom. There were slits where the windows had been, to let in air, and a slot where there'd been a door, to let in food. She lived cooped up alone in darkness and endless cold until 1614, when she died 'suddenly and without a crucifix and without light'. A Bohemian prince whose wife is also a descendant of her's tells me that the *on dit* is that the gaolers got fed up, crawled in, and strangled her. It's not a joyous tale. But, if this charming, eloquent but unhappily disconnected lady had never lived, I couldn't have been born to write this bloody review now.

Books & Bookmen

HORROR AND THE GIGGLES

The makers of Hammer Films have sensed to a nicety the inter-relationships between horrors and comics. Their recent rib-crackingly beastly funny film, *Theatre of Blood*, which deals with critics like me, is a case in point. Now Angus Wolfe Murray has edited, with an introduction, the *Comic Tales of Edgar Allan Poe* (Canonsafe Publishers, 1974), amusingly illustrated with line drawings by Stephen McKeown. At first the work might seem dated, but on reflection the works of the great don't date: they just go in or out of fashion. For example, Kipling went out of fashion for a bit, and we laughed a lot when the smarty-boots were confounded by their fashionable hero T. S. Eliot editing Kipling's verse with high praise. Poe won't date, and is always worth perusal.

I usually call Angus Wolfe Murray 'the Wolf of Moray', a complicated 14th century pun based on Murray being a different spelling of Moray and the Bishop of Moray's cathedral having been burnt down by King Robert III's brother, the Wolf of Badenoch. The Bishop had been impertinent enough to write to the Wolf suggesting he should give up one of his mistresses: had my vulpine forefather complied, I might never have been born.

But actually A. W. M. is called Wolfe, like all his branch of the Murrays of Blackbarony (a sinister name too), because his ancestor was the Godson of General Wolfe, who spent the evening before he was mortally wounded storming the Heights of Abraham, slaying the Marquis de Montcalm and taking Quebec, reading Gray's *Elegy* out loud and telling his bemused officers that he would rather have written those words than beaten the French tomorrow. Time passes: how many readers today realise how much I admired the verse but abhorred the sentiment, sitting on a warm afternoon on the green lawns of Stowe looking across the artificial lake towards the Temple of Ancient Worthies:

> The boast of Heraldry, the pomp of Power,
> And all that Beauty, all that Wealth e'er gave,
> Await alike the inevitable hour,
> The paths of Glory lead but to the Grave.

You will be aware that anyone with as nasty a mind as mine is acquainted with the creepy works of the late Edgar Allan Poe. But his *Comic Tales* had eluded me. Horror and the giggles are so closely interlinked, if only as a mercurial release from intolerable strain, that it's surprising to have been surprised that that brilliant hair-raiser did his brilliantine hair-smoothing by the skilful use of Humour.

And the Wolf has tracked down for the introduction the startling facts that Mr Poe was a typical square, left the University of Virginia because of gambling debts and became instead a *Regimental Sergeant Major* in the Army, which he left in order to write poetry. Sticking to his upper-crust background, he went through our usual gambits. It was 'only four years before his death that he received any kind of acclaim. During his most productive period he was fighting alcoholism – while his wife lay dying of tuberculosis. There followed . . . attempted suicide, brief desperate affairs with married women.' Eventually he enjoyed a 'three day blind from which he never recovered . . . Within a week he was dead'. Angus Wolfe Murray concludes on a more cheerful note about Mr Poe: 'He thrived on disappointment.'

The book is worth reading for its introduction alone. Comic tales rely on being unexpected, so can't fairly be reviewed. But who is the cat not prepared to die of curiosity (remember those nine lives, like Genghis Khan's *noyons* or heroes nine times forgiven the Death Sentence) to find out what comic tales the weird pre-Hammer film Mr Poe wrote? Wait for the moment when members of the orchestra 'broke out, with one accord, into "Yankee Doodle", which they performed, if not exactly in tune'. *Deus ex machina*, the Wolfe regurgitates for us an unexpected poe-full.

Books and Bookmen, April 1974

To the left of Genghis Khan

My grandmother only learnt the facts of life on her wedding night. Once, during my teens in the 1930s, as I sat at the foot of her candlelit London dinner table, she called disconcertingly down an avenue of distinguished guests: 'Are you hairy, Rupert Iain? Your grandfather was hairy.' So I rather think she'd got a bit of a shock that nuptial night in 1883 when my Esau-limbed Victorian grandfather first leapt on to her with hot passionate grunts. Certainly she always remained a widow from the age of twenty-one observing to me that she couldn't understand why anybody ever got married except to have children. For my own part, however, being taught the facts of life will ever remain inextricably mixed up with Genghis Khan.

At my last private school, Stone House at Broadstairs, it was the custom for each Sixth Former, aged about 13, to give a farewell lecture at the end of his last term. Eddie Anson, for example, gave a talk on the classic 18th-century voyage round the world of his famous ancestor, Admiral Lord Anson. My own lecture was on Genghis Khan. It was a great success. Forty years on, one of our schoolmasters still recalled that lecture and how a talented general who was present had been astonished by its grasp both of Mongol tactics and strategy. But I too remember that alert general, egging on young Bain to ask: 'Did the Chinese use wooden artillery in the time of Genghis Khan?' My curt reply was that the lecture was on Genghis Khan and not on Chinese artillery. But this gap in my adolescent omniscience rankled.

Next day came the long-awaited summons to the headmaster's study to receive the traditional but literally vital Revelation of the Facts of Life. We held Mr Arnold Churchill in mingled affection and awe, the more especially as he was rumoured to have been in the Secret Service in Russia after the Revolution. He said 'Sit down', so I sat respectfully on the edge of a chair. He said nervously 'I expect you know why I've sent for you?' and I replied 'Yes, sir.' He asked furtively 'Have you ever seen dogs doing it?' I lied (for I had urges but still no clear inkling of those mysteries) 'Yes, sir.' He looked relieved, and observed 'Human beings do it in much the same way.' Then, puffing at his pipe, he asked shyly 'Is there any question at all you would like to ask me? Any question in the world? Don't be embarassed.' There followed a long silence, during which he sat engulfed in embarassment. I was only longing to get out of the room and observe dogs doing it (which incidentally placed me under a misapprehension for quite some time), but at last, struggling politely to put him at his ease, I asked my $64,000 question: 'Did the Chinese use wooden artillery in the time of Genghis Khan?' The headmaster looked startled, explained that that wasn't quite what he'd had in mind (wrote to my future housemaster at Stowe saying that I was 'sexually rather immature') and said that although the Chinese had already discovered gunpowder they hadn't yet developed proper artillery by Genghis Khan's time.

But, and this is the nub, it seemed to me then, with the vision of boyhood when everything is so much more definitely black or white, that Genghis Khan, about whom we were taught so little, had had ultimately a far greater impact on our present-day situation and problems than had (for instance) Alexander the Great, about whom we were taught so much. Looking back, this view may well have been right. Cliché people on the telly talk of 'being slightly to the right of Genghis Khan.' But a moment's reflection will shew that this should run 'slightly to the *left* of Genghis Khan.' For there was nothing conservative about Genghis Khan: he was the greatest *radical* reformer imaginable. It would be easier to equate him to Stalin or even our Baader-Meinhof lefties than to conservative statesmen like Hailsham or Macmillan. It's the tanks of the successors to Genghis's empire, and not those of Mrs Thatcher, that the neutron bomb has been devised to deter. Indeed, it's perhaps in considerable measure to him that we owe the tiresome mould that has shaped communism. Whenever I see their clenched fist salute, I think of the baby Yemujin, the supercharged infant who grew to be Genghis

Khan; for this human dynamo was born with a clot of human blood torn from his very mother in his tiny archetypal clenched fist.

In *The Tartar Khan's Englishman* (1979), Gabriel Ronay conveys in clear black and white the driving ideology of the Mongol 'Emperor of All Men'. This is a book well worth reading as much for its general background as for its special tale – it's a feat of biographical detection – and then pondering its lessons in an attempt to trace the history of the Soviet hawks' outlook today. For successive rulers of his empire have inherited his sense of an inevitable mission to impose 'universal peace' by force or guile under their own sway, and with it his inexorable determination to prevent even a single individual marked out for their brand from escaping to any other way of life.

Thinking over the application of these lessons, perhaps one of the most interesting is the way an essentially religious concept can remain a driving force centuries after the spirit has been sublimated away. Why, for example, do bossy atheists who believe us to be but ephemeral beings like sophisticated cabbages still insist like holy do-gooders on forcibly postponing the present happiness of some in each generation for the conjectural gratification of others in some equally ephemeral generation human crops yet unborn: if there is no divine purpose, why not live and let live now?

To change the subject: the difficulty about any universal state is of course that, unless intolerably policed, it doesn't prevent civil strife in the last resort – it debases ordinary warfare into much more bitter civil war. With Genghis Khan this bossy concept of universal meddling – universal rule, 'universal peace' – was at a more understandable stage, for it was based on celestial mandate. Even in minor matters he felt the inspiration of religion: his sacred battle standard, the *kara sülde* of nine black tails from bay horses, was yet more sacred to him than the consecrated Colours that symbolise the spirit of the Scots Guards are to me; indeed, human hearts were still torn out in sacrifice to Mongolian war banners in the early 20th century. He had as clear an instinct of the ultimate godhead as most of us – poetically personified as *Mengke Koko Tengri*, the Eternal Blue Heaven – and his first reaction to Islam, for example, was that special pilgrimages to Mecca were pointless as the divine spirit is everywhere. He was very conscious of his star, and had discovered from experience, rather naturally to his own satisfaction, that he had a celestial mandate from the Eternal Blue Heaven to bring all men into his peace, even if they had to die in his attempt. This imperial concept of universal rule by divine right passed down to his descendant Ivan the Terrible (whose mother was a princess of the House of Genghis Khan) and has snowballed round the Muscovite nucleus up to the present day. But now, for the first time in human history, it is strangely animated – if that be not too ironic a word – by the only world-wide religion ever known that knows no God.

Thus, from the European point of view, one of the most lasting effects of the Mongol empire was that it enabled the Grand Princes of Muscovy, who followed the wise example of Alexander Nevsky of Kiev and Dmitri Donskoy in submitting completely to the Khans of the Golden Horde, to act as Tartar agents and use their position to subjugate their fellow Rurikid princes, before at last turning on their Tartar overlords and taking their place as autocrats. The old Russian principalities had been fairly democratic city states in the pre-Tartar olden golden days when the cry was 'If the prince is bad, into the mud with him'. This sort of cry was heard no more by the time Ivan the Terrible had imposed his quasi-Tartar sway on expanding Russia. Moreover, the Mongol destruction of Russia's principal cities eliminated the mercantile middle class, and though this vacuum was filled to some extent by the Ashkenazi Jews, many of them doubtless of Khazar origin, their different religion from the autocracy's notables and the peasantry prevented them from playing the liberalising role that minor capitalism (that nurse of independent thought and human progress) did in the West.

Quite apart from its after effects, Genghis Khan's life was shattering enough. A contemporary of our King John, he was the orphaned son of a minor Mongol chieftain. Captured in boyhood by a rival clan and made to live with a heavy wooden cangue locked round his neck, he eventually escaped by hiding underwater among reeds in a river, the cangue turning out useful at last to keep his head just above water. From this lonely vigil in that far-off river of desert Mongolia, he set out to make himself Emperor of All Men. I have a coin of his at Easter Moncreiffe that calls him 'The Just, the Supreme Zinghis Khan.' It was vengeful retribution that gave him his 'kicks'. As Gabriel Ronay reminds us, the great khan observed that the greatest happiness in life is 'to vanquish your enemies, to chase them before you, to rob them of their wealth, to see their near and dear bathed in tears, to ride their horses and sleep on the white bellies of their wives and daughters'. I see his point over the first and perhaps the last bits, though his chosen warrior companions, the Orlok, were rather surprised he didn't prefer falconry on a fine day. While the *Magna Carta* barons were making history in England, Genghis Khan burst through the Great Wall of China for ancestral vengeance on the Kings of Gold (the Jin dynasty in what is now Peking) who many years before had most unkindly made his great- uncle and the then ruling khan sit on wooden asses with pointed stakes instead

233

of saddles, so that they were impaled up the behind to die in agony for the edification of the citizens of Cathay.

He now proposed to kill off *all* the urban millions who formed the population of conquered Cathay (China north of the Hwai ho) in order to put the whole realm down to grazing for the Mongol herds. In similar vein, when we visited China last autumn, and called on the late Chairman Mao recumbent in a crystal case within his palatial tomb, we found that Mao had caused *all* the birds in China to be wiped out, to protect his crops; so that we travelled for thousands of miles without seeing a single bird, except for a few crows and magpies that had taken refuge within foreign embassy compounds in Peking itself. However, Genghis Khan heeded his wise future chancellor, Ye-liu Chu-tsai, one of the most admirable statesmen there will ever have been, himself a scion of the original Khitai dynasty after whom Cathay was named. The great statesman persuaded the great khan that human beings, especially artisans, properly administered and milked with reasonable taxation, were even more valuable to their owners than flocks and herds: whereafter the Chinese population were spared and cared for in the same pastoral way and for much the same reasons by their new Mongol masters.

Nevertheless, Genghis Khan could still be inexorable in penal warfare. He held that 'word-breaking is hateful in a ruler', and his great campaign that destroyed the empire of Mohammed II, the Khwarism Shah, was launched only because the Shah had murdered his ambassador, which turned out to be no joke even though the envoy's name was Bughra. The Arabian Nights cities of Bokhara and Samarkand were utterly demolished: I was in modern Samarkand for some days before discovering that the city destroyed by the Mongols was some miles away at ruined Maracanda. This time, although industrious artisans were still spared, Mongol punishment was thorough. Gabriel Ronay recalls that a captured prince 'tried to plead with Genghis against the senseless massacre of innocent millions, by appealing to his vanity. The prince reasoned that if the Mongols were to drown Khwarism in a sea of blood, 'no one will be left alive to harbour the memory of your bloodshed'. Genghis brushed aside the prince's reasoning and the underlying plea for mercy: 'What do these people matter to me?' he asked. 'There are other countries and many other races, and among them my fame will live on, even if in every corner of the land to which the hoofs of Mohammed's steed have strayed, such looting and killings should continue with my permission'. This pursuit of individual survivors of doomed races, kept up if need be for years, coupled with the total destruction of every land and city that harboured them, made all limited warfare and ordinary diplomacy impossible: for to cross the Great Khan's will was to offend the Eternal Blue Heaven. These pursuits had a snowball effect as country after country sheltered refugees.

The Shah's son, Jelal ad-Din, managed to escape to India 'with the Mongols doggedly chasing after him', as Mr Ronay tells us. For once, this didn't result in the addition of Hindustan to their empire. However, as a genealogist, it's irresistible to point out here that, curiously enough, the first and last Emperors of India were both descendants of Genghis Khan. The Grand Moguls descended from the marriage of a prince of the House of Tamurlane to a Genghiskhanid princess of Chagatai; and the late King-Emperor George VI was also descended from Genghis Khan by way of the original Dracula's kid brother, through Queen Mary of all unlikely people. Nevertheless, when the Mongol empire reached its widest extent after Genghis' death, his own grandsons reigned over China and Persia and Russia, even from the Mediterranean to the Pacific; and Marco Polo could make his famous journey in perfect safety for the first time in a thousand years.

The distances covered by Genghis's well-disciplined horsemen were incredible. The longest patrols in recorded human history were probably those carried out by two of my brother Scots Guards officers who in turn commanded the Guards Patrol of the Long Range Desert Group in the Second World War: Michael Crichton- Stuart covered over 4,000 miles of enemy territory in 45 days, and Bernard Bruce, posthumous son of the Viceroy Lord Elgin, made his way past Rommel from the Eighth Army to the First Army and back, some 3,800 miles in all. But this was in our modern days of motorised warfare. For distance in practice must be related to the speed of transport. Genghis Khan told his sons: 'Aided by the Eternal Heaven, I have conquered for you an empire so vast, that from its centre to its bounds is a year's riding'.

Last autumn, Hermione and I ourselves travelled across Genghis' erstwhile empire. We took the Chinese express on the Trans-Siberian Railway by way of Mongolia to Moscow, and thence by the Soviet express on to Ostend: eight days in comfortable well-hoovered trains instead of two weary years on horseback. We passed in through the Great Wall of China, which coils like a sleeping dragon along the mountain tops and is the only work of Man visible to astronauts on the Moon, and came out through the cold Berlin Wall, all floodlit and barbed wire. At every communist frontier – Mongolia, Siberia, Russia, Poland, East Germany – the guards searched only under our seat for people seeking to escape from paradise. And it's this unwillingness to let such people go that seems to me to owe more to Genghis Khan than to Marx.

Thus, when my own pagan Kipchak ancestor Kutyan, Khan of the Kumans — Mr Ronay gives his name in the Magyar form Kötomy — decided to emigrate from his steppe country beneath the Black Sea after twice repelling Mongol invasions, taking two hundred thousand of his people with him and accepting mass baptism as Christians in return for permission to settle in Hungary, King Bela IV of Hungary was warned that by sheltering 'the slaves of the Great Khan' he had himself become a foe. The result was the lightning overthrow in 1241 of both Poland and Hungary in a *blitzkrieg* master-minded after Genghis's death by his veteran general Subotai, one of the greatest soldiers in world history, as Chief of Staff to the dynastic commander Prince Batu. The full plan, which envisaged the destruction of Vienna and the subsequent conquest of the unprepared Holy Roman Empire, was only postponed and then cancelled because news arrived of the death of Genghis's successor, the Great Khan Ogodai, a full year's ride away in far Mongolia.

It was at this turning point in the history of Western civilisation, when England came so near to facing a Mongol armada, as indeed the Japanese did a generation later, or else to our joining an involuntarily integrated Eurasian continental state, that Mr Ronay's Englishman was recognised by Prince Frederick the Warlike of Austria among a party of eight Mongol officers captured near Wiener Neustadt. It would spoil his book to tell you how he has sought, by detective work, to reconstruct the traitor Englishman's extraordinary career. He is perhaps sometimes too positive in his assumptions, but all the same the tale he unravels holds together well, and if his evidence were produced at Minehead, Master Robert, erstwhile chaplain of the famous *Magna Carta* baron Robert FitzWalter, would certainly have a case to answer. Mr Ronay takes us through the difficulties of those English clergy who supported the barons against King John only to be excommunicated by the Pope and banished to the Holy Land, and thence with his particular quarry on divers adventures to the chancery of the Great Khan where the statesman Ye-liu Chu-tsai required interpreters who could if necessary be used as envoys on important missions. In tracking *The Tartar Khan's Englishman*, Mr Ronay has also unfolded for us an easily readable account of the foundation of the greatest land empire the world has yet seen.

Books and Bookmen, 1979

Lone Star

When I was asked, as Patron of Debrett, to write a foreword to an interesting book about Texan notabilities, I objected strongly to its being called a *Peerage*, and still do. To me the word 'peerage' has long become what may be termed a 'word of art' which limits its original meaning. There were the 'Twelve Peers of France' as early as the 12th century, for instance, and the Seven Peers of Champagne. Later, there were certain *duc-pairs de France* added and, at the Restoration, a whole peerage of France on English lines was in existence for a while. The character of the Peerages of England, Scotland, Ireland, Great Britain and the United Kingdom is well defined. Every member family of the Swedish *Riddarhuset* had a defined number within its rank. The Golden Book or *Libro d'Oro* of Venice, burnt by Napoleon, comes near to this category of reference.

But, to be fair, I was reminded that the word 'peer' originally only means 'equal' – as in *Magna Carta*'s stipulation that every man be tried by his peers – and that in every country and age, as George Orwell points out in *Animal Farm*, some are more equal than others. In effect, times still change and, since the mental association of *Debrett's Peerage* was with British historic families of achievement, a book published by Debrett about Texan historic families of achievement would be understood if called a *Peerage* nowadays in a rather jocular way: indeed it seemed I was being a bit of a fuddy-duddy in standing out for 'Texas Notabilities'.

That said, my great regret is never having had an opportunity to visit Texas, although we've travelled from Mongolia to the Straits of Magellan, and from Machu Picchu to Angkhor Wat. For everything they say about Texas is Writ Large: a generous, warm hearted country started by heroes like Sam Houston and everything larger than life.

Moreover, I'm happy and proud to be chief of the clan that includes such Texan notabilities as that tremendous but modest old wild-catter 'Monty' Moncreif, whose *sixth sense* as an oilman built up Moncrief Oil: the history of his branch's adventures from Georgia to Texas is chronicled in John David Scott's *True Legacy* (published privately, Fort Worth, 1982). The different branches of my scattered kinsmen spell our surname differently: but we all derive it from Sir Mathew of Muncrefe who was living here under the shadow of Moncreiffe Hill in 1248 and whose son rode a black charger in the wars of Robert the Bruce – many centuries before the first bronco bucked in Texas.

As I walk down St James's Street from my club in London, I often stop wistfully at the entrance to a little side turning called Pickering Place. Affixed to what are now Berry Bros. the wine merchants is a Lone Star within the inscription 'THE REPUBLIC OF TEXAS', and underneath it the brave words: 'TEXAS LEGATION. In this building was the Legation for the Ministers from the Republic of Texas to the Court of St James's 1842–1846' I salute you, and hope this book does their efforts honour.

At the bottom *of this proposed Foreword* to Debrett's Texas Peerage, *I. M. appended a 'Note to Printer'. It read*: myself personally *'Please spell my last word 'honour' as I am writing & I speak English* NOT *American! In the event I. M.'s Foreword was not published.*

VII

Mixed Bag

From the age of eleven, I.M. kept a Game Book. The observations he recorded in the 'Remarks' column would surely have proved an invaluable source for the memoirs which, alas, he never wrote. This part of the miscellany is devoted to a few extracts from the calf-bound volume (well worth publishing in its entirety one day).

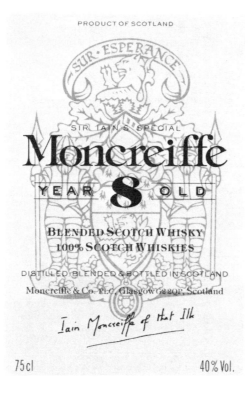

DATE	PLACE	BAG		GUNS	REMARKS
13 September 1930	Combe Court Surrey	Rabbits:	1	I.M.	My first rabbit. Shooting with a 28 bore with a cast-off stock because of being left-eyed. A sitting rabbit.
22 July 1931	Moncreiffe Loch (Loch Knowes) Perthshire	Perch:	5	I.M.	The loch at Moncreiffe was dug for the 6th Baronet to help keep down the numbers of those unemployed after the Napoleonic Wars.
20 January 1934	Moncreiffe	Pheasants: Rabbits:	4 7	Sir Guy Moncreiffe and I.M.	First pheasant shot (a Japanese cock). Took it back to eat at Stowe.
September 1934	Glentilt Atholl	Red Deer:	16	The Duke of Atholl, Admiral Sir Berkeley Milne; and Ian Lyle, yr of Glendelvine.	...staying with Cousin Bardie [*The Duke*] at Blair. A magnificent deer drive, which David (Moncreiffe) and I.M. watched as guests, lying in the heather on the slopes of Ben a' Chait. Between 900 and 1,000 beasts were gathered on the hillside opposite, but most of them broke away at the last moment, and only about 300 of the deer swept past the butts across the Tilt.
11 January 1935	Gloucestershire (Cotswolds)	Pheasants:	1	Kim Muir and I.M.	Out hawking with Kim Muir. Hawk failed to kill but Kim shot a pheasant on the wing with a service revolver (poaching).
29 August 1936	Cardney Woods Perthshire	Fallow Deer:	1	I.M.	First fallow deer shot. A doe, shot in the woods with a rifle. Out in the morning with Colonel Pinder without success. Succeeded in the evening with Dochie MacGregor. Shot just behind the shoulder.
23 January 1938	Jai Samand	Tiger:	1	The Maharana of Udaipur, Colonel Geoffrey Betham, Kitty Simpson and I.M.	Tremendous bandobast. Beaters were 2,000 spearmen and 18 elephants, controlled by the white-bearded chief herald with blasts on the sort of horn that Roland must have had at Roncesvalles. Camels, chained dogs and a

Date	Location	Game	Number	Party	Remarks
					squadron of turbaned cavalry with drawn swords in attendance near the tower. HH's courtiers and also Mrs George Keppel with us in the tower. The tiger broke the beat and got away, but the tigress (after slaying a huge boar) was shot by the Resident and finished off by the Maharana. I.M. missed a panther early in the drive.
24 January 1938	Jai Samand Menar State India	Boar: Sambar Deer:	3 1	H.H. of Udaipur, Colonel Betham (Resident in Menar), Kitty Simpson, various courtiers of the Menar durbar and I.M.	Unsuccessful panther beat. I.M. in a machan. Colonel Betham shot the sambar. The Inspector of Dancing Girls shot a sow by mistake, and was deprived of his rifle for the day.
30 January 1938	Gajner Bikaner Rajputana	Sand Grouse: Imperial Sand Grouse:	5 1468	The Maharajah of Bikaner, Lord Linlithgow (Viceroy of India), the Maharaj Kumar of Bikaner, the Maharawal of Dungarpur, the Jam Sahib of Nawanagar, Prince Karni Singhji of Bikaner, Lord Hopetoun, Lord Herbert, Count Zsiga Szechenyi, Lord Dundondald, the the Maharaja of Bhavnagar [et al including I.M.].	First imperial and grouse shot. All guns shooting morning only. The Viceroy with 3 guns and 2 loaders, I.M. with one light 16 bore. There were actually only 1447 imperial sand grouse picked up; many were lost, or carried away by buzzards, vultures, kites or eagles.

DATE	PLACE	BAG		GUNS	REMARKS
13 February 1938	Ramghat Jungle, near camp at Kua Khera, in Menar State	Tiger:	1	I.M.	First tiger shot. Shooting by the kindness of the Maharana of Udaipur ruler of Menar, who provided the camp and a special guard, and instructed his local baron, the Thakur of Nimri, to keep a friendly eye on us – and who owned the jungle. I.M. was accompanied by Lt. Col. Geoffrey Betham, Resident in Menar, and by Devi Lal, shikari to H.H. of Udaipur. an 8'7" tigress. Shot over a kill (tethered buffalo) from a hide in the grass across the partially dried-up Gonjali river bed. First shot entered behind right shoulder, passed downwards through lung, and found resting place beneath skin of left side. Second shot broke left forearm, but tigress crawled away mortally wounded into jungle. While buffalo were being gathered to locate wounded beast, shikari (without our knowledge) entered jungle on foot and was knocked down but not mauled. The old Thakur of Nimri appearing in the nick of time on an elephant, finished her off with both barrels of his heavy rifle. I.M. was using Colonel Betham's double-barrelled high velocity 360 rifle with dum-dum bullets.
19 February 1938	Pechola Lake Udaipur India	Crocodile:	1	I.M.	First crocodile shot. Only about 6 feet long. Some women had recently been attacked by crocodiles there.
4 September 1939	Novar Ross-shire	Grouse:	9	Tom Coats; Bill Coats and I.M.	(War with Germany was declared yesterday). Shooting afternoon only over dogs. Took the Loch Marie beat down wind, so many birds were put up too soon.

Date	Place	Quarry	Party	Remarks
13 January 1942	Beaufort Castle Inverness-shire	Pheasants: 18 Rabbits: 28 Woodcock: 12 Roe Deer: 3	Lord Lovat, Rory Fraser, Simon Fraser, Captain Rufus Clarke (Grenadiers), Roy Campbell (keeper), Beaton (keeper), George Ross (keeper) and I.M.	Walking up – very nicely mixed shooting. On leave from Pirbright, staying at Moniack Castle with Frasers. Met Maurice Baring, bedridden at Beaufort.
13 February 1943	Braidwood Lanarkshire	Hares: 4 Rabbits: 2 Snipe: 3 Wildfowl: 1 Moorhen: 1	Sir John Colville (Governor of Bombay), Mary Colville, Jim Scrymgeour Wedderburn, MP (Standard Bearer of Scotland) and I.M.	Very wet, but excellent walk. As Scottish Under-Secretary of State, Jim Wedderburn was responsible for the 1939 Act forbidding duck-shooting in February. He shot the duck.
7 December 1943	Monte Camino (2nd Battle of Italy)	15th Panzer Grenadiers: 1?	I.M. (Right Flank, 2nd Battalion Scots Guards)	Attacking in the mist near Rocca d'Evandxo. Shot at enemy face in window, but was advancing rapidly through scattered mines, so had no time to pick him up if he was bagged. Probably not, as am rotten pistol shot.
24 February 1944	An Italian Lake behind the front line near Mondragone	Snipe: 1 Wildfowl: 10	Captain the Hon. William Vestey, Captain Adam Stainton, Captain & Adjutant Michael Fitzherbert-Brockholes, Capt. Desmond Henderson and I.M. (all 2nd Bn. Scots Guards).	2 pintail and 8 teal. Michael using a tommygun, and I.M. a terrifying blunderbus of a hammergun that took ages to reload.

DATE	PLACE	BAG		GUNS	REMARKS
23 August 1945	Chequers Buckinghamshire	Rabbits:	2	Ivar Thorpe (Scots Guards) and I.M.	Out for a walk from the detachment guarding the Prime Minister's house.
6 September 1955	Glen Ogle Perthshire	Grouse: Hares:	23 1	Lord Dundee, Hon. James Cecil and I.M.	Charles Albert of Hohenlohe-Schillingsfürst staying at Easter Moncreiffe, and also out with the guns (Nicknamed 'Bumpo' by our children).
10 September 1955	Luss Dunbartonshire	Grouse: Hares: Chiefs:	14 4 1	Sir Ivar Colquhoun of Luss, Captain Rattray of Rattray, Seymour ('Timmy') Egerton, David Lubbock, Colonel Burge, Lumsden and I.M.	(One chief bagged another).
12 August 1959	Mar Lodge Aberdeenshire	Grouse: Snipe:	9 1	Captain Sandy Ramsay of Mar, three keepers (Rae, Dempster and Scott) and I.M.	Geldie Beat. Sandy managed remarkably with one leg.
25 November 1960	Montevoit Roxburghshire	Pheasants: Hares: Woodcock: Woodpigeon:	142 2 2 3	Lord Lothian, Lord Euston [now Duke of Grafton], Lord Ellesmere [now Duke of Sutherland], Major David Butter, Major Hugh Cairns, John Menzies and I.M.	Shot 6 birds with 6 successive shots: unusual for me. Tony Lothian, Mary Kerr, Fortune Euston, Lavinia Renton and Myra Butter out with us. Staying with Lothians at Crailing.
21 November 1961	Meikleour Perthshire	Hares: Wildfowl: Wild Geese:	1 1 3	Lady Lansdowne, Monsieur Jacques Peten, Hon. Robert Corbett, Aldred Drummond and I.M.	Shooting at dusk. Bar Lansdowne fell into the Isla – she missed her footing in the dusk and is already ill with 'flu.

Date	Location	Quarry		Guns	Notes
10 November 1962	Moncreiffe Perthshire	Pheasants: Hares: Rabbits: Woodcock: Wildfowl: Woodpigeon:	19 1 1 1 4 5	The Moncreiffe Syndicate (less Dr Watson), also Hon. Malcolm Napier, Dr Gavin Douglas, Dr Michael Oliver and (afternoon only) Lord Hay.	Merlin shot his first pheasant – a very good shot. He also shot the rabbit. He is using my old 12 bore with the cast-off stock because he is left-eyed, as I was before the War.
22 August 1964	Kinveachy Inverness-shire	Grouse:	18	Lady Hesketh, Lord Hesketh, Hon. Robert Fermor-Hesketh, Hon. John Fermor-Hesketh, Alexander McEwen and I.M.	Kinveachy taken by the American Ambassador [David] Bruce and Kisty Hesketh, who shot her first grouse. Walking up. Alexander Hesketh retired early with blisters, and his brothers after luncheon so 'Dead End Kids' got morning only. Rosie Lovat, Hugh Fraser, Sacha Bruce and her brothers, Jane Frick and Letitia Elliot out with us.
6 November 1964	Dochfour Inverness-shire	Pheasants: Hares: Woodcock: Wildfowl: Woodpigeon:	260 2 2 10 8	Lord Burton, Hon. Evan Baillie of Dochfour (afternoon only), Sir William Gordon Cumming of Altyre, Colonel Charles Cameron, Lt. Col. Angus Cameron of Aldourie, Andrew Forbes-Leith of Fyvie, Major Michael Leslie Melville, Captain Neil Hughes-Onslow and I.M.	Evan Baillie arrived home afternoon on long leave from Harrow. Angus Cameron shot at a buzzard; and later brought down a pigeon from a tree. That paragon of butlers, Beecroft, looks after our shooting luncheon daily. Wonderful autumn tints on trees – and splendid weather.

DATE	PLACE	GUNS	BAG		REMARKS
7 February 1965	Gajner Bikaner Rajasthan India	The Maharaja of Bikaner, Sir Ivar Colquhoun of Luss, General Paul W. Tibbets (US Air Force), Colonel Robert J Graham (Canadian Army) and I.M.	Wild Boar: Sand Grouse: Nilghai:	2 1 1	Morning only. Staying at Gujnex Palace with H.H of Bikaner. General Tibbets (who was captain of the aircraft that dropped the atom bomb on Hiroshima) had given us a lift the day before from Delhi to Bikaner in his C54 official aeroplane which he piloted himself. The Nilghai and one boar by shot by the Colonel, other boar by the General. Ivar Colquhoun and I.M both missed a nilghai blue bull.
13 February 1965	Narlai Jodhpur	Motored with Princess Baijilal of Jodhpur and Thakur chandra (former head of Shikar in Jodhpur State), also another Rathos Rajput called Kanwar Laxman Singh, to Narlai Village about 100 miles from Jodhpur city. There we were joined by the Thakur of Modewas, a Bhati Rajput who wore a beard and a turban and spoke no English though he offered me opium (refused) and later fetched their local drink *assa*, made from fermented sugar cane. As my other companions were all Rathos, and he belonged to the Bhati clan (whose chief is the Maharawal of Jaisalmer far out in the great desert), they ragged him in a friendly way – and the princess got him to draw and then scratch out his own portrait in the sand – he laughed and spat at it as well, to remove any bad luck owing to his presence. The village was full of old Hindu temples and weird temple music, and we were garlanded with artificial flowers by the villagers on arrival about six o'clock in the evening. A tethered goat on a platform had been killed by a panther the night before (while a few nights ago a panther had entered the yard of a house in the village itself, killed a goat and devoured it in spite of being stoned by 8 men). So last night two goats were tethered on platforms, one on either side of the hill (towards the end of last evening, the villagers claimed to have located three separate panthers, but in the event neither goat was killed). We waited on the outskirts of the village for a long time as night fell. There was bright moonlight, and two satellites (whether Russian or American) crossed each other's path from opposite		Panther: (Indian Leopard)	1	

sides of jackals, made a lot of noise, mingling with the village drumming, a torchlight procession and native music in the background. Our experienced driver was lurking near the poor goat, which only bleated thrice, but no panther came. We got colder and colder, and twice drove the jeep up to the chosen site 20 yards from the goat's platform, turning the spotlight on its surroundings. After some hours we drove to the other side of the hill and did the same near the other goat. On the rocky hill behind we saw the panther's eyes gleaming (Baijal was working the spotlight over my shoulder). We drove away and waited half-an-hour; but the excitement and crowding of the villagers a few hundred yards away had disturbed the panther and when we returned to the goat at about 10.30 p.m. the leopard's eyes still glinted from the same spot. I wanted to wait but the others had been instructed to stay on no longer than 8 o'clock (because of the princess) and were already restive. So Chandra Singh and I both fired at the shadowy form whose two eyes glared down at us from a high ledge of rock about 50 yards away. The leopard fell forwards into a gully below – the others maintained that both shots had hit it and that it was dead, but it was not to be approached until morning. I hadn't expected Chandra Singh to fire too except in case of need, but I suppose he was afraid of losing it in the darkness if I only wounded it. I used the late Maharaja's double-barrelled Holland 30 super rifle. We then motored back through the night, arriving at the Umaid Bhawan Palace in Jodhpur at 3.15 a.m. and had some food. The servants gave me 2 'gimlets' (gin and lime) to drink and after a hot bath and some reading, I put out the light at 6 a.m. The following morning we left Jodhpur and it was not until my return to India from Nepal that I learnt the panther had been found dead in a cave by the gully some days later (it had however been killed by the shots but had crawled into the cave while dying). Unfortunately one of the bullets had smashed one of its floating rib bones. It was 6 feet long.

| 10 September 1965 | Herdade das Pinheiras Portugal | Turtle doves: | 3 | The O'Neill of Clanaboy and I.M | Staying with Jorge O'Neill at Quintas das Machadas near Setubal. Shooting in pine and cork woods by a pond. Saw an egret. |

DATE	PLACE	BAG	GUNS	REMARKS
28 September 1966	Paal Forest Styria	Red Deer:	1	Staying with Prince Schwarzenberg (Fürst Karl VI) in a wooden hut which is one of his son's Austrian shooting lodges, 5000 feet up in the largest Zirbenwald in Europe: a great forest of tall Zirben fir-trees covering the mountain-sides. Hermione and I eat in the prince's bedroom, which we have to go through to our own: a stove connects the two rooms visually. The outside loo is built over a brook running downhill, so forms a perpetual water closet. My *Jäger* is Johann Hansmann, a bearded pipe-smoking old *Häger* from the (Communist seized) lost Schwarzenberg estates in Bohemia, who has a Scheiphund – a dog for tracking wounded beasts, whose drops of blood are known as *Scheiss* (literally 'sweat') – called Rüdan. We went out at dusk, and stalked a stag which I shot through the neck as his body was concealed by the trees. A bad head (a switch) but a difficult shot in the twilight. Hansmann then greeted me with the traditional '*Weidmannsheil*' and placed a sprig of fir (as no oak was available) in the Austrian hat lent me by the Schwarzenbergs. We returned to the hut after dark, and dined by oil lamps.
5 October 1966	Paal Forest Styria	Red Deer:	1	Our last chance. I got up at 4 a.m. with Charles Schwazenberg, and went stalking our separate ways. I went out with Hansmann and his dog Rüdan, while Hermione stayed in bed, as she had a long day's driving ahead. Too warm. No roaring. Saw a roebuck moving fast. Gave up at 7 a.m. and returned towards the hut to pack. About 400 yards from the hut I heard Prince Schwarzenberg fire a shot (although) a very accomplished marksman, he missed) and a few moments later the same stag passed me with some hinds. I shot him through the neck. *He was a Royal!* 12 points, 9 years old, with a good mane, part of which Hansmann cut off and stuck in the back of my hat together with the usual sprig of fir, as he shouted '*Weidmannsheil*'. Took the stag's teeth to make into buttons or cuff-links. We had luncheon in the Schwarzenbergs' local castle, Schloss Murau, where they have many fine heads and also the stuffed wolf that was shot on the estate a few years ago. Then Hermione drove Charles Schwarzenberg

and me to Vienna. A couple of days later in Vienna I acquired a wooden stag's head of about 1840, on which I had my Royal's antlers mounted on our return to Scotland; but unfortunately in mounting, the antlers had to be separately inserted (and thus severed from the skull) and in doing so nearly half the spread was lost.

10 December 1966 — Birkhill, Fife

Partridges: 2
Pheasants: 130
Hares: 1
Woodcock: 3
Wodpigeon: 10

Lord Dundee, Lady Dundee, Lord Kilmany, Rt. Hon. Quintin Hogg, MP, Captain Mervyn Fox-Pitt, Lt.-Col. Alastair Balfour of Dawyck, Alexander Wallace of Candacraig ('Dandy'), Capt. Richard Heriot Maitland of Errol, William Warde-Aldam and I.M

Patsy Dundee wearing the most beautiful crocodile-skin shooting boots, as usual. City of Dundee looking fine and almost Grecian across the Tay Estuary. Very pleasant day's shooting.

26 July 1967 — Easter Moncreiffe

Rabbits: 1

I.M

Shot from drawing room window, but unfortunately the big buck rabbit that does most damage to the roses got away again.

21 September 1967 — Rowallan Castle, Ayrshire

Snipe: 3
Wildfowl: 1

Hon. Robert Corbett, John Bowes-Lyon, Auberon Waugh, Duncan Davidson, Nicolas Paravicini and I.M

Staying for Caledonian Hunt meeting at Ayr. Shooting morning only.

DATE	PLACE	BAG	GUNS	REMARKS
23 November 1968	Langford Grove Essex	Pheasants: 193 Partridge: 1 Hares: 2 Rabbits: 3	Colonel 'Jubie' Lancaster, MP, Hon. Rupert Strutt, Roddy Macleod of Cadboll, Mr Forbes, Anthony Sebag Montefiore, Julian Jenkinson, Jim Stanton, Dr Lyster and I.M	Randolph Churchill came to dinner afterwards, looking as though he knew his life was ending. [*I.M seems to have got his dates confused here as Randolph Churchill had already been dead for five months by this time* – ED]
16 February 1969	Coipue Chile		Don Felipe Edwards, Dana Nadine Van Peborg de Ulloa, Mrs Maldwin Drummond, Don Manuel Ulloa, Gonsalo Martinez and I.M.	Picnicked by the River Toltan about 2 o'clock. The others rode there on horseback. Splendid picnic with open fire and log seats and tables (a fixture by the river bank). Gonsalo Martinez is of mixed Spanish/Araucanian Redskin blood; son of Ruffina the cook who is away with Doonie E. aboard his yacht. Then set out downstream in three boats, wearing ponchos and sombreros, fishing quietly though unsuccessfully as far as the ferry. Pleasant day; saw quervo and other birds and cattle drinking in the river. The Ulloas are in exile from Peru, as Nadine U's husband was Minister of Finance in Peru before the last Revolution there. However, her brother is the present Minister of Defence in the Argentine.

14 March
1969

Isla Alejandra
Selkirk
South Pacific

Cabrilla:

7

Dona Chavela
Eastman de Edwards,
Lady Moncreiffe and
I.M.

Flew across the Pacific Ocean for three hours yesterday from Santiago de Chile in a twin-propellered TAXPA Aerocommander (pilot and 5 passengers) and landed with difficulty in strong wind on a tiny makeshift airstrip on the island in the San Fernandez Archipelago where Alexander Selkirk (the original of 'Robinson Crusoe') was marooned 1704-1709. Indeed a small neighbouring island, bleak and uninhabited, has long been officially named 'Isla Robinson Crusoe'. We then walked some distance downhill to a boat, on board which was the most enormous lobster I've ever seen, while we sailed past tall and sheer rocky cliffs to the scattered little settlement in the hilly wooded bay where the German raiding cruiser SMS *Dresden* was sunk in 1915. We are staying as guests of Dona Blanca-Luz Brum de Bronson, whose husband is head of BRANIF airlines, because we are accompanied by Chavela Edwards (whose son 'Dounie' E. has made me a founder member of his new yacht club: the Cofradia Nautica del Pacifico Austral). There are still goats on the island, as when Daniel Defoe wrote. Today we sailed in a motor boat to the beach where Selkirk had his shallow cave. It is semi-circular about 5 yards deep and from 10 to 12 yards wide, and originally had a shelter built to cover all the front, as the post holes in the rock show. He had also carved niches in the sides of the cave, to act as cupboards just like the *aumries* in old Scots houses of that period. On the way back from the cave we fished in the ocean, looking at a rainbow shining up from *under* bright blue water. We caught 5 of one kind of fish and 2 of another – the two were much larger, shining yellow and almost translucent – but the boatmen called them all 'cabrillas'. Afterwards we met Don Fernando Rojas, Governor of Juan Fernandez, with the Greens, splendid characters who have a pet *coati* of great charm; as small mammals do.

DATE	PLACE	BAG		GUNS	REMARKS
17 October 1969	Easter Moncreiffe Perthshire			Hugo O'Neill of Clanaboy, Countess Boriska Karolyi and I.M.	Out taking turns with one gun. Missed various pigeon and pheasant. Usual Easter Monckers bag: NIL
23 January 1971	Birkhill Fife	Partridge: Pheasants: Rabbits: Woodcock: Woodpigeon: Roe deer:	1 119 1 5 23 1	Lord Dundee, Lady Dundee, Lord Scrymgeour, Sir David Erskine of Cambo, David Carnegy-Arbuthnott of Balhamoon, yr., Lewis Heriot Maitland of Errol, yr., Patrick Heriot Maitland, John Hutchison-Bradburne, Robert Tuscan, Captain Mervyn Fox-Pitt and I.M.	I.M shooting afternoon only as just out of bed after tearing ligaments in the back, (and also having temporarily given up Grouse whisky and Smirnoff vodka)
24 October 1971	Avalon Rhode Island USA	Pheasants:	121	Mrs Candace Van Alen, the Duke of Atholl, Elton Hydes, Smith Jackson, Messmore Kendall with Frank MacLear, Arturo Manas with Mrs Nellie Barletta, Mrs Marian O'Donnell with Austen Grey, John Vials and I.M.	Staying at Avalon with Jimmy and 'Candy' Van Alen, who rent a small aeroplane to fetch Hermione, Iain Atholl, Jeannie Campbell [*sometime wife of Norman Mailer* – ED] and me from New York, where we are part of a delegation of Scottish chiefs for the Scottish American Foundation ball (Jeannie Campbell representing her father). Sat at dinner next to Mrs Stuart Auchincloss (... the very intelligent and charming mother of 'Jackie' Kennedy/ Onassis) last night. The shoot today was in the American fashion – a 'Released Pheasant shoot',

as they call it – rather like clay pigeon shooting but with live pheasant. It's laid on in the wooded policies around a pond near the house, a yellow tape with numbered posts leading the guns from stand to stand within the grounds. Three pairs of guns were sharing guns, alternating at each stand. The wind was east-north-east 25 knots: the sky overcast, 360 birds were released altogether, to shouts of 'mark' from concealed traps behind the trees, high over which they rocketed past the waiting guns: 106 were killed and a further 15 picked up later. The shoot started after a comfortably late breakfast, and was over in time for an excellent luncheon.

DATE	PLACE	BAG	GUNS	REMARKS
15 January 1972	Foret de Sille-le-Guillaume Maine, France	Red Deer:	1	Staying with the Duc and Duchesse de la Force at the château de St Aubin. Lady Moncreiffe and I.M followed the Equipage Ralley Thiouze staghounds, with them in their motor car through roads in the deep woods of this forest (which British soldiers in the last War mis-called 'Silly William') while the hunt canterred down rides (*lignes*) cut through trees. Their son Henri-Jacques (Marquis de la Force) had led off at the Meet with much music of French horns, and we came upon the hunt from time to time, or heard more of the music in the forest. It was bitterly cold and twice we stopped to make thankful use of the contents of the motor boot, which the La Forces had provided with picnic of pâté sandwiches, ham sandwiches, white wine and rum. Once we saw the unfortunate stag, its mouth open and panting with exhaustion, fleeing through the trees parallel to us, hotly pursued by the baying black and white hounds. At last we heard a horn braying out the music of a kill, and stopped to find the poor stag newly dead, in a field just off our road: he had been caught at last in the rear by the fangs of the leading hounds, and had died of heart failure. The horn was being sounded by a bystander who had followed the chase in another motorcar and was first on the scene. Indeed it was a little while before any of the huntsmen rode up to join the group that was gathering around the dead deer. *It was a hart of nine points.* It was immediately grallocked, next flayed from the shoulders downwards, so that only its skin with antlered head were spread out on the ground rather like a tiger-skin rug. The carcase was then broken up and given to the patiently waiting but ravenous hounds, while the hunt stood around all clad in their romantic traditional uniforms. 'Cotte une rite barbare', observed the duchesse (*née La Rochefoucauld*) of this mingling of beauty and tragedy. After that the duke brought up and introduced to Hermione the Baron du Jancheray, Master of the Hunt, who presented to her the *honneures de la chasse*, one of the feet of the slain *cerf*, which our hosts' daughter Marguerite de Caumont La Force (who had been hunting) is going to have mounted for us in Paris. She then joined with her brother and all the rest of the hunt,

dismounted, in playing a long sorrowful, yet triumphant salute to Hermione on their French horns – The uniform of the Equipage Ralley Thiouze hunt consists of a pale 'Hussar blue' coat, with cuffs and pocket flaps and collar all of maroon velvet (whip's have gold edges), a gold-banded white belt with a hunting sword, and a great French Horn doubly encircling chest and shoulder. The Master wears a black velvet cap, some of the ladies had gold lace on black tricorne hats, and the rest of the hunt wore curly brimmed bowlers. The duke drove us back to the buildings (saddle-room, etc) where the Meet had been held and we awaited the return of the Hunt in a large raftered room with a blazing fire and a long table. On arrival they removed their blue coats, revealing beautiful gold-trimmed crimson velvet waistcoats with gilt buttons. We had several drinks with them; the barn-like room soon filled with smoke so that our eyes watered; but everyone was charming to us.

DATE	GUNS	BAG	PLACE	REMARKS
20th February 1972	Jilom ak Ussah (son of the old Iban sea-Dyak chief of the long-house at Murat)		Kampong Mujang Skrang River Sarawak	

Went up river and stayed last night with Hermione and the Colquhouns of Luss and a Frau von Knublock in the Murat long-house's new guest house. We all slept under mosquito nets on 'biscuits' as our Army call mattresses, in a bamboo floored common dormitory on stilts (which got much shaken by grunting pigs beneath scratching on them at dawn). Before going to bed we had been long entertained in the long-house itself (also on stilts) among the turmoil of the women and children and chickens and cocks and dogs of the 21 Iban families cooking and chatting in their long communal hall, off which they sleep in family apartments. Bansing ak Ussah, son of the chief, danced with *parang ilang* sword in hand, as did other Ibans (one of them a former head-hunter) in ceremonial sea-Dyak warrior's elaborate head-dresses of silver or fur from which rose long black and white hornbill's plumes, imitating as the warriors danced the movements of the monkey and sacred hornbill bird, to the music of the *gendang raiyab* gongs. During the dance the pretty Dyak girls smile, suddenly revealing their fashionable gold teeth that spoil the effect for a European. Most were bare breasted, but some spoilt the effect further by wearing white bras. Later I.M danced a strathspey and reel for them, but bumped his head into a bundle of about 20 smoked human skulls hanging from the communal roof, including the head of a man whom the old chief Ussah had slain. A ghost used to appear on the long-house verandah whenever the skulls got damp, so they had to be re-smoked – and when Ussah's long-house went on fire some years ago, the skulls all rolled out of their own accord. While we were staying there old Ussah the head-hunter chief sliced his little toe laterally almost in half while chopping jungle wood with his *parang*. Hermione and I.M could only treat what needed several nasty stitches with Dettol, panadol and a clean handkerchief for bandage. This morning a number of women and children attended our levée, giggling at I.M's nightshirt (made by Mr Yee Mee in Hong Kong), which has the Moncreiffe coat-of-arms complete with supporters and baronial cap on maintenance, on its top pocket. Today we set off back down river with Bansing ak Ussah, but our outboard motor long boat stopped for a moment by another sea-Dyak jungle village and we were greeted by a young hunter being taken off in a small canoe, armed with a single barrelled shot-gun, *parang* sword and a primitive native pouch. He was Bansing's brother Jilom, who had gone to live in accordance with old custom in his wife's village. He was just setting off up river to hunt, no longer human heads as his father Ussah had done, but wild pig, deer and monkeys in the jungle. Alighting from our boat on our return down river, we saw a beautiful Rajah Brooke birdwing butterfly and shared the sadness of the Dyaks that the Brookes no longer reign paternally over Sarawak.

About 30 Leeches

Went to see orang-utans being rehabilitated. They come out of the jungle at 4 p.m. to be fed, then all return except Joan, who has a baby and refuses to go back into the trees. They look just like Douglas-Homes. We then went along a jungle track for about half an hour, looking at the orang-utans' nests about 60 feet up on the gigantic trees: then fled crawling with leeches. The Colquhouns of Luss were covered in blood and Hermione had a leech that looked like a ripe plum on the sole of her foot. I.M had one leech in his armpit, one on the welt of his shoe, six on his trousers and one trying to enter past his fly-buttons, but none had sucked any of his blood. The native guide asked me if I drank a lot, and being an historian, I replied truthfully. He then observed that leeches don't like too much alcohol in the blood.

2 Colquhouns of
Luss and Hermione

Sandakan
North Borneo

25 February
1972

The Celestial Incarnation and the Star-Spangled Tortoise

Messengers of Impending Doom

In Max Beerbohm's *Zuleika Dobson*, the fateful telegram for the Duke of Dorset read 'DEEPLY REGRET INFORM YOUR GRACE LAST NIGHT TWO BLACK OWLS CAME AND PERCHED ON BATTLEMENTS REMAINED THERE THROUGH NIGHT HOOTING AT DAWN FLEW AWAY NONE KNOWS WHITHER AWAITING INSTRUCTIONS JELLINGS'. The Duke replied immediately, 'PREPARE VAULT FOR FUNERAL MONDAY DORSET.' For this was the customary warning of His Grace's impending doom. It is not at all unusual in ancient families to have such premonitions. With the ancient Irish royal dynasts, it's almost commonplace to have a family *ban-sidhe*, or 'fairy lady': – what is popularly known as a 'banshee'.

Perhaps the best known are *A'bhill*, hereditary banshee of the *Dalcassians*, who appeared to Brian Boru in his tent on the morn of his victorious death at the hands of the Vikings at Clontarf in 1014, and the equally sinister Mauveen who regularly bewailed the death of the O'Neill of Clanaboy at Edenduff Carrick, now called Shane's Castle.

Crossing the narrow Irish Channel to the West Highlands of Scotland, the omen-spirits came too. Thus we have Woden's ravens who assemble to mark the passing of the Woden-descended local representative of their god-spirit, the Duke of Argyll. Since he moved from the fresh water of Ardconnel on Loch Awe, to the more expansive seawater at Inveraray on Loch Fyne, the ever attentive ravens have moved with him.

There are other stories which I do not believe, such as the death of Lord Herries being heralded by the arrival of hedgehogs, because *herisons* is the French for hedgehogs, and they have three hedgehogs in their coat-of-arms, which is a pun upon their name. Since my childhood, I had been told that the hedgehogs came to attend the death of Lord Herries, but I don't believe it, because I don't think that the hedgehogs would know it was a pun on their name. Certainly, I don't suppose that they came for the late Bernard Duke of Norfolk, who was also Lord Herries, although I think he would have been much amused if they had. There are strange tales like the one of Maclean of Torloisk in the Isle of Mull, who in the 18th century told his wife that if he were to die a white rose would blow through his bedroom window. He went off to the wars abroad and perished, and a white rose did blow through her bedroom window.

When the squint-eyed Marquess of Argyll made a great raid with 5,000 men upon the bonny House of Airlie in 1640, a drummer boy was burnt to death. Ever since, whenever Lord Airlie is about to die the drummer boy is heard. The late dowager Countess of Airlie, who was a cousin of my first wife, told us that when her husband [*the 6th Earl*] was killed at the battle of Diamond Hill in the Boer War, she heard the drummer drumming. The Earl had led a cavalry charge to recover some guns, and gave the command 'files about gallop': at that moment he was hit and fell from his horse, and as he lay there his last words were 'moderate your language please Sergeant'. And at that very moment Lady Airlie heard the drummer boy drumming. I was an ensign in the Scots guards at the Tower of London in 1940, when the second-in-command in my battalion was 'Joe', 7th Earl of Airlie and we all knew about the drummer boy. Being naughty, we sometimes thought of beating a drum outside his bedroom door during the Blitz, but as he was a major and we were all subalterns we thought it would be both tactless and unwise.

The romantic house of Lusignan has a poignant ancestral spirit from whom the houses of Derby and Atholl descend, called Melusine, the tutelary fairy of their line. She was a spirit of the fountain of Lusignan, a forest spring in Poitou. The tale runs that once upon a time a young lord was wandering in the woods when he came upon a fair maiden and proposed to her. She accepted him on condition that he never saw her on a Saturday. They were married in style, and lived happily for a long time, while she bore him an heir and helped him build the castle of Lusignan. But one Saturday, her husband could restrain his curiosity no longer, and peeped at her secretly. To his astonishment, she had become a snake – symbol of water – from the hips downwards. He rashly gave himself away by exclaiming 'ha, serpent': whereupon Melusine gave a shriek and flew out through a window of the castle, never to be seen again. Ever since, the death of a member of the house of Lusignan was heralded by the cries of the fairy serpent. '*Poussez des cris de Melusine*' is still a popular saying.

Before the war I was staying with my great-uncle General Sir Ian Hamilton, who had been commander-in-chief at Gallipoli. There was also a sinister Russian staying, whose name I have forgotten. He told me a strange tale about an Irish family called O'Gorman, who had a strange affinity for foxes. No O'Gorman was allowed to hunt a fox. But one did. He became separated from the pack and found himself alone pursuing an enormous fox. It ran straight through the school playground where his daughter was a child and leapt into her arms. This story made a deep impression on my mind. Years later, I learnt of the strange story of the Lords Gormanston, premier viscounts of Ireland, so created in 1478. They were a family from Lancaster called Preston and their coat-of-arms is a straightforward Lancashire one, but one of their supporters is a fox and their crest is a fox, both of which they must have acquired in Ireland. Whenever Lord Gormanston is dying, all the foxes in the district come to the castle. The most celebrated occasion was in 1907, when the 14th Viscount lay dying, and the hunt was unable to find a fox anywhere, because as one old man said to them 'They'll all be over at the castle because the old lord is dying'. And so they were. That evening the Honble Hubert Preston, the late Viscount's son, went into the family chapel to pray by his father's coffin. There was a scratching at the door, and when he opened it there was a ring of foxes and one of them pushed passed him and scratched at the coffin.

Antiques Across The World, USA

Obituary

Among I. M.'s papers, there is the following unpublished scrap — presumably penned by his alter ego, *Dr R. I. K. Moncreiffe*:

Sir Iain Moncreiffe of that Ilk, 11th Baronet and 24th Chief, died yesterday at the age of 104. This master snob was also a crashing bore. Once, in the morning room of the Turf Club, he heard himself telling a story he had related many times before. Fed up, he hurried through to the bar, only to find himself telling another. He thought desperately of entering himself in his Game Book under 'VARIOUS: *Self* 1'; and then shooting himself. But curiosity about the sequel kept him alive.

At the age of four he was kidnapped by his nurse. His bedroom had been a bee-hive shaped hut made of mud and straw. Here he had baths in a portable tin hip-bath with hot water from a can with a handle. When the door of the hut was closed, there was a disgusting smell; and everybody said it was little Rupert (as he was then called). 'It subsequently transpired', as the cliché goes, that the hut had been built on top of a disused cess-pool.

Some 50 years earlier, as a schoolboy at Stowe, I. M. fashioned the following remarkable document – complete with blue ribbon – on his 15th birthday. It touchingly reveals the child as the father of the man we all miss so much:

The Last Will and Testament of Angus MacSnort of that Ilk and Auchinbuidle CSI

9 APRIL 1934 *Ao Dom. 1934*

This is the last Will of me, Angus MacSnort of Auchinbuidle, otherwise *An Mac-an-Snuirtalach Mor*, Chieftain of the Clan MacSnort, Hereditary Keeper of Ardcromach Castle, a Companion of the Most Exalted Order of the Star of India, an Honorary Knight Grand Commander of the Most Sumptuous and Magnificent Order of the Contemplation of the Celestial Incarnation of the Supreme Deity of Metempsychosis and of the Star-Spangled Tortoise of Eternal Bliss of Bhangee and Bhor, a Deputy Lieutenant for and in the County of Argyll, a Justice of the Peace, sometime a Colonel in the Army, whereby firstly I revoke all previous wills and testamentary dispositions.

WHEREBY SECONDLY I bequeath the Castle of Auchinbuidle, together with the whole lands and barony of Auchinbuidle, and the whole lands of Ardnacreac, Dalquhenzie, and Kenfunnel, in Argyllshire, including all rooms, tacks, steadings, goods and gear, and rights in woods, plains, moors, marshes, roads, paths, waters, pools, streams, meadows, grazings and pastures, mills, multures and their sequels, hawkings, huntings, fishings, petaries, turbaries, coal-pits, stone and lime, smithies, brewhouses, heath and broom, with court and their issues, hereyeldes, bludwits, and merchets of women, pit and gallows, sol, soc, thol, theme, infangthief, outfangthief, and all other and singular liberties, commodities, and easements and just pertinents as well named not as named, together with all such moveables, save only those that be hereinafter mentioned, as may be at the time of my decease in, under, or upon the aforesaid Castle and lands, and also the gold seal of Sir Lachlan MacSnort of Auchinbuidle, Knight Baronet, nineteenth Chieftain of the Clan, who, being slain at the battle of Culloden or Drumossie Moor in the year of God one thousand, seven hundred, two score and six, was attainted and forfeited of his title and estates, of

261

which only the last mentioned have been restored to our family, and furthermore six thousand (6,000) of my ten pound sterling (£10) shares in the Bhangee and Bhor Oil Company, Limited, to whomsoever of my lawful sons Ranald, Snort and Angus, who shall be or shall have been the first among them to beget a lawful son, according to the ancient and singular custom of the Clan MacSnort, whereby he of the Chieftain's blood, who first begets them an heir, is himself Chieftain among them and possessor of the lands and barony of Auchinbuidle.

WHEREBY THIRDLY I bequeath to those two of my sons Ranald, Snort and Angus, who shall not succeed me in the Chieftainship of MacSnort and as Laird of Auchinbuidle, the residue of my shares in the Bhangee and Bhor Oil Company, Limited, saving only such as may be hereinafter mentioned, to be shared equally between them in two parts.

WHEREBY FOURTHLY I bequeath to my son Ranald, otherwise Raoghnuill, the small bronze cat with which I was presented by Sukwallah Oofat Khan, the Zemindar of Madpai, on the occasion of my shooting a large tiger – stop the lawyer if you have heard this before – which was menacing the paths through the jungle even up to the very gates of the village of Madpai, and which I shot from my machan in a banyan tree on the twentieth day of July, between chota hazri and tiffin, in the year of God nineteen hundred and four, whereafter I was called by the natives Pukka Wallah Shikari Sahib.

WHEREBY FIFTHLY I bequeath to my son Snort, otherwise Snuirtalach, the *sgian dubh*, otherwise black knife, with the which I gralloched my first stag on *Ben'a Chait*, otherwise the Hill of the Cat, in Glentilt in Atholl.

WHEREBY SIXTHLY I bequeath to my son Angus, otherwise Aonghas, my toy rabbit Bunny, which I have cherished since my fifth birthday, when I had the measles, and which I recommend to his care, and to that of his descendants.

WHEREBY SEVENTHLY I bequeath to Rory, otherwise Roderick, otherwise Ruari, *MacPiobair*, Hereditary Piper to the Chief of MacSnort, to Ebenezer Erskine, Butler in my castle of Auchinbuidle, to Alexander, otherwise Alasdair, Stewart, Head Keeper of my lands of Auchinbuidle, Ardnacreac, Dalquhenzie, and Kenfunnel, to James, otherwise Seumas, MacGregor, Head Forester of my lands aforesaid, to Jock Ramsay Anderson, Head Gardener of my gardens at Auchinbuidle, and to Charles Duncan, otherwise Tearlach Donach, Stewart, Head Fisherman of my waters of Loch-an-Snuirtalaich and in the Sea, the sum of one hundred pounds sterling (£100) each, and recommend them to the especial care of my successor.

WHEREBY EIGHTHLY I bequeath to my Harper George, otherwise

Seoras, MacPiobair, the sum of fifty pounds sterling (£50), and recommend him to the care of my successor.

Whereby ninthly I bequeath to each several one of my servants, foresters, keepers, fishermen, gardeners, pipers, gillies, and dependents, as well not named as named, the sum of twenty pounds sterling (£20) each, and recommend them all collectively and individually to the care of my successor.

Whereby I remind my son Ranald (for inasmuch as he has already begotten a son, my grandson Angus, in spite of the malicious attempt of his younger brother Snort, who, in direct contravention to the ancient tradition of our family whereby the eldest son first of them marries, secretly married without my knowledge or permission, the outcome of which treacherous policy was the birth of a daughter, my granddaughter Dorvegelda, he it is who will be my successor in the Chieftainship of MacSnort and in the lands and barony of Auchinbuidle) that MacSnort of Auchinbuidle is one of the two Chieftains who, alone in all Britain, are permitted a trained bodyguard of two hundred (200) Highlanders, armed with firearms, and also two pieces of field artillery.

Whereby tenthly I bequeath to Ranald MacSnort, Younger of Auchinbuidle, my eldest son, and to Donald Roderick MacSnort of Ardnagory, my kinsman, Majors in my regiment of MacSnort Highlanders, to Angus MacSnort, my youngest son, to Godfrey Fitzbastion Alexander George, Earl of Scotstoun and Balchleuchries, KT, my nephew, to Snort MacSnort, my second son, and to James Angus MacSnort of Dunhallion, my cousin, Captains in my regiment aforesaid, to Kenneth Mackintosh of Inversporran, my nephew, Adjutant in my regiment aforesaid, and to the eighth gentlemen, my near kinsmen, Lieutenants in my regiment aforesaid, chosen from the Library at Auchinbuidle by each one, blindfold, pricking the catalogue with a drawn dirk, each gentleman one book.

Whereby eleventhly I will that Terence Patrick O'Duffy, formerly a master at Blenheim School, near Broadstairs in the county of Kent, be informed that the two hundred lines which he gave me on the morning of March the fourth, in the year of God eighteen hundred and seventy-eight were grossly unjust.

Whereby twelfthly I request my son Ranald to make search under the floorboards in my bedroom for a large ruby, commonly called the Rajah's Ruby, which I bequeath to the Temple of the Supreme Deity of Metempsychosis in Bhor, whence I stole it, the which theft I do now confess as follows:

In the year of God one thousand, nine hundred and eight, being appointed Military Adviser to the Royal Government of Bhangee and

Bhor (the Maharaja-dhirajah of which state is without power, and which is ruled by His Highness the Hereditary Ex-Finance Minister, lineal descendant of that Ex-Finance Minister who, in the year of God seventeen hundred, seized the power), and my excellent advice being supported with ease on the bayonets of sixteen battalions of the finest Gurkhas (it was on this occasion that I secured a monopoly of all the oil in that State for the Bhangee and Bhor Oil Company, two thirds of the shares of which I hold, after a polite call on His abovementioned Highness, when I was accompanied by a light escort of four battalions and two companies of Gurkhas), I spent one night while on shikar at the abovenamed temple, after the which night the ruby was missed which formed the eye of the god Sivaboonya-Sacramentadjoss, my Lieutenant, poor Thompson (the Afridi slew him in the year of God nineteen hundred and nineteen) being suspected but proved innocent, and I escaping all suspicion of the theft which I hereby confess.

WHEREBY I devise and bequeath the residue of my estate and effects to my son Ranald.

WHEREBY I will that my body be disposed of as follows:

At ten o'clock in the night the MacSnort Highlanders, will parade in full dress uniform, wearing on their left sleeves black crepe arm-bands, by the light of many torches borne by gillies wearing the Hunting MacSnort tartan, my son Ranald still wearing the two eagle's feathers of a chieftain's heir, my coffin, draped with the Union Jack which flew above my Residency in Bhangee, and covered with my plaid, on which my military sword and revolver, my broadsword and dirk, my bonnet with the Auchinbuidle crest, the MacSnort badge, and the three feathers of a Chieftain in it, and the sword of the fourteenth Chief, who served under Lord Reay in the wars abroad, will be laid, being borne in the midst of the men, preceded and followed by a banner of the regiment; and they shall march with my body from the Castle of Auchinbuidle down through Glen Donnachaidh until they reach the slopes of *Ben'a Creac*, where they shall bury my body without other mark than a boulder rolled upon the spot and carved with the initials A.M. and the year of my death (1936, for so the *taibhsear* has prophesied), so that I may become when but dust a part of my beloved country, and there shall be a beacon that night on the summit of *Ben'a Creac*, and another on the summit of *Monadh Croibhe*;

But my heart they shall carry back to Auchinbuidle in a silver casket engraved with my arms and with my name and with my badge and with the dates of my birth and of my death, and this they shall bury in the chapel at Auchinbuidle, and they shall lay above it such a stone as is laid above the grave of Angus Og Macdonald of Islay in the Cathedral of

Iona, save only that the galley-dexter of the Isles be exchanged to the galley sinister of Auchinbuidle, and that the words inscribed upon it shall be: HIC IACET CORPUS ANGUSII FILII DOMINI ANGUSI MACSNORT DE AUCHINBUIDLE; and the music that shall be played by Rory MacPiobair and his pipers shall be as follows:

Between Auchinbuidle and *Ben'a Creac* they shall play the Flowers of the Forest or the Lament for Flodden, the *Cumha Mhic-an-Snuirtalaich* or MacSnort's Lament, *Cuimknick Bas Snuirtalaich* or Remember the Death of Snort, the *Cumha Mhic-an Toisich* or Mackintosh's Lament, the *Cumha Mhic- Criomthainn* or MacCrimmon's Lament, the *Cumha Aonghais Mhic Raoghnuill Oig* or Lament for Angus Macdonald of Keppoch, the *Cumha Ghriogair MhicGriogair* or Lament for Gregor MacGregor, and *Mac-Griogair 'o Ruaru* or MacGregor of Roro, and between *Ben'a Creac* and Auchinbuidle they shall play the *Oran mu 'n Bhas* or Hymn of Death, the Atholl Highlander Slow March, the Atholl Highlander Quick March, the March of the Clan MacSnort, a *Brosnachadh* or Battle Song, Hey Tooty Tetty, now commonly called Scots wha Ha'e wi' Wallace Bled, the March of the Stewarts, and the Flowers of the Forest or Lament for Flodden; furthermore, of modern music they shall play the Road to the Isles, formerly called the Misty Hills of Jura; and if any of the evil Clan Colquhalzie are seen, who are our blood enemies and who wear trews, then shall Rory MacPiobair and his pipers play the mocking challenge, with the which the kilted Breadalbane men taunted the trousered Sinclairs in the Caithness creach by Iain Glas, to wit *'Bhodach nam Brigeis* or Knaves in Trousers;

And for the space of one week there shall be mourning in Auchinbuidle, and then there shall be held a great Deer Drive, and a Banquet, and there shall be many rejoicings for my son Ranald who will be Laird and Chieftain after me.

AND WHEREBY I give this my last advice to my beloved sons, that is to say:

Never shake a Colquhalzie by the hand, for in the days long past they slew many of our Clan; avoid all those who spell MacSnort Macsnort, for they demean our name; wash ever behind your ears, for there it is that the observant notice dirt; never wear aught beneath the kilt, for so to do is bad form; attend the kirk with regularity, for you must set an example to the Clan; always follow and slay a wounded beast, for this is the duty of a gentleman; be kind to your inferiors, friendly to equals, and loyal to your superior; and above all be white men.

AND WHEREBY lastly I commend to the care of my successor the ghost of Lacklan Dubh, the Black Laird of Auchinbuidle, who, as is well known, is yearly to be seen gazing from the window of the Banqueting

Hall onto the heights of Alt-na-cearc, where long ago he murdered his brother Mungo.

AND I HEREBY appoint the said Godfrey Fitzbastion Alexander George, Earl of Scotstoun and Balcleuchries, KT, and the said Donald Roderick MacSnort of Ardnagory, otherwise *Mac Mhic Aonghais*, the joint executors and trustees of this my last Will and Testament,

In token whereof I subscribe these presents with my hand this ninth day of April in the year of God one thousand, nine hundred, and thirty-four, before the witnesses also subscribing.

SIGNED, SEALED, AND DELIVERED BY
AUCHINBUIDLE BEFORE AND IN PRESENCE OF *Angus Macsnort of*
AUCHINBUIDLE BEFORE AND IN PRESENCE OF *Auchinbuidle,*
MacSnort

THE CHEVALIER MACOSTRICH *Jean MacOstrich*
a gentleman of no fixed abode

ANDREW JAMES MACTAVISH OF BLAIR TAVISH *Andrew James Mactavish*
Strathtavish, Argyllshire *of Blair Tavish*

Auchinbuidle Castle, 9 April 1934.

Index

Photographic Acknowledgements

All the photographs in the book are the copyright of Lady Moncreiffe of that Ilk, with the exceptions of the frontispiece (*Manchester Daily Mail*); Derek Hill's portrait (Tom Scott); 'Puffin' Countess of Erroll, and I.M. at the Argyll funeral (Brodrick Haldane); I.M. on Moncreiffe Hill (*Observer*); I.M. with Hermione outside Easter Moncreiffe and in the hall (*Daily Record*); I.M. in his Yucata (D.C. Thomson); I.M. at a shooting party (the Prince of Lippe); I.M. and a trophy, and the last photograph in the book (*Camera Press*); and I.M. with Chief Arogundade (Caroline Irwin).